PLAYING FOR KEEPS

IMPROVISATION, COMMUNITY, AND SOCIAL PRACTICE

A series edited by Daniel Fischlin

Books in this series advocate musical improvisation as a crucial model for political, cultural, and ethical dialogue and action—for imagining and creating alternative ways of knowing and being in the world. The books are collaborations among performers, scholars, and activists from a wide range of disciplines. They study the creative risk-taking imbued with the sense of movement and momentum that makes improvisation an exciting, unpredictable, ubiquitous, and necessary endeavor.

Daniel Fischlin
and
Eric Porter,
EDITORS

PLAYING FOR KEEPS

Improvisation in the Aftermath

DUKE UNIVERSITY PRESS · DURHAM AND LONDON · 2020

© 2020 Duke University Press
All rights reserved

Designed by Matthew Tauch
Typeset in Minion Pro by Westchester Book Services

Library of Congress Cataloging-in-Publication Data Names:
Fischlin, Daniel, editor. | Porter, Eric, [date] editor. Title:
Playing for keeps : improvisation in the aftermath / Daniel
Fischlin and Eric Porter, editors.
Description: Durham : Duke University Press, 2020. | Series:
Improvisation, community, and social practice | Includes
bibliographical references and index.
Identifiers: LCCN 2019027309 (print)
LCCN 2019027310 (ebook)
ISBN 9781478006800 (hardcover)
ISBN 9781478008149 (paperback)
ISBN 9781478009122 (ebook)
Subjects: LCSH: Improvisation (Music)—Political aspects. |
Improvisation(Music)—Socialaspects.
Classification: LCC ML3916 .P58 2020 (print) |
LCC ML3916 (ebook) | DDC 781.3/6—dc23
LC recordavailableathttps:// lccn.loc.gov/2019027309
LC ebookrec ordavailableathttps:// lccn.loc.gov/2019027310

Cover art: Randy DuBurke, from the series CIVIL JAZZ!
Courtesy of the artist.

Duke University Press gratefully acknowledges the
Social Sciences and Humanities Research Council
of Canada for its support of the Improvisation,
Community, and Social Practice (ICASP) project, at the
University of Guelph, which provided funds toward
the publication of this book.

for our beloved partners,
Martha Nandorfy and Catherine Ramírez

Contents

ix   ACKNOWLEDGMENTS

1   Playing for Keeps: An Introduction
Daniel Fischlin and Eric Porter

25   ONE. manifesto
Matana Roberts

29   TWO. *The Exhibition of Vandalizim*: Improvising Healing, Politics, and Film in South Africa
Stephanie Vos

55   THREE. The Rigors of Afro/Canarian Jazz: Sounding Peripheral Vision with Severed Tongues
Mark Lomanno

81   FOUR. "Opening Up a Space That Maybe Wouldn't Exist Otherwise" / *Holding It Down* in the Aftermath
Vijay Iyer in conversation with Daniel Fischlin and Eric Porter

94   FIVE. Experimental and Improvised Norths: The Sonic Geographies of Tanya Tagaq's Collaborations with Derek Charke and the Kronos Quartet
Kate Galloway

121   SIX. Nina Simone: CIVIL JAZZ!
Randy DuBurke

129   SEVEN. Free Improvised Music in Postwar Beirut: Differential Sounds, Intersectarian Collaborations, and Critical Collective Memory
Rana El Kadi

160   EIGHT. Street Concerts and Sexual Harassment in Post-Mubarak Egypt: *Ṭarab* as Affective Politics
Darci Sprengel

191   NINE. Improvisation, Grounded Humanity, and Witnessing in Palestine: An Interview with Al-Mada's Odeh Turjman and Reem Abdul Hadi
Daniel Fischlin

250   TEN. *Silsulim* (Improvised "Curls") in the Vocal Performance of Israeli Popular Music: Identity, Power, and Politics
Moshe Morad

275   ELEVEN. Three Moments in *Kī Hōʻalu* (Hawaiian Slack Key Guitar): Improvising as a *Kanaka Maoli* (Native Hawaiian) Adaptive Strategy
Kevin Fellezs

300   TWELVE. From Prepeace to Postconflict: The Ethics of (Non)Listening and Cocreation in a Divided Society
Sara Ramshaw and Paul Stapleton

325   CONTRIBUTORS

331   INDEX

Acknowledgments

This project began coming together during our first conversations with one another at a jazz studies conference, Lost in Diversity, at the Heidelberg Center for American Studies in November 2012. We thank Christian Broecking and the other conference organizers for making that connection. Subsequently, our rather broadly framed 2013 call for papers for a somewhat differently conceived version of this project elicited well over one hundred abstracts. Although we were able to include only a subset of those proposed projects in *Playing for Keeps* and two related volumes, the enthusiastic response to the call confirmed our impression that scholars—established and up-and-coming—were pushing critical improvisation studies in important transcultural and transnational directions. We therefore appreciate the efforts of all who responded to our call for helping us to understand the necessity of this project—the range of responses we received was a clear indication of the degree to which the field of critical studies in improvisation in general had begun to account for cultural difference as a largely understudied aspect of how improvisatory practices manifest globally.

We are especially indebted to the contributors to *Playing for Keeps* for their excellent scholarship as well as for their dedication to the project during a long and not always easy journey. Their timely and thorough responses to our editorial suggestions over several phases of the volume's development pushed us to sharpen its focus, and their patience and tenacity through a somewhat complicated review process kept our spirits from flagging. We were also encouraged by the ways many contributors bridged in some inspiring ways the gap between practitioners and scholars and scholar/practitioners—this volume gives voice to a wide array of case studies and experiences that hint at the enormous amount of inspiring work going on worldwide in this burgeoning area of inquiry.

The team at the International Institute for Critical Studies in Improvisation (IICSI) hosted by the University of Guelph was similarly dedicated through this process. We especially wish to thank our research assistant, Dr. Brian Lefresne, for his tireless work as liaison with authors, careful reader and copy editor, project manager, and keeper of the files. Rachel Collins provided invaluable work, yet again, assembling and formatting the manuscript during the two stages of submissions. Justine Richardson, IICSI project manager, and Ajay Heble, IICSI director, were unstinting in their support, providing much-needed assistance throughout the process. We acknowledge the Social Sciences and Humanities Research Council of Canada for its ongoing, significant contributions to both the Improvisation, Community, and Social Practice (ICASP) and IICSI projects.

Ken Wissoker of Duke University Press was supportive and encouraging throughout the conceptualization and review processes, and his keen analytic eye helped us refocus and reconceptualize at several key moments. We also value the work of his assistants, Elizabeth Ault and Josh Tranen, who kept us on track through review and production, and of senior project editor Liz Smith, who helped bring the project to conclusion. The insights of two anonymous readers led to valuable reconsiderations of aspects of our thinking and ultimately made this a better book.

Last but not least, we are grateful to our families, friends, and colleagues for their support and for giving us the time to work. And we thank those who improvise, as always, for the inspiration. Our title, *Playing for Keeps: Improvisation in the Aftermath*, points to the global importance of ongoing improvisatory practices discussed in the book, and the need for these to continue to flourish, and develops the implications of Sun Ra's observation in *Space Is the Place* that "the earth cannot move without music. The earth moves in a certain rhythm, a certain sound, a certain note. When the music stops the earth will stop and everything upon it will die."[1]

NOTE

1 Sun Ra in John Coney, dir., *Space Is the Place* (USA: North American Star System, 1974).

Playing for Keeps

An Introduction

DANIEL FISCHLIN AND ERIC PORTER

Improvisation: Reverberations of the Possible

Celebrated author Thomas King's history from below, *The Inconvenient Indian: A Curious Account of Native People in America*, opens with a short tale of a traditional First Nations drum group to which he belonged: "Anishinaabe, Métis, Coastal Salish, Cree, Cherokee. We have nothing much in common. We're all Aboriginal and we have the drum. That's about it."[1] The drum is a gathering point that is more than symbolic since its sound is a form of embodied endurance. The musicians "play for keeps"; that is, they play for people engaged in multiple struggles for survival. The crisis in Canada and elsewhere with respect to indigenous populations that have suffered a sustained attack on their communities, cultural traditions, and very existence has produced a payload of intergenerational misery—but also a sustained set of creative responses that have reclaimed political agency in spite of a settler culture still keen to eradicate their traditions, languages, and history. The drum betokens an improvised community that gathers around it even as it heralds a future yet to be made in the sound of playing together. It is the sound of resilience and solidarity with an outcome yet unknown. Survival, if not political certainty, is audible in the pulse that mimics the diastole and systole of the beating hearts that make it resonate.

Playing for Keeps explores the emergence and development of musical improvisation in settler-colonial, postcolonial, postapartheid, and postwar societies, with particular attention to the uses of it, successfully and otherwise, in negotiating lingering violence and uncertainty, and in imagining alternative futures, addressing trauma, sustaining resilience, and modeling, if not inspiring, solidaric relationships. Ongoing forms of empire and related structures of inequality continue to propagate—with the *post* in the relevant descriptors signifying not the end of but rather changing contours of terror and domination and a failure to address the pervasiveness of systems that rely on disproportionate wealth, modulated forms of enslavement, and technologies of alienation and disempowerment. In such circumstances, people are forced to improvise socially, politically, and culturally. Although musical improvisation's emergence in such contexts is never certain, and its politics often fraught,[3] this book shows how groups and individuals use improvisatory practices in compelling ways to make the aftermath of trauma, crisis, revolution, colonization, and inequality a site of emergent potential. Improvisation offers not only a means for coping with and responding to impossible and unthinkable situations but also an embodied strategy for analyzing the very structures of destruction and dominance that produce sustained misery and subject aggrieved populations to the implacable logic of violence and exploitation.

The globalized realities of expansive, systemic socioeconomic and racial inequalities, unparalleled ecological rapacity, the mutation of colonial power into its present transnational corporate forms, and the default violence deployed by overmilitarized nation-states, police forces, political groups, and individuals all sustain the crisis of the moment in myriad locally specific ways. Esteemed musicians Herbie Hancock and Wayne Shorter in a cowritten open letter addressed to the next generation of artists take note of how "we find ourselves in turbulent and unpredictable times. From the horror at the Bataclan, to the upheaval in Syria and the senseless bloodshed in San Bernardino, we live in a time of great confusion and pain." In response, they articulate the functional role of tactics deeply associated with their improvisatory experience of music: "Whether through the exploration of new sounds, rhythms, and harmonies or unexpected collaborations, processes and experiences, we encourage you to dispel repetition in all of its negative forms and consequences. Strive to create new actions both musically and with the pathway of your life. Never conform."[2]

Hancock and Shorter advocate a willingness to engage the unknown, and the risks associated with taking such action, as a fundamental part of their artistic practice: "The unknown necessitates a moment-to-moment improvisation or creative process that is unparalleled in potential and fulfillment. There is no dress rehearsal for life because life, itself, is the real rehearsal. Every relationship, obstacle, interaction, etc. is a rehearsal for the next adventure in life. Everything is connected. Everything builds. Nothing is ever wasted. This type of thinking requires courage."[3] In other words, in the aftermath of chaos and trauma, improvisatory modes of being provide generative alternatives based on risk taking and nonconformity rooted in cocreative connections.

This book argues that sonic improvisation and the musical and social practices and discourses that coevolve with various forms of it provide a powerful, if marginalized, tool for finding the grounds to negotiate, survive, analyze, and sometimes oppose what First Nations author Leslie Marmon Silko describes as "destroyer" culture in her 1977 novel *Ceremony*. Musical improvisation responds to destroyer culture in multiple ways. These can include the development of shared artistic practices that necessarily hybridize musical languages to find a common ground, or that find ways to say new things within the limitations of a specific form or within the confines of limited access to resources, or that expand the event horizon of the possible through attacks on convention and radical experimentalism, to list only a few of its methods and outcomes. Musical improvisation allows for, even encourages, differential encounters—with sound, with other humans, with the spirit, with the cosmos—that gesture toward their aftermath. In its "purest form," as improviser and composer Wadada Leo Smith argues, improvisation is "an arrangement of silence and sound and rhythm that has never before been heard and will never again be heard."[4] But its resonance—in thought, memory, practice, and affect—continues to shape the world, necessarily engaging and potentially transforming the societies where it is made and those to which it travels. These are not vacuous theoretical shibboleths but lived experiential realities, current in contemporary discourses about improvisation arising from multiple sites and practitioners, that musicians share in real time as part of the interchange that improvisation unfolds. Indeed, the material outcomes of these sorts of generative musical interchanges, even in their least successful iterations, are part of an aspirational form of human agency in which choice, context, resourcefulness, dialogue, plurivocality, independence, and reciprocity can be played with (quite literally) in the face of the systemic underpinnings of crisis.

As part of the Improvisation, Community, and Social Practice (ICASP) book series, *Playing for Keeps* falls within a trajectory of critical improvisation studies that is committed to understanding the possibilities, and limitations, of musical improvisation as a model for political, cultural, and ethical dialogue and action—for imagining and creating alternative ways of knowing and being known in the world even as it interrogates the ways in which aesthetic practices impact other forms of social practice. It argues for the value of the creative risk taking imbued with a sense of movement and momentum that makes improvisation an inspiring, unpredictable, ubiquitous, challenging, and necessary endeavor.[5] But we also intend this book as an invitation to think about how we might push the conversation in critical studies in improvisation in new directions. We recognize that "improvisation," as put into scholarly practice in North America and across much of Europe, has become a master trope that potentially erases elements of the multiple, differential, and sometimes radical practices to which it generally refers. Such monolithic discourses can obscure the culturally specific dynamics and meanings of improvisational practices across time and space. They can assume too neat a connection between liberation in performance and liberation in social practice. And they can also lose sight of the ways that the affective and political work that improvisation in the strictest sense—that is, unscripted, creative decision making in real time—accomplishes is often a product of its coproduction with other modes of musicking (composition, reproduction, repetition, and so on) and a wide array of culturally specific social activities.

Improvisatory human activity, as the chapters and case studies that follow make clear, has not developed simply in opposition to, or free from, these underpinnings of present-day crisis or the *longue durée* processes that constitute them. Improvisatory musical practices, the humans who create and listen to them, and the stories and critical discourses that make them intelligible beyond the scenes of their performative iterations are both the outcomes of and the alternatives to this tragic history. Improvising communities have long and often been riven by gendered, racial, ethnic, and class-based exclusions, conflicts, and symbolic (and occasionally real) violence. Further, the tropes that enable our understandings of the liberatory work improvisation can potentially do have deep roots in modernist, primitivist racial fantasies and their dispersals via critical discourse, literary performance, and the promotional practices of a global music industry whose economic practices help create the conditions, and often set the limits, for spontaneous musicking and its wider cultural dissemination. Yet it is precisely through improvisation's deep imbrication in overlapping, asymmetrical power relations that its efficacy as a practice for modeling alternatives to such relations may be explored.

As a social practice, improvisation is an important aspect of the public commons, "the assembly of people," as Thomas DeFrantz argues, "that aligns contingent interests and needs. The commons emerges to be different from sedimented concepts of community; the commons imagines itself to be contingent and ephemeral, momentary but stable.... The commons recognizes itself briefly and then moves away from itself, leaving traces of its achievement in Black Lives Matter, in the Occupy movement, in student uprisings against gun access and LGBTQ hate crimes."[6] To this list may be added multiple examples of the commons, through both social and musical forms, responding in the aftermaths of the crises that activate aspects of our shared humanity.

A devastating 2017 earthquake in central Mexico, for instance, saw rapid-fire responses from the commons in which *colectivos* in rural locations reconstructed devastated homes with an eco-friendly technique using materials easily at hand: PET (polyethylene terephthalate) plastic bottles filled with garbage and trash to create load-bearing bricks for new homes.[7] Luis D'Artagnan, a volunteer aid worker during the crisis, notes how "lo que proliferó y se diversificó con gran plasticidad y rapidez fueron las brigadas de ayuda" (it was the help brigades that proliferated and diversified with great flexibility and speed). These help brigades improvised a range of responses to the disaster: a group called the Bikers, who were able to quickly access remote regions that government vehicles could not, distributed basic necessities and provided medical assistance; other brigades identified damaged structures posing a risk to neighbors; and arts collectives addressed issues of morale, childcare, and the like for victims.[8] Similar DIY responses to disaster relief occurred in Puerto Rico after the 2017 Hurricane Maria, which saw a state response characterized by mismanagement, corruption, and incompetence—whereas the DIY grassroots response across multiple communities led to concerted actions like the Proyecto de Apoyo Mutual (Project for Mutual Aid), which "began by feeding hundreds of people a day ... [then] added a weekly health clinic.... A free meal delivery service for the elderly. Potable water. Even Wi-Fi."[9] Both examples point to the exceptional resilience of the commons to self-empower via improvised, DIY direct action in the face of disaster and state incompetence and neglect.

In music, improvisation is often a key component of direct engagements with forces that produce crisis. The freestyle cipher performed by Eminem as part of the 2017 Black Entertainment Television hip-hop awards fused aspects of community-based improvisatory practices with a scathing critique of the various crises brought on by the Trump presidency. Eminem's improvised rap occurs in the context of a circle of observers, the cipher—for whom he performs and with whom he is in improvised dialogue. These improvisatory forms are manifestly sites where a critical commons operates within and against a backdrop of hegemonic structures and institutional inertias that limit or foreclose on agency. The improvised spaces of the commons model contingency, respond to the ephemeral needs that require collective action and resilience, and underline the need to move away from inflexible, stagnant ways of expressing human community in all its wondrously specific manifestations.

Perseverance and resilience are critical to the survival of the commons in certain contexts, and these are closely tied to subtler ways of exercising agency and implicitly offering political critique. The case of Sara Akel, a young Palestinian pianist from the Gaza Strip and

> one of the Strip's greatest cultural assets, is typical of Gaza—exceptional talent overcoming obstacles that few of her peer group elsewhere could imagine. She had to wait seven years for a second-hand piano at home because of the shortage of the instruments in Gaza during the blockade. She first played on a toy keyboard, then mostly practised on a Yamaha "virtual piano." Before taking part in her first national Palestinian competition, she had to learn to use pedals at the conservatory. Moreover, she could only participate by video because she and her fellow competitors from Gaza had not been allowed out to the West Bank—an all too familiar enforcement of Israel's determined separation of Gaza from the West Bank.[10]

In Gaza, to express herself, Akel was forced to deploy all sorts of improvisatory practices to address the exceptional material challenges to her access to teachers, audiences, and even the very instrument on which she has displayed such exceptional talent. Similar acts of localized courage and persistence may be found in global northern contexts, where racialized violence takes other forms. Nisha Sajnani, director of the Drama Therapy and Community Health program at the Post Traumatic Stress Center in New Haven, Connecticut, points to "improvisation as a kind of 'disciplined empathy'" and places it at the core of her art-based research called Living Enquiry.[11] Living Enquiry is an outgrowth of "embodied non-scripted forms" that call on aspects of Keith Johnstone's developmental transformations, playback theater, and Augusto Boal's theater of the oppressed, and Sajnani has "drawn on Living Enquiry to enquire into the experiences of communities displaced by genocide and other human rights violations . . . and to explore and document the experience of oppression faced by racialized youths and adults."[12] Improvisation plays a key role in this form of inquiry. It blends testimony with embodied explorations of trauma and is predicated on principles closely tied to improvisatory practices: "opening to uncertainty," "attuning to difference," and "aesthetic intelligence," with Sajnani noting George Steiner's observation, "We do not have a word yet for this 'ordered enlistment of intuition.'"[13] Embodied theatrical play in which improvisatory unscripted performance both witnesses and addresses trauma and its aftermath presents a new vector for responding to crisis.

There is back of these examples a long history of decolonizing reverberations across the planet that were, in many ways, facilitated by the expansion of empire and the economic, military, and racial knowledge projects associated with it. W. E. B. Du Bois embodied some of these contradictions in his early twentieth-century writings about music. His Eurocentrism, racial essentialism, masculinism, and cultural elitism shaped his approach to writing about music and its political potential, including his unwillingness to engage significantly with the dynamic improvisational practice called jazz. While limited in many respects, he was still hailed—albeit through the lens of his Arnoldian take on culture—by emergent, decolonizing aesthetic practices. In *The Negro* (1915), Du Bois unabashedly links the creative output of African Americans with progressive outcomes, stating, "Already in poetry, literature, music, and painting the work of Americans of Negro descent has gained notable recognition. . . . Self-realization is thus coming slowly but surely to another of the world's great races, and they are today girding themselves to fight in the van of progress, not simply for their own rights as men, but for the ideals of the greater world in which they live: the emancipation of women, universal peace, democratic government, the socialization of wealth, and human brotherhood."[14]

Du Bois eloquently reflected on African American "sorrow songs," "the Negro folk-song—the rhythmic cry of the slave" that "stands today . . . as the sole American music" and "remains as the singular spiritual heritage of the nation and the greatest gift of the Negro people." The sorrow songs were "the music of an unhappy people, of the children of disappointment; they tell of death and suffering and unvoiced longing toward a truer world, of misty wanderings and hidden ways."[15] Du Bois precisely links the crises triggered by racism, colonization, slavery, exile, and historical erasure, among others, with the ways music addresses, if not arises from, these circumstances and is situated in their aftermath as an "unvoiced longing toward a truer world."[16]

Du Bois understood that the "market" for the spirituals, their growing popularity in the US and abroad, facilitated their potentially transformative power as a vehicle for Black recognition. What he subsequently missed, however, by not taking seriously jazz and its relations, were the decolonial imaginaries consolidated specifically through commodity capitalism and emergent technologies. Michael Denning, in his examination of the explosion of vernacular music from the late 1920s and early 1930s that emerged from an "archipelago of colonial ports," argues that such musical forms—on their own, as heard together, and when cross-fertilizing one another—remade the "musical ear" via their common articulations of noisy timbres, syncopated rhythms, "weird" vocal tonalities, and, with increasing emphasis, improvisation. Once committed to record, these sounds decolonized the ear, calling into question established cultural hierarchies based on race, color, and civilization and "remaking... the very structure of feeling as new sensibilities and new aesthetics become new ways of living."[17] This process, Denning argues, helped set the stage for decolonization as a constellation of social, political, and cultural movements, for "these vernacular phonograph discs were, in their very sound, a 'working out of the social order to come,' an improvisation of a postcolonial world."[18]

The political project of this vernacular music was contradictory, not least because embedded within it were forms of embodiment (singing, dancing, marching, playing instruments, and so on) and technologies carried across the globe by various forms of colonialism.[19] Moreover, the music

> often prefigured the contradictions to come, the trials and tribulations of the decolonizing movements and states: the divide between a democracy of improvisation, and a cult of populist stars and bandleaders; the divide between male instrumentalists, inheriting the craft ideologies of artisan music-making, and a now open, and openly sexualized, ambivalence toward the woman singing star; the divide within new territories, as the musics of particular regions and peoples became emblems of the nation; and the political metaphysics of rhythm—the inversion of the disparagement of rhythm and "rhythmic" peoples into the celebration of a sometimes essentialized, naturalized somatic rhythm.[20]

This contradictory and anticipatory scene played out via multiple reverberations—albeit with some, like jazz, more prominent than others—of local expressions across the globe.

Denning's observations on improvisation in settler-colonial contexts are particularly acute:

> Improvisation in music has... long existed, but, in nineteenth-century Europe and the European settler societies of the Americas, it lost recognition and value as printed composition came to dominate both art music and popular song.... Moreover, as improvisation declined in prestige, it became increasingly associated with subaltern castes of musical performers: "Extemporisation or improvisation," the 1927 edition of the authoritative *Grove's Dictionary of Music and Musicians* stated, is "the primitive act of music-making, existing from the moment the untutored individual obeys the impulse to relieve his feelings by bursting into song. Accordingly, therefore, amongst all primitive peoples musical composition consists of extemporization subsequently memorized."[21]

The *Grove's Dictionary*'s dismissive notion of improvisation as a form of primitivism is deeply racist and accounts, in part, for the way in which improvisation has been marginalized, ignored, or placed at the bottom of Western musical hierarchies of knowledge. And, as Denning observes, this movement is clearly coincident with colonization and Eurocentric values that were horrified by any threat to the aesthetic order that supported notions of restricted and exploitative political agency in relation to "subaltern castes." Yet the anxiety produced by jazz and other forms of improvised musical discourses in the face of Eurocentric, colonial values in the early twentieth century helped to consolidate their disruptive power. In short, the audio-politics of improvisation were radically at odds with hegemonic thinking but were also made audible by it, and this rupture helped set the stage for its deployment as a strategy for voicing various forms of resistance to the crises perpetuated by empire and its failures.[22]

The promise of vernacular music, improvised and otherwise, like the promises of the often-revolutionary freedom movements it anticipated and, at times, interfaced with, remains "unfulfilled" and "unfinished" given the persistence and mutability of "the racial orders of colonialism and settler colonialism."[23] Still, the reverberations of possibility as well as contradiction remain, on record and in live performance, and continue to be worked through via various modes of musicking. But it is improvisation, as a shared practice, that holds a particularly valuable potential for responding to the multiplicity of crises that have local and global historical roots. These crises continue to generate lived material consequences—from post-traumatic stress disorder and other forms of trauma through to the inability to access adequate resources; from intergenerational suffering brought on by war, disaster, or malicious forms of governance, among other causes, that produce life-and-death circumstances the world over.

"Playing for keeps" is, in such circumstances, a historically unfolding trope that articulates the stakes of responding to what Argentine-Mexican philosopher and social critic Enrique Dussel calls "transmodernity."[24] It is a response that will very possibly be determinative of what it means to be human in a future for which we are all struggling. Dussel's work, at the turn of the new millennium, aligns with that of other cultural theorists in advocating for pluriversality and linked forms of epistemic and biotic diversity, what Donna Haraway calls *sympoiesis*, or "making-with." "Nothing makes itself," Haraway argues. "Nothing is really autopoietic or self-organizing. . . . *Sympoiesis* is a word proper to complex, dynamic, responsive, situated historical systems. It is a word for worlding-with, in company. *Sympoiesis* enfolds autopoiesis and generatively unfurls and extends it."[25]

At odds with singularities and myths of autonomy, *sympoiesis* instead recognizes the cocreative, contingent aspects of multiple forms of connection that bind epistemic, historical, and material systems ineluctably together. It helps us understand how monocultural formations that threaten difference on a planetary scale need to be opposed by "imag[ining] multiple possible alternative worlds," as Ramon Grosfoguel puts it, in order to resist and subvert the crises brought about by a combination of postindustrial, hypertechnological, corporate self-interest and diminished rights environments that failed to address basic logics of sustainability and survivability.[26] Upholding reciprocal interests between larger biotic and human realities requires evolving creative forms of agency congruent with core human values. Playing for keeps entails thinking through where these forms of agency get modeled, reproduced, refigured, and tested. Our argument is that improvised performative, creative practices found in music, art, storytelling, and the like all have roles to play in shaping such interactions. We add the caution that such practices often sit at the margins of where the determinative practices of power and resources are located. A further caution recognizes that improvisatory interventions into practices of governance, whether intentional or not, may well be co-opted, assimilated, or subsumed into realpolitik practices deeply at odds with idealized notions of improvisatory liberation. Sometimes, such practices simply reproduce power and its constitutive elements. A struggle, in short, over the dominant epistemes associated with improvisation and the way they are shaped is ongoing.

Increasingly precipitate crises that accumulate over time, causing enormous material and psychic damage to millions of people globally, and the responses to those are now definitive of who we are in the process of becoming, how we are "making-with." Strategies of cultural transformation associated with improvisation need to be evaluated in relation to their capacity to effect material change in complex circumstances where crisis occurs. Critical studies in improvisation offers an opportunity for imagining how aesthetic models of cocreation may be linked to other forms of social practice, with full recognition that there are dangers in doing so, not least of which is that improvisatory practices are subject to repurposing in the name of the very hegemonic forces they ostensibly oppose. A further danger is the significant slippage that occurs when one discusses a musical performance in relation to the aftermath of an earthquake—is cocreative action for aesthetic purposes really thinkable in terms of life-and-death scenarios of the struggle to survive? While the initial sense of the Greek word *krisis* meant the "'turning point in a disease' (used as such by Hippocrates and Galen),"[27] it also carried with it the sense of *krinein*, that is, to judge, to decide, to be capable of informed critical thought. Improvisation figures in this scenario because it is the scene of turning points, the place where possibility collides with reality, the agency of hope with the inertia of despair: both a way out of no way, as Daniel Fischlin, Ajay Heble, and George Lipsitz argue, *and* a site where real-time information sharing, critical thought, and epistemic variation and diversity arise.[28]

To live on we must move on. The diverse case studies found in this book suggest that generative cocreation, however problematic and difficult to achieve, is indeed possible and is happening in multiple sites where improvised music and social practice collide. Envisioning and enacting material, lived alternatives to systemic structures of colonial inequity, racism, economic exploitation, and the radical disregard for equality across gender, ethnicity, and class is no facile challenge. Producing new models of solidarity and resilience out of both collective dialogue and epistemic diversity—that is to say, out of difference made manifest—is at the heart of what occurs in improvisatory musical practices in which the principles of proportionality, solidarity, complementarity, reciprocity, and correspondence are at stake. We emphasize that these are not pure forms inoculated against use in support of hegemony, as the chaotic Trump presidency has shown in all its improvisatory destructive power. How then to evaluate critically collective undertakings and principles that imagine meaningful responses to the array of crises that put the collective meaning of humanity to the question? Some of these principles include notions of hospitality, contingency, synergistic codependency, and obligate mutualism, among others. Improvisation provides one important frame for exploring what these mean and how they operate as a potential model for reorienting structures of thought and behavior that have abandoned these principles, let alone definitive structures of interaction with the biotic realities of the environment out of which humanity arises and without which it will not survive.[29]

Improvisation involves the readiness to remake things out of a paucity of materials, limitations, the crisis of having to risk in the here and now the immediacy of a decision—the responsibility to act creatively and in concert with others to reclaim a public commons under attack. Improvisation is not the answer, then, but a tool to create flexible, site-specific strategies that connect the creative and the critical—that negotiate stricture and unrealized possibility. The regenerative potential in improvisation thrives in opportunity, turning dissolution and degeneration into the potential for refiguration. Improvisation can, like fire pines, reproduce out of crisis and destruction.

As improvisation reproduces itself, it reproduces us as well, for better or for worse. In musical terms, improvisation challenges conformity—it teaches humility and contingency, but it also allows for dissonance and unresolved tension. Improvisation voices contingency, embodies agency, offers a practice to find voice in relation to the otherness that is omnipresently a part of self-definition, but improvisation also always risks an outcome that no one predicted, and even more so an outcome that not everyone agrees on. We hope not to be separated: by walls, by state-imposed constraints, by violence, by daily humiliations that abject and dehumanize the oppressors more so than the victims. Dignity arises from the power of creation embedded in community. But underlying who defines community are discursive regimes frequently based on violence and oppression: Wafaa Hasan, invoking the work of Sara Ahmed, notes how these discursive regimes must be understood before the "we" of collective politics can be made real: "Ahmed's insistence that the 'we' of such a collective politics is what must be worked for is importantly paired with her insistence on the details of how race, gender and other oppressions work to differentiate some others from other-others in particular socio-political contexts. Indeed, the work of dismantling those discursive régimes might comprise the struggle in itself."[30] Dissonance and improvisation go hand in hand. Critique and alternative voicings lie in wait in the next measure of an improvisation.

What might it mean to be faced with our potential end as an improvisation, to improvise an ending, or to end improvising? What might it mean to live in improvised time, in the time of improvisations overtaking crisis? For we struggle as victims; we struggle as perpetrators of conformity and violence; we struggle to free ourselves from imitating failed models of encounter and silencing. We struggle to affirm our empathy and respect for each other, and to re-create these on a daily basis. Improvisation gives us some of the tools for finding ways into this shared language, inspires and potentially models deep human needs to live free of violence, to respect others, to struggle toward a justice that recognizes the ongoing work of being human, to learn from differences, to embrace creative play as a way, *the way*, forward. The challenge is determining how to use these tools—without damaging something, or at least without damaging the wrong thing. And the struggle, going forward, as the essayists in this book collectively examine, is how to understand improvisation as a contested site whose meanings and uses remain to be determined, remain part of an ongoing struggle, a crisis in what it means to be relationally contingent, biotically codependent.

New Directions in Improvisation Studies: Voicing the Aftermath

Playing for Keeps is part of a multipart intervention that builds from a call for papers we issued in 2013. Our broader project now includes a special issue of the journal *Critical Studies in Improvisation/Études critiques en improvisation* (vol. 11, nos. 1–2, 2016), this book, and an additional book in progress. All of these volumes push beyond some of the initial cultural and political assumptions animating the ICASP series, as we ask whether some assumptions driving work in critical improvisations to date—and, more specifically, some of our own work—may obscure the complexity of dialogue and action that becomes increasingly evident when one examines improvisational musical practices across a range of geographic and cultural contexts. As such, in concluding remarks to the first publication we produced on the topic, we argued that "musical improvisation is no monoculture, nor is it meant to be a dominant discourse reduced to academic cant. It is predicated on sonic diversity, multiple practices of engaging with aurality, and unexpected convergences that are unpredictable and endlessly contingent. Its specificity arises from differential understandings of what it means in practice and in theory."[31]

In continuing to work on this topic, we asked ourselves, more specifically, whether field-defining interpretative paradigms—largely inspired by the liberatory sonic, intellectual, and political projects of African American improvised musicians and, to a somewhat lesser extent, by the broader terrain of European and US-based experimental music—assumed too narrow an understanding of the work that improvisation does or potentially does. If so, we asked, how might multiply sited investigations of improvisation call into question existing theoretical and political assumptions guiding its study? And how might the development of new theoretical and case-study analyses broaden critical improvisation studies, with its interdisciplinary reach and attention to political context, beyond North American and European sites delimited (largely) by specific forms like free jazz, spontaneous composition, and experimental music? The challenge to critical studies in improvisation generally is to avoid the familiar patterns of academic cant and rhetorical ossification, where universalist assumptions eradicate pertinent differences across diverse improvisatory musical and social practices.

Authors responded in various ways to the call for papers, with quite a few pushing back quite forcefully on ICASP's politically and ethically affirmative investments in improvisation as social practice—a chance for dialogue and learning we welcomed. This group of essays, however, along with a handful of artist-generated pieces we commissioned, is an extension of the ICASP project that makes clear that the theoretical and pragmatic role of improvisation, both as a social practice and as a musical discourse in relation to the specific circumstances arising in settler-colonial, postcolonial, postapartheid, and postwar societies, has been underexplored, in spite of the fact that improvisation plays such a key role in how people respond to crisis and to asymmetrical structures of power and access to resources. Taken together, the chapters that follow, based on case studies that identify improvisatory practices across a range of global sites, demonstrate that improvisatory responses to such circumstances are indeed multifaceted, determined as they are by the specifics of time and place as well as the range of practices under consideration. People play for keeps individually and collectively by drawing on (and changing) local tradition and traveling forms, onstage and in the classroom, through the shaping of sound-making materials and in the rarefied discourse about them, through meanings generated solely among performers, and through those created by others. How people choose to voice the aftermath, as these case studies show, has a great deal to teach about the connections between improvised forms of musical cocreation and larger solidaric practices in the face of complex social and political challenges.

Opening the collection, then, is sound experimentalist, composer, and reed player Matana Roberts's poem "manifesto." Framed as an improvisation on the preamble of the US Constitution, the piece imagines a more humane nation, defined by an expansively conceived and applied set of principles through which "the ever growing collective mongrel race" might survive the "United States of Hysteric-a," at this moment witnessing the crisis of the Trump presidency and the unleashing of the social and ideological forces that made it possible. Writing as a member of the Association for the Advancement of Creative Musicians, whose members' aesthetic and critical practice has long performed and analyzed improvisatory response to crisis as a global and transhistorical project, Roberts sets the stage for a collective project of examining and responding to a variety of aftermaths across the planet. And, importantly, Roberts locates the crisis in America in a misreading of a Constitution that "sums up our values" but fails to recognize that "we are improvised."

Stephanie Vos's "*The Exhibition of Vandalizim*: Improvising Healing, Politics, and Film in South Africa" shows how improvisational practices from the United States (namely, African American free jazz) are often used and transformed in response to localized conditions of crisis. She analyzes a filmed, improvised performance by composer and improviser Zim Ngqawana and his group that responded to the burglary and ransacking of Ngqawana's

Zimology Institute, an educational center dedicated to free improvisation pedagogy. Vos shows how Ngqawana and fellow musicians responded to this invasive act and the broader social environment in South Africa by performing distorted sounds on the instruments that were damaged by a group of vandals. She further theorizes how distorted sounds and images may provide particularly meaningful representations of precarious social situations. She highlights, in light of Ngqawana's own ideas about the same, the ritualistic healing (pace Victor Turner) and political voice (pace Jacques Rancière) that collective improvisation may offer in the face of real or symbolic violence. The outcome may not necessarily be healing in any complete sense but can still provide a glimpse of an alternative social order in the aftermath of destruction.

Mark Lomanno's "The Rigors of Afro/Canarian Jazz: Sounding Peripheral Vision with Severed Tongues" continues the examination of the politics of contemporary improvised music in Africa, although here the denial of the "Africanness" of this music informs the hegemonic structure that improvising musicians work within and against. Lomanno examines recent efforts by musicians from the Canary Islands, an autonomous community of Spain located west of Morocco, to create Afro/Canarian jazz. Such efforts assert an Afro/Canarian identity, and an attendant cultural critique, in the face of a long history of Spanish suppression of Canarian indigenous culture. Along the way, Lomanno argues that interdisciplinary, performance research stances attentive to the multiplicities of musical and social improvisations provide a mechanism for critiquing the conventions of academic disciplinarity.

An interview with Vijay Iyer returns the project to the United States, albeit with attention to issues that play no small part in generating crises elsewhere. Focusing on the collaborative performance/composition *Holding It Down*, Iyer discusses how US veterans'—and, especially, black and brown US veterans'—participation in this project as artists and listeners has helped them work through the traumatic aftermath of their participation in the perpetual wars of the early twenty-first century. Iyer positions the project within a genealogy of improvising artists—some of them veterans—commenting on war. But Iyer also interrogates the term *improvisation*, calling into question "the use of the word *improvisation* to stand in for freedom or liberation," when practices of domination and oppression may also involve improvisatory aspects. Speaking about *Holding It Down*, Iyer notes that the project involved spontaneous improvisations at different levels but also what he calls an "*annealing* process," a congealing of "a lot of [musical and lyrical] elements in motion" through contemplation and repetition over time. It is a process, he argues, that involves improvisation but also a kind of "*stripping away* [of] improvisation through coordinated collective actions."

Kate Galloway's "Experimental and Improvised Norths: The Sonic Geographies of Tanya Tagaq's Collaborations with Derek Charke and the Kronos Quartet" considers a geographic and cultural context, the Canadian North, that is relatively close to North American metropoles but, given histories of settler colonialism and extreme weather conditions, symbolically distant. Examining experimental Inuit throat singer Tanya Tagaq's collaborative works with Canadian composer Derek Charke and the US ensemble Kronos Quartet, Galloway emphasizes the potential of hybrid, cocreated improvised practices to promote cross-cultural understanding and indigenous survivance in the aftermath of sustained state violence against First Nations peoples. Galloway foregrounds the "performance ecology" of these collaborations as a means of both situating the work as a regionally specific articulation of indigenous modernity and accounting for the range of scripted and unscripted musical and extramusical activities on which the more visible, onstage and on-record improvisations are based. Galloway steers us toward questions of embodiment, which are crucial to her analysis; she draws attention to Tagaq's embodied knowledge of the Northern environment and the ways that her raced and gendered body as instrument "challenges the accepted norms of Indigenous female performance" while engaged in a cocreative process in physical proximity to differently raced and gendered bodies.

In "Nina Simone: CIVIL JAZZ!" illustrator Randy DuBurke offers eight drawings charting Simone's politicization during the early 1960s civil rights movement, culminating with the creation of her song "Mississippi Goddam" in the wake of the white nationalist terrorist bombing of a Birmingham, Alabama, church that killed four young girls and the murder of Medgar Evers, both in 1963. The stunning visual imagery evokes both direct acts of violence and the ever-present threat of violence—both state and vigilante—that haunted and inspired civil rights activists. Although Simone was particularly notable for her explicit political critique and her direct assistance to political organizations, she is but one of many improvising artists active in the 1960s who responded to the ongoing crisis of a society's refusal to extend full citizenship rights to a significant portion of its population. DuBurke, like Roberts, reminds us of this disgraceful element of US history that birthed an improvisatory movement that negotiated the present and imagined a better future.

Rana El Kadi's "Free Improvised Music in Postwar Beirut: Differential Sounds, Intersectarian Collaborations, and Critical Collective Memory" takes the discussion to the contemporary Middle East and a range of issues related to recent (and lingering) postcolonial and postwar violence. She considers the recent development of the free improvisation scene in Beirut, Lebanon, arguing that it has provided a unique vehicle for people to negotiate sectarian differences in this city torn by ethnic and religious factionalism and civil war. With particular focus on the work of Mazen Kerbaj, Sharif Sehnaoui, and Raed Yassin, El Kadi shows how this putatively "culturally neutral musical practice" with roots in the United States and Europe takes on particular cultural and political resonances in Lebanon. El Kadi's case study examines both the localized power of deployments of free improvisational forms drawn from elsewhere and the specific work done when such styles are fused with local sonic expressions. One such project, which had musicians improvising alongside a "collage" made of recorded sounds—artillery, political speeches, news broadcasts, music, and so on—from the era of the Lebanese Civil War, interrogates the "collective amnesia" about the conflict, used by some to absolve themselves of responsibility for it. El Kadi's work shows how improvised music in postwar Beirut models a civil society in which the striving toward open dialogue allows for working through conflict cocreatively.

Darci Sprengel's "Street Concerts and Sexual Harassment in Post-Mubarak Egypt: *Ṭarab* as Affective Politics" similarly looks at improvisation's role in modeling alternative social relations but foregrounds the site-specific transformation of local musical practices rather than the rearticulation of those imported from elsewhere. Sprengel explores the Mini Mobile Concerts project that came together after the 2011 revolution in Egypt. These concerts brought into the street *ṭarab*, a musically induced ecstasy created through interactions among performers and audience, which has usually been restricted to art-music contexts. Participants in this project sought to create an alternative public culture outside of the control of state authority and pursued this goal through this hybrid, embodied, affective practice rather than the kinds of direct political interventions that were soon stymied in the postuprising period. Intervening in the street, however, required this group, with significant female membership, to reconfigure the context of popular music performance to enable women in the group to inhabit the public sphere, free of sexual harassment. By thus enacting a reconfiguration of ethical relationships among its citizens in the arena of gender relations, the Mini Mobile Concerts fulfilled some of the goals of the 2011 uprising in the face of its ostensible failure.

An interview with Reem Abdul Hadi and Odeh Turjman, along with an introductory essay by Daniel Fischlin, addresses how the West Bank–based

Al-Mada Association for Arts-Based Community Development responds to the crisis of potential erasure—of land, of language, of equal rights, of mobility, and so forth—that besets Palestinians in the Occupied Territories. This erasure is linked to what Saree Makdisi describes as "a broad complex of Israeli policies that has come to define the rhythm and tempo of life for Palestinians, not only in the occupied territories but inside Israel itself."[32] The arts-based community work of Al-Mada seeks to redefine the rhythm and tempo of life in the refugee camps to be found throughout the Occupied Territories, demonstrating how a range of improvised small acts—among professional musicians and nonmusicians, in interactions of organizers and bureaucratic officials, help people, especially young people, survive settler-colonial occupation and militarized violence and the deep, painful psychological traumas that result.

Moshe Morad's "*Silsulim* (Improvised 'Curls') in the Vocal Performance of Israeli Popular Music: Identity, Power, and Politics" focuses on how elements of musical improvisation provide a means of negotiating difference on the other side of the militarized border—that is, among Jewish citizens of Israel. Morad shows how popular *mizraḥit/yam-tichonit* music, especially through its partially improvised vocal elements, has been coded vis-à-vis a series of binaries—Arab/Israeli, black/white, Ashkenazi/Sephardi—as it has gained (partial) acceptance in Israeli society. While practitioners, critics, and fans debated its merits, the music became a touchstone for conversations about the place of Jews from the Muslim world in Israeli society as well as a vehicle for Sephardic peoples' struggles against Ashkenazi cultural and social hegemony. The terrain is complicated. Morad examines the ways that prejudices against *mizraḥit/yam-tichonit* music (and Sephardic people more generally) stem in part from anti-Arab sentiment, even as many Sephardim support right-wing politicians who espouse similar views. Yet, although it has not been realized, *silsulim*'s popularity among Palestinians in the Occupied Territories suggests that this music possesses some potential to play a bridge-building function in the Palestinian-Israeli political context.

Kevin Fellezs's "Three Moments in *Kī Hōʻalu* (Hawaiian Slack Key Guitar): Improvising as a *Kanaka Maoli* (Native Hawaiian) Adaptive Strategy" attends to improvised performances of indigeneity that are rooted in traditional musical practices (albeit always-already hybridized), shaped by a specific physical environment, and in response to settler colonialism in Hawaii. Yet Fellezs focuses less on improvisation in specific performances than on the improvisatory strategies indigenous musicians use when developing their practice offstage: that is, when appropriating the guitar, developing pedagogical practices, "(re)inventing" their indigenous tradition musically and discursively, and negotiating the music industry as both economic actors and culture bearers. Critical to this strategic practice, he suggests, has been a willingness to engage and accommodate "the unexpected." This orientation helps us see that familiar models of improvisational liberation are not so easily applied in some contexts and that those improvised practices that are indigenous to these contexts—"patient yet active listening," "the creative (re)use of materials," and so on—enable the music and the people who perform it to persevere.

Finally, Sara Ramshaw and Paul Stapleton's "From Prepeace to Postconflict: The Ethics of (Non)Listening and Cocreation in a Divided Society" emphasizes the interface of external influence and local conditions in the production of another island-bound improvisational scene. Drawing significantly on the analyses of local musician-theorists, they chart the development of the free improvisation scene in Northern Ireland over the past several decades. Like others in this volume, they foreground the question of how improvisation might model future sociability, by emphasizing a "hospitable (non)listening to others" that enables cocreation in the sphere of performance without erasing difference. Ultimately, they argue, this culturally specific form of cocreation might model social interactions that productively engage and work through lingering divisions and conflicts in Northern Ireland.

Coda: The Integrity of Difference

In a packed, dark room in a community art space called Silence in the city of Guelph, Ontario, Thomas King sings a round dance while beating a traditional drum. Behind him a group of improvisers sit ready to respond to his call. Every time he sings the song it is the same—yet different. On this night, he is singing it for the second time in the performance, and his voice carries into the darkness and uncertain future a powerful message of resilience and strength. The song is part of a performance entitled *When You Were Gone* that brings together traditional First Nations song and rhythm, King's unpublished poetry, and improvised and composed responses to both in a structure created by Canadian composer and instrumentalist Rebecca Hennessey. The improvisers listen intently and join voices with King's powerful invocation of renewal, adaptation, healing, cultural identity, and social connection—all key symbolic figurations of the round dance. At his invitation the improvisers play with the musical motifs he has unleashed, and a new sound arises, inviting new forms of correspondence and dialogue.

Nothing less than survival is at stake. The sound of a voice singing its own agency in the face of uncompromising histories of oppression and racism is a powerful reminder of what it means to play for keeps, to erase erasure. One of the composition-improvisations in the suite takes King's words from a short poem called "Treaty":

Nothing passes for favour here,
all talk is razor-toothed.

Take nothing from the hand that offers
friendship.

In this place
all promises are bruises
in good suits.[33]

The lines resonate with an apocalyptic message from another portion of the suite, "We Will Destroy It All," that addresses betrayal by a culture predicated on destruction of aboriginal peoples and the land that is ineluctably tied to their being: "As for the garden, Adam after the fall, make no mistake he said, we will destroy it all."

In the contexts of the findings of the Truth and Reconciliation Commission of Canada (2012) about the brutal aftermaths of the residential school system that caused such damage to multiple generations of aboriginal peoples, King identifies the crises of failed encounter, and its aftermath, as ongoing. Remember that in 1883 the public works minister of Canada, Hector Langevin, a key player along with Nicholas Flood Davin in the construction of the residential school system that played a brutally critical role in the attack on indigenous cultures in Canada—and incidentally someone whose name was attached (until 2017) to the Langevin Block, where the Privy Council and the executive branch of the Canadian government were until very recently located—stated, "In order to educate the [First Nations] children properly we must separate them from their families. Some people may say that this is hard but if we want to civilize them we must do that."[34] Truth and reconciliation may be in the air, but powerful symbols of the ongoing alignment between state power and systemic injustice remain—as they do in the Langevin Block.[35] The truth of this reconciliation is that it has a long way to go before the historical landscape is sufficiently refigured in ways that respect the realities of meaningful reconciliation. The sustained crises of Canada's aboriginal peoples have included, as Langevin's racist assumptions reveal, a full-on attack on the most vulnerable members of their communities, which in turn produced incalculable multigenerational suffering and abuse.

When You Were Gone, a profound reflection on such erasures and disappearances, is also emblematic of resilience and new forms of political and aesthetic solidarity that arise when peoples provoked by utterly failed models of encounter with difference come together seeking new solutions, new ways to voice opposition to circumstances that produce systematized oppression, and alternative visions of what it means to find a grounded and shared humanity that improvises new iterations of solidarity and community.

Might such sites of improvisatory agency come to represent a response to the crises that arise from destroyer culture? Might they inspire us to renewed forms of generative agency in which reciprocity, contingency, hospitality, and respect for the integrity of difference thrive? As the essays in the volume tell us, the future is uncertain, but, at least for the moment, there is one in which improvisatory practices are alive with potential.

NOTES

1. King, *Inconvenient Indian*, x.
2. Hancock and Shorter, "Open Letter."
3. Hancock and Shorter, "Open Letter."
4. Smith, *Notes (8 Pieces)*, 4.
5. "Humming in the background of all life—and familiar and alien as breathing—is improvisation. Even the most regulated life has its perpetual micro-incidents of improvisation, periodically spiked by volcanic eruptions of haphazard behavior that release pressure. Settled situations are continually disrupted by crises both grave and petty; life, like improvised music, is a disturbing conflict between predictability and contingency." Toop, *Into the Maelstrom*, 1.
6. DeFrantz, "Identifying the Endgame," 13.
7. We are grateful to Luis D'Artagnan, a Mexican volunteer who assisted in the 2017 reconstruction efforts, for sharing this information.
8. Luis D'Artagnan, email message to author, October 20, 2017.
9. Crabapple, "Puerto Rico's DIY Disaster Relief."
10. Macintyre, "How Art Is Blooming."
11. Sajnani, "Improvisation and Art-Based Research," 83.
12. Sajnani, "Improvisation and Art-Based Research," 80.
13. Sajnani, "Improvisation and Art-Based Research," 83.
14. Du Bois, *Negro*, 138.
15. Du Bois, "Sorrow Songs," 536–38.
16. Du Bois, "Sorrow Songs," 538.

17 Denning, *Noise Uprising*, 137.
18 Denning, *Noise Uprising*, 167.
19 Denning, *Noise Uprising*, 141–42.
20 Denning, *Noise Uprising*, 167–68.
21 Denning, *Noise Uprising*, 206.
22 See, among others, Daniel Fischlin, Ajay Heble, and George Lipsitz's work on civil rights and improvisation in *The Fierce Urgency of Now: Improvisation, Rights, and the Ethics of Cocreation*, as well as Eric Porter's work on African American music and activism in *What Is This Thing Called Jazz? African American Musicians as Artists, Critics, and Activists*.
23 Denning, *Noise Uprising*, 233.
24 We have relied on three works by Dussel: *Ethics of Liberation in the Age of Globalization and Exclusion*; "¿Por qué la filosofía?"; and his preface to *Beyond Philosophy: Ethics, History, Marxism, and Liberation Theology*.
25 Haraway, *Staying with the Trouble*, 58.
26 Grosfoguel, "Wallerstein's Utopistics," 129.
27 See the etymology of "crisis" in the *Online Etymology Dictionary*, http://www.etymonline.com/word/crisis.
28 Fischlin, Heble, and Lipsitz, *Fierce Urgency of Now*, 55.
29 For a discussion of the vexed notions of what "human being" means, see Fischlin and Nandorfy, *Eduardo Galeano*, 107–16. "The OED definition [of *human*] does little to address the actual etymology of the word 'human,' which derives from Old Latin '*hemo* (whence *nemo*, nobody),' meaning the '*earthy* one, the *earth*-born' from, L *humus*, earth (soil, ground). . . . In this etymology . . . a more forthright definition of human is explicit: *the earth-born nobody*" (113).
30 Hasan, "Orientalist Feminism," 50.
31 Fischlin and Porter, "Improvisation and Global Sites of Difference," n.p.
32 Makdisi, "Israel's Policy of Erasure."
33 This unpublished poem is used with the permission of the author.
34 Epigraph to *Canada, Aboriginal Peoples, and Residential Schools: They Came for the Children*, by the Truth and Reconciliation Commission of Canada.
35 On June 21, 2017, National Aboriginal Day in Canada, Prime Minister Justin Trudeau announced that the Langevin Block would be renamed the Office of the Prime Minister and Privy Council. Coincident with the announcement was the decision to rename National Aboriginal Day as National Indigenous Peoples Day.

BIBLIOGRAPHY

Crabapple, Molly. "Puerto Rico's DIY Disaster Relief." *New York Review of Books*, December 2, 2017. http://www.nybooks.com/daily/2017/11/17/puerto-ricos-diy-disaster-relief/.

"Crisis." *Online Etymology Dictionary*. Accessed October 31, 2019. http://www.etymonline.com/word/crisis.

DeFrantz, Thomas F. "Identifying the Endgame." *Theater* 47, no. 1 (2017): 3–16.

Denning, Michael. *Noise Uprising: The Audiopolitics of a World Musical Revolution*. London: Verso, 2015.
Du Bois, W. E. B. *The Negro*. New York: Cosimo Classics, 2007.
Du Bois, W. E. B. "The Sorrow Songs." In *W. E. B. Du Bois: Writings*, edited by Nathan Huggins, 536–47. New York: The Library of America, 1986.
Dussel, Enrique. *Ethics of Liberation in the Age of Globalization and Exclusion*. Translated by Eduardo Mendieta, Camilo Pérez Bustillo, Yolanda Angulo, and Nelson Maldonado-Torres. Durham, NC: Duke University Press, 2013.
Dussel, Enrique. "¿Por qué la filosofía?" *La Jornada*, May 2, 2009. https://www.jornada.com.mx/2009/05/02/opinion/020a1pol.
Dussel, Enrique. "Preface." In *Beyond Philosophy: Ethics, History, Marxism, and Liberation Theology*, edited by Eduardo Mendieta, ix–xiii. Lanham, MD: Rowman and Littlefield, 2003.
Fischlin, Daniel, Ajay Heble, and George Lipsitz. *The Fierce Urgency of Now: Improvisation, Rights, and the Ethics of Cocreation*. Durham, NC: Duke University Press, 2013.
Fischlin, Daniel, and Martha Nandorfy. *Eduardo Galeano: Through the Looking Glass*. Montreal: Black Rose Books, 2002.
Fischlin, Daniel, and Eric Porter. "Improvisation and Global Sites of Difference: Ten Parables Verging on a Theory." *Critical Studies in Improvisation/Études critiques en improvisation* 11, nos. 1–2 (2017). https://www.criticalimprov.com/index.php/csieci/article/view/3949/3989.
Grosfoguel, Ramon. "A Critical View of Wallerstein's Utopistics from Dussel's Transmodernity: From Monoepistemic Global/Imperial Designs to Pluri-epistemic Solutions." In *Global Crises and the Challenges of the 21st Century: Antisystemic Movements and the Transformation of the World-System*, edited by Thomas Reifer, 118–31. New York: Routledge, 2016.
Hancock, Herbie, and Wayne Shorter. "Wayne Shorter and Herbie Hancock Pen an Open Letter to the Next Generation of Artists." *Nest HQ*, March 8, 2016. http://nesthq.com/wayne-shorter-herbie-hancock-open-letter/.
Haraway, Donna J. *Staying with the Trouble: Making Kin in the Chthulucene*. Durham, NC: Duke University Press, 2016.
Hasan, Wafaa. "Orientalist Feminism and the Politics of Critical Dialogue between Israeli and Palestinian Women." PhD diss., McMaster University, 2011.
King, Thomas. *The Inconvenient Indian: A Curious Account of Native People in America*. Toronto: Anchor Canada, 2013.
King, Thomas. "Treaty." Unpublished poem. 2017.
Macintyre, Donald. "How Art Is Blooming amid the Gaza Wasteland." *Guardian*, October 15, 2017. https://www.theguardian.com/world/2017/oct/14/art-blooming-amid-gaza-wasteland.
Makdisi, Saree. "Israel's Policy of Erasure." *Los Angeles Times*, November 18, 2013. http://www.latimes.com/opinion/op-ed/la-oe-makdisi-settlements-israel-palestinians-kerr-20131118-story.html.
Porter, Eric. *What Is This Thing Called Jazz? African American Musicians as Artists, Critics, and Activists*. Berkeley: University of California Press, 2002.

Sajnani, Nisha. "Improvisation and Art-Based Research." *Journal of Applied Arts and Health* 3, no. 1 (2012): 79–86.

Silko, Leslie Marmon. *Ceremony*. New York: Viking, 1977.

Smith, Wadada Leo. *Notes (8 Pieces) Source a New World Music: Creative Music*. Rev. ed. Bloomington, IL: Corbett vs. Dempsey, 2015.

Toop, David. *Into the Maelstrom: Music, Improvisation and the Dream of Freedom; Before 1970*. New York: Bloomsbury, 2016.

The Truth and Reconciliation Commission of Canada. *Canada, Aboriginal Peoples, and Residential Schools: They Came for the Children*. Winnipeg: The Truth and Reconciliation Commission of Canada, 2012.

ONE manifesto

MATANA ROBERTS

WE the PEOPLE
Are the ever growing collective mongrel race
WE the PEOPLE
Are never to underestimate the power and strength of the gathering of our differences
WE the PEOPLE
Are most powerful when we come together to battle that shame that ails us, the sick oft bawdry that pales us
WE
Laugh together.
WE
Cry Together
WE
Try Together

United States of America
United States of Hysteric-a
United States of
America.

In ORDER
To push along, we gather strong
In ORDER
To live free we know we must first see what afflicts us and destroy its song
In ORDER
To receive, we know we must give
In ORDER
To grieve, we know we must live

United States of America
United States of Hysteric-a
United States of
America.

UNION
Is the fusing of our like and unlike minds
UNION
Makes us celebrate what makes all our kind
UNION
Not some of us
UNION
Not some of them
UNION
All of us.

United States of America
United States of Hysteric-a
United States of
America.

JUSTICE
Is our birth right fought for, hurt for
JUSTICE
Can never die
JUSTICE
Is not supposed to lie, yet we struggle still in ways that pick us apart, destroy us

United States of America
United States of Hysteric-a
United States of
America.

TRANQUILITY
Is given if what we give is love, compassion, and understanding
TRANQUILITY
Is to honor for what love is to all humility
TRANQUILITY
To be
TRANQUILITY
Free

United States of America
United States of Hysteric-a
United States of
America.

WELFARE
Means care, not shame.
WELFARE
Means joy, not pain

United States of America
United States of Hysteric-a
United States of
America.

BLESSINGS OF LIBERTY
Is our right plain and simple
BLESSINGS OF LIBERTY
Is for what we claim in ample
BLESSINGS OF LIBERTY
Includes the joy and yes the pain
BLESSINGS OF LIBERTY
And though it was technically stolen
We have the power of mind as a bona fide group to now reframe the chosen

United States of America
United States of Hysteric-a
United States of
America.

POSTERITY
Gives us lessons for the ages
POSTERITY
Creates a visage that shines bright
POSTERITY
Makes darkness refreshed in new light

United States of America
United States of Hysteric-a
United States of
America.

CONSTITUTION
Points to a strength that exists within
CONSTITUTION
It is not a rules game
Or a blame game
Or a same game
CONSTITUTION
Sums up our values in one place that is the goal
Yet we suffer in forgetfulness, and petty points, and let hate roll
We are improvised, yet we should synchronize to bring the best of ourselves to fore
We have what it takes, there is just too much at stake
Please sing along

United States of America
United States of Hysteric-a
United States of
America.

United States of America
United States of Hysteric-a
United States of
America.

United States of America
United States of Hysteric-a
United States of
America.

(WE the PEOPLE of the UNITED STATES in ORDER to form a more just UNION

Establish JUSTICE, insure domestic TRANQUILITY

Provide for the common defense

Promote the general WELFARE

And secure the BLESSINGS OF LIBERTY to ourselves

And our POSTERITY, do ordain and establish this CONSTITUTION for the UNITED STATES OF AMERICA.)

TWO *The Exhibition of Vandalizim*

Improvising Healing, Politics, and Film in South Africa

STEPHANIE VOS

In January 2010 the Zimology Institute was vandalized.[1] Located on a smallholding on the outskirts of Johannesburg, the institute was established by the South African saxophonist, composer, and improviser Zim Ngqawana as a personal project devoted to the practice of free improvisation and the nurturing of young jazz musicians. Premised on Ngqawana's views of music, the Zimology Institute advanced an alternative vision of education: it spurned the idea of tuition fees, for "true education" is free and is "about love," and was furthermore dedicated to seeking a "universal consciousness" that was "free from race, class, and the specificity of history."[2] Ngqawana cited parents, village life, and his experiences as a student with Archie Shepp and Yusef Lateef at the University of Massachusetts, Amherst, as models of this holistic notion of education.[3] Moreover, the institute was underpinned by Ngqawana's philosophy of "Zimology," which he defined as the "study of the self" or "knowledge of the self," in which improvisation provided a central vehicle for this exploration.[4]

As far as crime goes, the vandalism of the Zimology Institute is but one instance of the petty metal theft that is rife throughout South Africa, an indelible reminder of the institute's location in a country where high levels of inequality and soaring crime rates imbue lives and livelihoods with precarity.[5] Whereas Ngqawana sought to transcend race, class, and the specificity of history in his teachings and practice, the act of vandalism brought their material manifestations to the Zimology Institute's door. If the vandalism of the Zimology Institute represents crisis, understood in its original Greek sense as the cusp that augurs a turning point, a transition, or a change, Ngqawana's response to the vandalism provides the starting point for this chapter's reflection on the threshold moment that the notion of crisis implies. In the wake of the vandalism of the institute, Ngqawana improvised a healing ritual, a performance of transformation and change. It is through this response that this inquiry reflects on the critical capacities of improvisation as a response to crisis.⁶

The healing ritual in response to the vandalism took the shape of a performance of free improvisation that Ngqawana titled *The Exhibition of Vandalizim*. Joined by the pianist Kyle Shepherd and the filmmaker Aryan Kaganof—both acclaimed artists in their own right—the group improvised amid the building rubble of the wrecked institute, using vandalized instruments and fragments of debris along with intact instruments.⁷ The event was attended by a small gathering of close friends of the institute, and in a subsequent extension of the initial project, the film of the original performance was reedited and screened during further live performances of *Vandalizim* at Gallery MOMO in Johannesburg, the Cape Town City Hall, and Star Metals scrapyard in Stellenbosch.⁸ This chapter focuses primarily on the film version of *Vandalizim*, although it takes into account how the film continued to inform and interact with the musical improvisations in subsequent performances.⁹

The Exhibition of Vandalizim is an artist's reconciliation with the destruction of a labor of love, the Zimology Institute, but it is also an aesthetic response to the broader social conditions that gave rise to desperate measures such as the vandalism of instruments for scrap metal. It invites us to consider the way that the aesthetic order interacts with the sociopolitical. Certainly, *Vandalizim* demonstrates the widely asserted connection between improvisation and social practice, as is evident in statements like Ekkehard Jost's that "free jazz shows precisely how tight the links between social *and* musical factors are."¹⁰ The question that remains compelling to musicians and scholars alike, however, is *how* the social could be understood as engaged through a nonrepresentational medium such as music.¹¹

This chapter reads *Vandalizim* to prompt further reflection on improvisation's critical potential and the connection between aesthetic and social regimes. As such, *Vandalizim* is a springboard to a series of theoretical deliberations, bringing together diverse frameworks to explore improvisation as a form of social agency and critical practice. The sections that follow each consider an aspect of *Vandalizim* that dovetails with the next to probe this interaction between the aesthetic and the sociopolitical. The first two sections ask how the social is inscribed in aesthetic regimes such as improvisation and film. Revisiting the model of improvisation as dialogue, these sections suggest how the troubled social environment of South Africa in the wake of apartheid becomes inscribed in the performance through different notions of interaction, and then consider how film as a medium might be understood to widen this dialogue as an engagement with the broader sociopolitical context. The last two sections consider how improvisation constitutes critical engagement. By reading ritual alongside improvisation, the third section overlays Victor Turner's conception of the transformative and conscientizing function of ritual with similar claims made for free improvisation. The fourth section delves further into what happens in this transformative and conscientizing moment. This question is explored through Jacques Rancière's notion of politics as the disruption of the status quo, located in the moment where the imperceptible becomes perceptible and the distribution of the sensible shifts.

Introducing *Vandalizim*; or, The "Error" and Its Recovery

The spirit of hopefulness that marked South Africa's transition to democracy in the 1990s has since dimmed to a simmering discontent as the ruling party, the African National Congress, has only partially delivered on its 1994 election slogan that promised "a better life for all." Recent spates of service-delivery protests over the insufficient provision of basic amenities such as water, electricity, sanitation, and housing demonstrate the level of frustration among the country's poorest with the lack of meaningful change. South Africa remains one of the most unequal countries in the world, with the gap between affluence and poverty even more pronounced than in India, according to indicators used by the World Bank.[12] While the removal of racial constraints to economic prosperity after 1994 meant that the spread of wealth at the top end of the economic scale now includes Africans in a sector formerly occupied almost exclusively by whites, the better life that the political sea change of South Africa's transition to a democracy augured has since become a reality for far too few.[13]

What this means in the day-to-day life of South Africa's poor emerges in accounts such as Adam Ashforth's description of the insecurities that characterize life in Soweto. In this sprawling suburb south of Johannesburg, widespread poverty and unemployment (estimated at 34.9 percent across the entire South African population in 2015) prevail; notoriously high crime rates and levels of physical violence are met with no assurances of the "law standing above all"; and poor health services buckle under the onslaught of HIV.[14] Ashwin Desai's account of living conditions in several other townships echoes Ashforth's descriptions but tells the story of communities' responses. In the absence of formal infrastructure and services, communities employ improvisational tactics in self-organizing to secure basic services, often in dissonance with local authorities.[15] Such tactics draw attention to the social practice of improvisation as a function of necessity and a mechanism of community mobilization, which simultaneously becomes a means of empowerment.[16] Moreover, they demonstrate Daniel Fischlin and Martha Nandorfy's conception of community not as a stable, given entity but rather as a metaphor that is continually forged through relational contingencies.[17] Community, then, can be understood as an ephemeral formation that is constituted through its performance—galvanized in the face of crises like the lack of basic services or evictions.

Although metal theft presents a different order of improvised livelihood outside the system (and the law in particular), it arguably emerges from the same matrix of systemic failure. Metal theft has been a growing problem since the 2000s, with the province of Gauteng, where the Zimology Institute was located, proving to be a hotbed.[18] Small-scale metal theft, such as the looting of the Zimology Institute, is most commonly ascribed to "subsistence" or "bread-and-butter" thieves (those who are unemployed and steal for survival).[19] The vandalism of musical instruments for pieces of scrap metal serves as an acute and literal reminder of the inextricability of Ngqawana's music practice from this environment of precarious living conditions and improvised livelihoods that many people in present-day South Africa confront.

In *The Exhibition of Vandalizim*, Ngqawana, Shepherd, and Kaganof subject these realities of everyday life to aesthetic contemplation, inscribing the events and context that prompted the performance—the vandalism of the Zimology Institute—through their improvised responses to it. Both the sounds of the improvisation and the visuals of the film index the place and context in evocative ways. From the outset of the film, the materiality of the music-making process—the performance environment, the instruments, and the bodies that perform on them—is visibly and audibly conspicuous. No narration accompanies the film, and only a brief contextual note, introducing the *Exhibition of Vandalizim* as a response to the institute's vandalism, is given up front. Hence, the viewer is plunged into the aural testament to the vandalism and the camera's depiction of the damage. Visually, the film alternates between color and black-and-white, using footage filmed in daylight and at night, indoors and outdoors, providing a sense of landscape, place, and time. Scenes show the entrance to the smallholding, focusing on the cables that hang limply from a telephone pole, clipped and stripped of their copper wire, then proceed to the inside of the Zimology Institute building, where pianos balance precariously on their sides, wheels pillaged, and a double bass stands muted against the wall, pegs removed, and thus relieved of the tense potentiality of its strings. Wires protrude from the wall where a light switch used to be, the hollow chamber of the bathroom is cleared of its built-in conveniences, and in a chapel-like recital room a piano without legs shares the floor with a dislocated washbasin, toilet cistern, and kitchen cupboards. The film follows the performers moving from room to room, improvising as they survey the destruction that surrounds them.

With the exception of two scenes at the entrance gate of the Zimology Institute, all sounds are diegetic, and thus the improvisation is rendered visible through the camera's eye. It makes for curious viewing: the intactness of the instruments the musicians brought along—Shepherd's *uhadi* (San bow) and violin, Ngqawana's flute and saxophones—stands in stark contrast with the broken instruments, instrument fragments, and debris that the musicians requisition to join the ensemble in the course of the performance.

In the opening scene, Ngqawana plays a frantic torrent of notes reminiscent of John Coltrane's "sheets of sound" at an open fire that flickeringly illuminates his image in the otherwise dark outdoor surroundings. It is a mystical setting, evocative of traditional African gatherings. Five minutes into the film, Ngqawana is first featured speaking, introducing his intention to raise awareness about the vandalism of the Zimology Institute through the improvised performance. Five further short statements by Ngqawana, ranging from thirty seconds to four and a half minutes in length, appear over the course of the forty-seven-minute film. Otherwise, the film presents a continuous cascade of improvised sounds and images.

The improvisations themselves are pan-tonal, and the improvisatory strategies range from spontaneous utterances, often in the extreme ranges of the instruments, to more pensive improvised melodies and repeated riffs in the instruments' middle ranges. As the musicians move from room to room, they relay each other or play in ensemble—sometimes from different rooms. The use of instruments is striking: Shepherd, who is best known as a pianist, is first seen playing an *uhadi* but uses a modern violin bow to elicit sound rather than striking the string with a thin reed as it is traditionally played; Ngqawana, who is principally known as a saxophonist and flautist, plays on the institute's damaged grand piano in a blurry cluster of notes as the strings continue resonating (the damper pedals, we later notice through the film footage, have been removed). Every object can serve as a sound source: Shepherd toes the tuning pegs of the double bass, broken off by the vandals, around the floor to make percussive, grating sounds. Ngqawana, in a sonic reprise of Marcel Duchamp, uses a broken toilet cistern simultaneously as

FIGURE 2.1 Zim Ngqawana singing into the broken toilet cistern, flute in hand. Still from *The Exhibition of Vandalizim*, courtesy of Aryan Kaganof.

an echo chamber that distorts his voice as he sings into it and as a drum on which he beats a rhythm (see figure 2.1).

The trope of dialogue and interaction has been widely used to describe improvisation as a process.[20] Besides the interpersonal interaction between musicians in the course of performance, dialogue and interaction also characterize the musical process itself. Robert Hodson, for instance, depicts free improvisation as "continual interaction in which each musician's improvised output . . . [serves] as input to which the other performer may respond."[21] In a slightly different take on interaction, as taking place not between players and the sounds they produce but within the sequence of notes produced by a single performer, Frederic Rzewski significantly calls the "first idea" that commences the improvisation an "error, a wrong note, a fumble in which the ball is momentarily lost." What follows is "the graceful recovery of the fumbled ball, a second 'wrong' note that makes the first one seem right," thus modeling improvisation as a perpetuation of "errors" and "recoveries."[22] We can thus think about improvisation-as-interaction in *Vandalizim* happening on an interpersonal level between Ngqawana and Shepherd, on a musical level in the sounds each musician produces that serve as impetus for the other's response, and on an intramusical level within each musician's playing, where he salvages the sounds that came before, to paraphrase Rzewski.

This model of interaction becomes more complex when taking into consideration an aspect that renders this performance particularly remarkable:

the idiosyncratic and eclectic use of intact and vandalized instruments, as well as of found objects as instruments. What Derek Bailey calls the "instrumental impulse" is arguably another force in the interaction complex that critically shapes improvisation. As Bailey explains, "it is the attitude of the [free improvising musician] to the tactile element, to the physical experience of playing an instrument, to this 'instrumental impulse' which establishes much of the way he plays. One of the basic characteristics of his improvising, detectable in everything he plays, will be how he harnesses the instrumental impulse. Or how he reacts against it. And this makes the stimulus and the recipient of this impulse, the instrument, the most important single factor in his musical resources."[23] If the instrument is central to the improvisation as a musical resource (both "stimulus" and "recipient"), what happens to the improvisation when the instrument is disfigured? Whereas an element of unpredictability is germane to free improvisation performances with normal, or even prepared instruments, an intensified unpredictability enters where instruments have been vandalized, resulting in often unforeseen distortions or, where found objects are commandeered as instruments, opening novel possibilities of sound production.[24] This precipitates new responses, by both the player and his ensemble partner(s). For Ngqawana, this has greater significance than merely dealing with contingency. As he states in the film, "I am grateful to the thieves and the thugs . . . whoever did this to this place, for giving us such inspiration to improvise further . . . [to] expand our vocabulary . . . from your conventional instruments to the instruments that are not known."[25]

Shepherd's and Ngqawana's creative reactions to the unexpected distortions of sound, and indeed their deliberate elicitation of this distortion, create a third force that, in turn, following Bailey, determines the musicians' actions. In their responsiveness the musicians are attuned not only to one another but also to the manifestations of the vandalism in the distortion of instruments' sounds. The vandalism, in other words, becomes *instrumental* to the performance: an integral part that conditions the improvisation itself.

Ngqawana's statement suggests that we think of the metonymic presence of the vandals through the distorted sounds. This presence profoundly locates the performance within a chronological sequence of events and a particular performance environment that is South Africa. The improvisation becomes a response to an "error" (the vandalism) and performs its "recovery" through the healing ceremony. To extend the analogy of "error" and "recovery" even further, the scrap metal theft could be regarded as an improvised and disruptive response to poverty, thus constituting the original "error" that is "recovered" through the performance of *Vandalizim* as a response. In this way, Ngqawana and Shepherd can be understood to enter into a symbolic dialogue with the social conditions described above that gave rise to the vandalism, for which the distorted sounds and fragments serve as metonyms.

The Paradox of the Improvising Film

My ability to describe the improvisation in the performance of the *Exhibition of Vandalizim* in such detail hinges on the paradox the film presents: recording something as ephemeral as improvisation.[26] In this section I suggest that the film does not operate as a *representation of* improvisation so much as it actively participates in, and extends, the improvisatory process, bringing the temporal and spatial aspects of *Vandalizim* into sharper focus. Authors like John Corbett posit that improvisation is defined exactly by its resistance to the reification that enters in the act of recording, a stance that reveals improvisation's entanglement with the idea of liveness. "Records of improvised music," Corbett writes, "are not the same as improvisation, but are instead a more refined form of inscription, of composition."[27] From the perspective of performance art, Peggy Phelan argues along similar lines that "preserving" performance art through the reifying process of writing or filming renders the record of the "performance" on the page or screen fundamentally different from the event that it captures.[28] Yet the film *The Exhibition of Vandalizim* problematizes such neat categorization as mere recording in several ways.

The filming, done with only a single handheld camera, is highly responsive to the sound improvisations it captures, veritably improvising the filming process through the steep angles in which the subject matter is framed (often a forty-five- to ninety-degree tilt), or by panning and zooming in quick, jagged movements, visually elaborating (or contrasting) bursts of frantic sounds that emanate from the music improvisations. The filming does not efface the camera's presence, nor does it merely record the scene in a passive sense. Rather, the filming as a visual response to the sounds as they are improvised becomes part of the improvisation itself. The camera's movement and its angles of portrayal do not make for complacent viewing. It is therefore debatable whether this is part of an improvisatory or compositional approach in Corbett's dichotomy.

The reediting of the film for the purpose of subsequent live performances by Ngqawana and Shepherd (as mentioned in the introduction) again challenges easy classification as part of an improvisational or compositional act. While a compositional gesture undoubtedly enters when a prolonged performance is cut to forty-seven minutes, when sounds are superimposed nondiegetically (even though this is the exception in *Vandalizim*), or when images are rendered in monochrome or color, I would argue that more than "inscription" or "preservation," which Corbett and Phelan respectively refer to, takes place. In the same way as Hodson describes the improvisatory process as the (re)entry of improvised material into a system that generates new responses, the reedited film served as a visual impulse for subsequent improvised performances of *The Exhibition of Vandalizim* at Gallery MOMO in Johannesburg and Star Metals scrapyard in Stellenbosch.[29] The editing of the film thus fits into the trope of improvisation as dialogue and interaction. Or, as Corbett would put it (following Roland Barthes), it renders the "readerly" text "writerly," shifting the emphasis from *product* (where meaning is authoritative, reified, rendering the reader the passive consumer of the preordained meaning of such a text) to *production* (in which the reader, or listener, actively participates in the processual production of meaning).[30] Viewed as such, the film *Vandalizim* forms an additional mode of improvisation to the otherwise musically improvised performance. If the film provides a "visual layer" of improvisation additional to the sound improvisations, it is possible to conceive of the editing process as a *performative* filmic act, a further visual improvisation responding to the musical improvisation that thus extends the temporality of the performance beyond the duration of the musical performance in the strict definition of the word.

The two dimensions that *Vandalizim* as film heightens, the contextual and the temporal, contribute to a consideration of how social context inheres within an aesthetic medium such as improvisation. In addition to the aural presence of the vandalism through the distortions of the sounds, the visual images of the destruction reinforce the metonymic presence of the vandals. It is amplified by inclined camera angles that disorientate the viewer's spatial perception of up and down, floor, wall, and ceiling. It mirrors the disorientation of a piano toppled on its side, stripped of its wheels (see figure 2.2). As the film pauses, focuses, angles, and zooms in on or out from the destruction of the vandalism, it powerfully spatializes the improvised sounds, heightening the viewer's awareness of the destruction that gave rise to the performance. It invites contemplation of the social and political context that precipitates vandalism for scrap metal. The film thus heightens the sense of context that is made sonically present through the unusual sounds of the musical performance. This is one of the ways in which an improvisation practice conceived of as universal becomes differentiated and profoundly situated in its immediate South African environment.

FIGURE 2.2 Kyle Shepherd playing on an overturned grand piano. Still from *The Exhibition of Vandalizim*, courtesy of Aryan Kaganof.

Ngũgĩ wa Thiong'o's theorization of performance space provides a useful framework to unpack the ways the Zimology Institute relates to its broader environment. Performance space, he reminds us, is never empty space. It is shaped by the relations between performer and audience within the venue's confines, but is also subject to the performance space's relationship with the broader environment and power structures in which it is located, as well as with the histories of the space (what came before, which shapes the present).[31] This helps us to think about the ways that the spatial and temporal dimensions of improvisation conjoin in *Vandalizim*. The improvisation is shaped not only by relations among the performers, the audience, and the immediate performance space within the Zimology Institute at the time of its performance but also by its locus in South Africa and the history of events leading to the performance: the incidence of vandalism. Understood this way, a much broader contextual and historical dimension to the performance is ingrained in the fabric of improvisation.

Drawing on Rzewski's model of the first idea of the improvisation as the "error," followed by its "recovery," we may think further about the temporal parameters of *Vandalizim*. In a narrow understanding of the word *performance*, *The Exhibition of Vandalizim* is hedged by the first and last note of the improvised healing performed on January 30, 2010, at the Zimology Institute itself. The film *Vandalizim* presents yet another sense of sequence, as the edited footage presents a longer time frame for which the improvisation on January 30, 2010, is the starting point, and the editing process and subsequent screening-improvisations at Gallery MOMO, the Cape Town City Hall, and Star Metals scrapyard are part of an extended performance. But the "first idea" or "error" that was the impulse for the performance (or series of performances) altogether is arguably the act of vandalism itself; and the vandalism itself could be seen as a response to systemic failure in South Africa. Within this broader view of performance, the "first idea" or "error" occurs much earlier than the sound of the first note of the performance of *Vandalizim*—whether in the film or the actual performance thereof.

Playing with the parameters of the improvisation goes beyond a mere exercise in thinking through, or challenging, theories that describe and circumscribe improvisation. An extended perspective of the interactions through which *The Exhibition of Vandalizim* is constituted enables us to contemplate a more holistic view of improvisation: how the social is inscribed in performance, and how improvisation could be conceived as a response to broader concerns within the society in which it is located.

Improvising Ritual, Liminality, and *Communitas*

So far, this chapter has focused on how social context is made present in *Vandalizim*: through sound, harnessing the instrumental impulse of vandalized instruments and debris, thereby integrating the product of the vandalism in the improvisation; and through film, prompting an extended understanding of the temporal and spatial dimensions of improvisation so that social context is understood as part of the impetus to which the performance of *Vandalizim* is a response. The remainder of the chapter considers how *Vandalizim* engages with these social concerns through ritual, healing, and the enactment of politics.

Vandalizim invokes ritual in several respects: the opening scene is set at the fireside in darkness, where Ngqawana performs amid a circle of onlookers, a mystical setting evocative of African ritual; and the performers' subsequent movement from room to room, improvising while observing the destruction, brings to mind gestures of exorcism or anointment. Similarly, the musicians' use of the vandalized remnants as mnemonic devices invoking the vandalism suggests improvisation as a musical meditation on the events. Among the hallmarks of shamanic conceptions of healing are extended notions of temporality and context beyond that of the present ritualistic performance. This is evident in Michael Titlestad's summary of Mircea Eliade's ideal-typical features of shamanic conceptions of healing. "In the act of healing," Titlestad writes, "the shaman narrates the creation myth, confronting the first entry of disease into the world and, in its turn, the advent of the gift of healing. The particular process of recovery emerges, then, as an affirmation of the whole of creation by situating both the healer and the 'patient' in the grand narrative of the clan's origin and history.... Shamanism is, then, also a narrative process of (re)integration and (re)membering."[32] It is worth dwelling on the notions of temporality and community in this description, as they link to the exploration of how *Vandalizim* invokes a broader context discussed above. From Titlestad's description we glean several notions of time: the performance of healing through narration in the present; the history of the people and the onset of illness in the past as recounted in the narrative that draws it into the present; and the progression of the narrative act itself through time. These notions map onto the problematic of locating the boundaries of performance in *Vandalizim*. "Performance" in the strict sense corresponds with the narration of healing as it unfolds in the present; the advent of the illness corresponds with the "error" or "first move" (the act of vandalism, or even the broader social conditions in South Africa that it betokens, as I have argued), which is brought into the present and thereby recovered through the act of narration, or, in the case of *Vandalizim*, through improvisation. Most important, in Eliade's conception of shamanic healing the past is invoked to right the present—to reinstate wholeness within a fractured community. In *Vandalizim* this process is symbolically enacted through a musical process of playing (or recovering) vandalized instruments, thus performing a musical (re)membering and (re)integration through improvisation.

Music understood as a form of healing is not unprecedented in Ngqawana's work. Two of his albums' titles, for instance, refer to the role of the musician as a healer and to music as integral to healing practices in African societies. The album title *Vadzimu* means "traditional healer" in isiXhosa, and the title of another album, *Ingoma*, literally translates as "song" but also refers to singing and handclapping at festive occasions or divination ceremonies in Nguni healing practices.[33] As Ngqawana explains in an interview, "You know that the whole continent understands music as Ingoma? And even understands certain instruments, and certain dances, as Ingoma? The whole concept of Ingoma means *healing*. And that is the true purpose of music."[34]

Even as this statement suggests Ngqawana as a bearer of tradition in casting himself in the role of the healer, it should not be taken as a straightforward continuance of an established cultural practice. While Ngqawana would have been familiar with Xhosa healing practices from his upbringing in the Eastern Cape, an area that is still the heartland of Xhosa traditional practices, he qualifies that as an artist—"living in an urban center—one realizes that you cannot continue practicing your tradition the way it used to be practiced in the days of old. So you need to refine and update and adopt the techniques that are used to create that music, within the right context."[35]

This reconfiguration of tradition is more than a response precipitated by encounters with modernity, or processes of urbanization and globalization. As Jean and John Comaroff suggest, "the practice of mystical arts in postcolonial Africa . . . does not imply an iteration of, a retreat into, 'tradition'" but is "often a mode of producing new forms of consciousness; of expressing discontent with modernity and dealing with its deformities. In short, of retooling culturally familiar technologies as new means for new ends."[36] In this light, the reconfiguration of indigenous practice functions as a form of critical practice that rethinks and reforges ways of being in and engaging with the world.

Even as Ngqawana reconfigures tradition in an indigenous South African sense, it is simultaneously conversant with another tradition across the Atlantic—that of American improvisation building on the legacy of jazz. Ngqawana looks especially to John Coltrane as a keystone in his conception of improvisation as a vehicle of self-expression and spirituality. Having first encountered Coltrane's music as an adolescent in Port Elizabeth, he later studied with Coltrane's erstwhile associates, Pharoah Sanders, Archie Shepp, and Yusef Lateef during a year's sojourn at the University of Massachusetts.[37] This study reinforced the resonance he felt with these American musicians who understand jazz "as a spiritual journey."[38]

As a case in point, consider the correspondence between Ngqawana's notion of Zimology, described as "the study of the self" or "knowledge of the self" through improvisation, and Lateef's definition of autophysiopsychic music as "music that comes from the physical, mental, spiritual, and intellectual self."[39] In Eric Porter's discussion of Lateef's thought on improvisation, it is especially striking that Lateef conceives of improvisation as a form of therapy.[40] "The musician," writes Lateef, "is expected to skillfully filter his profoundest sensations in order to extract their properties and recompose them in performance. This is a process which compels the musician not only to recall his feelings but, to analyze and understand. If we look at the emotion-memory squarely, we see not only an improvizational tool but, a great boon for the ego, a therapeutic toy."[41] By means of performance, the therapeutic quality of autophysiopsychic music furthermore extends not only to the improviser but also to the listener.[42] Following Lateef's line of thought, healing in *Vandalizim* could thus be understood as a function of

Ngqawana's and Shepherd's improvisation (also rendered through the film), through which they delve into and analyze their emotional response to the vandalism, which engages listeners through performance.

The hybridity of influences evident in Ngqawana's reinvention of tradition underscores Titlestad's observation that Ngqawana "simultaneously refers to and constructs versions of memory, history, tradition and nationalism."[43] This syncretic reinvention of ritual does not fit one strand of thinking about ritual that regards it as an essentially conservative endeavor that entails repeated practices that communities, conceived of as fixed and stable, have agreed on.[44] As a highly idiosyncratic performance that taps into local as well as transnational senses of community, ritual in *Vandalizim* emerges as a transformative or perhaps even a transgressive practice that responds to incongruities within the social fabric. It is closer to Victor Turner's conception of ritual in the context of social drama, as a response to a "disharmonic social process [that arises] in conflict situations."[45]

In the resolution of social drama, the moments of crisis (understood as the moment when the original breach comes to a head, such as the act of vandalism) and recovery (the process to resolve the dispute, such as Ngqawana's performance in response to the vandalism) are characterized by a state of liminality. The word *liminal* derives from the Latin for "threshold" (*limen*) and marks a state of transition or change typical of ritual practices.[46] In this liminal state, the usual hierarchical structures that regulate political, economic, and social order are radically reordered or suspended, enabling the emergence of a particular mode of egalitarianism that Turner calls *communitas*, which emphasizes the *performance* of community rather than its tacit, and static, existence.[47] As Turner puts it elsewhere, "communitas emerges where social structure is not."[48] Turner's communitas indeed recalls Fischlin and Nandorfy's notion of community as a metaphor for relational contingency—something that does not exist in and of itself but is, instead, constituted through its performance.

In reading Turner's description of ritual with an eye (or ear) trained on improvisation, as *Vandalizim* prompts us to do, several parallels with descriptions of improvisation emerge. Similar to the liminal space of ritual, improvisation provides a performance space in which existing structures are suspended and challenged. Bailey's formulation of improvisation, for instance, draws attention to the subversion of the hierarchy of the tonal impulse and conformity to meter, the resistance to preordained structure and extension of timbral possibilities.[49] The suspension of structure is imbued with an added sociopolitical significance when George Lewis refers to free improvisation as "a symbolic challenge to traditional authority" that is engaged in the recovery of the black voice from its historical silencing.[50] Lewis's statement corresponds with Turner's notion of communitas as an enactment of egalitarianism, that is, the creation of a platform where those usually silenced are heard in the liminal space of the performance.

Turner's concept of ritual helps us to think about how improvisation as liminal space fosters transformation. In the suspension or reordering of structure, both ritual and improvisation provide a forum where the social fabric is open to critique and to reconfiguration, thereby enacting transformation. It becomes a space where the weak have a voice and the ability to chastise and conscientize the powerful. Communitas is not achieved or maintained only in states of ritual or liminality, however; it is also permanently embodied in the figure of the weak and inferior that unsettles any stable sense of community (and we may think of the vandals in *Vandalizim* as such a disruption to a stable sense of community), or in states of outsiderhood like the vocation of shaman or healer (such as Ngqawana).[51] The status of being an outsider enables the shaman "to criticize all structure-bound personae in terms of a moral order binding on all, and also to mediate between all segments or components of the structured system."[52] This may in turn serve as a description of the role of the socially engaged improviser.

Commensurate with both Eliade's and Turner's description of the narrative and conscientizing functions of the healer, Ngqawana points to the root of social ill, of the vandalism, in a statement two minutes before the end of the film:

> We used to play music here, before they vandalized it. You see it is strange that people can go to this extent of vandalism. To me it shows the extent of what has happened to them: the vandalism of the soul, the vandalism of the heart, of the mind. These people were not born like this, they have been created by a system that we live under, a system of barbarism, of ignorance. I am talking about the political system, that has turned people into barbaric creatures, that has retarded people, kept them in ignorance through their lousy system of education, religions, political systems. . . . I'm not looking at this vandalism, I am looking at the vandalism of the soul. And this system is responsible for this. . . . All society is responsible for this.[53]

This statement supports the argument this chapter advances that improvisation in *Vandalizim* figures vandalism as a metonym of broader social ills confronting South Africans and presents a form of social engagement and critique. Using the liminal space of the performance, Ngqawana locates the root of the vandalism in the systemic violence that keeps people in their place—or what

Turner calls "structure." The performance of healing in *Vandalizim* may be directed toward the actual vandalism of the institute, but symbolically extends to a critique of structural oppression, in which free improvisation is symbolically significant as a medium of performance. Given the South African sociopolitical context, where the state fails to meet the basic needs of communities, *Vandalizim* presents trenchant criticism that joins discourses over basic human rights and the conditions for human dignity.

In anthropology there has been resistance to a loose definition of the term *ritual* that elides the differentiation between ritual and performance, arguing that it empties ritual of its usefulness as a theoretical concept.[54] Yet it is exactly in this slippage, where it is difficult to disentangle notions of musical performance as artistic, aesthetic practice and ritual, that *Vandalizim* operates. In the reconfiguration of ritual in imaginative ways that defy anthropologists' neat definitions, the improvisational aspect of *Vandalizim* is particularly evident.

Rancière and the Politics of Free Improvisation

Let us now use the idea of liminality to think further about the ability to critique through an aesthetic practice like improvisation. What exactly in the suspension of order allows sounds to serve as critique? And how does improvisation, as a means of sounding critique, invoke communitas—an articulation or enactment of a more egalitarian society? One thinker who is particularly concerned with the juncture between aesthetics and politics implicit in these questions is Jacques Rancière.[55] His notion of the distribution of the sensible offers a particularly evocative framework to think about the relationship between music and politics.

The distribution of the sensible refers to the moment when those who are usually not seen or heard become apparent. The exclusion of the lower rungs of society from participating, or being heard, in the order of things, justified by the Platonic idea that they have neither the time nor the talent to do so, is what Rancière refers to as "the originary wrong." Politics, rather than referring to an omnipresent tension characterizing power struggles in various relationships, occurs in the moment when the silence of those who are rendered mute, or supposed to be mute, is broken. At this moment, the distribution of the sensible shifts—those who are, in the common order of things, unheard become audible; those who are invisible become perceptible. It is sense, both as a mode of perception and as comprehensibility, that is transformed.[56] The French verb *partager* (translated as "distribution") refers both to the division (parting) between those who are heard and those who are muted and to participation in political speech acts. Thus, for Rancière, the aesthetic dimension of politics is not concerned with art or beauty per se, but with the realms of perception and the sensory. The problem of the *sans-part*, literally "those without a part," is not only that they are not heard but that their complaints, when raised, are not recognized as meaning-bearing language.[57]

Sound operates as a central metaphor in Rancière's thesis. The capacity to be *heard*, or to have a voice, forms the hinge between politics and aesthetics: politics is crucially located in the act of breaking silence. The radical act of speech, of sounding a voice that is not (usually) heard, can be understood to disrupt, question, suspend, or even invert the usual structures that regulate speech. The sociopolitical significance Rancière ascribes to the capacity to speak recalls George Lewis's view of free improvisation as the assertion or recovery of the black voice, mentioned earlier. Even before the power of speech can be exerted, there is the question of who has the right to speak. As Daniel Fischlin, Ajay Heble, and George Lipsitz have argued in relation to recent thought on the relationship between improvisation and human rights discourses, improvisation presents a "symbolic staging of the right to speak freely, the capacity to take action" and, as such, "embodies publicly a basic human right—to make music, to be creative."[58]

How might this understanding of politics be illuminated through *The Exhibition of Vandalizim*? Ngqawana recognizes the source of the vandalism inflicted on the institute as rooted in social inequalities brought about by the "system of education, religions, political systems" that disregards its poor. This disregard corresponds with Rancière's notion of the originary wrong of the sociopolitical status quo that renders certain social strata effectively mute. The way that both Rancière and Ngqawana envisage a solution is through breaking the silence. Here, I would argue that through its *exposure* of the sociopolitical issues at the heart of the vandalism—as the word *exhibition* implies in the title Ngqawana devised for the performance—*The Exhibition of Vandalizim* serves as an exemplary disruption of the status quo. The act of performing the vandalism inflicted on the Zimology Institute shifts the distribution of the sensible and makes perceptible the metonymic presence of those who were mute and of the social disregard that this represents.

As significant as the act that breaks the silence is the means employed in the performance—improvisation. As I have argued, improvisation itself also enacts the radical suspension of conventional structures, and the practice in itself could be understood as performing communitas in Turner's sense of the word. If Rancière is read along with discourses on improvisation and ritual as egalitarian spaces, it further textures an understanding of how the disruption of the sensible could be conceived in music practice in particular. The suspension of musical hierarchy that Bailey describes in his theorization of free improvisation creates the sonic mechanisms and means through which the imperceptible might become perceptible. Rancière's notion of politics thus articulates the political significance of the moment when the domain of the sensory is radically opened. Improvisation might therefore also be understood in terms of this political framework that explains how music could be conceived as an articulation of politics.

We could think about the disruption of structure—that which sets crisis in motion—in the performance of *Vandalizim* as the linchpin between the conceptual frameworks I have introduced. As argued in the previous section, free improvisation as a suspension or disruption of structure makes it particularly compatible with Turner's notion of the liminal as a context within which *Vandalizim*'s performance can be explored. These are also the conditions that are at play in Rancière's speech act, in which the disruption of silence transforms the prevailing order, if only momentarily. For Rancière, the speech act is connected with the recognition of a fundamental humanity, defined as the capacity to speak and be heard—that which South African society's poor are not afforded in being overlooked in the provision of basic means to obtain a livelihood and opportunities for betterment. Interlinked with the disruption of structure in the liminal space or the speech act is the radical democratization of sound. One way of thinking of this in *Vandalizim* is in Bailey's assignment of central importance to the musical instrument in free improvisation—in this case the material produced by the vandalism. The metonymic invocation of those who are not heard is musically enacted through musical dialogue with the distorted sounds of the vandalized instruments or the harnessing of building rubble as sound sources; it is veritably democratized by using these in conjunction with intact instruments used in similarly novel, sound-effecting ways. This musical act is a symbolic performance of the radical equality that Rancière advocates.

The appeal of Rancière's definition and conception of politics in relation to improvisation lies in its understanding of politics as action, as performance, something that occurs in a particular moment rather than being latent and omnipresent. Improvisation, too, appears in a bounded moment (in a wider or narrower sense). It is performed and enacted—it encapsulates a moment of intervention in the order of things. Understood this way, improvisation is an apt expression of Rancière's notion of politics. The performative aspect of Rancière's politics and of improvisation furthermore maps onto an understanding of community not as a stable referent, but rather as emerging through performances of relational contingencies. I am suggesting the interaction of these conceptual frameworks not by means of equating them, nor to suggest that they mutually substantiate or substitute for each other, but rather to show how they converge and overlap, as demonstrated in *The Exhibition of Vandalizim*. Moreover, this convergence helps us to think in more nuanced ways about the liminal or threshold moment that inheres in the notion of crisis.

Improvising at the Threshold: *The Exhibition of Vandalizim* as a Response to Crisis

Crisis is at the core of *The Exhibition of Vandalizim*. Crisis, in the form of the vandalism of the Zimology Institute, gave rise to the performance, and the same crisis inheres in the performance through the improvisation as an interaction with the destruction—both on a metaphorical level (as a response to the vandalism) and on a literal level (the instrumental impulse provided by the debris left by the vandalism that enters into the sound of the improvisation). The crisis, however, is broader than the act of vandalism and the literal damage it wrought on the buildings. In Ngqawana's interpretation (an interpretation elaborated in this chapter), the vandalism is symbolic of a broader vandalism perpetrated by systemic failures that negate a basic recognition of humanity. This is the true crisis to which *The Exhibition of Vandalizim* responds. Film, in *The Exhibition of Vandalizim* as a performance, draws out this broader symbolism and amplifies it through the visual imagery and its resistance to complacent viewing.[59]

Ngqawana's response is a reinfusion of humanity in its fullest sense. This response is contextualized through two paradigms in which I discussed Ngqawana and *The Exhibition of Vandalizim*. The first is the spiritual paradigm invoked through the notion of ritual, which interprets crisis in holistic terms. This notion of spirituality is at once local, traceable to the Xhosa background of Ngqawana's upbringing, and also connected to a transnational network of improvisers who regard their practice in spiritual terms, notably Coltrane and Lateef. Crucially, this notion of spirituality forms part of a counterhegemonic discourse and may therefore be interpreted as a critique of the modernity that led to the present order of things.

The second context is the reinfusion of humanity embraced in Ngqawana's response, namely, that of free improvisation. Improvisation entails the same suspension of structure as ritual does: whereas in ritual this might be narrated in terms of social hierarchy and structure, improvisation gives musical content to the same suspension through sonic means. The liminality of ritual—the name given to the space-time in which this suspension and radical reordering take place—is at once a characterization of crisis as the moment of change, of transformation, and a description of the performance space in which improvisation is located. In activating the dialogue or interaction, improvisation refuses systemic muting (the relegation into imperceptibility) and reinfuses a sense of human voice and agency.

Crisis is a threshold moment; it is the cusp where the antecedent and the consequent meet. It is a turning point where causes are divined, and possible remedies are considered. It requires all the critical faculties of analysis and interpretation of that which brought one to the threshold as well as additional imagination and creativity to envision what will take one over, past, through, and further in its aftermath. The threshold suggests both the barrier (the limit crisis brought one to) and its traversal (enlisting creativity to find the means to go beyond). Yet the surpassing of the limit promises no certain outcome: crossing the threshold is stepping into the unknown. In the medical origin of the word *crisis*, the turning point of the disease bodes either recovery or death. This quality of uncertainty is also an attribute of improvisation: it involves the risk of the turning point—the surpassing of the threshold of the known into the unknown. As such, improvisation is an apposite form as a response to crisis, and Rzewski's notion of the recovery involved in improvisation is an evocative pivot between the paradigms of healing and improvisation.

I resist an affirmative reading of *Vandalizim* that poses it as a complete resolution or healing in the aftermath of crisis, for it is debatable whether Ngqawana's extraordinary response effected any lasting, material change. Some obituaries of Ngqawana, who passed away in 2011, suggest that he never fully recovered from the blow of the vandalism to his highly personal, aesthetically expressed project (the Zimology Institute was, after all, a manifestation of a personal philosophy and practice). Yet I do not discount the power of symbolic intervention, for it is a powerful means of analysis and creates the capacity (and means) to shift perspective and envision a different future. I therefore argue that *The Exhibition of Vandalizim* demonstrates the confrontation of crisis, although the outcome remains in play.

In this sense, *Vandalizim* is congruent with improvisation, which always plays at the edge of the unknown and embraces that risk, as well as the ephemerality of the moment of its performance. Following the interactive model of improvisation, in a certain sense *Vandalizim* presents a recovery, yet, as in improvisation, it is ephemeral and merely serves as the prompt for another response. The "recovery" in *Vandalizim* outlines the possibility of an alternative reality or order. Yet its power lies in its ability to disrupt the present order of things for the ephemeral moment of its performance, during which it allows the glimmer of an alternative order to shine through. This is indeed an enactment of politics in the Rancièrian sense.

Perhaps this is the role of improvisation (or the aesthetic) in the aftermath of crisis: it is the torch that illuminates the crisis and divines the way forward, but it is not the hands nor the feet. This moment of acuity shows the promise of an alternative order, and therein lies its alchemy: that in its response to crisis it turns destruction into a generative force, which creates the impulse for the next response.

NOTES

1 I thank Aryan Kaganof, who introduced me to the music of Zim Ngqawana and sent me a copy of the film *The Exhibition of Vandalizim*. Ngqawana passed away on May 9, 2011, at the untimely age of fifty-two. The Zimology Institute was not rebuilt before his passing.
2 Kakaza, "Healing with Music."
3 See Kakaza, "Healing with Music"; and Van Wyk, "Zim Ngqawana."
4 Ngqawana, quoted in Kakaza, "Healing with Music"; and Mabandu, "Zimbol of Free Sound." The inscription of his name in the titles of his projects is one of the ways in which Ngqawana inscribes himself in his artistic endeavors.
5 In 2011, 72,533 incidents of metal theft were reported to the police, amounting to an estimated seven billion rand in losses to the economy. See Pretorius, "Criminological Analysis," 31, 48.
6 See Kaganof, "Exhibition of Vandalizim," 26. The description "musical ritual" was used on the website of Stellenbosch University's Documentation Centre for Music (DOMUS), which hosted a live performance of *The Exhibition of Vandalizim*: http://www.domus.ac.za/content/view/56/5/; and "healing ceremony" appears in Philip Kakaza's "Healing with Music" in the *Mail and Guardian*, which served as publicity for the live performance of *Vandalizim* at Gallery MOMO in Johannesburg. These are apt descriptors, as will become clear in the following discussion.
7 With six albums and several music awards to his name, Kyle Shepherd has gained prominence in South Africa as well as abroad. As a musician and cultural activist, he is concerned with the reclamation of Khoisan cultural heritage, as evident in an album like *South African History X!* or the *Afrikaaps* hip-hopera, for which he was musical director, which foregrounded the creole history of Afrikaans. Kaganof is an independent filmmaker, poet, and visual artist best known for his award-winning films that explore politically charged and provocative subject matter. A number of his films focus on music, including *Blue Notes for Bra'Geoff* (on one of the father figures of jazz in Pretoria, Geoff Mphakati), *An Inconsolable Memory* (on the history of South Africa's first opera group), and *Death and the Archive* (on the South African veteran pianist Tete Mbambisa).

8   See *Mail and Guardian*, "Healing Ceremony," 17.
9   The film is available on Vimeo at https://vimeo.com/108982799.
10 Jost, *Free Jazz*, 9 (emphasis in the original).
11 Born, "Music, Modernism and Signification," 166.
12 The Gini coefficient is a widely used indicator that measures the spread of wealth and access to resources, with 0 representing perfectly equal distribution. In 2011 South Africa's Gini coefficient was pegged at 65, compared to India's 38 for the same year. See World Bank, "Gini Index." Comparing the sets of data used across different studies, Jeremy Seekings concludes that South Africa's levels of inequality are increasing. Seekings, "Poverty and Inequality," 28–30.
13 Seekings, "Poverty and Inequality," 30.
14 See Ashforth, *Witchcraft*, 20–62; also see Comaroff and Comaroff, "Occult Economies," 292. The unemployment statistic is from Reuters; see *Times Live*, "South Africa's Unemployment Rate."
15 Desai's *We Are the Poors*, based on his own involvement and fieldwork in grassroots movements, provides a moving account of the tactics communities employ in the struggle for daily survival. For a brief summary, see Desai, *We Are the Poors*, locs. 130–52 of 2560.
16 Silver, "Incremental Infrastructures," 799.
17 Fischlin and Nandorfy, *Community of Rights*, 87.
18 Pretorius, "Criminological Analysis," 24.
19 Pretorius, "Criminological Analysis," 127–29.
20 Texts expounding this model, such as Ingrid Monson's *Saying Something: Jazz Improvisation and Interaction* (especially chapter 3) and Paul Berliner's *Thinking in Jazz: The Infinite Art of Improvisation* (especially chapters 6, 7, and 13), have become standards in jazz literature. Daniel Fischlin and Ajay Heble's edited volume *The Other Side of Nowhere: Improvisation, Jazz, and Communities in Dialogue* also advances the premise of improvisation as dialogue.
21 Hodson, *Interaction*, 117.
22 Rzewski, "Little Bangs," 379.
23 Bailey, *Improvisation*, 115.
24 On unpredictability in improvisation with normal instruments, see, for instance, Corbett, "Ephemera Underscored," 222–23.
25 Ngqawana in Kaganof, *Exhibition of Vandalizim* (film), 7:09–7:38.
26 Jarrett, "Cutting Sides," 321.
27 Corbett, "Ephemera Underscored," 219.
28 Phelan, *Unmarked*, 148.
29 Hodson, *Interaction*, 117.
30 Corbett, "Ephemera Underscored," 219.
31 Ngũgĩ, "Enactments of Power," 12–13.
32 Titlestad, *Making the Changes*, 205–6.
33 Following the definition in Tshabe, Shoba, and van der Westhuizen, *Greater Dictionary of isiXhosa*; also see Friedson, *Dancing Prophets*.
34 Ngqawana, "Zim Ngqawana."
35 Ngqawana, "Zim Ngqawana."

36 Comaroff and Comaroff, "Occult Economies," 284.
37 It is difficult to establish the extent of Ngqawana's studies at the University of Massachusetts, as the biographies available on Ngqawana, written mostly for concert publicity or journalistic purposes, are vague on the details. Piecing together snippets of information from various websites, it appears that Ngqawana attended the International Association of Jazz Educators Convention in the United States as a member of the South African group the Jazzanians and was subsequently offered scholarships to attend the Max Roach/Wynton Marsalis Jazz Workshop hosted by the University of Massachusetts, Amherst. Following the workshop, he received a Max Roach Scholarship to attend the University of Massachusetts, where he studied with Shepp and Lateef.
38 Ngqawana, "Zim Ngqawana." While the focus on ritual as a conceptual framework in this section does not permit me to go into greater detail, it is clear that the circulation of ideas about jazz, spirituality, and ritual between the African continent and diaspora in Ngqawana's musical practices and thought merits further discussion. In many ways his statement can be read in parallel with Steven Feld's accounts of jazz musicians' relationship with Coltrane's music and thought in Accra. See Feld, *Jazz Cosmopolitanism in Accra*. Ngqawana's perspective on African notions of spirituality and ritual as a direct influence on his jazz practices, enhanced by ideas on African spirituality that circulate in the African diaspora and are brought back to the African context, would provide a fascinating complement to American texts situating ritual through its diasporic ties to American blues and jazz, like Samuel A. Floyd Jr.'s *The Power of Black Music: Interpreting Its History from Africa to the United States* and Travis A. Jackson's "Jazz Performance as Ritual: The Blues Aesthetic and the African Diaspora."
39 Lateef, quoted in Porter, *What Is This Thing Called Jazz?*, 242.
40 Porter offers an extended discussion of Lateef's thought on music in chapter 6 of *What Is This Thing Called Jazz?* See especially pp. 242–46.
41 Lateef, quoted in Porter, *What Is This Thing Called Jazz?*, 244.
42 Porter, *What Is This Thing Called Jazz?*, 245.
43 Titlestad, *Making the Changes*, 213.
44 J. Lewis, *Anthropology of Cultural Performance*, 56.
45 Turner, *Anthropology of Performance*, 74.
46 Turner, *Ritual Process*, 94. In Turner's discussion, liminality typically involves the inversion, or suspension, of typical social, political, and economic rungs, which are reinstalled with greater wisdom and sensitivity to the welfare of the whole community after the rite of passage is completed.
47 Turner, *Ritual Process*, 96–97.
48 Turner, *Ritual Process*, 126.
49 Bailey, *Improvisation*, 110.
50 G. Lewis, *Power Stronger than Itself*, 41–42.
51 Turner, *Ritual Process*, 109–10, 116.
52 Turner, *Ritual Process*, 117.
53 Ngqawana in Kaganof, *Exhibition of Vandalizim* (film), 40:30–42:30.
54 J. Lewis, *Anthropology of Cultural Performance*, 44.
55 Rancière's *Aesthetics and Its Discontents* deals extensively with the relationship between aesthetics and politics. The scope of this chapter and the particular focus of my

inquiry mean that the discussion is limited to one aspect of a much wider theorization that most resonated with my reading of *The Exhibition of Vandalizim*.
56 Rancière, *Aesthetics and Its Discontents*, 24–25.
57 Davis, *Key Contemporary Thinkers*, 91.
58 Fischlin, Heble, and Lipsitz, *Fierce Urgency of Now*, 100.
59 The film of *Vandalizim* also performs another important function: it creates an impulse that refuses the improvisation, that makes subsequent performances in different locations possible. It engenders, in other words, a series of ephemeral moments that perform the healing again and again, each time in a new iteration.

BIBLIOGRAPHY

Ashforth, Adam. *Witchcraft, Violence and Democracy in South Africa*. Chicago: University of Chicago Press, 2005.

Bailey, Derek. *Improvisation: Its Nature and Practice in Music*. Ashbourne, UK: Moorland, 1980.

Berliner, Paul. *Thinking in Jazz: The Infinite Art of Improvisation*. Chicago: University of Chicago Press, 1994.

Born, Georgina. "Music, Modernism and Signification." In *Thinking Art: Beyond Traditional Aesthetics*, edited by Andrew Benjamin and Peter Osborne, 157–76. London: Institute of Contemporary Arts, 1991.

Comaroff, Jean, and John L. Comaroff. "Occult Economies and the Violence of Abstraction: Notes from the South African Postcolony." *American Ethnologist* 26, no. 2 (May 1999): 279–303.

Corbett, John. "Ephemera Underscored: Writing around Free Improvisation." In *Jazz among the Discourses*, edited by Krin Gabbard, 217–40. Durham, NC: Duke University Press, 1995.

Davis, Oliver. *Key Contemporary Thinkers: Jacques Rancière*. Cambridge: Polity, 2010.

Desai, Ashwin. *We Are the Poors: Community Struggles in Post-apartheid South Africa*. New York: Monthly Review Press, 2002. Kindle.

Feld, Steven. *Jazz Cosmopolitanism in Accra: Five Musical Years in Ghana*. Durham, NC: Duke University Press, 2012.

Fischlin, Daniel, and Ajay Heble, eds. *The Other Side of Nowhere: Jazz, Improvisation, and Communities in Dialogue*. Middletown, CT: Wesleyan University Press, 2004.

Fischlin, Daniel, Ajay Heble, and George Lipsitz. *The Fierce Urgency of Now: Improvisation, Rights, and the Ethics of Cocreation*. Durham, NC: Duke University Press, 2013.

Fischlin, Daniel, and Martha Nandorfy. *The Community of Rights, the Rights of Community*. Montreal: Black Rose Books, 2012.

Floyd, Samuel A., Jr. *The Power of Black Music: Interpreting Its History from Africa to the United States*. New York: Oxford University Press, 1995.

Friedson, Steven M. *Dancing Prophets: Musical Experience in Tumbuka Healing*. Chicago: University of Chicago Press, 1996.

Hodson, Robert. *Interaction, Improvisation, and Interplay in Jazz.* New York: Routledge, 2007.

Jackson, Travis A. "Jazz Performance as Ritual: The Blues Aesthetic and the African Diaspora." In *The African Diaspora: A Musical Perspective,* edited by Ingrid Monson, 23–82. New York: Garland, 2000.

Jarrett, Michael. "Cutting Sides: Jazz Record Producers and Improvisation." In *The Other Side of Nowhere: Jazz, Improvisation, and Communities in Dialogue,* edited by Daniel Fischlin and Ajay Heble, 319–49. Middletown, CT: Wesleyan University Press, 2004.

Jost, Ekkehard. *Free Jazz.* New York: Da Capo, 1994.

Kaganof, Aryan, dir. *The Exhibition of Vandalizim.* With Zim Ngqawana and Kyle Shepherd. Filmed at the Zimology Institute, Elandsfontein, South Africa, January 30, 2010. Available on Vimeo: https://vimeo.com/108982799.

Kaganof, Aryan. "*The Exhibition of Vandalizim.*" *Art South Africa* 10, no. 1 (Spring 2011): 26.

Kakaza, Philip. "Healing with Music." *Mail and Guardian,* December 4, 1998. http://mg.co.za/article/1998-12-04-healing-with-music.

Lewis, George. *A Power Stronger than Itself: The AACM and American Experimental Music.* Chicago: University of Chicago Press, 2008.

Lewis, J. Lowell. *The Anthropology of Cultural Performance.* New York: Palgrave Macmillan, 2013.

Mabandu, Percy. "A Zimbol of Free Sound." *Mail and Guardian,* January 15, 2010. http://mg.co.za/article/2010-01-15-a-zimbol-of-free-sound.

Mail and Guardian. "The Healing Ceremony." April 30–May 6, 2010, 17.

Monson, Ingrid. *Saying Something: Jazz Improvisation and Interaction.* Chicago: University of Chicago Press, 1996.

Ngqawana, Zim. "Zim Ngqawana: Sound, Song and Humanity." Interview by AAJ Staff. *All about Jazz,* May 12, 2011. http://www.allaboutjazz.com/zim-ngqawana-sound-song-and-humanity-zim-ngqawana-by-aaj-staff.php?&pg=1.

Ngũgĩ wa Thiong'o. "Enactments of Power: The Politics of Performance Space." *Drama Review* 41, no. 3 (Autumn 1997): 11–30.

Phelan, Peggy. *Unmarked: The Politics of Performance.* London: Routledge, 2004.

Porter, Eric. *What Is This Thing Called Jazz? African American Musicians as Artists, Critics, and Activists.* Berkeley: University of California Press, 2002.

Pretorius, William Lyon. "A Criminological Analysis of Copper Cable Theft in Gauteng." Master's thesis, University of South Africa, 2012.

Rancière, Jacques. *Aesthetics and Its Discontents.* Translated by Steven Corcoran. Cambridge: Polity, 2009.

Rzewski, Frederic. "Little Bangs: A Nihilist Theory of Improvisation." *Current Musicology* 67/68 (Fall 1999): 377–86.

Seekings, Jeremy. "Poverty and Inequality in South Africa, 1994–2011." In *After Apartheid: Reinventing South Africa?,* edited by Ian Shapiro and Kahreen Tebeau, 21–51. Charlottesville: University of Virginia Press, 2011.

Silver, Jonathan. "Incremental Infrastructures: Material Improvisation and Social Collaboration across Postcolonial Accra." *Urban Geography* 35, no. 6 (2014): 788–804.

Times Live. "South Africa's Unemployment Rate Down." July 29, 2015. http://www
.timeslive.co.za/local/2015/07/29/South-Africas-unemployment-rate-down.

Titlestad, Michael. *Making the Changes: Jazz in South African Literature and Reportage.* Pretoria: University of South Africa Press; Leiden: Koninklijke Brill, 2004.

Tshabe, S. L., F. M. Shoba, and P. N. van der Westhuizen, eds. *The Greater Dictionary of isiXhosa.* Vol. 2. Alice, South Africa: isiXhosa National Lexicography Unit, 2003.

Turner, Victor. *The Anthropology of Performance.* New York: PAJ, 1986.

Turner, Victor. *The Ritual Process: Structure and Anti-structure.* New York: Aldine de Gruyter, 1995.

Van Wyk, Lisa. "Zim Ngqawana: The Silence between the Notes." *Mail and Guardian,* May 10, 2011. http://mg.co.za/article/2011-05-10-silence-between-the-notes.

World Bank. "Gini Index (World Bank Estimate)." Accessed September 25, 2015. http://data.worldbank.org/indicator/SI.POV.GINI.

THREE The Rigors of Afro/Canarian Jazz

Sounding Peripheral Vision with Severed Tongues

MARK LOMANNO

> Canary Islands musicians have drunk from many cultural fountains: Africa, [the] continent to which they belong geographically; Europe, [the] continent to which they belong politically; and America, [the] continent to which Canarians have had thousands of historical ties through emigration & immigration.
> —ENRIQUE "KIKE" PERDOMO, program notes for "Volcano Music"

Critical Interruptions

On Thursday, June 5, 2014, I delivered an unexpectedly brief preperformance lecture at the Instituto Cervantes in New York City. "Volcano Music," a concert headlined by saxophonist Enrique "Kike" Perdomo and guitarist Diego Barber, along with bassist Joseph Lepore and drummer Jeroen Truyen, featured modern interpretations of *música tradicional canaria*, arrangements of autochthonous folk songs from the Canary Islands. Perdomo and Barber had invited me to preface the show with a brief history of the Canary Islands as context for any audience members who might have been unfamiliar with las Islas.

Informing the audience that there would be a question-and-answer session after the concert, I began my prepared remarks by situating las Islas (off the coast of Morocco and Western Sahara) and discussing some differences between las Islas and Latin American and Caribbean countries. At that point, I was cut off—interrupted by an audience member who began shouting at me about the inaccuracy of my information and accusing me of eschewing "the facts" for my own personal biases. Emboldened, he stood up and accused me of lying to the audience. He did not specify to which facts he objected but suggested that he and the other Canarians "knew better." Equally flustered by the tone of his interjection and frustrated that he had drawn attention away from the musicians and las Islas, I placated this concertgoer by offering him an opportunity to speak with me after the performance and attempted to redirect the audience's attention by pivoting quickly to introductions of the personnel. The frame of the performance had been ruptured, though. The hopes the musicians and I had discussed for making this rare performance an opportunity for dialogue about las Islas and their relatively unknown musical culture had been undermined by one individual, who would later buttress and amplify his claim of authority—and justify his actions—by tracing his family lineage in las Islas back to its early Spanish colonial aristocracy.

The musicians' instrumental performance proceeded without any further interruption. Their repertoire elaborated on the performance's program notes—quoted at the beginning of this chapter—and included, for example, an adaptation of the *baile del vivo* that featured mixed meter, extended chromatic harmony, and large sections of solo and group improvisation.[1] Each composition and the entire performance were greeted with ample applause—including from the man who had disrupted my remarks. When he and I spoke after the concert—in a carefully choreographed, yet improvised switching between Spanish and English—this man, a Spanish diplomat, expressed distress over the concert's program notes and promotional materials, and admitted to attending with the intention of echoing publicly his grandmother's opinion that "las Islas tienen nada que ver con África."[2] Taken aback by such a definitive negation of many connections to Africa expressed by and experienced firsthand with my Canarian friends and interlocutors, I responded that my presentation was informed by years of research but, more importantly, by others' self-identification as Afro/Canarian. After he left (undeterred), several audience members approached me, apologizing for his interruption and expressing regret that a more open dialogue had not been possible.

Three days after the concert I was on a flight to Tenerife, one of the Canarian archipelago's two central islands, for a six-week visit in which I continued my research, reconnected with friends, and performed as a pianist in several concerts. About a week after the "Volcano Music" concert, I attended a rehearsal of the group Ait Nahaya, at which I recounted the story of the Spanish diplomat who insisted that las Islas "tienen nada que ver con África," an absurd viewpoint according to these musicians whose project foregrounds the historical and current connections between Canarian and Amazigh (Berber) music in language, performance practice, repertoire, and instrumentation.[3] Their music reflects the easily observable local truth that African influences abound in las Islas: in language, toponomy, cuisine, ecology, music, and many other realms. No solo se puede descubrir África en las Canarias—in touch, taste, and, in the case of these and many other musicians, sound; pero también, on the easternmost islands in the archipelago—Fuerteventura and Lanzarote—se puede ver África desde las Islas.[4] So, given both historical accounts and the present, intercultural interactions between Africa and las Islas, how might we understand that diplomat's interruption and his dismissal of these commonalities? How do we understand his applauding support of the musicians' sonic performance but not our spoken or written texts associated with it? What kinds of listening and vision is this person practicing?

The incident at the "Volcano Music" concert reiterated a well-worn, insidious trope about the Spanish colonization of las Islas as the arrival of civilization and beginning of historical time. Despite the passage of over five hundred years since colonization, however, traditional Afro/Canarian culture has persevered amid persecution, violence, enslavement, and marginality. This diplomat could not let me finish even the most basic recounting of Afro/Canarian history because speaking of (or writing about) Afro/Canarian culture as an observable recent history and present—measured in discrete actions and moments of time—destabilizes the dominant epistemic perspectives that would maintain the Afro/Canarian as an atemporal, prehistoric myth. The self-perpetuating, exclusionary modes of perception like those practiced by this Spanish diplomat have long histories rooted in politically motivated silencings of Afro/Canarian identity and in debates about indigeneity, the genealogy of cultural practices in colonial and settler contexts, and authenticity. Relegating the African presence and present in las Islas to the realm of ahistorical myth, this silencing erases precolonial history with the goal of destabilizing contemporary Afro/Canarian communities and acts of cultural belonging.

Yet what the diplomat failed to see and hear was that Perdomo, Barber, and their accompanists performed this past and present *afrocanariedad* through sound. As they relate to Afro/Canarian identity formation, the practices of music making can actuate potential for subverting these exclusionary modes of perception in ways that spoken and written language cannot. With its inherent ephemerality and multiplicity, improvisation—as both musical and cultural practice—is particularly effective in asserting

Afro/Canarian identity as uniquely pluralistic, emergent, and subject to contestatory interpretations. Perdomo and Barber's "Volcano Music" concert sounded markedly different from the Ait Nahaya rehearsal, but both expressed Canarian identity as African and Afro/Canarian. Improvisation figures prominently in both groups' performance practices and in their selective sampling from and interpretative taste for the many cultural "fountains," as Perdomo has written (see epigraph), from which musicians can drink. While these multiple forms of Afro/Canarian identity and the subjective and polysemous nature of improvised instrumental music can undermine the efficacy of these musical counternarratives, the flexible plurality and independence from institutional modes of communication inherent in improvisatory acts can provide at least some subversive potential—some alternate means of expression. Listening for these alternatives and working them into research should be a priority for ethnographers and jazz studies scholars, two groups that, while subscribing to disciplinary conventions that purport to elevate individuals and celebrate the collaborative and diverse nature of their methodologies and scholarly work, still risk perpetuating entrenched political and social histories of silencing and erasure because of their dependence on the dominant discursive modes through which these histories have been constructed all along.

Improvisation performs a crucial role in exposing, undermining, and creating alternatives to the structures (aesthetic, political, social, etc.) that have informed the diplomat's perception and his refusal to perceive. Inasmuch as improvised sound slipped past the diplomat's silencing rebuke of spoken language at "Volcano Music," finding ways to fold sonic improvisation into scholarship can just as adeptly undermine the prevailing written histories from which Afro/Canarians have been excised for centuries. By augmenting an ethnographic text and the methodologies that produce it with the presence and practices of these improvising musicians, we can expose and undermine some of the scholarly conventions that have quite literally and violently cut the Afro/Canarian out.

Heeding Carol A. Muller's call for establishing localized contexts in jazz studies, this chapter explores Afro/Canarian jazz as acts of resistance against histories of silencing via a trenchant and often-debated origin story about las Islas—the myth of *lenguas cortadas* (severed tongues).[5] This myth documents the exile of rebellious North Africans from the Roman colony of Mauretania to las Islas. When the uprising could not be quelled locally, the single Roman legion tasked with enforcing imperial law in North Africa was dispatched to restore the Roman government's control. The leaders of the uprising (those "que se levantaron contra los Romanos") were exiled to las Islas, and as further punishment, "les cortaron las lenguas" (their tongues were removed) so they could not speak of their revolt.⁶ This myth perpetuates the memory of colonial disempowerment and violence, and continues to undermine local claims to sovereignty grounded in indigenous land claims by characterizing the indigenous Afro/Canarian as "not a viable category of personhood," a mute(d) subject incapable of linguistic communication.⁷

As both the Perdomo/Barber ensemble and Ait Nahaya demonstrate, musicians perform Afro/Canarian identities by circumventing linguistic modes that, because they necessarily rely on colonial epistemologies, have invited, and continue to invite, interruption, silencing, and erasure. In order to highlight these Afro/Canarian improvised musical practices as just one set of coping strategies in the larger framework of responses to settler-colonial violence around the world, I will gloss Afro/Canarian improvised musical practice, afrocanariedad, and the lenguas cortadas myth through a discussion of "the cut," a concept explored at length in Fred Moten's *In the Break: The Aesthetics of the Black Radical Tradition*.⁸ As an aesthetic practice and a cultural phenomenon, "the cut" sheds light on the tactical artistry of these Afro/Canarian musicians. Even as they are isolated from globalized flows of cultural and economic industries, these musicians are drawing on some of the same practices of African American jazz and Afro-diasporic consciousness that Moten understands via "the cut." I am not suggesting, though, that Afro/Canarian jazz should be viewed first *through* the African diaspora, African American jazz, or "the cut." Rather, as a peripheral group within the diaspora, Europe, and the world more generally, Afro/Canarians cut "the cut": while Afro/Canarian improvisational musicking and ideas of fusion relate to Moten's cut and his ideas of montage, Afro/Canarians riff on these, demonstrating how adopting diasporic and globalized musical practices—even mimetically—can create new meanings and worldviews tied to emergent conceptions of indigenous and hyperlocal identity. These recontextualizations are alternate visions of Afro/Canarian culture and history, improvised, contestatory responses that simultaneously implicate and work around the dominant epistemologies and normative scholarly practices that have looked past them for centuries. For this reason, hearing Afro/Canarian jazz only as a localized form of global jazz culture or Afro-diasporic culture not only betrays its own history and present but also reifies the Afro/Canarian as a muted subject unable to articulate without recourse to more legible referents. Last, folding Moten into the mix acknowledges my positionality as a jazz pianist and academic trained in the music and scholarship of the

Afro-Atlantic world. Inasmuch as Moten's and my voices figure into this essay's mix, I intend to augment that mix by foregrounding Afro/Canarian perspectives, highlighting the potential of emergent, improvised, and collaborative practices in las Islas to articulate alternatives to dominant settler-colonial and diasporic epistemologies. These improvisatory performance practices can also serve as critical responses to and revisions of scholarly epistemologies, modeling more practice-based approaches where normative research methodologies and formats have perpetuated a centuries-long tradition of silencing the Afro/Canarian.

Foregrounding Afro/Canarian Histories

Partly owing to colonial historiography and a scholarly predilection for natural history, much more is known about the ecological origins of las Islas than those of its human populations. Although archaeological and genetic research has definitively established a connection between las Islas' earliest inhabitants and North African peoples, these peoples' histories and exact geographic origins are not well documented.[9] Historical accounts attest to regional trade with the Phoenicians and the Romans, while Portuguese, Genovese, and English conquerors all established ports and trade interests in las Islas before the Spanish colonized las Islas in 1496, when, after laying siege for almost a hundred years, they defeated the inhabitants of Tenerife, the last of las Islas' populations to be subdued.[10]

Las Islas remain under Spain's political aegis today as one of the nation's seventeen autonomous communities, a designation that belies systemic dependencies on the nation-state that impede any potential movements toward self-governance. These dependencies are present in every facet of Canarian life, including state education, which promotes a historical narrative that collapses Afro/Canarian history in las Islas: concentrating on the arrival of western Europeans as the beginning of local, "verifiable" history relegates the African influences in las Islas and the Afro/Canarian to a mythological past.[11] Las Islas' natural history as one inclusive of its precolonial inhabitants has been reworked and naturalized into a set of timeless myths about exotic island-scapes with their indigenous populations conveniently dehumanized as primitive savages.

As part of this constructed past, the lenguas cortadas myth attempts to explain the arrival of las Islas' first inhabitants.[12] Despite archaeological evidence proving that las Islas were inhabited long before this exile would have happened, this cultural myth lingers as debate over historically verified facts continues. The myth has also been invoked to explain why indigenous Canarians were not seafaring people (because they were unable to verbally instruct subsequent generations) and why inhabitants of La Gomera communicate in *silbo gomero*, a so-called whistle language, "el lenguaje más extraño de todos los países de por acá . . . como si no tuvieran lengua."[13] Even basic silbo speakers can quickly point out the fallacy in this ex post facto colonial teleology, though: you simply can't whistle without a tongue.[14]

Historical fallacies and physiological impossibilities aside, the lenguas cortadas myth has taken root in the Canarian social imaginary as a well-known narrative about precolonial Afro/Canarian life. Associating the Afro/Canarian with physical deformity and disorder, this "distorted origin story"—yet another form of settler-colonial silencing that marginalizes the Afro/Canarian—also legitimizes Spanish conquest by implying that the Spanish had at least as much claim to sovereignty in las Islas as those they conquered (since no one could make a verifiable claim to indigeneity). I would suggest that, as they have with other myths, Afro/Canarians are using this lack of history—or excess of historicities—to their advantage, reappropriating these erasures to perform fluid, changeable—even improvised— identities that draw critically on these accounts.[15] Bolstered by more recent research that debunks these myths, Afro/Canarians are filling in the historiographical gaps and breaks, creatively and deconstructively rewriting las Islas' multiple histories, thus reenvisioning their present and future through collaborative sonic performance. In their plurality, these alternate histories sound decolonizing riffs against settler-colonial power and silencing.

But glossing the Afro/Canarian as just another variation on the theme of reappropriation by a marginalized group would overlook important differences that have isolated las Islas, their inhabitants, and their histories *within* the African diaspora, Europe, and Western scholarly epistemologies more generally. The continued erasure of the Canary Islands in discourses on Atlantic, diasporic, African, and European musics suggests the potential in a specific application of Moten's comment, "These institutions cut it up and made it invisible. . . . They cut it up and thus made any apprehension of its totality all but impossible to us who pursued it."[16] Here Moten's multiple references to the cut could refer both to the multiple, institutionalized silencings of the Afro/Canarian and to the plurality of approaches Afro/Canarian musicians adopt in their improvisatory sonic reconstitutions of themselves and their histories in the aftermath of such silencings.

Emergent Performance and Afro/Canarian Irruption

As Perdomo's program notes for the "Volcano Music" concert outlined, the Canary Islands' plural histories—written, influenced, and composed by multiple cultures—provide contemporary Afro/Canarians with a wide range of traditions on which to draw as inspiration for formulating their identities. The concept of *tricontinentalidad* localizes this multiplicity of influences as a particularity of Canarian culture. Derived from a historically informed understanding of las Islas as an intersection of European, African, and American cultures, it functions as a means of both commemorating las Islas' historical importance in global economies and reasserting those associations in contemporary circumstances. Despite its emphasis on transcultural fusion of multiple cultures from various geographic locations, tricontinentalidad is an autochthonous phenomenon, rooted in Afro/Canarian sociocultural landscapes.

Tricontinentalidad acts in part as a counterbalance for another operative force in the Canarian social imaginary that arises from the knowledge that las Islas' more cosmopolitan moments are in the past. *Aislamiento* describes the many ways in which las Islas and their inhabitants have been isolated from history and continue to exist at the world's margins, a condition amplified and institutionalized through las Islas' status as one of nine outermost regions of the European Union.[17] Aislamiento is used to describe the condition of the Afro/Canarian within las Islas, and of las Islas in relation to mainland Spain, the Caribbean, and the world. Aislamiento as a phenomenon similarly references both a general condition of island life and a uniquely Canarian experience. And while tricontinentalidad attempts to counteract this Canarian isolation from the African and European continents and within the diaspora through celebrations of archipelagic diversity, only certain kinds of diversity are audible, only certain gaps bridged.

Nowhere are the inequities within present-day ideas about tricontinentalidad and Canarian diversity more audible—the "epistemological abyss" more apparent—than in the continued erasure, isolation, and subjugation of Africa and Africanness in the Canarian social imaginary and institutional discourses, in which state-sanctioned models of an ahistorical, exoticized precolonial past overwrite an already peripheral community and its cultural memory. Musical practice cuts against the exclusionary potential of these presumably inclusive models of community just as improvisational music making constantly critiques systematized constructions of improvisation. Musicians such as Kino Ait Idrissen of Ait Nahaya foreground these subjugated cultures and histories not only through collaborations that draw on the repertoires and traditions of North Africa, Ireland, and India—all prominent cultural legacies within las Islas that do not figure into Canarian conceptions of tricontinentalidad—but also through a virtuosic mobility across these traditions. This changeable plurality resists the kinds of institutional codification that perpetuate the silencing of the Afro/Canarian past and present.

So, in addition to personal histories, competencies, aesthetics, and aspirations—in addition to the cultural histories, social imaginaries, and political motivations—concepts such as tricontinentalidad and aislamiento inform performances of pluralistic Afro/Canarian identity. Beyond critiques of fixed or static identity, though, lie the specific histories of indigenous Canarians, shrouded in myth and ambiguity—at times intentionally so—such that the lack of collective consensus about who and what these people were and are makes Afro/Canarian identity particularly diffuse. Because of this void, though, reconstructing critical Afro/Canarian indigeneity can be highly personal and creative work. This multitude of identities is referenced locally through endonyms, of which *afrocanario* is just one.[18]

Beyond the archipelago, local forms of aislamiento are reproduced in popular and academic discourses. Owing to various factors related to geography, racial politics, and what Rosi Braidotti calls "methodological nationalism," las Islas and their inhabitants do not quite fit in Latin America, the Spanish Caribbean, Iberia, Africa, Europe, postcolonial studies, or the Black Atlantic.[19] And so the multiply marginalized Afro/Canarian can assert cultural identity only through performances that irrupt into discourses from which they are excluded through historiographical default and ideological assumptions. For the emergent, ephemeral, and pluralistic characteristics of this identity and its relation to the others it references, improvisation is a particularly productive musical practice and discursive framework for enacting and understanding Afro/Canarian cultural formations. By creating space—ruptures—within everyday, mundane structures through the repeated cuts and polysemous performances of silenced perspectives, improvisation more accurately reflects the position of the peripheral Afro/Canarian "in but not of" the institutions that deny them.[20]

Collective, improvisational Afro/Canarian music making responds critically to aislamiento, normative tricontinentalidad, and the settler legacy of lenguas cortadas by constantly reperforming sonic afrocanariedad in ways that refuse the logocentric canonizations that have silenced and overlooked Afro/Canarians for centuries. These Afro/Canarian musicians are performing what Moten describes as "the augmentation of vision with the sound that it has excluded, the augmentation of reason with the ecstasy it has dismissed—that improvises through the determinations of lack and alienation, not via some direct adequation between word and object, but through the object's transferential reproduction in and as the (re)production of sound and of an ensemblic, dynamic totality."[21] Countering the colonial violence against Afro/Canarians that is reinforced through epistemic acts like the diplomat's interruptions requires a paradigm shift that does not just make space for but celebrates Afro/Canarian epistemes. Because of improvisers' inherent ability to rework existing systematized logics—including, for example, the excisive settler epistemologies on which language must rely—this shift is unfolding through successive, emergent waves of improvised Afro/Canarian sonic performance.

Contingencies and Creating in the Act

Inasmuch as the beginnings of jazz in the Canary Islands—like the origins of its peoples—are diffuse, sporadic, and highly varied, collective discourse around the beginning of *jazz canario* usually coheres around Jazz Borondón. Formed in the early 1980s, the group featured the aforementioned saxophonist Kike Perdomo, bassist José Carlos Machado, guitarist Ruskin Herman, drummer Alfredo Llanos, percussionist José Pedro Pérez, and others. The group modeled their compositional and performance practice after jazz-fusion groups like Weather Report, Return to Forever, and the Mahavishnu Orchestra. When I first arrived in Tenerife in 2010 and told people of my project about "jazz canario y jazz hecho en Canarias," people spoke of this group's authenticity in near-mythic terms—as in "el primero verdadero," "el principio," and "la canariedad auténtica." Their albums *Borondón* (1990) and *Botaraste* (1992) mark some of the first attempts at fusing jazz with traditional and folkloric Afro/Canarian music.

Jazz Borondón combined the melodies, rhythms, and instruments (especially *chácaras*, wooden castanets) of música tradicional canaria with other signifiers of Afro/Canarian identity—including silbo gomero, song titles ("Arrorró," "Berlina," "Tango"), compositional elements, and performance techniques—and the aesthetics of synthesizers, drum machines, and postproduction processing adopted from contemporary US and British jazz-rock fusion bands. And while many of these elements can be heard simultaneously in most tracks, the group's use of sampling amplified this plurality of influences by foregrounding individual elements, cutting them into and on top of the overall mix. Jazz Borondón's fusion aesthetic and its use of samples and quotations improvised on las Islas' multiple histories, translating them into a musical mode.

Like Afro/Canarian identity more generally, the Canarian *tango* (unrelated to the South American tango) as a song form subsumes many different performance practices, theorized origins, and artistic interpretations within las Islas. Jazz Borondón's tango (from the album *Botaraste*) features a binary form that oscillates between a vamp in which the bass and drums perform the traditional tango rhythm in two, simultaneous divisions of 6/8 (two groups of three eighth notes and three groups of two eighth notes), and a jazz-rock setting of a traditional tango melody, performed by the late guitarist Ruskin Herman, in 4/4 time. The ensemble cycles through this structure several times: the first establishes the foundation, a polymetric representation of pluralized Afro/Canarian identity; the second revises, adding a keyboard improvisation; and the third and final iteration restates the first iteration but augments it with a choir accompanying Herman's melody. As the melody and track fade (back) into silence, Herman further elaborates, superimposing and improvising embellishments above the choir, who perform the melody as scripted, "scatted" nonlinguistic phonemes. Here again, the Afro/Canarian sounds outside, around, and in spite of its linguistic isolation, expressing the incisive mobility and ambiguity of paralinguistic sound by highlighting not one, distinctive, sonic element or voice but the process through which a changeable plurality of possible voices and continually reworked elements can emerge.[22]

On their album *Borondón*, the group's arrangement of an *arrorró*, a traditional lullaby, exemplifies Afro/Canarian critical reappropriation of cultural identity through performed arrangement of preexisting phenomena. "Arrorró" exemplifies Jazz Borondón's aesthetic of fusion especially well: along with elements of jazz-rock, the ensemble begins the track with a sampled recording of música tradicional canaria. The sampled arrorró is one of several recorded by Valentina la de Sabinosa (Valentina Hernández, 1889–1976), an icon of música tradicional canaria. As the track begins, the sampled recording sounds alone, filtered through a highly produced, heavily layered reverb that simultaneously casts Valentina's voice at a great distance and creates a large auditory space for the ensemble. The sample ends abruptly—at which time the ensemble enters—but with a melody culled from an arrangement of the arrorró by composer Teobaldo Power (1848–1884), whose version, excerpted from his suite titled *Cantos Canarios*, has been adopted as the state anthem of the Canary Islands. Within the first thirty seconds, Jazz Borondón has again orchestrated a polyvalent range of coexistent sonic signifiers and performance aesthetics. Whereas "Tango" reflected this primarily through polymeter and the fusion of multiple musical practices, Jazz Borondón's treatment of the arrorró reflects the plurality of Afro/Canarian identity within a single (jazz-fusion) aesthetic via melodies laden with the arrorró's extramusical connotations as both hyperlocal Afro/Canarian tradition and nationalist, Europeanized appropriation thereof.

While Valentina's sample sounds soloistically and completely, the group adopts a critical stance toward Power's arrorró, treating it as a text to be continually reworked through reharmonization, modal manipulation, and fragmentation. Power's melody is deconstructed, interrupted, elaborated on, reduced to a motivic fragment, halved, and sutured to various counterstatements that Jazz Borondón composed as a surplus of possible responses to Power's initial call. One of these is a keyboard improvisation that plays out the Afro-diasporic cut exactly as James A. Snead defines it: the improvisation begins where the listener expects another rephrasing of Power's melody but instead re/listens to the ensemble's arrangement of Power's theme.[23] Though following the arrangement's formal structure, in his improvisation keyboardist Luis Fernández exercises a critical reading of Power and audiences' expectations for it. The solo concludes with the second half of Power's initial melodic phrase, reattached to the excised and truncated call, creating a space of one complete minute in between the melody's two halves, which Jazz Borondón has re/composed as an Afro/Canarian critical response to western European periodicity, sentential structure, and normative time.

The piece ends with a final statement of Power's melody, once again fragmented and re/arranged by Jazz Borondón with a percussion break and long fade. As Jazz Borondón ruptured the well-composed lines of Power's arrorró to represent more fully the plurality of Afro/Canarian identity, the precedents the group set for improvised music making influenced by global jazz-rock aesthetics similarly opened up space in which subsequent generations of musicians have elaborated. The interpretative vocal and lyrical improvisations (of which Valentina's music is an archetype) and the polyphonic, polymetric percussion parts of música tradicional canaria are all part of a local performance practice of improvisation, which Jazz Borondón sutured to practices culled from globalized musical forms and the African diaspora, including jazz, sounding out a new pathway on which present-day Afro/Canarian musicians continue to add successive layers of sonic afrocanariedad.[24]

One such musician, guitarist Diego Barber, lives in New York City, where he is quickly gaining a stature in that jazz scene similar to the one he has held among Canarian jazz musicians for a while. Bassist Larry Grenadier and drummer Jeff Ballard—both internationally renowned artists known for working with pianists Brad Mehldau and Chick Corea, among others—joined Barber on his second recording, *Calima*, released in 2009. In a review of the album, one writer adopts a positive tone, drawing parallels among Afro/Canarian musical ecologies: "'Calima' es . . . el viento . . . aportando calor, arena y recordando que África no esta lejos. . . . Se oye la voz propia de Barber en esos pasajes más flamencos, más enraizados que despiden un aroma distinto al de otros guitarristas."[25] Despite calima's more negative and widespread associations as a pollutant—a meteorological irritant swept in from Africa that brings heat and sand that must be wiped away and washed off—for this album reviewer calima suggests a generative potential, a pollinating catalyst that infuses and inspires Barber's music. And while close connections to Africa carry cachet within jazz literature and historiography lacking within Spanish and some Canarian "nationalist" discourses, Barber and his music are cast in terms familiar to Canarians: those of transcultural fusion, cross-pollination, and the reach toward "la voz propia" that distinguishes the Afro/Canarian subject through extralingual means (the smells and sounds of proximal Africa). Interestingly, the reviewer conflates Barber's distinctive sonic "aroma" with flamenco, a genre Barber has studied and to which he alludes in the album's liner notes. Unlike the state's importation of white African sand (*arena*, not *calima*) to cover las Islas' black volcanic sand Barber celebrates the diverse roots of his music by juxtaposing many different influences within each performance rather than supplanting them with a single genre or approach.

The recasting of calima as generative speaks to improvisational practices as critical engagements around and within existing structures infused with the potential for creating alternate worldviews. Barber's music draws on Afro/Canarian culture, música tradicional canaria, jazz, Western classical music, flamenco, and many other influences, but overlaying one genre title, or even multiple titles, cannot sufficiently represent the plurality of his musical identity. So while Nathaniel Mackey's suggestion that "all that has black sounds has *duende*" could apply to Canarian beaches, Barber's music, and many other aspects of afrocanariedad, Barber—and the Afro/Canarian more generally—invokes the diaspora, Europe, and global jazz aesthetics but cannot be contained within or covered by them, or any other rubric.[26]

This uncircumscribable plurality—of which Barber's musical and cultural identities as expressed in his album *Calima* are just one example—is what the particular sounds, histories, and practices of Afro/Canarian improvisation expose, inspire, and propagate.

In the album's liner notes, Barber posits that *Calima* is his improvised attempt at working out a sonic resolution to the "*dilema*" of his pluralistic identity: its confounding surplus arises from a voice—or a spliced, sutured, tricontinental fusion of multiple voices—that cannot be contained within (genre) boundaries but instead emerges, like the Afro/Canarian counteracting aislamiento through historically rooted knowledge, collectively and continually "de comienzo incierto," from an unknown origin.[27] In formulating his response to this *dilema* of articulating the cross-pollinating potential of calima in his diverse, personalized understanding of sonic afrocanariedad, Barber makes special mention of the insight gained from one of his mentors, Costas Cotsiolis, with whom he studied in Athens: "El periodo en Grecia . . . supone la adquisición del rigor, la capacidad de 'ver.' Fue para mí de una ayuda inestimable."[28] Through collaborative, improvisational consideration and incorporation of sounds, sights, aromas, and tastes from many "fountains," Barber has acquired the truly rigorous vision of an Afro/Canarian who articulates his identity with a "troubled" voice that, like Jazz Borondón, relies on nonlinguistic sound to amplify, assert, and augment itself amid relentless interruption.[29]

With Cut Tongues

The rigor of which Barber speaks is distinct from the rigor deployed in positing lenguas cortadas as the foundation of silbo gomero. Through his open interpretation of calima, Barber explores the fluid plurality of afrocanariedad, drawing simultaneously on Miles Davis, Johann Sebastian Bach, flamenco, and música tradicional canaria, with an approach that defies and exceeds categorization—learned in Lanzarote, refined in Greece, and recorded in New York City. It is particularly telling that Barber calls this rigorous ability to articulate his perspective on Afro/Canarian identity "la capacidad de 'ver.'" When settler-colonial epistemologies continually reinforce that there's nothing of Africa to be seen in las Islas, seeing the Afro/Canarian—and seeing as an Afro/Canarian—continues to be an elusive and difficult practice. Barber approaches this, his dilemma, through sounding a plural vision—of styles, collaborators, and influences—correcting the myopia of normative, naturalized sight with a sonorous diplopia.³⁰

Barber's work since *Calima* bears this out. *The Choice* (Sunnyside Records, 2011) again resolves this *dilema de afrocanariedad* with new and different improvised responses. The first half of the album features some of the finest jazz musicians in New York City—Seamus Blake (saxophone), Larry Grenadier (bass), Ari Hoenig (drums), Mark Turner (saxophone), and Johannes Weidenmueller (bass)—while the latter half is an extended classical composition, *Sonata Banc D'Arguin*, that Barber performs as a soloist. This three-part piece furthers Barber's attention to grounding his music in biotic space—*Banc D'Arguin* (the Bay of Arguin) refers to both the body of water and the national park that spans over 450 miles of the Mauritanian coast.³¹

In 2013 Barber riffed on the history of jazz fusion, electronics, and sampling in Canarian jazz on *411* (Origin Records), a collaboration with fellow *lanzaroteño*, electronic composer, and DJ Hugo Cipres. Also featuring Blake, Weidenmueller, and Hoenig, the album's compositions continue to reference place. "Timanfaya," the first track on the album, is not "Volcano Music" but music for a volcano—the irruptive, pollinating force that created the island of Lanzarote ex nihilo—and recalls Jazz Borondón's electro/acoustic sampling fusions with an overlay of time signatures, timbres, and instrumental voices. In this brief introductory track, these voices are not melodic, though, but rather repetitive riffs amid waves of digital sound that create a framework on which the musicians elaborate throughout the rest of the album. Barber celebrates and commemorates his collaboration with producer Hugo Cipres on *Tales* (Sunnyside Records, 2014), a duet record with pianist Craig Taborn. This album has garnered Barber the most critical attention from US and international jazz media, primarily for the musicians' ability to transcend rigid demarcations of musical genre and those between improvised and composed music.³² The second track on *Tales*, "Cipres," runs nearly thirteen minutes in length—replete with multiple melodies (composed and improvised) and shifts in tempo, meter, aesthetic, tonality, and foregrounded soloist—but this music's afrocanariedad is not readily perceptible. It can be heard as such only with a particularly situated listening practice—*una adquisición del rigor, una capacidad de "ver"*—that is receptive to this emergent history of improvised collaboration between two *músicos canarios*, reconstituted, augmented, and amplified with new personnel and places, and continually recontextualized with a plurality of new, polyphonic sounds, the sum total of which defies categorization. Through constantly shifting his focus but maintaining his "rigorous" vision through subsequent releases, Barber is enacting an improvised, resilient, and diverse afrocanariedad that refuses category and flows uninterrupted.[33]

Perdomo's recorded output is similarly diverse and shifting, though more prolific—in part because he has been continually active for the past thirty years as both a musician and producer. Perdomo has toured extensively throughout Europe with his own group and with pianist Chano Domínguez. In addition to recordings where he was the leader, Perdomo has participated in many collaborative projects even more wide-ranging in their stylistic breadth and cultural diversity than Barber's. Of particular note are *Baba Djembe* (Multitrack Records, 1998) with Senegalese percussionist Ismaila Sane; *Macaronesis* (Macaronesis, Hesperides Producciones, 2001), a celebration of Macaronesian identities; and *Atlántida* (Big Band de Canarias, 96K Music, 2011), a big-band recording featuring arrangements of música tradicional canaria in collaboration with US saxophonist Dick Oatts. The year before the "Volcano Music" concert, during a visit to New York City, Perdomo recorded the aforementioned *Celebrate Brooklyn I and II* (96K Music, 2013), a double release featuring his compositions on the first disc and on the second a collection of arrangements I wrote for a working quartet we formed during my first residency in the Canary Islands. In the liner notes, which Perdomo wrote (in English and Spanish), he calls attention to the value of collaboration: "Hay momentos en los que todo transcurre de una forma muy rápida. Casi sin darte cuenta te encuentras rodeado de grandes músicos y además todo fluye de una forma muy natural. Y cuando eso ocurre hay que celebrarlo."[34] Perdomo's directive is in part self-referential: his visits to New York City and participation in that scene represent important moments when aislamiento has been neutralized temporarily. These temporary reprieves facilitated additional performances of sonic afrocanariedad through new collaborations and in new environs, to which Perdomo would return for the "Volcano Music" concert that served as this chapter's initial inspiration. *Celebrate Brooklyn*'s simplistic cover lists the title, the personnel, and one other word: "listen." Including such a basic instruction on the cover of a recording might seem redundant; however, as the diplomat's interruption at the "Volcano Music" concert reminds us, listening to and for Afro/Canarian music and musicians requires particularly situated practices and *una adquisición del rigor*. Perdomo's and Barber's calls to "listen" and "see" are subversive, multisensory, and plurivalent acts aimed at opening up the very dialogues that the Spanish diplomat attempted to sever.

Afro/Canarians have been coping with and responding to such acts of epistemic violence for centuries. Reappropriating obscurity and isolation as mobility from within, continual waves of improvised identities—of which Barber's and Perdomo's are just two—have produced a sonorous plurality of afrocanariedad that celebrates the constructive and productive potentialities of aislamiento in part through language but most especially through sound, "the ongoing improvisation of a kind of lyricism of the surplus—invagination, rupture, collision, augmentation."[35] This multiply tongued, polymetric, collaborative improvising irrupts from within dominant discourses about and mythic constructions of las Islas and their inhabitants with "an ongoing shiftiness, a living labor of engendering to be organized in its relation to a politico-aesthesis."[36] Listen again to Moten's take on the cut in light of "Volcano Music," Jazz Borondón's aesthetics of fusion, Barber's rupturing of genre boundaries, Perdomo's mobility, and the persistent epistemic violence commemorating Afro/Canarian lenguas cortadas: "Such blackness [read: afrocanariedad] is only in that it exceeds itself; it bears the groundedness of an uncontainable outside. It's an erotics of the cut, submerged in the broken, breaking space-time of an improvisation. Blurred, dying life; liberatory, improvisatory, damaged love; freedom drive."[37]

Nada que ver: Listening for the Afro/Canarian

This chapter is about improvising with and in spite of epistemological violence. That the diplomat's interruption precedes everything else is crucial: using necessarily ambiguous nonlinguistic means simultaneously to circumvent and levy critique against exclusionary logocentric practices is one primary way in which Afro/Canarians can respond to the conditions of aislamiento that deny them access to the institutions and frameworks of postcoloniality, repatriation, the African diaspora, and autonomy or self-governance. And while the violence in this chapter is only epistemological, it connects to a much longer history of physical violence tied to the Canary Islands and more generally to settler colonialism.

Repeated acts of epistemic violence—of which my being heckled by the Spanish diplomat was just a single example—perpetuate a challenging condition in contemporary Canarian society metonymized in the lenguas cortadas "distorted origin story." The lenguas cortadas myth, like tricontinentalidad and aislamiento, represents an ongoing dilemma—or what Gloria

Anzaldúa calls "una herida abierta," an open wound—with which Afro/Canarians must constantly cope.[38] Apart from his contestations against my spoken and Perdomo's written words, the diplomat took no issue with the ensemble's performance, even though the musical sound illustrated the same concepts of Afro/Canarian identity he so vehemently opposed when expressed verbally. Despite these critiques' reliance on more specialized sensory competencies and arguments more susceptible to ambiguous interpretations, this dichotomy suggests the emancipatory, critical power of nonverbal modes of art, the ameliorating conditions of hope on which newly emergent epistemes and communities can be founded.

We must listen even more acutely precisely because of this necessary ambiguity: not just to the sounds themselves but also to the emergent re/combinations of situated sounds. In our quests for the adquisición del rigor, we must remain open and flexible to necessarily incomplete interpretations of such polyvalent performative acts. As I continue to work on this project, the Spanish diplomat's interruption has forced me to confront anew how language fails afrocanariedad. During my initial trip to las Islas I interpreted these failures somewhat self-consciously: as a personal inability to communicate properly in the Canarian Spanish dialect owing in part to my ongoing language learning.[39] At the "Volcano Music" concert, the Spanish diplomat's heckling interruption and our exchange that followed, because it mostly occurred *in English* (my native tongue), point to linguistic failure on a much deeper level, as a pathological inability—brought on by the logocentric politics of settler-colonialism—to articulate afrocanariedad.

In formulating responses to this condition, listening for and seeing Afro/Canarian bodies and contextual histories through an embodied research posture can help to parse these sounds, especially in articulating local meanings of seemingly globalized aesthetics or performance practices. And so, as with earlier instantiations of this work, I am compelled back to the piano bench, to compose empathetically, as part of an ensemblic collective, and with ears open to sonic afrocanariedad and "the kind of meaningful aural expression that improvises through the distinction between the paralinguistic and the metalinguistic."[40] Through their performances Barber, Perdomo, Ait Nahaya, and others are expressing alternative, viable Afro/Canarian identities that accommodate lenguas cortadas, celebrating—not excising—African biotics in spite of histories of epistemic and physical violence against Afro/Canarians and the actions and agents that would perpetuate those histories.

Just as African sands are either commodified as *arena* or pathologized as *calima*, Afro/Canarian culture is treated as either an exotic veneer that spruces up las Islas' state-sponsored, historicized folklore or a pollutant that needs to be swept aside lest it sully the utopian vistas that western European imaginations have mapped onto las Islas since antiquity. This is the rigorous myopia that willfully unsees the Afro/Canarian—the cartographic eye that carefully triangulates the location of the mythic St. Brendan's Island but glosses over autochthonous claims of indigeneity and silences those who would make them.[41] Through sound, Afro/Canarian musicians are constantly repositioning these many misinterpreted, mistranslated, and miscalculated appropriations of autochthonous culture.

The promises and dilemmas of contending with Afro/Canarian identity lie in its polyvalence; as Perdomo says, "nuestra identidad es el mestizaje."[42] While its lack of fixity resists writerly technologies of representation—a symptom of epistemological violence in las Islas—finding a way to fold the multiple responses/resolutions of the Afro/Canarian back into those technologies can effect a methodological shift, an "irruption into discourse" informed by Afro/Canarian performance practice that Moten says signals "the difference between ostension and improvisation. Ostension is an enactment on the other side of linguistic failure; improvisation is sounding in linguistic failure."[43] Though he does not explicitly invoke improvisation in his formulation of critical indigeneity, Bernard Perley accentuates the qualities of mobility, contingency, risk taking, and multiplicity that characterize these emergent sonic performances of afrocanariedad: "These practices of being Indigenous are neither mutually exclusive nor temporally distinct because, when viewed as a sequence of embodied experiences over time, the practices of being Indigenous are not totalizing or fixed. When the stakes for Indigenous practices of everyday life determine the competence of individual enactments of Indigenous identity, when unexpected elements introduce uncertainty, then the complex interactions of subjectivities become intuitive responses based on experiences and anticipations of critical Indigeneity in action ... [the] 'contingencies of emergence.'"[44]

Inserting Afro/Canarians into existing models of scholarship positions them liminally without dismantling the historiographical centers and disciplinary conventions that have occluded them; to rupture existing modes of scholarship through foregrounding Afro/Canarian bodies and the sonic improvisations they perform simultaneously cuts against the linguistic failures of those modes and creates openings within them, through which successive waves of improvised identities can flow: this is the rupturing, hope-filled accommodation of Anzaldúa's wound as (un)natural bridge; or as Perdomo has said, "se rompen los moldes y todo es posible."[45]

In listening to and amplifying these performances through scholarship, we should remain attendant to the dissonances of cultural polyphony, the dilemmas of categorization, and contestatory ideas about how—or whether—to resolve them. Though fluid and fleeting, calima is as persistent and omnipresent an architecture as the Spanish buildings that have occupied Afro/Canarian space for the past 550 years. Distinguishing between calima as pollutant and pollinator falls to the myopic eyes that would overlook afrocanariedad, and to the intact yet ineffectual tongues that attempt to articulate it through verbal language, but even more so to the attendant ears that would listen for it in spite of all the centuries of silencing. The failure of language to describe calima as either an Afro/Canarian architextural pollutant or a pollinator (or as both) points to the inability of logocentric, scholarly methodologies to represent sonic afrocanariedad.[46] Ethnographers and scholars need to embrace and embody new forms of rigor, employing a multiplicity of practices for coping with the polyvalent responses from the periphery: to attune, for instance, listening and writing practices to how Barber's improvisations of calima based on recontextualized influences of música tradicional canaria, western European classicism, African American jazz, and Andalucian flamenco can enrich analyses by creating openings for not just Afro/Canarians but the improvised self-representations of all silenced peoples.

Having echoed the often-repeated call for attention to local knowledge in ethnography, invoking Fred Moten, Gloria Anzaldúa, Rosi Braidotti, Nathaniel Mackey, Bernard Perley, and others throughout this chapter might suggest a methodological blind spot—a further occlusion of afrocanariedad—by rendering the Afro/Canarian knowable and legible through outsider epistemologies. I wonder if we might resolve this by thinking of these writers and the role their scholarship performs here in relation to situated listening practices. Inasmuch as the Spanish diplomat exposed his biases at the "Volcano Music" concert, in this chapter I am outing my identity as a US ethnographer and performer based in grounded histories and embodied competencies of Afro-Atlantic music and scholarship by exploring lenguas cortadas as an Afro/Canarian expression of "the cut/wound," two of the many ways that Afro/Canarian culture can be read/heard. I don't see (or hear) these as impositions on the musicians or las Islas, but rather as responsive, text-based amplifications born from resistance that would not be permitted in the Canary Islands (again, the diplomat's interruption shows this), written by scholars whose perspectives are informed by similar histories of settler-colonial violence. Simply put, Moten, Anzaldúa, and all the others are part of the ensemble through which I'm formulating my response to interruption. And so, for me, listening to and for sonic afrocanariedad through collaborative, improvisational ethnography at the piano bench necessarily entails listening with and through their work, too.[47]

My choice to include these related theories is as much about implicating my position in the products of ethnographic process and highlighting the kinds of improvisational resonances and translational relationships that can arise in those processes as it is about finding ways to amplify Afro/Canarian voices through those with similarly silenced voices and recuperating bodies. I see the choice to self-implicate as a disciplinary and methodological intervention—new only in the sense that I'm drawing on the practices of improvisational music making to inform scholarship in fields that are in the process of making turns toward more practice-based approaches. So, I don't think it's about mapping other experiences or perspectives onto Afro/Canarian ones; it's about shedding preconceived notions about how culture operates and is organized, and facilitating emergent resonances that amplify and augment all involved in diverse and unequal ways. Preserving the polyphony of interlocutors, cited scholars, and discursive modes through creative arrangement in the writerly mix presents epistemic alternatives as critical interventions in established modes of thought that have perpetuated the inequities against which these musicians and scholars are positing their rigorous visions for alternate ways of being.

This last point moves critical improvisation studies forward from understanding improvisation as a socially embedded set of musical and cultural practices toward an even more dynamic set of processes wherein research methodologies themselves are the result of similar interactions of exchange, reciprocity, unforeseen hybridizations, and emergent aesthetic and cultural practices. Adopting collaborative improvisation as a framework for research allows us to play deconstructively on normative and naturalized paths of research methodologies and scholarship. In his chapter on "The Sentimental Avant-Garde," Moten suggests that "while Ellingtonian meaning swings in a way that Freud probably can't quite reach," "in this swing there's something that Freud might help to illuminate even as whatever light he sheds is cut and augmented, if not eclipsed, by Ellington's sound."[48] Riffing on Afrodiasporic ideas of the cut, then, and transposing them through afrocanariedad, we can see and hear how Afro/Canarian tactics of fusion as multiple pathways back from a history of silencing teach us about making room for alternate modes of listening—phonomethodologies?—in critical improvisation studies research.

NOTES

I'd like to thank all the musicians listed for their invaluable time in conversation and on the bandstand; Anna Reidy and Dr. Meta DuEwa Jones, who read early drafts of this chapter; Dr. Veit Erlmann, who supervised the dissertation project on which this is based; and this volume's editors, Daniel Fischlin and Eric Porter, and its blind reviewers for their insights. This chapter is unquestionably better for their collective feedback and attention.

1. This arrangement of the *baile del vivo*, a traditional song from the island of El Hierro, was based on one that I wrote for a collaborative project with Perdomo, *Celebrate Brooklyn II* (96k Music, 2013). The concert itself was not recorded but was a clear development from earlier work by Perdomo and Barber that fuses música tradicional canaria with jazz performance practices, including improvisation. See below.
2. Personal communication with the author, Instituto Cervantes, New York, June 5, 2014. The expression *nada que ver* is usually translated into English as "nothing to do [with]," even though the Spanish verb *ver* means "to see."
3. To hear the performance that inspired this project, see Ait Nahaya, "Mustafá—Ait Nahaya." According to Kino Ait Idrissen, one of the group's members, as with his own name, *ait* means "hij@ o hij@s de." For the meaning of *nahaya*, he copied and pasted from the archaeolinguist Ignacio Reyes's online dictionary of Tamazight in Canarian Spanish: "de 'nahagga' . . . hombre digno." Personal communication with the author, November 10, 2015. For more information, see the group's Facebook page: https://www.facebook.com/AitNahaya/.
4. Distances of less than seventy miles—shorter than the distance between Miami and Havana—separate Morocco and/or Western Sahara and several points along the shores of Fuerteventura and Lanzarote.
5. Muller, "Musical Echoes of American Jazz."
6. Fr. Alonso de Espinosa, quoted in Álvarez Delgado, "Leyenda erudita," 53. See also Farrujía de la Rosa and del Carmen del Arco Aguilar, "La leyenda del poblamiento de Canarias por Africanos de lenguas cortadas."
7. Perley, "Living Traditions," 43.
8. See also Snead, "Repetition as a Figure," 71–72: "The 'cut' overtly insists on the repetitive nature of the music, by abruptly skipping it back to another beginning which we have already heard. . . . The ensuing rupture does not cause dissolution of the rhythm; quite to the contrary, it strengthens it, given that it is already incorporated into the format of the rhythm. . . . This peculiarity of black music—that it draws attention to its own repetitions—extends to the way it does not hide the fact that these repetitions take place on the level of sound only."
9. Carbon dating has confirmed that las Islas were inhabited as early as 200 BCE, although estimates based on genetic analysis suggest that las Islas were inhabited several centuries earlier; see Maca-Meyer et al., "Mitochondrial DNA Transit." Mitochondrial DNA analysis connected these inhabitants to the North African Amazigh; see Fregel et al., "Maternal Aborigine Colonization."

10 This precolonial internationalism informs a collective memory of the Canary Islands as an intersection of diverse cultures and economic prominence even before the archipelago became more cosmopolitan during the colonial era. For the reasons discussed above, as with most positive celebrations of precolonial culture, music (as a nonverbal art) plays a prominent role in expressing this cultural memory. See below on *tricontinentalidad* and *aislamiento*.

11 This politicized pedagogy is supported in part by a dearth of historical accounts—a break in the timeline—between the end of the Roman era and the rediscovery of las Islas by the Genovese and Portuguese in the fourteenth century.

12 The cutting out of tongues was a fairly common punishment, having been documented in Roman times and also in the Byzantine era. See Lascaratos and Dalla-Vorgia, "Penalty of Mutilation."

13 Fr. Alonso de Espinosa, quoted in Álvarez Delgado, "Leyenda erudita," 56.

14 Silbo gomero, recently recognized by UNESCO as intangible cultural heritage, is more accurately described as a language system in which certain intoned whistles correspond to language phonemes. Silbo gomero is this system applied to the Spanish language spoken on La Gomera, but the system functions with other languages.

15 For an account of the mythic St. Brendan's Island and its place in the Afro/Canarian imagination, see Lomanno, "Emergence and the *insula improvīsa*."

16 Moten, *In the Break*, 157.

17 See Lomanno, "Emergence and the *insula improvīsa*."

18 I have chosen the exonym *Afro/Canarian*, or *afro/canario*, as a means of signifying the myriad associations and engagements among the African continent, Amazigh culture, las Islas' multicultural histories, and the current inhabitants of las Islas that may come into play in any one improvised performance of sonic afrocanariedad. In reference to the virgule ("/"), Jennifer DeVere Brody writes that it "performs the interactivity and intersubjectivity of making/seeing that is a central tenet of postmodernism, poststructuralism, performance studies, and even psychoanalytic thought." Brody, *Punctuation*, 22.

19 See Braidotti, "Nomadism"; and Lomanno, "Jazz Nomadism."

20 Harney and Moten, "University," 101.

21 Moten, *In the Break*, 179.

22 Perdomo further accentuates this focus on process in his description of Jazz Borondón: "Fue un proyecto de fusionar . . . para traspasarlas a un grupo de jazz." He then elaborates on this "running-through" by describing the conceptual, compositional, and collaborative labor necessary to produce the group's repertoire. See Perdomo, "Entrevista," 97.

23 See note 8 above.

24 See Perley, "Living Traditions," in which he describes critical indigeneity as "the everyday embodiment of Maliseet worlds by Maliseet people in and on their own terms, thereby constantly re-creating Maliseet worlds. The importance of this strategy lies in creating possibilities for Maliseet futures as variously conceived by members of the community" (47).

25 Bosquesonoro, "Diego Barber."

26 Mackey, "Cante Moro," 182. I would suggest that the same failures of language that isolate the Afro/Canarian are perhaps why Gabriel García Lorca suggested that, in terms of *duende*, "ningún filósofo explica." Duende is not just a struggle but a struggling—*luchar*—the ongoing, irruptive emergence "de creación en acto" that sonic blackness (and afrocanariedad) requires to break into and against its isolation. See Lorca, "Teoría y juego del duende."
27 Barber, liner notes to *Calima*.
28 Barber, liner notes to *Calima*.
29 Mackey, "Cante Moro," 182.
30 This sonic double vision recalls Moten's discussion of Eric Dolphy as "multiply tongued" and reiterates the importance of using multiple voices—severed, troubled, and/or alternate—in the representation of the Afro/Canarian. See Moten, *In the Break*, 38.
31 This compelling, dichotomous sound-image conflates Western European classical performance and compositional practice with African geography and biodiversity.
32 For example, see Farberman, "Diego Barber and Craig Taborn."
33 Barber continues to record, most recently releasing *One Minute Later* on Sunnyside Records in May 2017.
34 Perdomo, liner notes to *Celebrate Brooklyn I and II*. Perdomo included his own translation: "There are times when it all goes very quickly. Almost without realizing it, you find yourself surrounded by great musicians and everything flows very naturally as well. And when that happens you have to celebrate it."
35 Moten, *In the Break*, 26.
36 Moten, *In the Break*, 24.
37 Moten, *In the Break*, 26.
38 Anzaldúa, *Borderlands/La frontera*, 25.
39 Thinking back to my first trip to las Islas, sitting in my room experimenting with how tongue placement affected my ability to correctly sound Canarian and articulate the Spanish language (and my subjectivity) seems even more compelling. While the lingual and the linguistic may seem inextricably linked, in those moments lingual inaccuracies neutralized linguistic competence and negated my ability to communicate. Noticing the relationship between my tongue and my ability to communicate highlights the paralinguistic power of sound to critique language and logocentrism.
40 Moten, *In the Break*, 48.
41 See Lomanno, "Emergence and the *insula improvīsa*."
42 Perdomo, liner notes to Big Band de Canarias, *Atlántida*.
43 Moten, *In the Break*, 142.
44 Perley, "Living Traditions," 42.
45 Perdomo, "Entrevista," 95. Also see Anzaldúa, "Let Us Be the Healing."
46 See Lomanno, "Improvising Difference," 281–89.
47 In fact, the reader may find the irruption of languages in the present text more unsettling than Moten's presence. As I explained in an email to the editors of this volume: "Including passages in Spanish without literal translation is an instantiation of the improvisational manipulating of the mix that I suggest is the hallmark of Afro/Canar-

ian cultural practice. Rupturing the frame of discourse to allow for polyvocality and multiple perspectives is precisely the root of Afro/Canarian critical experience.... With this arrangement I think the chapter can be both a call for methodological revision and a suggested interpretation of that call. The work the reader has to do to understand the piece draws attention to the process of knowledge production and how it can be subjective and polysemous. Furthermore, having to reconcile the quotes ... with the rest of the chapter mimics the process of listening to collaborative improvised performance where allusion, tangents, and interreferentiality must be worked out by the listener in real time."

48 Moten, *In the Break*, 25.

BIBLIOGRAPHY

Ait Nahaya. "Mustafá—Ait Nahaya." Video, 6:08, published June 3, 2014. Recorded in Teatro Leal, La Laguna, Tenerife, December 2013. https://youtu.be/iJtO1tlSqgs.

Álvarez Delgado, Juan. "Leyenda erudita sobre la población de Canarias con africanos de lenguas cortadas." *Anuario de estudios atlánticos* 23 (1977): 51–81.

Anzaldúa, Gloria. *Borderlands/La frontera: The New Mestiza*. San Francisco: Aunt Lute, 1987.

Anzaldúa, Gloria. "Let Us Be the Healing of the Wound." *The Gloria Anzaldúa Reader*, edited by AnaLouise Keating, 303–17. Durham, NC: Duke University Press, 2009.

Barber, Diego. *Calima*. Sunnyside Records SSC1210, 2009, compact disc.

Barber, Diego. *The Choice*. Sunnyside Records SSC1272, 2011, compact disc.

Barber, Diego. *One Minute Later*. Sunnyside Records SSC1481, 2017, compact disc.

Barber, Diego. *Tales*. Sunnyside Records SSC1346, 2014, compact disc.

Barber, Diego, and Hugo Cipres. *411*. Origin Records 82641, 2013, compact disc.

Big Band de Canarias. *Atlántida*. 96K Music TF640, 2011, compact disc.

Bosquesonoro. "Diego Barber 'calima.'" *Globedia*, July 20, 2011. http://globedia.com/diego-barber-calima-canarias.

Braidotti, Rosi. "Nomadism: Against Methodological Nationalism." *Policy Futures in Education* 8, nos. 3–4 (2010): 408–18.

Brody, Jennifer DeVere. *Punctuation: Art, Politics, and Play*. Durham, NC: Duke University Press, 2008.

Farberman, Brad. "Diego Barber and Craig Taborn: *Tales*." *Downbeat*, June 2014, 70.

Farrujía de la Rosa, A. José, and Maria del Carmen del Arco Aguilar. "La leyenda del poblamiento de Canarias por africanos de lenguas cortadas: Génesis, contextualización e inviabilidad arqueológica de un relato ideado en la segunda mitad del siglo XIV." *Revista Tabona*, July 2002, 47–71.

Fregel, Rosa, José Pestano, Matilde Arnay, Vicente M. Cabrera, José M. Larruga, and Ana M. González. "The Maternal Aborigine Colonization of La Palma (Canary Islands)." *European Journal of Human Genetics* 17, no. 10 (2009–10): 1314–24.

Harney, Stefano, and Fred Moten. "The University and the Undercommons: Seven Theses." *Social Text* 22, no. 2 (2004): 101–15.

Jazz Borondón. *Borondón.* Centro de Cultura Popular Canaria, 1990, compact disc.
Jazz Borondón. *Botaraste.* Manzana Records JJCD-15, 1992, compact disc.
Lascaratos, John, and Panagiota Dalla-Vorgia. "The Penalty of Mutilation for Crimes in the Byzantine Era (324–1453 AD)." *International Journal of Risk and Safety in Medicine* 10, no. 1 (1997): 51–56.
Lomanno, Mark. "Emergence and the *insula imprōvīsa*: St. Brendan's Islands and Afro/Canarian (Jazz) Fusion." *Shima: The International Journal of Research into Island Cultures* 7, no. 2 (2013): 106–20.
Lomanno, Mark. "Improvising Difference: Constructing Canarian Jazz Cultures." PhD diss., University of Texas at Austin, 2012.
Lomanno, Mark. "Jazz Nomadism and Bojan Z's Xenophonic Ideal." Paper presented at the Fourth Rhythm Changes Conference: Jazz Utopia at Birmingham City University, Birmingham, United Kingdom, April 17, 2016.
Lorca, Gabriel García. "Teoría y juego del duende." 1933. http://usuaris.tinet.cat/picl/libros/glorca/gl001202.htm.
Maca-Meyer, Nicole, Ana M. González, José Pestano, Carlos Flores, José M. Larruga, and Vincente M. Cabrera. "Mitochondrial DNA Transit between West Asia and North Africa Inferred from U6 Phylogeography." *BMC Genetics* 4, no. 1 (2003). https://bmcgenet.biomedcentral.com/track/pdf/10.1186/1471-2156-4-15.
Macaronesis. *Macaronesis.* Hesperides Producciones TF-639, 2001, compact disc.
Mackey, Nathaniel. "Cante Moro." In *Paracritical Hinge: Essays, Talks, Notes, Interviews,* 181–98. Madison: University of Wisconsin Press, 2005.
Moten, Fred. *In the Break: The Aesthetics of the Black Radical Tradition.* Minneapolis: University of Minnesota Press, 2003.
Muller, Carol A. "Musical Echoes of American Jazz: Towards a Comparative Historiography." *Safundi: Journal of South African and American Studies* 8, no. 1 (2007): 57–71.
Perdomo, Kike [Enrique]. *Celebrate Brooklyn I and II.* 96K Music TF875, 2013, compact disc.
Perdomo, Kike [Enrique]. "Entrevista a Enrique Perdomo, saxofonista." By Francisco Guerra de Paz and Encarnación Ruiz Valdivia. *Ateneo de La Laguna* 3 (December 1997): 95–99.
Perdomo, Kike [Enrique]. "Kike Perdomo and Diego Barber: Volcanic Music." Instituto Cervantes de New York. Accessed January 28, 2019. http://nyork.cervantes.es/FichasCultura/Ficha94849_27_2.htm.
Perdomo, Kike [Enrique], and Ismaila Sane. *Baba Djembe.* Multitrack Records EMCD-032, 1998, compact disc.
Perley, Bernard. "Living Traditions: A Manifesto for Critical Indigeneity." In *Performing Indigeneity: Global Histories and Contemporary Experiences,* edited by Laura R. Graham and H. Glenn Penny, 32–54. Lincoln: University of Nebraska Press, 2014.
Reyes, Ignacio. "Diccionario Ínsuloamazig." 2011–2018. https://imeslan.wordpress.com/.
Snead, James A. "Repetition as a Figure of Black Culture." In *The Jazz Cadence of American Culture,* edited by Robert G. O'Meally, 62–81. 1984. New York: Columbia University Press, 1998.

FOUR "Opening Up a Space That Maybe Wouldn't Exist Otherwise" / *Holding It Down* in the Aftermath

VIJAY IYER IN CONVERSATION WITH DANIEL FISCHLIN AND ERIC PORTER

INTERVIEWERS: *Your work speaks directly to this volume's attention to improvisation in the aftermath of what we're loosely calling crisis—but in fact entails thinking about improvisation in the aftermath of any number of scenarios involving violent encounters (whether past or present), trauma, and uncertainty about the future. You've talked about* Holding It Down: The Veterans' Dreams Project *as part of a trilogy of works with poet Mike Ladd that both examines life in the shadows of the wars in Iraq and Afghanistan and addresses the aftermath, the impact of American militarism in the US especially.*[1] *So one general question we'd like to start with: Can you talk a little bit about the role that creative improvised music plays in* Holding It Down?

VIJAY IYER: Sure. So, this project, as you said, was the third in the series. We didn't necessarily start out trying to make a series; it's just that we didn't stop. We found ourselves returning to the large-scale interdisciplinary performance format based on working with music and text and a certain kind of casual ethnography, building from interviews. The first project of its kind was called *In What Language?*, and that was about people of color in airports post-9/11. So, we tried to examine the common predicament that seemed to unify this disparate assortment of communities, which had to do with the common experience of surveillance and hyperpolicing across this transatlantic Brown superset of communities, you might say.

So that started with Mike Ladd doing these casual interviews of people he'd run into in transit, because both he and I, I guess, get mistaken for a lot of different ethnicities—he especially, being a light skinned African American, who people think is Lebanese or Puerto Rican or whatever. So, he found himself being able to suddenly slip easily into these conversations with people with pretty widely divergent backgrounds from his own, and they would find themselves suddenly divulging a lot of intimate details about what they'd just been through post-9/11: the random checks and holds, the extra scrutiny, the sense of anxiety associated with travel.

So that was the beginning of what felt like a way of working. You know, we didn't really have a genre in mind; we were just starting from what each of us knew and building from there. So that's what became *In What Language?*, the multidisciplinary evening-length work. Our original performance had a subtitle: "A Song Cycle of Lives in Transit." We produced an album and managed to tour the project a bit.

Based on the strength of that piece, we were invited to do another large-scale project that became *Still Life with Commentator*. This was in 2006, as we were observing the birth of the blogosphere and the hyperexpansion of social media and of personalized relationships to information itself. And so that's what that project was about: the flow of information within twenty-four-hour news culture in a time of war, and the relationship of the individual to the state under the so-called global war on terror. It actually feels as relevant now as it did then.

Later, when we were a couple years outside of that project and started to reassess what we had done, it felt like what we had been doing was toeing around the issue of war without really taking it on, except at a distance. What we needed to do next was not just make a project *about* war, but actually collaborate with people who'd been *in* it. We wanted to enact a gesture of listening between veterans and civilians, build something together, and create community through that process.

That meant that we had to find people from the veterans' community who wanted to work with us, and specifically we wanted to work with veterans of color. All of these community-facing music projects have been offering a Black and Brown perspective on post-9/11 life. Of course, we're so far into it now that it's hard to remember that there was a pre-9/11, where you didn't have to pay to check a bag, you could bring a bottle of wine on the plane with you, and so forth. Anyway, things have changed so drastically over these last years that we're in a very different place now.

Holding It Down was about trying to address what we had been skirting the whole time. By working directly with people whose lives were affected by war, it also meant that we had to put aside our knee-jerk politics. In order to build community with people who signed up for military service, us "do-gooder/liberal/pacifist types" have to check our own degrees of complicity with the whole enterprise of war. We pay taxes to send them there, don't we? The other thing is that, as I've said elsewhere, being an all-volunteer army in an unequal society like ours means that people actually enlist not just out of desire to defend their country, but also (and maybe more often) out of a sense of economic need or perceived need, or a sense of having no other recourse, or no other options. The US military conducts what has been called "predatory recruiting" in cities, especially in minority communities. These people are led to believe that they're going to be given a good education and set up for a lifetime of services, and maybe also get some technical training of some kind. And that is a big lie, because what the system is really doing is recruiting people to put their bodies on the line in combat.

These lowest rungs of the military are therefore primarily populated with people from disadvantaged economic communities, who tend disproportionately to be people of color, particularly African Americans, Latinos, and working-class Asians. That recognition is what emerged from the process of us finding these folks and talking to them. Mike did a whole bunch of interviews, and we also worked with a brilliant theater director and kindred spirit named Patricia McGregor, who did a lot of interviews specifically with women veterans of color. Partly because both Patricia and Mike are African American, they were able to win the trust of vets from communities of color, including the Afro-Caribbean community. The specific topic of these interviews was the veterans' dreams, because that was a space for their own subjectivities to shine through, and also a space where some of their darkest secrets remained raw and unprocessed. Sometimes that made it very hard to talk about.

We also worked directly with two veterans who wrote themselves into our piece and performed with us—and continue to perform with us. One is Maurice Decaul, an ex-marine who served in Iraq, and the other is Lynn Hill, who served in the US Air Force, including a year piloting drones. So, she was a very new kind of veteran. The world was just learning about what it means to have the kind of experience that Lynn had—to pilot planes in a combat environment from *an office* in Las Vegas. She'd go on breaks, and she'd go to Starbucks and stand in line, after dropping bombs on people and watching the aftermath. She'd drive home every night. So, every day she saw combat, and every day she had a veteran's experience of returning to civilian life.

That situation created its own kind of trauma or stress disorder that hadn't really been addressed or assessed publicly yet. I remember in the course of making the project, Lynn revealed to us some things that she had never said to anyone before, especially about self-destructive thoughts she'd had. These even appear on the track on the CD. It's basically a real-time revelation that happened in the course of making the music. So, to get back to your question about creative improvisation. What did the music do, for example? One thing it did is it elicited a certain *quality of voice* or quality of stance from those who were speaking; it became a heightened performative environment for storytelling, which is something like a *truth*—but something else too. I mean, it's not *not* truth, but it's somehow intensified. She is telling us something about herself that she has never told anyone before.

This is a moment in the track on the album called "Capacity," where she reads a poem about her experiences and her dreams, across this rhythm that I'm sending in from my laptop. I'm controlling and manipulating the track, so it kind of breathes and stutters, and it does different things, accompanying her, lifting her up, and giving her space. Then Mike interviews her in the booth, in the recording studio, immediately following that performance of the poem, and we kept it on the album as a way of exposing our process. It's in that moment, while she's answering Mike's questions, and in the *way* she's answering, there's a musicality in it. It's supported by these rhythms and patterns, and she's moving with it and taking breaths that are in the music. Somehow, in that process, she gets to this part where she tells us that she wanted to drive off a cliff.

And she'd never said that—not even to a therapist. So, as soon as we finished that take, I stopped and said, "Okay, that doesn't need to be on the record." She said, "Yes, it does. People need to know." A few months later I read a story on the front page of the *New York Times*. This study was released that revealed that people in these drone pilot positions experience a kind of PTSD-type syndrome that's entirely similar to that experienced by people in physical combat. So that's one thing we learned—that the *process of telling*, especially when carried by music, can function as a way of opening up a space that maybe wouldn't exist otherwise.

And then the other thing that I wanted to say was that we didn't really know who the audience would be for this project. What I can tell you is that the jazz business has *no* interest in any of these projects. I mean, they'll write about it occasionally, and it'll be basically the critical equivalent of a pat on the back for doing good work, but there's this sort of . . . like, it's held at arm's length. It does not satisfy the desires of the jazz culture industry. It doesn't perform some kind of ecstatic release, and the way it puts difference on display is challenging. It's more unsettling than affirming.

And there's the whole premise to begin with. I mean, this is the very problem that we chose to address. In fact, this has been a pattern of ours, trying to make art out of stuff that no one wants to talk about. We even developed a term for it. We call it *irritainment.*

So, this is why Americans don't talk about veterans' issues, why those issues never really become part of the national conversation. Veterans just become tokenized and instrumentalized for political discourse, usually for self-serving politicians who get photographed standing next to them on a podium or something like that. Actually sitting down with, listening to, and building community with veterans is a rare thing, and it's not something that has a kind of buzz to it. It's not something that people want to buy tickets to, or spend a weekend night checking out. People don't even want to buy a record like that.

So, you enter the project knowing that that's going to be the case. Then you think, well, who, at all, will engage? Maybe we'll get some engagements at performing arts centers here and there; maybe the album will circulate in its own way, on its own time. Maybe it will take years to have the impact it needs to have.

But there have been a couple of moments where the work, after the fact, or even through performance or through circulation in another way, opened up another kind of space. One was in Philadelphia last year, when we did a performance at the Kimmel Center. In the months leading up to it, we did a series of workshops with local veterans of color in Philadelphia, which led to them basically making their own *Holding It Down*. They wrote their own poems about their experiences, and those poems were compiled into a book that was published by the Kimmel Center and given out to the entire audience. They made a thousand copies, given out for free, under the title *Holding It Down: Philadelphia*. I believe the Kimmel Center still makes copies available.

That was stunning, you know, to see that: a real, physical book that now lives on a thousand people's shelves. Also, they performed with us. We created an opening set with some of them reading their works with some music. So now there's *Holding It Down*, our specific project, but there's also *Holding It Down*, the process, and the fact is that that process will never end. So it's been validating, to see how the project and the idea can continue to do the work that they need to do.

What I meant to say about Lynn is that—and not to make a trophy out of her or something like that—but she told us that after doing this project she stopped having nightmares and was able to leave therapy and start a family. And now she has three little kids. So that was a healing moment, where the listening and the telling actually gave rise to the literal transformation of a person's life.

The third thing I wanted to say is that the album got assigned in this class on post-9/11 literature at Linfield College near Portland, Oregon. The students sat with the album; they went through all the lyrics and listened to the whole thing together. Then I did a Skype visit to the class, and we talked about it. People had a lot of interesting questions, and there was even one young woman in the class who had served in Iraq. She herself was a veteran in her early to mid-twenties, when she had been out there, basically as a teenager, eighteen, nineteen years old—and so that was an interesting experience.

But after that, I received an email forwarded to me by the professor from one of the students in the class who hadn't said anything during the conversation. In the email the student thanked us all for the project and for doing that kind of work, and she said that her father had served in Iraq. When he returned, she said, he was a very different person, and he had exhibited all the symptoms associated with these stress disorders. He was jumpy, and certain things would trigger him, including seeing a person in a turban, or any loud, sudden sounds. But she also said that he was very silent about his experiences. She'd never really heard him talk about it. And he would have these violent nightmares. So, her father was a mystery to her. Eventually he passed away due to injuries sustained in combat. What she said in this email was that when she sat with the album and the music and the lyrics, she felt as if it was her father talking to her, and she finally was able to make peace with what she felt she had lost. It was actually this very emotional and crucial transformative moment that she experienced through the music. And it still makes me tear up to even think about that. All of us were profoundly moved and shaken by that email.

This experience helped us realize that the audience is not just veterans and civilians. It's also people who are right at that interface, particularly the family members who are right on the frontier between veterans and civilians every day. It was also an overwhelming realization for us that the project could have its impact years later—a drastic impact on a single person. It eclipses any conventional ideas of artistic, critical, or popular success (or lack thereof) that might otherwise be used to measure the impact of works like this.

INTERVIEWERS: *We had wanted to ask you about the life of this record, whether it's been used for therapeutic purposes, and how veterans or families of veterans have responded to it. So, it's good (and very powerful) to hear you talk about these experiences. It is also great to hear about Lynn Hill and how* this process was cathartic for her. That piece, "Capacity," is one of the most powerful musical expressions we've heard in recent years. Both of us have recommended this record (and that piece in particular) to people interested in the aftermath of 9/11 and the effects of the subsequent wars on veterans and others.

We have a couple of follow-up questions, the first of which builds from what you were saying about the ethnographic aspects of the project and Mike Ladd's "casual ethnographies" in particular: we were curious about the different layers of improvisation that went into making this recording. Especially beyond what was actually happening in real time in the studio, as in, for instance, how you pulled together the different people who were involved in the project. It would be interesting to hear more about keeping the tape on in the studio, having Mike go back and ask Lynn Hill questions after she had read her poem, which seemed like a spontaneous, intuitive thing to do on some level.

VIJAY IYER: I guess it was semistaged, in that we kind of knew that that would happen. It was more that it was unscripted.

INTERVIEWERS: *You didn't quite know how it would come about?*

VIJAY IYER: We knew that Mike would interview Lynn. But it was really that we wanted to capture a live moment, but we didn't know what would come from the unforeseen, *l'imprévu*—and so it meant that we wanted to make space for the unforeseen in the work, which is basically what I'm used to doing anyway, even when I make music for the trio or sextet or create music with Wadada [Leo Smith] or whatever else I'm doing. Or even working with classical musicians: how do you insert opportunities in the musical form or structure to pin us to the present? And that can happen in a lot of different ways.

I should say that I've grown a little bit wary or skeptical about the use of the word *improvisation* to stand in for freedom or liberation. There's almost nothing we do that isn't improvised. I'm saying this after having led a graduate seminar at Harvard called Theorizing Improvisation a couple of times, having been through this process of amassing a lot of critical literature and digesting and meditating on contemporary perspectives on improvisation. Of course, George [Lewis] was one of my mentors, and I'm very much a shill for that entire project. But having said that, I reached a critical perspective on the entire thing. I feel like too often we're cherry-picking moments that we feel are expressing a certain ideal of freedom. Freedom is such a problematic concept, you know, at this moment, more than ever. In American history it could be argued that despite "freedom" being in our founding documents, it was constructed under conditions of extreme hypocrisy, you know?

Thomas Jefferson had an underage Black concubine named Sally Hemings with him at the time that he hung out with Marquis De Lafayette and he talked about *liberté* and *égalité* and all that stuff. So, you know, freedom exists in the context of unfreedom. It's basically this rhetorical idea that was introduced in order to excuse and conceal the brutalities that actually supported the regime. So, I find that when we talk in these slightly misty-eyed ways about improvisation, we're actually falling prey to that rhetorical trap. I guess I'm just saying that I'm careful about supporting that thesis. But I will say that, like everything we do, this project was born of a certain coming-together, and moving-together, and listening-together, and sounding-together. And all of that involves a relational process of making decisions and acting on them.

So you can call that improvisation. I mean, it's not untrue; that's what that is. It's also not miraculous; I guess that's what I want to say. Improvisation is actually quite quotidian. It's how most things happen. What I will say is that this project took years to make, so it involved improvisation, but it also involved what I would call an *annealing* process. Basically, you have a lot of elements in motion, and then over time they congeal and become a little bit more predictable, or a little bit more specific, or a little bit more *known*, as we try it again and again and again and again.

And so that's basically how I work: very patiently, over years, trying to make something from what feels like almost nothing. We might all come in with different sketches: a few poems, a few tracks, and a few miniscores. Often after reading a poem or just sitting with some of the information that we had or even just listening to some of these interviews, you know, I would create small fragments. Sometimes an interview would be a prompt for me to understand, "Wow, that person needs a space to exist." So I'd make a space for that person, you know? That was how the music would come to be. But then we'd sit with these things together and say things like, "Why don't you try that poem with *this*?" I might say, "Well, that's just a mismatch." Then we'd ask, "Is it a *productive* mismatch?" Sometimes it was. Sometimes something that felt wrong was exactly the right feeling, as if the wrongness of it was exactly what we needed to set it off as its own thing. So you could call all that improvisation. But that's like calling every conversation an improvisation, which it is, also, but that's a bit of a banal observation. It's more a question of, How do we build it into something? How does it harden, or how does it settle? That's the real question, and that only comes from repetition.

And each repetition, each iteration, teaches us something new, you know? And a repetition is not necessarily the same as improvisation. It's like, okay, let's start again with the same premise, with the same set of elements, and see if the same thing happens, you know? It could be described as a process of *stripping away* improvisation through coordinated collective actions.

INTERVIEWERS: *So, it sounds like—as someone who teaches improvisation studies, teaches critical approaches to improvisation—you are looking for an alternative set of terms and principles to better describe, in contextually specific ways, a process that's much more complicated than can be, really, just described through just one term. Does that make sense?*

VIJAY IYER: We want to refine what we mean by *improvisation*. The potential to use the word *improvisation* is not an end in itself. We have to be able to say something beyond that, and not merely just point back at that word as some sort of validating principle or force. There's also the sort of improvisation associated with evil.

For example, are Donald Trump's tweets improvised? They sure seem that way, but maybe they're *constructed* to *seem* that way . . . to give you the feeling of spontaneity. After all, a lot of fingers are in the pie.

INTERVIEWERS: *Selective improvisation or the illusion of improvisation—both effective for imposing a political will?*

VIJAY IYER: Yeah. The thing is, it *looks* like a shambles, but meanwhile they're seizing more and more power every day. So they're not failing whatsoever, actually. They're enjoying a series of successes under the guise of failure.

INTERVIEWERS: *Right. We have to contend with the fact that improvisation as a social practice includes the inner workings of governmental institutions and what happens in the corporate boardroom and other sites where power is manipulated.*

VIJAY IYER: Well, it's like I said—improvisation is never not present. So even in cases where we think it is, has it really been banished—like in scripted situations or in the pageantry of classical music performance, for example, where we think everything is scripted? There's still the possibility of things falling apart at any moment, and sometimes that does indeed happen and people have to recover. I wrote a violin concerto this past year, for instance, that was premiered by this incredible violinist, Jennifer Koh, and she performed it three times. The third time was at Tanglewood. There's a cadenza toward the end that ends with a series of firm pizzicatos, and she was so energized in that moment that she knocked her bridge out of position, and her G string plummeted in pitch. Then the next thing she was supposed to do was play a bunch of open Gs in rhythm.

She had four bars of that and then had to play this really fast run. So, during that open G moment she tuned the string back up to pitch, in the span of four bars, and then just jumped right in on the next downbeat and played this run. So that's improvisation in the context of a nonimprovised piece. It's responding to a certain condition, adapting and solving a problem, and moving on. And that's what Jennifer did, right? This word that we think is banished from the stage in a supposedly scripted, unimprovised situation actually revealed itself to be quite natural and necessary, and indeed she demonstrated great skill in the moment.

INTERVIEWERS: *You talked earlier about there not necessarily being a plan for this trilogy, but we're wondering if you ever think about the trilogy as part of a tradition of pieces of music, compositions, performances, and recordings that comment on war or militarism or the experience of veterans?*

VIJAY IYER: For sure, there's been a whole body of points of reference for us. Maurice Decaul studied with Yusef Komunyakaa, who you may know was a poet and Vietnam veteran. Komunyakaa made war a central element of his work, particularly a Black perspective on war. There's a whole series of books that were important points of reference for us. There's a book called *The Things They Carried*, and there's a film called *Restrepo*, a documentary of young marines stationed in Afghanistan. And then other works by veterans, you know, including members of the creative music community who were vets, like Henry Threadgill, Butch Morris, Billy Bang, and Michael Carvin.[2] And there was this intergenerational experience among veterans that was present. This project was commissioned by Harlem Stage, and when we performed there, they invited a lot of people from different veterans' communities in the area, including people who served in the first Gulf War in the early 1990s and some elders who were Vietnam vets. They met Lynn and heard her perspective on things, and shared what they have in common. People who piloted planes over Vietnam had also had this painfully *remote* experience of inflicting suffering.

And that's dehumanizing in its own way. One of the things that Lynn said was so harrowing for her was that she had this omniscient satellite view of everything. So she could see on both sides who was perishing, which is totally different from when you're on the ground and you lob a grenade or fire a few rounds and then duck behind something, and you don't really know what happened. From her console she had this perspective where she could see everything happening in real time, and that's what stayed with her. It affected her more than anything. This omniscient view caused her to see too much, more than anyone was used to seeing. So, these elders who flew planes over Vietnam had something in common with her that they didn't expect to have.

But Lynn was doing this work while sitting in an office—that was the experience that brought her to the breaking point and led her to leave the military. After a couple of years of sitting in that office, she felt, no, this is not who we are. She realized the extreme hypocrisy of the enterprise. So she no longer wanted any part of it.

INTERVIEWERS: *Is there anything else in the works in this vein?*

VIJAY IYER: Yeah, so there's actually another . . . it's not a trilogy anymore, sorry. There was already a companion piece to *Holding It Down*. That came about because we wanted to include voices from the other side, so we developed this project called *Sleep Song*, which was a collaboration that included Mike, Maurice, me, this French guitarist named Serge Teyssot-Gay, and two other artists, a poet and a musician from Baghdad. And we performed several times in France mainly, and we tried to do it in the US, but we couldn't get visas for the Iraqis.

INTERVIEWERS: *Not surprising.*

VIJAY IYER: But then the other thing is that there's a new project in the works now, which Mike has been spearheading, that we started to hatch last month, in July 2017. It's called *Blood, Black and Blue*. He's taking up a project he started in the 1990s actually. He's rebuilding it from the same premise, which is dealing with African Americans in law enforcement. He's been interviewing dozens of people in Philadelphia in particular—prison guards, police, beat cops. Mike has been learning that many of them have friends or family members who are incarcerated, and what often leads them into that professional choice is a desire to change the system from within, because of what they and their families have experienced. So that's often what's happening.

We performed *Holding It Down* in Molde, Norway, in July 2017. I was an artist in residence at this festival there, so that's one of the things we did. Usually I have to force it in because it's not like the festival's going to voluntarily sign on to a project like that. But sometimes I can say, look, if you want me to be artist in residence, and I'm doing five concerts, this is going to be one of them. It's not like it's impossible to listen to. There's a liveness to it that's very cathartic and appealing in its own way. Anyway, Lynn was having her third child, so she couldn't be a part of the festival in Norway, so what we decided to do, rather than try to replace her—she's irreplaceable—was to start incorporating elements of this new project into the performance. We performed four or five new pieces that were built around some of the interviews and content from that new project about African Americans in law enforcement.

INTERVIEWERS: *And did that involve Mike Ladd doing spoken-word versions of the interviews?*

VIJAY IYER: Well, it took on different sonic identities. There were samples of the interviews that were set to the music. It was quite electronic overall. We had a vocalist, Imani Uzuri, and another electronic musician named HPrizm, and Mike was actually freestyling, which is an element that hasn't really been present in any of these other projects of ours. He's an incredible spontaneous poet. I've known him for close to twenty years now, and Mike freestyling is one of the most amazing things I've ever seen. It's just an incredible thing to behold in general. I guess I've been spoiled by knowing a lot of amazing improvisers who can spin something from what seems like nothing, and take you to a new place by doing it—and Mike's one of those people.

And it's funny, when he freestyles he becomes, like, a thousand-year-old man. His whole face changes, and it's like he sees really far into the future and gets one of those thousand-yard stares. He's looking way past everything, and his whole body changes. He delivers something that just lands in the room with this incredible power. And so that's basically what he did in Norway, from all the information he's amassed. You hear these individual figures present in the music, but you also hear Mike as a kind of interlocutor or commentator. And then also Imani, the vocalist, works from these interviews, kind of meditates on them and extracts a phrase or two and, again, spins them into something new. So, the performance had a pretty distinct identity from *Holding It Down*. I would say it was quite different, sonically and otherwise. Because it's actually dealing directly with law enforcement in the United States, which dates back to slave catchers. That's basically what this performance was, a consideration of all of this current pain as part of the afterlife of enslavement.

INTERVIEWERS: *And are there plans for a record?*

VIJAY IYER: It's probably a bit far in the future, but we're thinking of it as a multimedia project involving maybe documentary work. But we don't really know. It's like we don't know what shape these things are going to take until they develop. I guess it's sort of, like, when Meredith Monk starts creating pieces. She just gathers all the people in a room, but she doesn't know if it's going to be a theater piece or a song cycle or a dance piece or whatever: it's whatever emerges from the doing. You have to trust the process to yield something. Maybe that's what we call improvisation.

NOTES

1 *Holding It Down: The Veterans' Dreams Project*, by Vijay Iyer and Mike Ladd, was commissioned by Harlem Stage, where it premiered in 2012, and was released on Pi Recordings in 2013. The previous Iyer-Ladd collaborations are *In What Language?* (commissioned by Asia Society NYC, where it premiered in 2003, and released on Pi Recordings in 2004) and *Still Life with Commentator* (co-commissioned by the Brooklyn Academy of Music and Carolina Performing Arts, premiered in 2006, and released on Savoy Jazz in 2007).

2 See, for example, Bang's 2001 album, *Vietnam: The Aftermath* (Justin Time Records), featuring Carvin, Morris, Ted Daniel, Frank Lowe, John Hicks, Sonny Fortune, Curtis Lundy, and Ron Brown—an ensemble consisting entirely of African American Vietnam veterans.

BIBLIOGRAPHY

Bang, Billy. *Vietnam: The Aftermath.* Justin Time Records Just 165-2, 2001, compact disc.

Iyer, Vijay, and Mike Ladd. *Holding It Down: The Veterans' Dreams Project.* Pi Recordings P149, 2013, compact disc.

Iyer, Vijay, and Mike Ladd. *In What Language?* Pi Recordings P109, 2004, compact disc.

Iyer, Vijay, and Mike Ladd. *Still Life with Commentator.* Savoy Jazz SVY 17628, 2007, compact disc.

FIVE Experimental and Improvised Norths

The Sonic Geographies of Tanya Tagaq's Collaborations with Derek Charke and the Kronos Quartet

KATE GALLOWAY

With Canadian composer Derek Charke and the innovative American new-music ensemble the Kronos Quartet, experimental throat singer Tanya Tagaq has created a body of collaborative works that use improvisation to negotiate cultural difference and articulate dynamic and modern perceptions of North. These collaborations reposition Northern cultural life for Indigenous and non-Indigenous audiences using a combination of improvisational traditional and contemporary throat singing, notated and improvised instrumentation, electroacoustics, digital music production, and field recordings. These works illustrate how the sonic geographies of the North—both the North as a physical location and the constructed ideas of North circulating in cultural imaginaries—are contingent on sociocultural identities.[1] Participating in the Indigenous modernities movement, Tagaq's vocal practice is an example of how Indigenous artists retool sound traditions through modern iterations and express affective connections to place.[2] Indigenous modernity is expressed in various ways, including new musical forms that reclaim and recontextualize preexisting representations of Indigenous community and place and expand the definition of "traditional" culture to include hybrid practices. Hybrid practices such as these incorporate disparate sound cultures to resonate with urban First Nations people as in, for example, A Tribe Called Red's "Electric Pow Wow" night that brought traditional powwow to the club setting, creating "powwow step," which fuses and remixes traditional powwow music with instrumental hip-hop, electronica, dubstep, and DJ culture; and the cross-cultural collaboration between Cree-Canadian writer Tomson Highway and Chinese-Canadian composer Melissa Hui in the opera *Pimooteewin: A Journey* (2008).

This chapter engages with the politics of sound in collaborative arts that use improvisation to negotiate the cultural and musical differences of Inuit throat song and practices of new music while portraying contemporary perceptions of North and Indigenous modernity. Serving as forms of artistic redress in a settler-colonial society, with its attendant racial and gender violence, Tagaq's collaborations counteract notions of a fixed, singular, primitive culture and of the North, contesting fetishized and exoticized representations of Indigenous culture. I sketch out here how Tagaq and her collaborators use improvisation as a catalyst for the exploration of contrasting and complementary responses to community, place, and expressive culture. I use the following three projects, *Nunavut* (2006), *Tundra Songs* (2007), and *Nanook of the North* (2012), to address how improvisation is used as a mode of understanding and responding to imagined and lived experiences of place in the Canadian North. In collaborations with non-Indigenous artists who share Tagaq's aesthetic sensibilities and political perspective, Tagaq ruptures dominant stereotypes of the Inuit community and the North. Although Tagaq seeks to destabilize cultural and geographic stereotypes, her personal politics do not reflect those of the entire Inuit community. Her performance practice illustrates how improvisational soundscapes communicate a discursive and transgressive contemporary North for both Northern and non-Northern audiences.[3]

Sovereignty in Tagaq's collaborations is a creative act in which she has agency and actively participates in processes of self-representation and geographic representation that undermine stereotypes of the Inuit community and its culture, as well as typical representations of the North. She employs the improvisational aesthetic of traditional throat singing and experimental singing grounded in extended vocalization techniques to carve out this sonic sovereign space. Giving place and people a voice supports the creative and intellectual health of the community.

By considering the collaborative dynamics of Tagaq's sonic sovereignty, an improvisatory politics that challenges colonial stereotypes of Indigenous performance and Northern identity, this chapter points the way toward those aspects of performance that are inaccessible without a consideration of the ecology and politics of improvised cocreation among disparate creative actors and cultural influences. A close examination of these sonic cultural exchanges discloses the kinds of social and political dialogue and action that can take place in collaborative, integrative process-based works. Tagaq, the Kronos Quartet, and Charke have all experienced the North and its communities, but the complexity and nature of these experiences varies. As Dylan Robinson explains, "even if a composer is to travel to the North to understand the harshness of the landscape, spend time in a community, and consult with a cultural 'representative' for permission to use a throat song or other song, there remains the question of who is able to speak for the community and give permission."[4] These three projects collectively express diverse ways of knowing the North, illuminating how local sonic experience is filtered through geographic, cultural, and biographical perspectives.

The Performance Ecology of Collaboration and Hybrid Traditions

Tagaq's collaborators engage her aesthetic and cultural politics, fostering reciprocal forms of collaboration and performance ecology. I use *ecology* as both a metaphor and a theoretical model for examining the complex relationships among place, politics, musical practices, and networked artists. Internationally known for their support for new music and emerging composers, the Kronos Quartet is a vital cultural force in the commissioning and dissemination of a new-music repertoire that cultivates innovative sound practices, cross-cultural exchange, diverse genres, and multicultural sources. David Harrington, the violinist and artistic director of the ensemble, first heard Inuit throat singing in 1981. In throat singing he heard potential for intercultural and intermusical collaboration with the Kronos Quartet, considering it the most "string-like" sound he has heard produced by the human voice.[5] In 2002, as Harrington listened to Tagaq on a compilation distributed by *fRoots* magazine, he located his ideal collaborator. Attracted by the way Tagaq shaped sound, Harrington was fascinated by the aural profile of her performance. This realization of a productive site of creative synergy was akin to Harrington's exposure to Derek Charke's compositions during the "Kronos: Under 30 Project" fellowship competition. Although Charke was not awarded a fellowship, the groundwork for a rich continuing collaborative relationship was laid.

The performance ecology of collaboration and reciprocity intensifies Tagaq's creative process and performance projects. Benjamin Piekut in his discussion of actor-network theory similarly conceptualizes the interconnections between human and nonhuman actors in contemporary experimental music as an ecology. He writes, "An ecology is a web of relations, an amalgamation of organic and inorganic, or biological and technological, elements that are interconnecting and mutually affecting. Like experimentalism, an ecology is an emergent hybrid grouping that connects different kinds of things, diverse ways of being. It has real boundaries that mark it off as distinct from its surrounding environment, but those boundaries are variable and open."[6] For Tagaq, collaboration reveals new patterns of thinking and *sounding*. This variety of collaborative approaches has exposed a diverse demographic to shifting styles of contemporary Indigenous expression, revealing how improvisation is employed to converse among musical practices and encourage artists to acquire new skills.

Inuit throat singing (*katajjaq*) is traditionally an everyday activity with roots as a sounding, breathing game. In recent years, however, throat singing has undergone significant stylistic diversification. Traditionally, two women participate in vocal exchange and mimicry, collaborating, improvising, and co-composing the vocal counterpoint until one participant laughs—a physical reaction signaling the end of a throat song. The structure and the semantic and sonic content of throat song reflect the local environment, incorporating words and syllables from nature and the locale (e.g., place-names, plant and animal species), onomatopoeic words, and mimetic sounds representative of sounds heard in and absorbed from everyday life. Through the practice of throat singing, vocalists are grounded in a sense of belonging to the community, traditions, and the environment.[7] Bruno Deschênes summarizes this perspective: "Inuit throat-singing is not singing per se. Ethnomusicologists suggest it should be viewed as vocal games or breathing games more than anything else."[8] Although, as Jeffrey van den Scott has concluded from his fieldwork in Arviat, Nunavut, throat singing is increasingly mobilized as a live performance art form by many factions in Northern communities.[9] In contemporary Inuit communities of the late twentieth and twenty-first centuries, throat songs are multifunctional in Indigenous public and private spaces. Once a traditional game performed in the home, throat singing is increasingly encountered as a form of contemporary Inuit public performance during festivals, on the public international stage (as witnessed at the 2010 Vancouver Olympics opening ceremony), in youth groups, and as a feature in intercultural collaborations (as illustrated in Björk's collaborations with Tagaq). Throat singing is improvisational in nature, as vocalists respond to, mimic, and sound in response to their partner, drawing on a personal archive of remembered and experienced sounds. In her solo practice Tagaq breaks from the convention of singing with a partner, replacing the human partner with a microphone and amplification system. And in her collaborative work, she sings against and in collaboration with musicians from divergent cultural backgrounds, combining free improvisation, extended vocal techniques, and traditional throat singing.

With origins in home entertainment, katajjaq is grounded in embodied and sonic intimacy. Throat singing is characterized by spatial and physical closeness, a face-to-faceness between two female vocalists. This intimacy is retained in Tagaq's practice but taken in new performative directions. The interpersonal and spatial intimacy of Tagaq's collaborative creative process is highlighted through her physical interactions with her collaborators, audience, and technology. Through rigorous experimentation Tagaq weds the sonic worlds of throat singing, free improvisation, electronics, and digital music production. Freely adapting throat singing into a solo vocal practice, instead of one done in pairs, Tagaq, aided by sound technology, improvises in a highly rhythmic, temporally active, and frequently sexualized stylistic manner, interpolating guttural cries, shrieks, and vocal pulses alongside traditional oral machinations of environmental mimesis. Throat singers, like Tagaq, embrace Indigenous modernity, a process of adaptation where traditional Indigenous practices are revised for contemporary use and community expression. Tagaq reworks the participatory and spatial facets of traditional throat singing in the performance ecology of her collaborative practice. Instead of mimicking, listening to, and responding to another vocalist, Tagaq's "partners" are the instrumentalists, their instruments, and technologies (e.g., microphones, amplifiers, pedals).

Throat singing serves as a cultural and aural link between place and tradition. Conventional throat singers draw on a repertory of sounds that evoke their culture, soundscape, and life experiences, improvising with a personal archive of sonic markers of place. Tagaq developed her personalized style through self-study in cultural isolation, listening to and mimicking audiotapes of throat singing sent by her mother in Cambridge Bay while Tagaq was living in Halifax attending the Nova Scotia College of Art and Design. Tagaq builds on the vocal traditions of Inuit throat singing, hybridizing the practice by incorporating amplification and audio-processing technologies and vocal experimentation, but as Beverley Diamond explains, Tagaq is "so experimental as to defy an emphasis on traditionality at all."[10] Electronic sonic manipulation, sound effects, multitracking of additional layers, and transformation of syllables and accompaniments are the traces of a creative artist who builds on networks of experiences and memories.

Sonic Geography and the North

Sonic geography is the aural equivalent to physical geography, just as R. Murray Schafer's concept of soundscape is the aural equivalent to landscape. In the 1960s, Schafer suggested a radical approach to hearing the everyday environment. The acoustic environment is an unpredictable improvised composition to which all of society contributes. Society must "try to hear the acoustic environment as a musical composition and, further, realize that we own responsibility for its composition," Schafer suggests, and compose ethically with ecological (human and nonhuman) relationships in mind.[11] Sonic geography values the aural markers of place and considers how place is mapped through sound. What does the sonic spectrum of a collapsing iceberg in the Arctic Ocean sound like to the urban ear? Tagaq uses her voice and collaborations with the Kronos Quartet and Charke to interpret the North, answering questions such as this.

The Canadian North is not static. "Constantly changing," the North is, as Sherrill E. Grace asserts, "an idea as much as a physical region that can be mapped and measured for nordicity."[12] Grace observes how Canada has oriented its gaze northward from a vantage point anchored tightly along the country's southern border. In her work addressing the politics of artistic representational practices and the Canadian North, she considers how artistic statements function as enunciative actions in semiotic systems.[13] As an assembly of ideology, rhetorical moves, and performative representations that are shifting, irreducible, and unstable, North as a discursive formation shows us the "crucial constitutive activity of discourse at work."[14] Through Tagaq's work, diverse artistic expressions of the North are produced and publicly circulated where these sonic impressions of nordicity and the cultural life of the North gain currency with Indigenous and non-Indigenous audiences of experimental music.

Embodying Culture and Improvisational Play in *Nunavut*

The omnipresence of throat singing in popular culture, whether featured on the soundtrack of a televised Historica Canada *Heritage Minute* recounting the story of the inukshuk, performed in the 2010 Vancouver Winter Olympics opening ceremony alongside the Games' inukshuk logo, or heard in Tagaq's vocals on Björk's *Medúlla* (2004), throat singing has become internationally identified as a sonic marker of the Canadian North. The paradoxical celebration of the contemporary throat singing revival and hybridity by Indigenous and non-Indigenous listeners, as Drew Nelles explains, is complex: throat singing "has joined Inuit carving and the Inukshuk for the dissonant distinction of representing Canadian culture abroad, even though these traditional practices were systematically threatened by colonialism."[15]

Nunavut (2006), co-composed by Tagaq and the Kronos Quartet, experimented with structured improvisation to maneuver between contrasting musical backgrounds and languages during the collaborative process. Tagaq and the Kronos Quartet traveled to Whitehorse, Yukon Territory, to spend three days collaborating on the development of the performance framework for the improvisation-based piece *Nunavut*, listening to the North through recreational outdoor activities. The collaborative process is documented in the film *A String Quartet in Her Throat* and the narrative of the film highlights the interpretive moves among the Kronos Quartet, Tagaq, and the performance ecology of *Nunavut*'s collaborative spaces, inside and outside the studio.

The collective developed a system of colors to guide the improvisational structure. Pencil-crayon color swatches on individual white squares of paper served as a linear graphic score where the colors could be rearranged and juxtaposed according to the affective qualities each member associated with an individual color.[16] Finding common ground through the interpretation of color, the artists discussed their personal responses to the associative properties of each color, linking each color to one of Nunavut's seasons. Drawing on Tagaq's knowledge of the regional environment, the collective mulled over the affective properties of the seasons. The graphic score serves as a creative arbitrator between the Kronos Quartet's use of Western notation and Tagaq's oral tradition as they improvise in response to the hues.

To prepare the framework for the live performance of *Nunavut*, the Kronos Quartet recorded a range of Tagaq's vocalizations to map her stylistic vocabulary onto the performance capabilities of the instruments in the string quartet, and improvised in response to these recordings by mimicking her vocal gestures. From there, the quartet created an underlying compositional structure out of Tagaq's grammar of sounds and vocal inflections, a set of building blocks that allow for improvisation by both the quartet and the vocalist. The performers engage in a call-and-response exchange, with the instruments of the quartet assuming the function of the second voice in the throat song, responding to and "competing" with Tagaq's vocalizations.

Nunavut is grounded in group experimentation that explores the physical and expressive bounds of the instruments and sensitive cross-cultural aesthetic dialogue. Tagaq is rarely required to take on the postures of a member of a Western ensemble. She must only adhere to the duration of the composition. The string quartet, however, is required to improvise and adapt their playing techniques to Tagaq's vocal idiom. Collaborating with an experimental music ensemble and adopting specialized instrument preparations (the placement of objects on or in the instrument to modify its sound) to work with Tagaq's distinct vocal timbre is a logical marriage of divergent sound practices. Throat singing has been compared to extended vocal techniques, which occupy a prominent position in the experimental music palette. As Diamond explains, "audiences who enjoy these 'classical' compositions [e.g., Luciano Berio's *Sinfonia* or Peter Maxwell Davies's *Eight Songs for a Mad King*] are often attracted to the diverse sounds of throat singing."[17] The Kronos Quartet maps Tagaq's sonic vocabulary onto the string quartet using preparations and amplifying their instruments. The cello, for instance, has a wooden clothespin affixed to each of the first and third strings, altering the timbre. The sonic iconicity of the instrument is masked. The cello sounds less like a cello. These instrument preparations serve as one response to the Kronos Quartet's inquiry into how Western string instruments can participate in throat singing.

Translating throat singing games for alternative performance situations is not unheard of. Similar cultural transformations are taking place within both rural and urban communities. The Inuit community, particularly its youth, is reclaiming its cultural traditions and placing a contemporary spin on these practices to suit current aesthetic taste. In recent years, throat singing has experienced a revival by Inuit youth in the community, hybridizing the vocal practice with other forms of music, sound art, and performance practice. Charity Marsh explains in her discussion of "throat-boxing" (a fusion of throat singing and beatboxing) that hybrid practices enable "a re-working of contemporary Inuit identity. As part of this re-working, Inuit youth mediate representations of themselves and their current lived experiences through mobile technologies and local networks, challenging common stereotypes and reified identities that continue to circulate in political, cultural, and national discourses."[18]

Her virtuosic exploration of the human voice locates Tagaq within the lineage of avant-garde female artists pioneering new extended vocal techniques, including Joan LaBarbara, Meredith Monk, and Laurie Anderson, but also within what Anishinaabe author, activist, musician, and public intellectual Wab Kinew has called the "contemporary Indigenous music renaissance" in Canada.[19] The contemporary Indigenous music renaissance reimagines traditional idioms through the use of novel sound technologies and the infusion of ultramodern sounds. Through hybridized musical expression the Indigenous community, particularly Indigenous youth, witnesses how their culture is a vibrant part of the world they live in. The fusion of Western experimental music, extended vocal techniques, and technology with throat singing allows Tagaq to challenge and rewrite representations of her culture and situate her community and its practices in the modern world.

The creative process extended beyond the studio as Tagaq and the Kronos Quartet sought out recreational activities in Whitehorse. By knowing place through embodied engagement (e.g., dogsledding, hiking through diverse weather conditions), the Kronos Quartet listened to place. Tagaq served as an aural guide with insider knowledge of the Northern environment. For instance, she directed Harrington to observe that with each step taken in the snow, a different sound is produced, and the color of that sound shifts as one's weight and pressure vary. These sound qualities of the Northern environs were integrated into *Nunavut*. The crunching sound of the brittle crust of ice on the surface of the snow underfoot was mimicked by an amplified violin bowing the wooden back plate, producing a low grinding tone. Through the use of extended bowing techniques on amplified instruments that imitate the sounds from the environment, the instruments of the quartet participate in the representational practices of depicting the Northern environment.

The throat games between Tagaq and the Kronos Quartet are adapted from ludic, competitive, virtuosic sonorous improvised games between two female singers into a co-compositional event grounded in improvisation and extended techniques, where the instrumentalists must learn how to manipulate and adapt their bodies to Tagaq. *Nunavut* is an affective intercultural improvisation, because, as Robinson explains in his study of the politics of aesthetics in contemporary encounters between First Nations/Inuit and early music traditions, "rarely do we find an orchestra [or in this case a string quartet] asked to play an entire work from memory, as in Indigenous oral traditions of performance. Instead, First Peoples and their cultural practices are included in art music as long as composers can find ways to script those musicians (who frequently do not read Western music notation) into the art music genres within which the composers work."[20] In the case of *Nunavut*, the members of the Kronos Quartet are scripted into Tagaq's personal style of throat singing.

Gesture and physical interaction are characteristic features of *Nunavut*. Each member of the string quartet takes a turn as Tagaq's throat singing partner, as Tagaq holds a microphone between each instrument and her mouth. The improvisational exchanges grounding *Nunavut* translate the structure and aesthetic of the throat game, as Tagaq enters into dialogue with each string player individually and then, at the conclusion of the composition, with the whole string quartet. Inuit throat singers engage in vocal exchange in intimate proximity, their faces mere millimeters apart. The physical closeness between Tagaq and each instrumentalist maintains this practice. The physical proximity and face-to-faceness is replicated in *Nunavut*'s staging.

The face-to-faceness of Tagaq's performances is frequently described by audiences and the popular press as "sexual," "erotic," and "intimate"; it is also recurrently othered and exoticized as "primitive" and "animalistic." Yet Tagaq is better understood as presenting a performing female body that challenges the accepted norms of Indigenous female performance with an aggressive and expressive sexuality and unrelenting intensity. By challenging expected conventions of Indigenous female performativity, Tagaq promotes cultural growth and diversifies the sound and image of Indigenous performers circulated by popular media through the intensity, intimacy, and Tagaq's challenging physical proximity to her collaborators. The improvisatory intimacy, or erotics, of Tagaq's live performances embodies her reactive politics challenging stereotypes shaped by colonial histories that dictate how Indigenous peoples, particularly women, conduct themselves and perform in the public sphere. Tagaq explains, "People talk about the performances being sexual, but I feel like I'm just owning my femininity."[21]

In interviews Tagaq addresses the social, economic, and political issues at play in the culture of violence and abuse inflicted on Indigenous women and in the animal-rights sanctions that restrict traditional Inuit ways of life, like seal hunting. Expressive culture is a platform for activism. Speaking candidly in conversation with Drew Nelles for the *Walrus* about her personal encounters with the oppressive social problems that plague rural and urban Indigenous communities, Tagaq told Nelles that she uses her improvisational practices to "draw attention to the plight of Indigenous peoples in Canada, and to de-stigmatize the discussion of these issues in Inuit communities."[22] Her performances and her activism can cause discomfort, however, as audiences work through these uncomfortable moments, sounds, and social realities toward awareness and social action.

At the outset *of Nunavut*, Tagaq sings into the resonant body of the cello, the microphone positioned between her mouth and the f-holes. They breathe and "sing" to, and into, each other, sounding together like traditional throat singers. They are so close they can use each other's sound cavities as resonators. It is as if the cello is the responding second singer.[23] The resonant cavity of the cello is akin to the resonant space of a throat singer's mouth. The cellist, Jeffrey Zeigler, imitates and responds to Tagaq as she initiates and leads the sonic interplay. He percussively strikes the body of the cello, mimicking Tagaq's percussive vocal sequence. As Tagaq transitions to a higher register, inserting harmonics, he glides his bow across the prepared first and third strings, producing glassy timbres. The exchange between Tagaq and violist Hank Dutt is particularly stimulating as the two performers replicate the impression of joyful, humorous sonic play, reviving the cultural roots of throat singing as a sonorous game. At the midpoint of their improvisation, Dutt is at the edge of laughter as he struggles (successfully) to maintain pace in the improvisation as Tagaq accelerates and increases the level of musical challenge and complexity. He mimics her gestures with increased accuracy, and challenges Tagaq by further embellishing her original line. Dutt and Tagaq's final sonic acrobatics accelerate to such a degree that what was originally a canon becomes melodically entangled, breaking the rhythm of the exchange, and thus concluding the "song." In another "game" Tagaq and the violinist John Sherba exchange birdcalls, performing environmental mimesis.[24] Tagaq's voice and Sherba's violin mimic the timbre, rhythmic pattern, and melodic intricacies of the birdlife Tagaq encounters in the North. Physical and embodied sonic dialogue among the ensemble members expresses their individual and collective understanding of the North's sonic geography. Ultimately, in *Nunavut* a space is created in which Inuit cultural practices expose, challenge, and ultimately reshape ideological assumptions about art music when performers from different backgrounds forgo concert stage etiquette, and musical exchanges are simultaneously song and play.

The Sonorous North and a Soundscape in Flux in *Tundra Songs*

Tagaq and Charke's collaboration *Tundra Songs* (2008) extends the musical and aesthetic ideas concerning cross-cultural exchange and sonic geography that Tagaq and the Kronos Quartet explored in *Nunavut*. *Tundra Songs* sonifies the contemporary North in three ways: the inclusion of human and nonhuman field recordings, the use of mimetic extended string techniques informed by practices of Inuit throat singing, and the presence of a live improvising experimental throat singer. Commissioned by the Kronos Quartet and the Los Angeles Philharmonic Association, *Tundra Songs* for string quartet, throat singer, and a Northern electroacoustic soundscape is structured in five continuous movements with descriptive titles. Each movement explores a different Northern sound world Charke observed while field-recording: (1). Ice, (2). Water, (3). Sedna's Song, (4). Lament of the Dogs, and (5). Trickster "Tulugaq." *Tundra Songs* diverges in style from Charke's first collaboration with the Kronos Quartet on *Cercle du Nord III* through its inclusion of a live throat singer as a cultural and musical collaborator. Through this act of inclusion, as well as the weaving in of the Inuit creation myth of the marine goddess Sedna, *Tundra Songs* affords space and agency for Inuit indigeneity to sound.

Charke's aesthetic choices in *Tundra Songs* address the politics of representing the culture and soundscape of the contemporary North. "The soundscape of the north has changed. I wanted to reflect this change. Rather than create an ethereal sonic landscape of the idyllic north I choose to look for something more fitting of our times," Charke writes, challenging the popular constructions of North typically encountered by non-Northerners.[25] For instance, many soundmarks (to borrow a term from Schafer) in Charke's field recordings—such as a group of children playing hockey on a makeshift outdoor community ice rink in *Tundra Songs*—are not exclusive to the Far North. "The physical North," as Andrew Baldwin, Laura Cameron, and Audrey Kobayashi explain in their introduction to *Rethinking the Great White North*, "establishes a point of reference, meliorates cartographic anxiety, and founds Canada's spatial imaginary as both location and expanse. In both cartographic and mythical terms, the 'North' is a mutating landscape whose horizons seem forever in retreat. Its meaning has shifted significantly over time."[26] As the North changes, so too do its sounds.

Charke has featured Inuit throat song as a sonic marker of North in a number of his compositions, including *Netsiksiuvik* (1999) for mixed chamber ensemble, *22 Inuit Throat Song Games* (2002/2005) for amplified string quartet, *Cercle du Nord I* (2003) for amplified string quartet, *Cercle du Nord II* (2003) for multiple-channel electroacoustic diffusion, and *Cercle du Nord III* (2005) for amplified string quartet. Some of these works do not feature an actual singer, live or prerecorded. Rather, by using recordings and transcriptions of throat song, Charke devises instrumental techniques that imitate the approximate timbres and gestures of throat singing rather than the cultural and sonic specifics of the vocal practice. In *22 Inuit Throat Song Games* Charke explains his process: "The vocal transcriptions then became the source material for the string games. Alternations of techniques—circle, vertical and ordinary bowing; hocketing a certain effect between two instruments; or continuing a certain texture—became much more important than retaining any semblance to the original material. Because of this, melodies, words, dynamics, pitches and many other parameters were discarded and the concept of a particular sound or game took on a new life."²⁷ In such cases the voices of the Inuit are merely a new sound world, or syntax in the musical vocabularies of non-Indigenous composers and string ensembles, and thus little more than an exotic source material for the exploration of new techniques for string instruments. Yet in other cases—for example, his 2005 revision of *22 Inuit Throat Song Games* for the Kronos Quartet—the inclusion of a live throat singer who regains sonic sovereignty and identity is an act of compositional redress.

Charke's knowledge of throat singing comes from listening to and transcribing archival tapes of tradition bearers, observing the vocal game practices of community members in the regions he visited, and being exposed to Tagaq's distinctive vocal practice.²⁸ Extended bowing techniques are used as a method of tone production to allude to the sonic characteristics of throat singing. Examination of the score reveals that Charke writes very specific bowing instructions at the beginning of each movement; he also leaves interpretive space for variation and improvisation, essential aesthetic components of Inuit throat singing, experimental new music, and the soundscape. Charke explains, "Variation and improvisation is essential [in *Tundra Songs*]. Most of the games are of an indeterminate duration, usually with one or more repeat signs that state approximately how many times, or for what duration that section should continue. Simple things such as dynamics are deliberately left to the player's discretion (for the most part these pieces are to be performed loud)."²⁹

Charke goes on to suggest improvisatory techniques that include using medium to hard bow pressure against the strings for heavier grinding sounds and thicker textures; using light or extralight pressure to create ethereal sounds and lighter, more "transparent" textures; using circle bow techniques *sul tasto* for less high harmonics, and/or circle bowing near the bridge (*sul ponticello*) for higher harmonics; and using microtones and adding more rhythmic variations.³⁰ At first glance, the score appears to skew the improvisational aesthetic of throat singing. Crucially, improvisation is retained in the ways the string quartet executes Charke's guidelines and in the stylized vocal lines of the live throat singer. Charke notates both the recorded and live throat singers as a guide for future performers, but in performance the notated part for the live throat singer is actually improvised. Charke and the Kronos Quartet did not want to restrict Tagaq's creative process. There are, however, descriptive notes in the score that guide Tagaq's improvisations. For instance, Charke indicates that the recorded soundscape features the sounds of ice cracking and high-velocity winds whipping across the frozen ice fields. The throat singer is directed to perform "multiple techniques: wind and ice," suggesting a vocal imitation of natural phenomena. The throat singer performs a form of environmental mimesis, a throat song between human voice and the nonhuman soundscape.

The extended techniques used by the string quartet are a product of experimentations in timbre and texture. The coarse, gritty, grinding tones of amplified circular and vertical bowing using an untypical amount of pressure emulate the "guttural" tones Charke first heard on archival recordings of katajjaq. Similar to the prepared piano, these sonic effects are enhanced when the instruments are prepared with clothespins affixed to the string adjacent to the bridge. Just as throat singers alternate between breathing and sounding, listening and sounding, Charke assigned "breathing in" parts to two instruments while the two remaining instrumentalists are "breathing out."[31] The vocal exchange and contrapuntal texture that define throat singing are adapted to the capabilities of the string quartet. The string quartet, although virtuosic, is limited and cannot replicate the technical and sonic complexity of throat song. And while the live throat singer emerges as a virtuosic presence at key points in the score, the singer often assumes a coloristic accompaniment role.

The electroacoustic soundtrack was recorded primarily during an extended trip to Iqaluit, Nunavut, in 2007. In his field recordings, Charke recorded the sonic activity in the isolated environs beyond the margins of the community, and both the human and nonhuman, as well as the natural and urban sonic, life in the community. These field recordings archive the sonic spectrum of the modern North's soundscape. The soundtrack is punctuated by electronic sounds recorded and processed in Charke's home studio. The source of each sound is not immediately identifiable. Some sounds, while evocative, do not retain their sonic iconicity when digitally played back and removed from their physical source.

Field recordings and throat singers convey the cultural and physical environment. Speaking on the referential potency of sound and Tagaq's vocality, violinist Jesse Zubot comments, "What she does is about the moment, and about channeling a place. Most people may not understand where that place is, but they feel it."[32] In these moments of spontaneity in Tagaq's improvisational exchange, she dips into her personal archive of sonic memories, ultimately grounding her sonic practice in the specific spaces she inhabits, imagines, and has experienced.

During his field-recording excursions Charke improvised with the physical materials of the region, experimenting with different sound combinations and recording perspectives. He would leave his field recorder turned on in different locations, recording how the soundscape unfolded. Guided by Arctic explorer Matty McNair, who runs North Winds Polar Expeditions and Arctic Adventures, Charke embarked on a two-day trip by dogsled out onto the remote ice fields beyond Iqaluit. At the edge of an ice floe, the divide where the floating pack ice meets land, Charke submerged his hydrophone below the surface of the frigid ocean, recording the sounds of shrimp, krill, seals, whales, and other Arctic marine life.

To contrast his recordings of stark expanses of frozen glacial ice and tundra, Charke recorded the sonically animate community of Iqaluit. There were sounds he wanted to record but was unable to locate in the soundscape; however, the soundscape provided other points of aural interest. Charke recalls, "Over the next week I wandered the streets with my recording gear capturing daily life in the north; a group of kids playing shimmy street hockey, snowmobiles racing around town, airplanes coming and going, a dog sled race, someone carving a soapstone sculpture, the beeps of the water trucks backing up, howling wind and dogs tied up in front of homes. I was invited to a Country Feast. We ate polar bear, seal, caribou, whale and Arctic char. After the feast the tale of 'Sedna,' the Inuit goddess who created all living beings, was vividly recounted."[33] This lexicon contained the vast array of sonic activity, including the fragile icy timbres that have become commonly associated with the "Great White North" through popular culture, and the less familiar sounds of children playing hockey, the hum of electric and gas-powered generators working overtime in the deep cold, and the festive commotion of cultural events at the local community center. The multifaceted sound design of *Tundra Songs*, then, in which the dynamic unpredictable soundscape is combined with the improvisatory aesthetics of throat singing, ethnographic field recording, and experimental music, represents the varied and personal ways of knowing the North.

Revising and Reclaiming *Nanook of the North*

In *Nanook* (2012) Tagaq revises and reclaims American filmmaker Robert J. Flaherty's black-and-white silent film *Nanook of the North* (1922), which reproduces stereotypical representations of Inuit culture and the North.[34] These problematic images are the product of the time period's patronizing colonialist mentality. Tagaq's revisionist *Nanook* is an intermedia collaboration among Tagaq, improvisation artists Jean Martin (percussion) and Jesse

Zubot (violin), and a prerecorded multichannel soundscape composed by Charke. Flaherty's *Nanook of the North* tells the story of Inuit hunter Nanook and his family as they struggle to survive in the harsh environmental conditions. Tagaq, Martin, and Zubot perform live, improvising alongside Charke's soundscape and in response to the silent visuals of Flaherty's film, giving the place and its people a voice. By speaking back to Flaherty's film through performative intervention, Tagaq engages in a decolonial cultural practice in the present, reclaiming Indigenous agency (via a contemporary Inuit sounding body) in the representation of Inuit culture and the North.

In contrast to *Tundra Songs*, Tagaq assumes a prominent role in *Nanook*. The staging places Tagaq front-and-center, flanked on either side by her co-improvisers. Using a series of separate loudspeakers controlled backstage, Charke's soundscape is stereophonically diffused; the audience is *in* the soundscape. Above center stage hangs a screen. It hangs high enough so that the visuals and intertitles of Flaherty's film are unobstructed by the performance activity onstage.[35] With each live performance Tagaq's reinterpretation of an iconic but aesthetically problematic film depicting Canada's North in the early twentieth century is encountered by a Southern audience in the twenty-first century.

Tagaq's improvisations are a palimpsest of current responses to the film, memories of first viewing the film as a child, and her reactions to stereotypes of Inuit culture in the media. Tagaq sent these recorded improvisations to Charke, who composed the *Nanook* electroacoustic soundscape by combining field recordings and electronic music composed in response to her improvisations with reworked sections of her recorded improvisations. Charke's soundscape is synchronized with the film and includes two prerecorded vocal tracks by Tagaq improvised in response to the film; electronic samples and permutations of Tagaq's improvisation; short edited segments of her singing, speaking, and imitating Northern sounds; and a dense soundscape of field recordings Charke collected at Pond Inlet, a small, predominantly Inuit community located on Baffin Island.[36]

Flaherty paved the way for modern documentary with his contentious but significant chronicle of a year in the life of Nanook and his family, a family of Itivimuit. *Nanook of the North* was filmed in Inukjuak (formerly Port Harrison), at the Inukjuak River in northern Québec, Canada. *Nanook of the North* is known as a semi-fictionalized staged ethnographic documentary that problematically circulated the already-stereotyped image of the Inuit as childlike, fur-clad, and joyful people that are "close to nature." Joseph E. Senungetuk, an Inupiaq scholar from northwest Alaska, summarized this stereotype that characterizes Southern representations of Indigenous culture from all regions of the North: "a people without technology, without a culture, lacking intelligence, living in igloos, and at best, a sort of simplistic 'native boy' type of subhuman Arctic being."[37]

The Canadian Pacific Railway hired Flaherty in 1910 as an explorer. In this position he experienced the North firsthand and was moved to express his experiences on film. Armed with modest filming equipment, including a Bell & Howell camera, a portable developing and printing machine, some modest lighting equipment, and rudimentary training in cinematography, he spent 1914 and 1915 filming the North and its inhabitants. After the accidental destruction of his footage in 1916, it took Flaherty another four years to secure funding for an additional filming expedition. From August 1920 to August 1921, funded by the French fur company Revillon Frères, Flaherty refilmed his project. This time he focused on the life and activities of a single Inuit family.[38]

Audiences watch Nanook and his family performing everyday culturally specific activities in a friendly, livable North, but only through staged scenarios. They are costumed in traditional clothes and use historic hunting tools when modern ammunition technologies were widely used by local hunters. Flaherty also renamed his amateur actors (e.g., Nanook [Allakariallak] the hunter), giving them names he assumed a Western non-Indigenous audience of the 1920s would find accessible and, in line with the stereotypes circulating in popular culture, more Inuit sounding. "Nanook" is pronounceable, conjures a familiar-unfamiliar exoticism, and adheres to the cute aesthetic that was similarly used in the portrayal of the cartoon Inuit boy used in the marketing of Eskimo Pie ice cream treats and other popular products of the 1920s that drew on the newly circulated Northern culture. Flaherty did not want to depict the Inuit community in their current state but, rather, as he thought they lived prior to non-Inuit contact.

In the early 1920s, the perception of the vanishing Northern cultures proliferated through Western preservationist ideology. The film participates in the tradition of salvage ethnography, where ethnographers, fearing the loss and dilution of culture owing to intercultural contact, sought to preserve traditions for posterity. Often these ethnographers ignored the inevitable cultural change that had already occurred, taking strides to reverse the evidence of intercultural exchange using theatrical devices such as reenactment. Flaherty, for instance, emphasizes the "primitive" aspects of Inuit life, employing reenactment of "endangered" traditions. Under Flaherty's cinematic authorship these cultural traditions would not be lost; they would be forever immortalized on celluloid. Tagaq juxtaposes her improvisations with Martin, Zubot, and Charke's electroacoustic soundscape against Flaherty's film as a performative statement to her audience to question what these images of the Inuit and the North communicate.

Tagaq doesn't excavate the sonic past. She interprets what the North sounds in the present. Tagaq draws on her family's history in northern Québec and her Nunavut childhood to reclaim Flaherty's film, problematizing the director's cultural portrayal of the far North, its culture, and its people, revising the mediascape for contemporary use and a contemporary gaze. Tagaq's family moved to Cambridge Bay, where she experienced the cultural trauma inflicted by the residential school system, leaving two years after the move to attend a residential school in Yellowknife.[39] Cultural materials like their native language and throat singing were no longer practiced, erased from the community through years of disuse. Although she was raised in Cambridge Bay, Tagaq did not grow up listening to throat singing, which had been banned by the Catholic Church along with the local language. Tagaq recounts, "Cambridge Bay was heavily affected by residential schools." "Not a lot of people spoke, or still speak, Inuinnaqtun, and there was no throat singing. Now, people are starting to use their Inuk names again, but back in the day that wasn't where it was at."[40] Tagaq's intervention with Flaherty's *Nanook of the North* serves not only to destabilize the stereotypes of Northern life and Inuit cultural practices depicted in the film and popular culture but also to provide a form of cultural redress. The project uses improvisation as a remedy for cultural taxidermy, illustrating to non-Northern audiences that the North and its culture are vibrant and living, and cannot be frozen as a product of history for the non-Northern gaze and ear.

Charke's soundscape lends melodic, rhythmic, and geographically regional soundmarks for Tagaq, Martin, and Zubot to respond to and manipulate.[41] In his artistic statement on *Nanook*, Charke states, "My artistic goal has been to create a highly captivating and interesting sonic vocabulary that captures the spirit of the time and place depicted in *Nanook* while putting a contemporary spin on it."[42] Likewise, Tagaq sought to perform a transgressive intervention with a problematic film, rehabilitating it through the inclusion of a nondiegetic score saturated with modern sounds, electroacoustics, field recordings, extended vocal and instrumental techniques, and free improvisation that destabilizes mythologized perceptions of the North as a frozen, empty, quiet, unpeopled hinterland. Tagaq's North, conversely, is sonically intertextual, aligning with the perspective that works representing the North should be the product of lived experience.[43]

The austere black-and-white landscape of the film suggests cultural and geographic isolation, a landscape that could be perceived by viewers as silent, but the nonhuman environment is aurally dynamic. Through audio recording, sensory exploration, and mimicry of the diverse wildlife and weather, the sonic practices of Tagaq and her collaborators record and interpret the unpredictable and spontaneous improvisations of the soundscape's ecology and supplement the film's narrative. For instance, the addition of crunching sounds to the visual depiction of Nanook's feet trekking with enthusiasm in the snow correlates an appropriate sound to the visual action as Nanook rejoices over his successful hunt. *Nanook*, too, voices sounds of the North that are ignored or perceived as silently absent—the sounds of walking and running on sheets of ice, the sounds of pack ice colliding with the shoreline, and the sounds produced by the friction of the dogsled traveling across the snowfield. As Tagaq knows from her youth, and Charke learned living and traveling in Canada's North during his formative years, the North is sonically robust. *Nanook* is a composite soundtrack of the artists' vast and varied individual and collective experiences.

Tagaq uses improvisation to arrest the attention of the viewer during culturally problematic scenes. Near the start of the film, a white Southern trader introduces Nanook to a gramophone. Nanook and his family have traveled by kayak to the trading post to exchange his hunt for the year for goods. Having never before seen such a device, Nanook inspects the machine, gazes at it from all sides, touches its components, and listens as the trader cranks the mechanism to play music. Nanook appears to inquisitively ask after the function and purpose of the technology.[44] His haptic engagement with the gramophone is ludic, as he tries to understand this new technology. This scene intends to communicate to the audience that Nanook and his community are primitive, untouched, and inexperienced with Western culture, despite the prominence of trading companies posted throughout the North. Tagaq found that the scene where Nanook appears to first encounter modern technology and the sounds of the South reinforced inaccurate ahistorical stereotypes of Inuit culture and identity. Nanook stares at the gramophone and clenches the shellac record between his teeth. The intent is to elicit laughter from the audience, but its effect is to reinforce negative primitivism.

To accompany the narrative action of Nanook at the trading post, turntable scratches, sounds Nanook might create as he uses the technology in an inexperienced manner, overlay an archival 78 rpm recording of an early 1920s New Orleans jazz standard, "Choo Choo Blues," performed by the Virginians. The turntable scratches also suggest the technological treatment of the turntable, where the sounds of misuse—or scratching—are deemed musical and used improvisatorially in hip-hop, a popular genre adopted by Indigenous youth. Tagaq vocally reclaims this scene. As a child, she recalls she found this scene ridiculous. But as an adult she understands the politics of visual representation taking place and is offended by the way members of her community were instructed to perform for the camera. Reacting to these visuals, Tagaq confronts the representation with expressive vocables and a combination of Inuinnaqtun and English, shouting and repeating with sharp enunciation, "Colonizer—Colonizer—Colonizer," immediately after the gramophone is presented to Nanook on-screen.[45] Her improvisations are based on memories accumulated from the many times she has viewed the film and been subjected to misrepresentations of Inuit culture.

Flaherty's docudrama portrays the "noble savage" in his own habitat, as an astute, intelligent survivor, but diminishes Nanook when he is placed in a Western milieu. While both are stereotypes, the former demands some degree of respect from the viewer, while the latter infantilizes Nanook. Flaherty portrays the trading post as a positive space where North and West meet, a space of transcultural exchange, where the North is enlightened about the modern technologies of the Western South.[46] To Tagaq, this excerpt is "embarrassing."[47] Her visceral unscripted vocal reaction to the gramophone scene destabilizes the attitude that the Inuit were unfamiliar with technological advances and the misconception that there was a firm divide between Northern and non-Northern culture. In fact, this film ignores the Inuits' adoption and understanding of new hunting technologies, and this scene erases their imperative role in the production of the film behind the scenes and behind the camera.

Tagaq's *Nanook of the North* revisionist project works to reanimate and revoice Inuit peoples, their situated lives, and past and contemporary cultural practices. Situated in the current cinematic environment, Tagaq's *Nanook of the North* collaboration works toward equalizing the imbalanced representational power relations in the current film industry, which shapes how Indigenous bodies and voices are heard and seen on-screen. *Nanook* encourages contemporary audiences to watch *Nanook of the North* again, revisiting the film to think about these past and present perceptions of the North and its communities, and to participate as educated and ethical viewers. As Peter Geller explains, "as viewers, part of our work is to go beyond passively viewing the object before us to actively seeking out understanding, exploring the unfolding relationships between viewer and subject, us and them, insider and outsider, past and present."[48] Although each performance is improvised, Tagaq selects from an archive of sounds and musical ideas she has cultivated to represent contemporary Inuit life and culture. Improvisation, like culture, place, and community, is in a constant state of flux. Improvising to the film provides Tagaq with the agency to communicate one potential representation of Inuit modernity to an international audience.

Nanook sets the stage for Tagaq as an *agente provocateuse* who uses improvisation to manipulate boundaries and highlight issues that impact the cultural heath of Indigenous communities. In her 2014 Polaris Music Prize acceptance speech for the album *Animism* (2014), Tagaq spoke of the sustainable and reciprocal relationship between Indigenous communities and the nonhuman environment.[49] She critiqued veganism as a by-product of colonial structures and advocated for the consumption and use of seal products as a sustainable resource central to Indigenous life, using performance to advocate for Indigenous heritage in the face of PETA's protests and aggressive offensive social media attacks. Leading up to her Polaris appearance, Tagaq received unprecedented social media backlash for her participation in the #sealfie social media movement, a political campaign of contemporary Inuit political expression opposing Western colonial understandings of animal rights that do not accommodate the cultural practices of Northern Indigenous communities. Open-access digital platforms such as Twitter, YouTube, and Facebook, as Kathleen Rodgers and Willow Scobie explain, were used "to bring together images, texts, as well as facilitate dialogue across northern communities and beyond their borders, [and] Inuit were able to engage with and dispel myths, outdated claims, and point to the ongoing relevance of seal hunting."[50]

Tagaq's public-facing indigeneity redirects her celebrity to participate in the Indigenous activist conversation, using everyday improvisatory acts (such as speech and voice) to alter public opinion on this issue.[51] As she put it in an interview: "We don't get a ton of money from the natural resources that are being extracted from Nunavut, but we do have one resource and that's seals. We eat them and we always have and there are plenty of them, but for some reason there's a level of discrimination happening that one of the smallest minorities on the planet isn't allowed to reap the benefits from their own resources. It just seems like there's a lot of oppression happening from too many sides."[52]

Animism thrust Indigenous issues and ways of knowing into public consciousness. The album thematically calls into question the separation of society from nature, addressing issues of place and culture that concern both Indigenous and non-Indigenous audiences. *Animism* is sonically and politically challenging. Recorded within the grounding practices of improvisation, *Animism* is compiled from sessions of free improvisation and collaboration, and reassembled in the production studio post hoc. It uses improvisation as a communicative tool to address society/nature dialectics, including the relationship of Northern fossil fuel and natural resource extraction to colonial power dynamics, society's relationship with the natural world, and the scarring social issues that mark the everyday lives of Indigenous communities.

The lack of a directly articulated message promotes political efficacy. Rather than preaching to listeners a singular perspective, Tagaq's mostly wordless onomatopoeic sound mimesis, combined with some words in English and Inuktitut, opens up the conversation to sonic interpretation and political nuance. Tagaq unpacks the choices she made in shaping her vocality in "Fracking," a direct environmental critique of the Canadian oil industry: "I wanted a song to be unlistenable, so ugly and disgusting, so I imagined my whole body was the Earth and that someone was doing fracking on me."[53] Tagaq sonifies the visceral disruption of the landscape as pressurized steam is forcibly pumped beneath the earth's surface to extract valuable oil—the sounds of a humanity that exploits nature for capitalist gain. "The more you remove yourself from nature, the more you think that the Earth belongs to you, and not that you belong to the Earth," Tagaq says. "I wanted to have a voice for what the Earth is trying to say to us."[54] In her most recent solo projects and carefully cultivated social media presence, Tagaq continues to sophisticatedly combine political activism, improvisation, and expressive culture as she becomes increasingly vociferous in using her musical work to remedy the crises of Indigenous rights, oppression, and systemic violence in Canada.

Tagaq's collaborations with the Kronos Quartet and Derek Charke are examples of how contemporary Indigenous artists are creating alliances to challenge harmful Indigenous stereotypes and provide alternatives. These collaborations illustrate how the improvisatory practices of throat singing, experimental music, and soundscapes are used as political tools to highlight the dynamic cultural and musical hybridity of Indigenous modernity. To change how Inuit people, their sonic culture, and the sonic geography of the North are represented and identified in the contemporary world, the sounds and performance structures used must change. By forging affective alliances among music, sound, and emplaced lived experience, improvisational sonic culture is powerfully used to foster cross-cultural understanding and social activism. In the collaborative context in which Tagaq operates, improvisational sound is meaningfully connected to representations and lived experiences of the contemporary North and Inuit life, working against cultural and sonic stereotypes circulated through popular culture that essentialize, suppress, or erase Inuit culture and the sociopolitical issues entangled with its survivance.[55]

NOTES

1. See Sherrill E. Grace's *Canada and the Idea of North*, where Grace examines images, ideas, texts, and sounds of the Canadian North in Canadian thought, art, and popular culture. Glenn Gould also explores physical and cultural imaginings of North as a place and as an idea in his radio documentary *The Idea of North*, produced in 1967, in which five speakers provide contrasting views of northern Canada.
2. Beverley Diamond, Kati Szego, and Heather Sparling explain in "Indigenous Modernities," "Indeed, the very application of the concept of 'modernity' to Indigenous cultures is part of a broad movement to decouple the idea of the modern from Euroamerican centrism" (2). Also see Diamond, "Music of Modern Indigeneity."
3. It is in her most recent solo work that Tagaq's politics have developed a razor-sharp focus, and she has seamlessly linked her musical work to the crisis in Canada over Indigenous rights. This has been made possible because she does not have to attend to the performance ecology of collaboration and the presentation of a multivocal representation of the contemporary North and modern indigeneity. Tagaq's recent projects that address Indigenous politics warrant a more extensive study that is outside the scope of this chapter.
4. Robinson, "Politics of Aesthetics," 234.
5. See Lawrence, "Kronos Quartet."
6. Piekut, "Actor-Networks in Music History," 212.
7. See Nattiez, "Inuit Vocal Games"; Diamond, "Decentering Opera"; Diamond, "'Re' Thinking"; and Stévance, "Analysis of the Inuit Katajjaq in Popular Culture."
8. Deschênes, "Inuit Throat-Singing," par. 10.
9. See van den Scott, "Experiencing the Music"; van den Scott, "Throat Games or Throat Songs?"; and Stévance, "Analysis of the Inuit Katajjaq in Popular Culture."
10. Diamond, "Sound Reviews," 95.
11. Schafer, *Tuning of the World*, 205.
12. Grace, *Canada and the Idea of North*, xii.
13. Grace, *Canada and the Idea of North*, 127.
14. Grace, *Canada and the Idea of North*, 27.
15. Nelles, "Why Tanya Tagaq Sings."
16. See the excerpt from *A String Quartet in her Throat* in Lawrence, "Kronos Quartet," 1:44–2:23.
17. Diamond, *Native American Music*, 58.
18. Marsh, "'Don't Call Me Eskimo,'" 112.
19. Quoted in Kinos-Goodin, "A Tribe Called Red."
20. Robinson, "Politics of Aesthetics," 244.
21. Quoted in Nelles, "Why Tanya Tagaq Sings."
22. Nelles, "Why Tanya Tagaq Sings."
23. See Lawrence, "Kronos Quartet," 6:54–8:38.
24. See Lawrence, "Kronos Quartet," 8:46–10:00, for the exchange with Dutt, and 10:11–11:28, for the ludic interplay of birdsong between Tagaq and Sherba in *A String Quartet in Her Throat*.

25 Charke, *Cercle du Nord III*, Programme Note, n.p.
26 Baldwin, Cameron, and Kobayashi, "Introduction," 2.
27 Charke, *22 Inuit Throat Song Games*, Programme Note, n.p.
28 In his introductory program notes to the score for *22 Inuit Throat Song Games*, Charke details a selection of his sources of Inuit throat song:

> Inspiration for these works came from Katajak I transcribed for two or three voices. These were taken from three albums: JVC World Sounds, "Canada, Songs of the Inuit," Jean Malaurie, "Chants et Tambours Inuit de Thulé au Détroit de Béring" and ULO, "The Circumpolar Heartbeat." The vocal transcriptions then became source material for the string quartet games. Alternations of techniques—circle, vertical and ordinary bowing; hocketing a certain effect between two instruments or continuing a certain texture became much more important than retaining any semblance to the original material. Because of these melodies, words, dynamics, pitches and many other parameters were discarded and the concept of a particular sound or game took on a new life. However, some resemblance is inevitably retained as a comparison between the originals and the string quartet reveals. The titles of the works have also been retained from the original Katajak.

29 Charke, *22 Inuit Throat Song Games*, Programme Notes, n.p.
30 Charke, *22 Inuit Throat Song Games*, Programme Notes, n.p.
31 Charke, *22 Inuit Throat Song Games*, Programme Notes, n.p.
32 Quoted in Everett-Green, "Primal Scream."
33 Charke, *Tundra Songs*, Programme Notes, n.p. See also Altman, "Derek Charke Embraces the Arctic with Sound," 20–28.
34 To differentiate between Tagaq's *Nanook of the North* and Flaherty's *Nanook of the North*, I will refer to the former using the abbreviated title *Nanook*.
35 For photographic footage of the event, see Luminato's official Flickr photo stream with photos by Tom Beedham: "Tanya Tagaq presenting 'Nanook of the North' live @ David Pecaut for Luminato 2014," https://www.flickr.com/photos/98855002@N07/sets/72157645276623759.
36 Pond Inlet (Baffin Island) is not, however, the filming location of *Nanook of the North*.
37 Senungetuk, *Give or Take a Century*, 25.
38 See Barnouw, *Documentary*, 33–35, for further details into the history of Flaherty's experience in Canada's North and the making of *Nanook of the North*.
39 Nelles, "Why Tanya Tagaq Sings."
40 Quoted in Dickie, "Tanya Tagaq Grabs," 30.
41 For further explanation of the lexicon of soundscape terminology developed by the World Soundscape Project, consult Schafer, *Tuning of the World*.
42 Charke, *Nanook*, Programme Notes, n.p.
43 Hulan, *Northern Experience*, 3.
44 See Flaherty, *Nanook of the North*, 12:34–14:07.
45 This observation was made at the 2014 Luminato Festival performance of *Nanook* outside Roy Thompson Hall in Toronto, Ontario, on June 10, 2014.
46 See Raheja, "Reading Nanook's Smile"; and Rony, *The Third Eye*, 99–128.
47 Gordon, "Inuk Throat Singer Tanya Tagaq."

48 Geller, *Northern Exposures*, xv.
49 A video recording of Tagaq's appearance in an interview on CBC's *The National* following her Polaris Prize win and gala performance can be viewed on YouTube at https://www.youtube.com/watch?time_continue=3&v=4wKRz562MY8.
50 K. Rodgers and Scobie, "Sealfies, Seals and Celebs," 71.
51 For further discussion on Indigenous forms of publicness and public performances of identity through expressive culture, see Dueck, *Musical Intimacies and Indigenous Imaginaries*. See also Hoefnagles and Diamond, *Aboriginal Music in Contemporary Canada*.
52 *Chart Magazine*, "Inuk Throat Singer Tanya Tagaq Talks."
53 Quoted in S. Rogers, "Tanya Tagaq's New Album."
54 Quoted in Everett-Green, "Primal Scream."
55 Vizenor, *Survivance*, 1–23.

BIBLIOGRAPHY

Altman, W. L. "Derek Charke Embraces the Arctic with Sound." *Musicworks* 113 (Summer 2012): 20–28.

Baldwin, Andrew, Laura Cameron, and Audrey Kobayashi. "Introduction: Where Is the Great White North? Spatializing History, Historicizing Whiteness." In *Rethinking the Great White North: Race, Nature, and the Historical Geographies of Whiteness in Canada*, edited by Andrew Baldwin, Laura Cameron, and Audrey Kobayashi, 1–15. Vancouver: University of British Columbia Press, 2011.

Barnouw, Erik. *Documentary: A History of the Non-fiction Film*. Oxford: Oxford University Press, 1993.

Björk. *Medúlla*. One Little Indian Records/Elektra, 2004.

CBC News: The National. "Tanya Tagaq on the Polaris Prize, the Seal Hunt and the 'Sealfie.'" Video, 8:27. Uploaded September 26, 2014, by CBC News: The National. https://www.youtube.com/watch?v=4wKRz562MY8.

Charke, Derek. *Cercle du Nord III*. Self-published, 2005.

Charke, Derek. *Nanook*. Self-published, 2012.

Charke, Derek. *Netsiksiuvik*. Canadian Music Centre, 1999.

Charke, Derek. *13 Inuit Throat Song Games*. Canadian Music Centre, 2009.

Charke, Derek. *Tundra Songs*. Self-published, 2007.

Charke, Derek. *22 Inuit Throat Song Games*. Canadian Music Centre, 2002/2005.

Chart Magazine. "Inuk Throat Singer Tanya Tagaq Talks Animism, Pixies and #Sealfies." May 29, 2014. http://www.chartattack.com/features/uncharted/2014/05/29/uncharted-tanya-tagaq/.

Deschênes, Bruno. "Inuit Throat-Singing." *Musical Traditions: The Magazine for Traditional Music throughout the World*, March 1, 2002. http://www.mustrad.org.uk/articles/inuit.htm.

Diamond, Beverley. "Decentering Opera: Early Twenty-First-Century Indigenous Production." In *Opera Indigene: Re/presenting First Nations and Indigenous Cultures*, edited by Pamela Karantonis and Dylan Robinson, 31–56. Aldershot, UK: Ashgate, 2011.

Diamond, Beverley. "The Music of Modern Indigeneity: From Identity to Alliance Studies." *European Meetings in Ethnomusicology* 12, no. 22 (2007): 169–90.

Diamond, Beverley. *Native American Music in Eastern North America: Experiencing Music, Expressing Culture*. Oxford: Oxford University Press, 2008.

Diamond, Beverley. "'Re' Thinking: Revitalization, Return and Reconciliation in Contemporary Indigenous Expressive Culture." In *The Trudeau Foundation Lectures, Volume III, 2011*, 118–40. Montreal: Trudeau Foundation of Canada, 2011.

Diamond, Beverley. "Sound Reviews: 'Medúlla'; 'Sinaa.'" *Journal of American Folklore* 124 (2011): 95–97.

Diamond, Beverley, Kati Szego, and Heather Sparling. "Indigenous Modernities: Introduction." *MUSICultures* 39, no. 1 (2012): 1–6.

Dickie, Mary. "Tanya Tagaq Grabs the World by the Throat." *Musicworks* 188 (Spring 2014): 28–36.

Dueck, Byron. *Musical Intimacies and Indigenous Imaginaries: Aboriginal Music and Dance in Public Performance*. Oxford: Oxford University Press, 2013.

Everett-Green, Robert. "Primal Scream: Inuk Throat Singer Tanya Tagaq Is like No One You've Ever Heard." *Globe and Mail*, May 30, 2014. http://www.theglobeandmail.com/arts/music/primal-scream-inuk-throat-singer-tanya-tagaq-is-like-no-one-youve-ever-heard-anywhere/article18923190/.

Flaherty, Robert, dir. *Nanook of the North*. 1922. DVD. Irvington, NY: Criterion Collection, 1999.

Geller, Peter. *Northern Exposures: Photographing and Filming the Canadian North, 1920–45*. Vancouver: University of British Columbia Press, 2004.

Gordon, Holly. "Inuk Throat Singer Tanya Tagaq on Reclaiming *Nanook of the North*." *CBC News*, January 25, 2014. http://www.cbc.ca/news/aboriginal/inuk-throat-singer-tanya-tagaq-on-reclaiming-nanook-of-the-north-1.2508581.

Gould, Glenn, Marianne Schroeder, W. V. Maclean, James R. Lot, R. A. Phillips, and Frank G. Vallee. *The Idea of North: A Sound Documentary*, 1971. Sound recording.

Grace, Sherrill E. *Canada and the Idea of North*. Montreal: McGill-Queen's University Press, 2007.

Historica Canada. "Heritage Minutes: Inukshuk." Video, 1:00. Uploaded March 9, 2016, by Historica Canada. https://www.youtube.com/watch?v=JD7rAD_S-fE.

Hoefnagles, Anna, and Beverley Diamond, eds. *Aboriginal Music in Contemporary Canada: Echoes and Exchanges*. Montreal: McGill-Queen's University Press, 2012.

Hulan, Renée. *Northern Experience and the Myths of Canadian Culture*. Montreal: McGill-Queen's University Press, 2003.

Kinos-Goodin, Jesse. "A Tribe Called Red, Wab Kinew, Tanya Tagaq on the Indigenous Music Renaissance." *CBCMusic*, August 18, 2014. http://music.cbc.ca/#!/blogs/2014/8/ATribe-Called-Red-Wab-Kinew-Tanya-Tagaq-on-the-Indigenous-music-renaissance.

Lawrence, Mark, dir. "Kronos Quartet and Tanya Tagaq—*A String Quartet in Her Throat*." Excerpt from the film *A String Quartet in Her Throat*, 2007. Video, 7:16. Uploaded March 23, 2009, by Kronos Quartet. https://youtu.be/nCSxNOdZEww.

Marsh, Charity. "'Don't Call Me Eskimo': Representation, Mythology and Hip Hop Culture on Baffin Island." *MUSICultures* 36 (2009): 110–29.

Nattiez, Jean-Jacques. "Some Aspects of Inuit Vocal Games." *Ethnomusicology* 27, no. 3 (1983): 457–76.

Nelles, Drew. "Why Tanya Tagaq Sings." *Walrus*, January 15, 2015. http://thewalrus.ca/howl/.

Piekut, Benjamin. "Actor-Networks in Music History: Clarifications and Critiques." *Twentieth-Century Music* 11, no. 2 (2014): 191–215.

Raheja, Michelle H. "Reading Nanook's Smile: Visual Sovereignty, Indigenous Revisions of Ethnography, and *Atanarjuat (The Fast Runner)*." *American Quarterly* 59, no. 4 (2007): 1159–85.

Robinson, Dylan. "Listening to the Politics of Aesthetics: Contemporary Encounters between First Nations/Inuit and Early Music Traditions." In *Aboriginal Music in Contemporary Canada: Echoes and Exchanges*, edited by Anna Hoefnagles and Beverley Diamond, 222–48. Montreal: McGill-Queen's University Press, 2012.

Rodgers, Kathleen, and Willow Scobie. "Sealfies, Seals and Celebs: Expressions of Inuit Resilience in the Twitter Era." *Interface: A Journal on Social Movements* 7, no. 1 (2015): 70–97.

Rogers, Sarah. "Tanya Tagaq's New Album Captures the Spirit of Good and Evil." *Nunatsiaq Online*, May 16, 2014. https://nunatsiaq.com/stories/article/65674tanya_tagaqs_new_album_captures_the_spirit_of_good_and_evil/.

Rony, Fatimah Tobing. *The Third Eye: Race, Cinema, and Ethnographic Spectacle*. Durham, NC: Duke University Press, 1996.

Schafer, R. Murray. *The Tuning of the World*. Toronto: McClelland and Stewart, 1977.

Senungetuk, Joseph E. *Give or Take a Century: An Eskimo Chronicle*. San Francisco: Indian Historian Press, 1971.

Stévance, Sophie. "Analysis of the Inuit Katajjaq in Popular Culture: The Canadian Throat-Singer Superstar Tanya Tagaq." *Itamar—Revista de investigacion musical: Territorios para el arte* 3 (2010): 79–85.

Tagaq, Tanya. *Animism*. Six Shooter Records, 2014.

Tagaq, Tanya, with Jean Martin, Jesse Zubot and pre-recorded soundscape by Derek Charke (Studio Recording, Kentville, Nova Scotia, 2012). *Nanook*. Luminato Festival, Toronto, June 10, 2014. Live performance.

van den Scott, Jeffrey. "Experiencing the Music: Towards a Visual Model for the Social Construction of Music." *Studies in Symbolic Interaction* 42 (2014): 3–19.

van den Scott, Jeffrey. "Throat Games or Throat Songs? The Changing Inuit Perspective of a Traditional Practice." Paper presented at the Annual Meeting of the Canadian University Music Society at the University of Victoria, Victoria, British Columbia, June 6–9, 2013.

Vizenor, Gerald, ed. *Survivance: Narratives of Native Presence*. Lincoln: University of Nebraska Press, 2008.

SIX Nina Simone

CIVIL JAZZ!

RANDY DuBURKE

SEVEN Free Improvised Music in Postwar Beirut

Differential Sounds, Intersectarian Collaborations, and Critical Collective Memory

RANA EL KADI

Lebanon has long been home to myriad cultures and religions, and the fates of its citizens, whether social, economic, or political, have historically been aligned with the fates of its religious groups. Through intense clashes over power sharing, potent sectarian identities were created and utilized to fuel political instability and violent conflict, the worst of which was the fifteen-year civil war (1975–91). Growing up in Beirut, I witnessed the ravages of civil war and political instability, which to this day continue to threaten social unity and the maintenance of a functioning government. This left me plagued by questions regarding the formation and preservation of sectarian identities and the way that a brutal history of civil war may continue to influence contemporary intersectarian relations, particularly when such a war failed to resolve any of the country's long-standing political issues.

My involvement in Beirut's music scene, both as amateur performer and as audience member, led me to discover the local practice of free improvised music while attending the sixth annual Irtijal (Arabic for "improvisation") festival in April 2006.[1] Besides its challenge to my understanding of what constitutes music, I was particularly intrigued by the notion that it may be possible to create a sonic-musical identity that is devoid of any "cultural" signification. Unbeknownst to many at the time, free improvisation had materialized in Beirut in 2000, within a religiously and socioeconomically homogeneous circle. This practice initially emerged elsewhere in the 1960s, out of the twin influences of jazz and the classical avant-garde, leading to a rich Euro-American history of musical freedom and creative risk taking. It has since led to the development of a highly transnational free improvisation scene, which currently stretches all the way from Europe to the United States and from the Middle East to East Asia.

Despite the transnational community's dispersed and divergent nature, ethnomusicologist David Borgo states that free improvisers generally agree on a number of defining characteristics; these include a sense of freedom and discovery, an emphasis on process-over-product creativity, and the prominence of dialogic real-time interaction.[2] But how might these values interface with local histories and sociopolitical issues when free improvisation is practiced in the Lebanese capital? What role may such a presumably culturally neutral musical practice play in the postcolonial, conflict-ridden, highly globalized context of contemporary Beirut? My master's thesis in ethnomusicology centered on these questions, which took on a particular urgency with the onset of the Lebanese-Israeli war in July 2006, merely three months after I attended the Irtijal festival in Beirut. Residents who had lived through the civil war were suddenly plunged back into the violent physicalities, psychologies, and sonorities of warfare.

This chapter is based on ethnographic data I collected during several fieldwork trips over a one-year period (May 2008–April 2009). My research methodology included attending public and private free improvisation concerts as well as private dinners and after-parties hosted by Irtijal festival organizers for visiting international musicians, in-depth interviews with key Lebanese improvisers, and a survey of international album reviews, CD liner notes, music websites, and blogs. I argue that the output of three key Lebanese musicians exhibits the emergence of a differential improvisatory practice that is deeply rooted in their localized, generational struggle with three layers of crisis: colonialism, sectarianism, and civil war. I contend that in a postcolonial society still coming to terms with the atrocities of civil war, sectarianism, and constant political instability, the practice of free improvised music provides a unique space for musicians to "play for keeps." These musicians use free improvisation to engage with cultural and religious differences, negotiate the lingering violence and uncertainty, engage with collective memory of civil war, and communicate critical alternatives for national politics and intersectarian social relations. By focusing on Lebanese free improvisation within the first decade of the third millennium, this chapter contributes to our knowledge of the distinctive meanings and social utility of improvisation in the aftermath of crisis.

A Musico-Political History of Lebanon

Surrounded by Syria, Palestine/Israel, and the Mediterranean Sea, Lebanon possesses a lengthy history of cultural contact arising from imperial conquest, colonialism, international trade, and migration. During the fifteenth and sixteenth centuries, most of the Arabic-speaking countries in the Middle East and North Africa were integrated into the Ottoman Empire, which was based on Islam. By the end of the eighteenth century the Ottoman Empire had begun to decline as new European powers challenged its control over the region. Historian Albert Hourani argues that this decline was accompanied by the emergence of a discourse of self-doubt within the Arab territories; part of this discursive shift translated into an obsession with musical "reform."[3] Eventually, European influences and technological developments brought about a number of significant changes in Arab musical life. Musical compositions, for instance, became lighter in character, improvisation decreased, Western instruments and teaching methods dominated, and Western-inspired orchestras replaced the traditional small ensemble. At the same time, the emphasis shifted from individual virtuosity to collective discipline and well-tempered harmony, while musical pieces were eventually standardized and shortened to conform to phonograph and radio restrictions.[4]

After its defeat by the Allies in World War I, the Ottoman Empire's collapse led to the division of its Syrian provinces among the British and the French, with the present territory of Lebanon falling under the French mandate until Lebanon gained its independence in 1943. Hourani notes that while European control in the Arab world officially ended following World War II, the local regimes that took over were heavily influenced by European-borrowed nationalist ideals.[5] Around this time the concept of "Lebanese music" materialized and was actively promoted by the Lebanese government and media. Characterized by a melding of rural Middle Eastern music and European art-music principles, this new style was practiced by composers and musicians who performed regularly at historical sites and international festivals in the country. Interestingly, as ethnomusicologist Thomas Burkhalter argues, this new style did not draw on the highly influential classical Arabic music that was practiced by famous twentieth-century composers and performers within Egypt, the regional capital of musical production at the time.[6] It seems that as early as the mid-twentieth century, a number of mainly Christian Lebanese composers were attempting to differentiate their music from other traditions in the Muslim-dominated region, particularly by avoiding the use of Islamic influences and referents.

This attempt at musical differentiation was merely a reflection of the general sociopolitical climate in Lebanon. Caught among a diverse set of ethnic and religious groups and a multitude of conflicting cultural influences, Lebanese citizens have long possessed discordant definitions of cultural and national identity. Historian Kamal Salibi even goes so far as to say that political conflict in Lebanon is strongly intertwined with opposing visions of collective identity, where Muslims identify themselves in terms of pan-Arabism, and Christians in terms of Lebanese particularism with a non-Arab connection to the ancient Phoenicians.[7] Lebanese sociologist Samir Khalaf notes that within Lebanon, kinship, fealty, and confessional loyalties have long overridden those to the nation, state, or political party; as such, "a Christian is first a Christian, a member of a given family, and from a specific region before he is a Lebanese."[8] Historically, this has meant that most Lebanese citizens have been ready to take up arms whenever directed to do so by their confessional leaders.

As the Lebanese economists Samir Makdisi and Richard Sadaka demonstrate, the sectarian formula for power sharing that was put in place on the eve of Lebanon's independence from France played a major role in instigating armed interreligious conflicts and eventually led to the onset of the Lebanese Civil War in 1975. Within the framework of a consociational democracy, this formula essentially divided power among the three leading religious communities in Lebanon: the Maronite Christians, the Sunni Muslims, and the Shi'a Muslims. Makdisi and Sadaka note that this political system afforded Maronites more political privileges—owing to this, coupled with their historical socioeconomic dominance, the Maronites emerged as the single most influential religious community up until the 1970s. In the decades leading up to the civil war, Muslim political leaders in Lebanon persistently called for more equal power sharing between Christians and Muslims. Meanwhile, the military power of resident Palestinian organizations increased, making southern Lebanon their base for operations against Israel. This led to intermittent armed clashes between the Palestine Liberation Organization (PLO) and the Lebanese army along with Christian political parties, until one such clash in a Beirut suburb finally ignited a civil war that persisted for fifteen years. During the civil war, there were two main warring camps: on the one hand, the Maronite Christian parties, which were generally aligned with the Lebanese state and army, and, on the other, the PLO along with several Muslim-dominated parties. The complexity of the war lay in its multifaceted nature, the frequent intermilitia fighting within each camp, and the unpredictable shifting alliances among the primary contenders and their external supporters.[9]

Predictably, the protracted civil war succeeded in destroying the country's infrastructure and large sectors of its economy. Lebanon's musical life changed drastically, as the country's international festivals and orchestras ceased operations. At the same time, owing to the acceleration of technological progress and domestic access to radio and television, Lebanese citizens were exposed to an international mixture of popular music, particularly through jingles and commercials with eclectic influences. According to Burkhalter, these included mixtures between "Lebanese music" in the style of the Rahbani Brothers and rock 'n' roll, rock, funk, big-band jazz, reggae, French chanson, country, and other styles of Western popular music.[10] It is important to recognize that most of the fighting in the capital city took place on either side of the so-called Green Line, a demarcation that separated the Palestinian and Muslim warring factions in West Beirut from the Maronite Christian Front in East Beirut. As civil conflict raged on for fifteen years, the strict geographic segregation of the city's religious communities resulted in the development of popular music along two distinct trajectories. According to Burkhalter, West Beirut's music scene was led by the likes of Ziad Rahbani, Marcel Khalife, and Khaled el Haber, composer-musicians who fused Arabic music with Western styles such as jazz and rock, while strongly promoting the Lebanese Communist Party's left-leaning, pro-PLO ideologies.[11] On the other side of the Green Line, East Beirut became home to numerous rock, heavy metal, and death metal bands that exclusively performed renditions of existent European and American songs.[12]

The civil war significantly shaped the personal and musical lives of four musicians (Mazen Kerbaj, Sharif Sehnaoui, Christine Abdelnour, and Raed Yassin) who have played key roles in developing the contemporary Lebanese free improvisation scene. The son of famous stage actor Antoine Kerbaj and renowned visual artist Laure Ghorayeb, Mazen Kerbaj was born in Beirut in 1975 and has lived there until recently. After studying at l'Académie Libanaise des Beaux-Arts, Kerbaj began to earn an international reputation for his innovative work in illustration and cartooning.[13] Sehnaoui was born in 1976 and grew up in East Beirut. During the civil war, he and his family were displaced first to the town of Mansourieh for a couple of years and then to neighboring Cyprus for a year, after which he returned to Beirut around the age of twelve. Since Sehnaoui descended from an affluent Christian family, he was able to move to France to study philosophy at the age of twenty. As for Abdelnour, her wealthy parents emigrated to the former colonial metropole during the civil war, and she was born in Paris in 1978. Finally, Yassin was born in Lebanon in 1979 and has been living there ever since. He began publishing Arabic poetry in local newspapers at the age of fifteen, while taking flute and double bass lessons at the Lebanese National Higher Conservatory of Music.[14]

All four musicians discovered jazz and improvisation during early adulthood. Kerbaj developed an interest in free jazz and free improvised music in his early twenties, after being exposed to the recordings of landmark figures such as John Coltrane, Evan Parker, and Peter Brötzmann.[15] His interest in playing free jazz led him to take lessons with a jazz trumpet player who taught at the Lebanese National Higher Conservatory of Music; Kerbaj apparently discontinued those lessons after incessant arguments with his teacher about "what is music and what is not."[16] He eventually began to perform live after switching to the saxophone. Sehnaoui discovered jazz in Paris. Following his piano lessons during childhood, he had taken up rock guitar and drums during adolescence. Once in Paris he began taking lessons in jazz and later classical guitar techniques. Sehnaoui eventually developed an interest in free jazz and free improvisation, particularly after witnessing the impressive extended techniques of world-renowned improvisers such as Evan Parker and Barry Guy. He subsequently began to develop his improvisation skills while participating in several experimental and improvisatory orchestras in Paris.[17]

As a young adult, Yassin chose to focus on the double bass and began taking private jazz and fusion lessons from an American musician residing in Beirut. Soon thereafter, he enrolled in a university theater program; he claims that he was more interested in studying video art installation, but unlike Sehnaoui and Kerbaj, Yassin could only afford to attend the publicly funded Lebanese University, which did not offer such a program.[18] Today he is recognized as a visual/video artist as well as a musician. As for Abdelnour, she first discovered improvised music in France at the age of nineteen; she has been engaged in a process of "self-taught study and sound experimentation" on the alto saxophone ever since.[19] Despite her early contributions, Abdelnour is permanently stationed in Paris and has not been as heavily involved as the three other musicians in developing the Lebanese free improvisation scene; therefore, her work will only be touched on briefly in this chapter.

Avant-Garde Music in Postwar Beirut

In October 1989 the civil war was finally settled through an agreement on national reconciliation. Known as the Ta'if Accord, this agreement essentially reaffirmed the principle of sectarian power sharing, but modified its contents to create a more equitable formula for Muslims and Christians. The hostilities ended a year later, but not before an estimated 144,000 people had lost their lives, tens of thousands had been internally displaced, and around 990,000 people had emigrated.[20] Notably, a law of general amnesty was passed in 1991, allowing for a clean slate while keeping political leaders in their positions despite the numerous crimes they had committed during the war; the slogan of "la ghalib la maghlub" (Arabic for "no victor, no vanquished") was officially used to justify Lebanon's shift from war to peace.[21]

In the years that followed, Lebanon's "culture of sectarianism" persisted, as the country underwent an intensive process of physical reconstruction. This collided with an accelerated process of globalization and digitalization, which significantly altered the musical landscape in the Arab world.[22] On the one hand, substantial technological developments in music and video production led to powerful shifts in the region's musical consumption habits and the operations of its popular music industry. Ethnomusicologist Michael Frishkopf states that given the development of pan-Arab satellite radio and television channels and the ease of electronically manipulating the voice, the emphasis shifted from the pop singer's vocal ability to his or her visual style and physical appeal.[23] As a result, most Arab pop singers today sing catchy, formulaic songs in a variety of regional dialects, thereby targeting a multitude of populations within the Arab world and its diasporic communities.

On the other hand, music from all over the world became progressively more accessible through digital form and via the internet. As Burkhalter notes, instead of waiting for international CDs to be imported or smuggled into the country from remote locations, musicians in Beirut began to listen to and download all kinds of music; this allowed them to stay apprised of the latest developments in their specific niche music genres. Equally important was the emergence of technological developments that began to democratize the means of music production and distribution, particularly through laptop culture. This meant that musicians could inexpensively produce and distribute their music across transnational networks, thus reaching an unprecedented level of international exposure within their niche music circles. Burkhalter argues that these changes are key features of the "digital mediamorphosis" that has recently swept across the Arab world, Asia, Africa, and Latin America, leading to the development of a geographically multisited musical avant-garde, comprising commercial as well as experimental styles like free improvised music.[24]

Within Beirut, for instance, a small but vibrant music scene began to emerge in the decade following the civil war, bringing together young performers who played a variety of musical styles, including rap, rock, death metal, jazz, electroacoustic music, free improvisation, and Arabic music.[25] Although these musicians belonged to various religious backgrounds, many of them could afford to attend American or French private schools and universities in Lebanon, as well as travel to Europe and North America on a regular basis. These musicians were cognizant of the latest trends in their niche music genres owing to the global digital revolution; at the same time, their relatively high levels of education made them well versed in these musics' underlying histories and philosophies.

According to Burkhalter, the musical avant-garde to which Lebanese improvising musicians belong seeks to "challenge 'ethnocentric' perceptions of 'place' and 'locality' in music, and attack the focus on musical 'difference' in Euro-American music and culture markets." These Lebanese musicians generally refuse to cater to the exoticizing demands of the imperialist Western market, which categorizes music from the Arab world under the patronizing label of world music and includes only classical, rural, or folk music from the region.[26] Further, they vehemently repudiate the mainstream pan-Arab pop music industry for pumping out inexpensive, catchy, and, in their opinion, superficial albums. Since these musicians are generally interested in retaining their creative freedom while producing "high-quality" music, they resort to recording, producing, and distributing limited-edition albums through their own small, independent record labels.[27] Additionally, they promote and sell their music through personal websites, music-streaming services, blogs, and social media fan groups. Their performances often occur at trendy clubs, public music festivals, cultural centers, theaters, and independently managed performance spaces, as well as private apartments and houses.

Although avant-garde musicians in Beirut often experiment and collaborate across genre and ensemble boundaries, it is possible to discern a distinct free improvised music circle in the city. The practice of Lebanese free improvised music officially materialized in 2000, when Kerbaj, Sehnaoui, and Abdelnour founded an association called Musique Improvisée Libre au Liban (MILL). One of the association's main goals was to organize an annual festival called Irtijal. Kerbaj states that their inaugural minifestival was "probably the first improvised music concert in the Middle East"; it was held at Strike's Pub in Hazmieh, a Christian-dominated neighborhood on the outskirts of Beirut.[28] Over the past two decades, Irtijal has grown into an international festival that attracts world-renowned artists who participate in live performances, offer public workshops, and collaborate with Lebanese musicians on recording projects. Furthermore, MILL members' frequent musical performances and collaborations at worldwide festivals have earned them a solid reputation within the transnational free improvised music scene. Notably, Lebanese improvisers depend on nongovernmental organizations, festivals, and media channels in Europe and the United States for funding and international exposure.[29] These Euro-American relationships of patronage are a strong indication of the lingering postcolonial influences to be found in contemporary Beirut.

Intersectarian Improvisatory Encounters

In a country with a brutal history of sectarianism and closed religious communities, a highly versatile and socially interactive practice such as free improvised music was bound to reflect and engage with social tensions. In what follows I show how this practice facilitated a unique intersectarian exchange by critically engaging with the postwar desegregation realities of a generation born at the outset of the civil war. Sehnaoui states that back in 2000, it was quite possible that Lebanese free improvisation could have remained a purely "Christian-Christian thing," and MILL musicians then did not know that it could be any different.[30] In the late 1990s, it was natural that Sehnaoui, Kerbaj, and Abdelnour were mostly acquainted with Christian friends, communication channels, and neighborhoods. Lebanon, after all, was still emerging from a horrific fifteen-year civil war, during which most Christians in East Beirut had spent their childhoods within the confines of their own religious group and geographic area, forbidden from interacting with the "enemy"—in this case, the religiously heterogeneous but Muslim/Palestinian militia–dominated West Beirut.

Consequently, although the war had ended ten years earlier, most audience members who attended MILL's early concerts were friends of the performers who belonged to the same religious background and "financially comfortable" class.[31] This is unsurprising, given the persistence of a culture of sectarianism in postwar Lebanon. According to the Foucauldian reading provided by Lara Khattab and colleagues, the political economy and ideological hegemony of Lebanon's postwar sectarian system were sustained through a complex combination of institutional, clientelist, and discursive "practices of governance" that manufactured docile sectarian subjects.[32] It was therefore quite a surprise to the founders of MILL when Raed Yassin, "a Shi'ite from West Beirut," suddenly "popped out of nowhere" in 2001 and expressed interest in playing with Kerbaj. Soon thereafter, Sehnaoui, Kerbaj, and Yassin formed the A Trio collective. Despite emerging from previously physically

FIGURE 7.1 Cover of A Trio's debut album, *A*, released by Incognito in 2003.

segregated communities, the three musicians were able to establish points of commonality through their shared experiences of sound during the civil war. According to Sehnaoui, "it was funny [the three of us] talking together when we discovered what was in common ... the same TV advertisement, the same songs we heard, basically the same TV programs, the same politicians."[33]

In 2003 the three musicians released their first album as the A Trio; it was eponymously entitled *A*. In retrospect, Sehnaoui agrees with the other musicians that this was probably their worst recording ever because they were still inexperienced and had not been improvising collectively for long. Nonetheless, the three improvisers were cognizant of the various barriers they were breaking through this collaboration. Kerbaj and Sehnaoui in particular decided to highlight their dissimilar religious backgrounds in the album's liner notes, because Yassin's presence constituted an extremely momentous occasion for them at the time; they knew for a fact that they could not have even made his acquaintance ten years earlier.[34] The liner notes that Sehnaoui subsequently wrote state, "It is probably worth mentioning at this point that Kerbaj and Yassine [sic] come from different parts of the city of Beirut, East and West, once closed to one another, often at war. Part of the thrill from their duo comes from this new testimony of music bringing more and more barriers to the ground.... This is where we stand in Lebanon: gates between cultures, bridges between differences, you can cross, but you cannot break the gates open, and you should not bring the bridges down."[35]

Here the reader might question why Sehnaoui refers to "cultural" instead of "religious" differences when referring to intersectarian conflict in Lebanon. In fact, this is not an uncommon understanding of Lebanese identity politics. As Khalaf explains, the boundaries between different religious neighborhoods during the civil war were not merely spatial. Even though the boundary was sometimes an imaginary "green line," a bridge, or a road, members of different religious communities began to sense and create psychological, cultural, and ideological barriers that left them reluctant to cross over. Khalaf's comments demonstrate how powerful the process of othering can be in instigating segregation and prolonging conflict. In particular, the civil war had an enduring impact on children, since they grew up knowing nothing but war and segregation until they were in their twenties. According to Khalaf, besides perceiving differences in religious background as profound differences in cultural, ideological, and political values, whole generations of children and adolescents grew up believing that their social world was restricted to the small communities within which they were confined.[36] This was certainly the case for the A Trio musicians, who were merely children during the war, but even more so for Sehnaoui and Kerbaj; unlike West Beirut, their East Beirut community was religiously homogeneous. As such, the trio's first collaborative album represents a significant testimony to the religious-cultural boundaries that were challenged and overcome in the process of creating today's Lebanese free improvisation circle.

Individual Identities, Differential Techniques, Context-Specific Sounds

According to my research, free improvisers in Beirut value this musical practice because, on the one hand, it helps them shed the burden of an enforced religion, culture, and history; and, on the other, it provides them with the freedom to negotiate and perform their individual, fluid identities through personalized improvisatory techniques and differential context-specific sounds.

First, Kerbaj and Sehnaoui separately mention their gravitation toward free improvised music because, unlike jazz, which is resolutely associated with a geocultural area or ethnic group, it is allegedly nonidiomatic and free from cultural association. In fact, it is often celebrated for its "resistance to labeling."[37]

> Kerbaj: The good thing about [free improvised music] is you can take it wherever you want in the world and totally make it your own. It has zero identity. Its identity is your identity as an *individual*, not even as a Lebanese.[38]

> Sehnaoui: One of the reasons I like this [improvised] music is because it has no clear identity. . . . It can start anywhere and everywhere. . . . It's new tradition and new subcultures of the modern world. . . . Anyone can take it and just make it his own. I don't feel I'm playing someone else's culture—I'm playing my *own* culture. This is very important. . . . You create your own identity, which is not traditional, which is individual.[39]

Second, Lebanese improvisers value the individual creative freedom they find in this musical practice. Free improvisation in principle lacks many of the restrictions that other musical practices impose in terms of style, instrument, technique, and cultural affiliation; instead, it encourages musicians to utilize any sound source, point of reference, and combination of influences.

In what follows, I shall provide an overview of the three musicians' development of differential improvisatory techniques. They all believe in the importance of creating personalized techniques that manipulate and expand the aural capacity of their instruments, as a path toward individual style. Subsequently, I shall discuss the way that Kerbaj and Yassin further differentiate their improvisatory practices by incorporating and interacting with culturally specific sounds and images, in order to create recordings and audiovisual performances that are unique to the Lebanese context.

Sehnaoui is known for using prepared, extended, and percussive improvisatory techniques, specifically by holding his guitar in a horizontal position on his lap and using mallets to strike the strings. In his review of Sehnaoui's solo album *Old and New Acoustics* (2010), for instance, music critic Massimo Ricci states that "Sehnaoui develops entrancing circularity and obsessive rhythmical geometries improved by nonstop sparkling discharges and mind-influencing irregular accretions. This system considers the stringed body as a substitute cimbalom—or hammered dulcimer."[40] Notably, Sehnaoui switches back and forth between electric and acoustic guitar at different points in time, and he finds both the sound and the physical experience of playing totally different on the two instruments.[41]

Kerbaj prepares his trumpet with a variety of mouthpieces, mutes, and rubber hoses, while masterfully employing every conceivable part of his instrument when improvising.[42] He is renowned for his innovative extended techniques that allow him to expand the aural-producing capabilities of the trumpet, particularly when utilized in tandem with an assortment of blowing, sucking, and percussive techniques.[43] As I mention elsewhere, his signature extended techniques include "blowing through a long tube that is wrapped around his stomach, placing his trumpet vertically between his legs or a tin can on the bell of the trumpet, and even filling the instrument with water to create bubbling sounds."[44]

As for Yassin, he is considered a "master of extended techniques" by *The Wire* magazine's Andy Hamilton; in addition to regular bowing and finger techniques, he employs "woody thumps and percussive string strikes" on his double bass, as noted by Matthew Wuethrich in a review.[45] I have also watched Yassin utilizing found objects such as a metal sheet or a bent fork, which he places between the bass's strings to create new timbres. In fact, he says he uses his instrument as "a sound-machine."[46]

As evidenced by the discussion above, these Lebanese musicians have succeeded in developing distinctive personalized improvisatory techniques on their respective instruments. In what follows I show that Yassin and Kerbaj, in particular, have taken free improvisation's built-in freedom even further. Yassin has long been collecting audio and visual samples from Arab pop song recordings and television and radio channels, as well as feature and documentary films produced between 1950 and 1990. He has been working on an extensive multimedia research project that aims to deconstruct Arab pop culture through the production of solo and collaborative audiovisual pieces.[47] Despite his proficiency on double bass, Yassin is perhaps even more renowned for his skillful, innovative work with tape manipulation, electronics, and turntables. Music critic Bill Meyer, for example, extols the musician's technique in his duo with American percussionist Michael Zerang on *Cedarhead* (2006): "Yassin tugs tape over playback heads, obtaining stuttering sound bites with the facility of a hip-hop turntablist. He adroitly mixes snippets of radio broadcasts with synthetic swooshes and whistles to create a dizzying ride, driven by Zerang's galloping darbekki."[48] Through the production of audiovisual collages that deconstruct and reconstruct Arab pop culture, Yassin manipulates his audience's collective memory—what he refers to as "the collective unconscious." In fact, as journalist Kaelen Wilson-Goldie states,

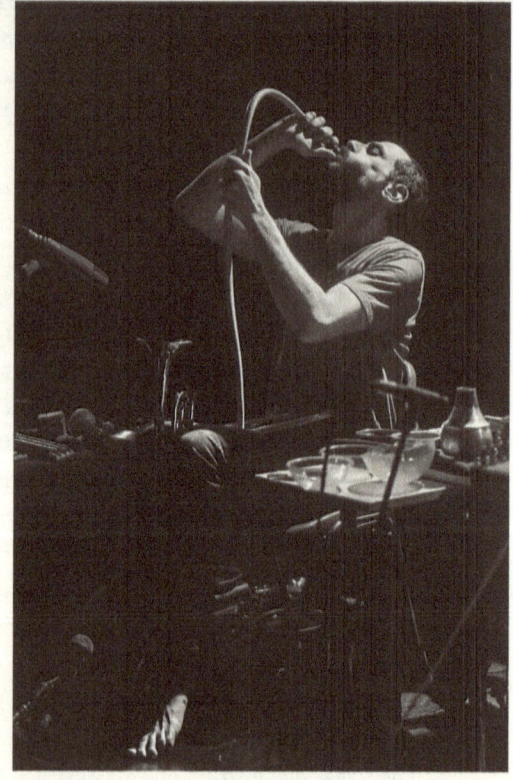

FIGURES 7.2–7.3 Sharif Sehnaoui playing his acoustic guitar (photograph by Tanya Traboulsi) and Mazen Kerbaj playing his trumpet (photograph by Micke Keysendal).

FIGURES 7.4–7.5 Raed Yassin playing his double bass (photograph by Tony Elieh) and manipulating his electronics and video projections at the Irtijal Festival in April 2009 (photograph by Tanya Traboulsi).

"for [Yassin], rather than an abstract notion, collective memory is a vibrant jumble of pop-cultural cues."[49]

Unlike Kerbaj and Sehnaoui, Yassin openly acknowledges that the general Lebanese public considers free improvisation abstract, elitist, and inaccessible. In response, he has founded an improvisatory ensemble called Grendizer Trio that tries to "meet the audience halfway," particularly by connecting with the pop culture experiences of people in Lebanon and the Arab world. The trio held its first performance in Beirut in March 2006, featuring Yassin, Kerbaj, and two other Lebanese improvisers (Bechir Saade and Charbel Haber) in a concert called "Ya Habibi Ta'ala."[50] The musicians played their usual free improvisation sets on their respective instruments, but Yassin also incorporated tape samples of well-known Arab songstresses from the mid-twentieth century, such as Nour el-Houda, Leila Murad, and Asmahan.[51]

Somewhat similarly, Kerbaj has been able to expand his improvisatory practice by moving beyond instrumental extended techniques to incorporate context-specific elements of the Lebanese soundscape. He recalls that he had been improvising for several years when a friend, Austrian trumpet player Franz Hautzinger, remarked that some of Kerbaj's trumpet sonorities sounded like war machines.[52] This notion intrigued Kerbaj, so much so that he began to collect and improvise with sounds from the Lebanese Civil War, such as rifle shots and bomb explosions.[53] In an interview Kerbaj explains that the aforementioned exercise served two purposes: first, it allowed him to explore the extent to which "belliphonic" sounds—that is, those produced by armed combat—from his childhood may have subconsciously impacted his present improvisatory techniques; and, second, it provided him with an opportunity to examine whether these sounds were aesthetically compatible with his trumpet improvisations.[54] Interestingly, the discourse linking some of Kerbaj's techniques to the belliphonic began to gain momentum after the release of his solo album *Brt Vrt Zrt Krt* in 2005. Wilson-Goldie quotes from an interview with Kerbaj: "'I hate to say this in Lebanon,' he says, but there is something in [this] work that betrays 'a nostalgia for soundscapes in times of war. It's more afterward that I realize this, but "Tagadagadaga" [the album's fifth track] sounds like a rifle.'"[55]

Barely a year later, Lebanon was plunged back into a state reminiscent of the civil war: on July 12, 2006, Israel declared war on Lebanon after Hezbollah (literally, "party of God") captured two Israeli Defense Force soldiers at the southern border. The Israeli Air Force began to shell Beirut, allegedly in an effort to drive Hezbollah out of its stronghold in the Shi'ite-dominated southern suburbs. Within a few weeks, the country's infrastructure was severely damaged, thousands of Lebanese civilians were injured or killed, and about a million people were displaced. Thirty-three days later, on August 14, international pressure finally led to the cessation of the war.

Given his interest in the belliphonic, Kerbaj quickly realized that it would be "more effective" to record his improvisations with live air raids instead of prerecorded sounds. While sitting on his apartment balcony, he ventured to record nine hours of live trumpet improvisations with the Israeli shelling on July 15 and 16. Soon thereafter, Kerbaj uploaded a six-minute excerpt on his personal blog; he called this track "Starry Night" and referred to the Israeli pilots as "sound artists."[56] Kerbaj was not personally in danger because, given its location, his apartment building was not likely to be shelled. He told me, however, that he was very stressed because "the explosions signified people being killed." Far from intending to produce an innovative or aesthetically pleasing recording, he claims that he had wanted to see whether he would "have the guts" to improvise with a bomb while it was exploding nearby.[57] In an interview with NOW, Kerbaj states, "If I play music while the bombs were falling, my brain will shift from fear to action, and I end up analyzing the bomb as a sound like any other that you have to work with and around."[58] Therefore, as I argue in my case study of "Starry Night," the practice of free improvisation allowed Kerbaj to psychologically face—and sonically grapple with—some of his childhood demons.[59] This demonstrates the role of improvisation in addressing war trauma on the individual level.

Collective Improvisation as an Intersectarian Social Model

Despite Kerbaj's and Sehnaoui's primary focus on individual musical expression, their participation in collaborative music making gradually heightened their interest in the social politics of collective improvisation and its implications within Lebanese postwar society. As Sehnaoui recounts, A Trio's first album was "a bit of a struggle aesthetically"; he claims that although the musicians were all inexperienced in free improvisation at that point, Yassin in particular was "not the player he is today—he was much more of a jazz player." This constituted a problem for Sehnaoui and Kerbaj, who shared a more "abstract" and "minimalistic" aesthetic vision. Apparently, this aesthetic difference led the two musicians to exclude Yassin from the sound-mixing process and lower the double bass's volume as part of the "correction" process.[60] Sehnaoui's confession is arguably symptomatic of what Ang refers to as "the fundamental *uneasiness* inherent in the global condition of togetherness-in-difference"; it also reinforces ethnomusicologist Jason Stanyek's argument that interculturality in musical encounters does not necessarily imply a preservation of difference.[61]

But was there more to this aesthetic struggle than "creative differences"? According to Yassin, the three musicians had arrived at this collective with diverse musical backgrounds and interests. It is often the case that differences in musical aesthetics do not merely reflect personal preferences but are also indicative of people's socioeconomic, educational, and religious or cultural backgrounds. Sehnaoui and Kerbaj (both Christian residents of East Beirut), for instance, use French as their primary language and are strongly cognizant and appreciative of European (and particularly French) philosophy, literature, art, and music, but they know little about Arabic musical traditions. Meanwhile, Yassin—a Shi'ite resident of West Beirut—uses Arabic as his primary language and is very cognizant and appreciative of Arabic music, poetry, and film. Indeed, he has strong views about the way Arabic music and pop culture have historically been treated in Lebanon; during an interview, he problematizes some commonly held beliefs regarding music categories. He says he finds it disturbing that "certain groups in the country" grow up believing that Arabic music is somehow beneath them, as opposed to Western music, which is often perceived as more elevated and civilized.[62] As Islamic studies scholar Mahmoud Ayoub illustrates, many people in Lebanon (especially Christians) have historically identified with the West and considered Lebanon as "part of the Arab East in geography only."[63] This explains the emergence of a Christian-led drive to create a distinctive "Lebanese" musical style during the mid-twentieth century, particularly through the Rahbani Brothers' massive musical output.

Yassin explains that the Rahbani Brothers were attempting to counter Egyptian music's (Islamic-influenced) "invasion of the Arab world" by capitalizing on their compositional talent, industry connections, and proficiency in adapting catchy melodies from eclectic sources. According to Yassin, the Brothers succeeded in constructing a musical standard of "high art," which immediately relegated all other Lebanese music to the category of "low art." Examples of the latter include styles in which Yassin is personally interested, such as *sha'abi* (literally, "*popular* music") and the aggressive style of *dabke* that is usually played on the microbus ride from Beirut to the Shi'ite-dominated town of Ba'albek.[64] He also argues that "the Rahbani phenomenon" created such a powerful hegemonic pole of musical production that it "trampled on" a considerable portion of popular music from that period, so much so that the latter has been permanently erased from the country's history, leading to the erroneous labeling and misunderstanding of Lebanese music.[65] Yassin resentfully states that "there is useless pretension due to a gap in [musical] history," which translates into "elitist groups in Lebanon" listening to older music in a rather Orientalist manner—even regarding it as "cute," as if it is something very exotic.[66] This concern no doubt fuels Yassin's aforementioned efforts to create a pop culture archive that highlights, among other things, the sound material that was produced during the civil war but has since been lost or forgotten.

Given Lebanese society's long-standing adversarial visions of collective identity and the fact that musical taste may unwittingly identify one's religious, cultural, and ideological background, even a seemingly mundane musical dialogue can become fertile ground for intersectarian conflict. That is precisely why I contend that, owing to its resistance to labeling and its relative genre neutrality, free improvisation seems to have provided just the right space for Lebanese musicians of diverse backgrounds to come together following protracted sectarian conflict and geographic segregation. Because this musical practice lacks a conspicuous association with any culture or religion, it translated into a common, *neutral* ground—and thus a tabula rasa—where musical dialogue could take place, unfettered by an excess of cultural baggage. As Sehnaoui puts it: "You know, getting together, after all these years and doing common music, which is neither our identity or yours—it's a common thing."[67] This account leads one to construe free improvisation as a potential tool for negotiating the lingering violence of sectarian identity in a postwar society.

Of course, Kerbaj and Sehnaoui's attempts to erase Yassin's musical voice demonstrate their initial inability to relinquish control over the final product, which resulted in an inequitable creative relationship. Yet my interviews with Kerbaj and Sehnaoui in 2008 and 2009 demonstrate a significant shift from the views they held during the first A Trio project. In those interviews the two musicians demonstrate a more compassionate attitude toward their musical collaborators, as well as a more dialogic approach toward improvisation, where the process is valued over the final product. Kerbaj, for instance, states that ideally free improvisation ensembles do not require a designated leader; instead, the music is the leader, and all members share equal responsibility for the success of the performance. This aligns with Daniel Fischlin, Ajay Heble, and George Lipsitz's argument that "improvisatory musical practices open up abiding questions of trust, relatedness, responsibility, and social obligation, or what [Ien] Ang aptly refers to as 'togetherness-in-difference.'"[68] Echoing Sehnaoui, Kerbaj speaks about the centrality of the interchange between individual and collective agency: free improvised music is "simultaneously personal

FIGURES 7.6–7.7 "They've Got a Bomb!" concert in Beirut, January 2009: Mazen Kerbaj and Sharif Sehnaoui setting up their instruments and found objects (photograph by the author), and (*from left to right*) Charbel Haber, Mazen Kerbaj, and Sharif Sehnaoui having a verbal discussion before the performance (photograph by the author).

and community expression.... You can have totally free personal expression but are aware that your expression can't erase somebody else's expression and also has to live with the expression of the other people." Furthermore, he states that in order to achieve this balance within collective improvisation, musicians must exercise humility, and their goal should not be individual exposure. He refers to the guidelines that German trumpet player Axel Dörner provided at the Irtijal 2006 workshop: "It's like in the workshop of Axel when he tells you, 'Don't play a sound unless you feel that if you don't play it, the music will be shit—unless you feel it's *totally* necessary that you play this sound.'"[69]

Kerbaj's and Sehnaoui's accounts clearly portray their contemplative engagement with various free improvisation discourses and practices. These sociomusical values take on particular significance when placed against the backdrop of continuous sectarian clashes and protracted civil conflict. In fact, one may draw a parallel between collective musical improvisation and Lebanese society. On the surface, a Beiruti free improvisation ensemble may appear to mirror contemporary Lebanese society in its "lawlessness" and "laissez-faire" characteristics.[70] The improvisation ensemble differs in that it proposes a *dialogic* model for postwar intersectarian interaction. According to Kerbaj, much like a free improvisation ensemble, Lebanon cannot succeed as a whole if each religious sect puts its own interests ahead of those of the country. He believes that a collective project such as nation building requires patience, respect, humility, open-mindedness, tolerance, listening, and give-and-take from all parties involved.[71] As such, it may be argued that these musicians are utilizing the process of free improvisation as a testing ground for new kinds of Lebanese intersectarian relationships, where the focus is on dialogue, plurivocality, and reciprocity.

Countering Collective Amnesia through Critical War Memory

As I have shown so far, the A Trio musicians grappled with the experience of sectarian conflict and war through musical means as well as interpersonal relationships. I argue that whereas their initial musical interchanges reveal their struggle with cultural and religious difference, some of their subsequent initiatives represent a profound social critique of Lebanese postwar society and the complex relationship among sectarianism, violence, and collective memory of the civil war. In this section I shall demonstrate that this social critique is particularly evident in the socially engaged multimedia performances instigated by Yassin and Kerbaj.

Yassin's aforementioned Arab pop culture project commenced while he was collecting sound files from the Lebanese radio archives of the civil war period.[72] He has produced a number of sound collages out of this material, one of the most prominent being the twenty-three-minute-long *Civil War Tapes*. This collage brings together daily radio sounds from the civil war, from political speeches by military or clan leaders, sounds of explosions, and news broadcasts to commercials, radio jingles, jazz-rock, synthesizer pop, and propaganda music.[73] Interestingly, Yassin claims that it was most difficult for him to get hold of the political speeches made by militia leaders, although these speeches are widely known and supposedly cannot be hidden from the public. In fact, many people interrogated him suspiciously throughout the process: "Why do you need this material? Where are you from?"[74] Yassin recognizes that collecting civil war material has inescapable political connotations, particularly given the widespread mood of national forgetfulness—or "collective amnesia"—that was instituted following the postwar law of general amnesty. Sune Haugbolle, a specialist in Middle Eastern media and politics, argues that incorporating the war's events into the nation's collective memory and identity has proven problematic, largely because many citizens believe that opening the civil war to public dialogue will lead to renewed warfare. He adds that for older people who survived the war and have memories of suffering as well as guilt, collective amnesia functions as a post-traumatic coping mechanism, while sectarian and political identities provide consolation for the guilt and embarrassment.[75] Consequently, dredging up militia leaders' speeches might be considered problematic because, as Yassin puts it, these speeches "were made from all sides, and it is obvious from them that [militia leaders] are the ones that destroyed this country."[76]

Following the Lebanese-Israeli war of July 2006, Yassin again sought to utilize radio samples in his improvisatory practice with Grendizer Trio. Unlike in the first concert, however, Kerbaj joined in with samples of his own. Held on October 18, 2006, at Théâtre Monnot in Beirut, the concert was entitled "Grendizer Trio Plays with July's War," and it featured Kerbaj on trumpet, amplifications, found objects, and recorded sounds and Yassin on double bass, radio, tapes, and laptop.[77] As Lebanese music journalist Bechir Sfeir recounts, although Grendizer Trio's performance was intended to recall or represent the experience of war, it was anything but programmatic. Instead, it portrayed "the present reality in all its horror," for the audience heard the sounds of warplanes and bombs, all of which were produced by the musicians' instruments, accessories, and electronics. They also heard ambulance sirens and the echoes of everyday life during wartime, where revolutionary songs, political speeches, and victory cheers merged with radio product commercials, news segments, and breaking-news notifications.[78] By incorporating and improvising with Yassin's civil war radio recordings and Kerbaj's July war field recordings of the belliphonic, the musicians melded into one framework all the wartime sonic details that the audience had collectively experienced within the Lebanese context. Yassin explains that "one can refer to this as a 'site-specific concert' since it tackles material that the people have already lived through within their collective memory."[79]

Yassin seems quite confident that Grendizer Trio's initiatives have helped to bring the Lebanese audience closer to the otherwise-abstract practice of free improvised music.[80] Yet it is equally important to note that in the process of connecting with local audiences, the trio has succeeded in foregrounding a dimension of Lebanese collective memory that is usually cloaked in whispers. As I mentioned earlier, the previously segregated members of A Trio were able to establish initial points of commonality through their shared civil war experiences of radio and television media. Likewise, I believe that through their war-related improvisatory performances, Yassin and Kerbaj have been able to tap into civilian listeners' *sonic* memories of the civil war by providing them with a familiar platform of armed-combat sounds, political speech excerpts, and pop culture references from that period. What is truly radical is the way the musicians, through improvisation, deconstruct and reconstruct these audiovisual elements in an effort to *manipulate* audience members' individual memories and propose a collective, nonpartisan memory of the civil war. In *Civil War Tapes*, for instance, Yassin does not highlight one-sided political speeches or distinguishable instances of violence, such as specific massacres that had clear victims and perpetrators—these would have communicated a politically partisan perspective of the civil war. Instead, he decides to meld sounds from *all* opposing sides into a single musical framework. Similarly, Kerbaj and Yassin later combined sounds from the July 2006 war with sounds from the civil war within their "Grendizer Trio Plays with July's War" concert. Besides demonstrating the continuity of war across generations, this strategy demonstrates the musicians' general aversion to violence, regardless of the perpetrator or victim. This view is evident in Yassin's assertion about the civil war: "West Beirut was the leftist pole ... which was the enemy for people in East Beirut. At the same time, East Beirut's ideologies were considered the enemy in the West. And this is why we ultimately did not believe either side because the civil war ended in a ridiculous manner, which made you see that it was not worth it from the beginning—all the blood that was wasted was not worth this ridiculous cause. Thus, it was very difficult to side with anyone."[81]

Yassin and Kerbaj concurrently deploy the versatile practice of free improvisation to communicate and affectively amplify sonically what some scholars have been claiming for decades—that despite their perceived differences, all Lebanese people share a common experience of fear, grief, and trauma.[82] In fact, according to film scholar Lina Khatib, the most striking similarity among people on either side of the historical Green Line is the division between militias and civilians, "where each community seems to be oppressed by its supposed 'protectors.'"[83] By juxtaposing various militia leaders' propaganda speeches with contextually indistinguishable bomb sounds, the musicians' war-related improvisations indiscriminately critique *all* militias involved in the civil war, thereby promoting an antisectarian stance. When performed for a religiously heterogeneous audience, these improvisations also challenge the widespread Lebanese perception of personal victimization and private communal memory; alternatively, they propose a sonic dichotomy between civilian and militia culture, thereby highlighting the audience's shared civilian experience of the war.[84] Such initiatives thus challenge both collective amnesia and a nondiscriminatory flood of memory, instead supporting a third option known as "selective amnesia." Initially proposed by Lebanese historian Fawwaz Traboulsi, this process has been described as "constructive forgetfulness" or "artfully selective oblivion." According to Haugbolle, selective amnesia would entail a "balanced, historical understanding" of the civil war that focuses on the reasons for the war and the lessons that can be drawn from it, while forgetting the gruesome details that inform private memory and fuel sectarian enmity.[85]

"Playing for Keeps" in Postwar Lebanon

Throughout this chapter, I have detailed the ways in which improvisatory interchanges model and potentially facilitate changes that have implications for broader aspects of Lebanese society. My analysis of Lebanese musicians who ascribe to the practice of free improvised music in postwar Beirut suggests that this practice is valuable precisely because it moves beyond parochial views of identity.

Since free improvisation lacks conventional stylistic constraints, its built-in freedom provides a largely inclusive space for practitioners to construct and express their individual identities. Kerbaj and Yassin have in fact been able to cultivate uniquely Lebanese sonic-musical identities by incorporating and interacting with context-specific audiovisual elements such as belliphonic sounds and Arab pop culture samples. Concurrently, owing to its resistance to labeling, free improvisation seems to have provided just the right space for Lebanese musicians of diverse backgrounds to come together following protracted sectarian conflict and geographic segregation. After all, this music's lack of association with the cultural or religious backgrounds of A Trio's members translated into a common, neutral ground where musical dialogue could be initiated, unfettered by an excess of cultural baggage. Furthermore, free improvisation's malleable nature, coupled with its ideals of creative freedom and collective dialogue, resulted in a unique intersectarian exchange that provided a model on which A Trio members based their visions of a functional postwar society.

My analysis further reveals the ways in which free improvised music contributes to a Middle Eastern society still addressing the atrocities of civil war and a fractured social fabric. Building on the versatility of this practice, for instance, Grendizer Trio has been able to connect to local audiences through the semantically abstract art form by nostalgically referencing culturally familiar sonic elements. The trio's sound collages and improvised audiovisual performances shed light on otherwise-silenced collective memories, thus deconstructing and challenging the official war memory. These performances contribute to a larger discourse that critiques Lebanese society's so-called collective amnesia, calling instead for a more informed, plurivocal memory of the war that strives to learn from the past and promote national—as opposed to sectarian—identity and solidarity. Although further research is needed to determine the range of interpretations that their work invokes, it is evident that these Lebanese improvisers are challenging social norms by interrogating deep-seated taboos in their society while offering a theoretical model for social interaction and postwar reconciliation.

In closing, I argue that free improvisation allows Kerbaj, Sehnaoui, and Yassin to transcend the violence of sectarian identity; it provides a neutral ground for the sonic encounter of difference. The cocreative and generative nature of free improvisation further enables these musicians to interrogate local histories of intersectarian violence, while deconstructing collective memory of the civil war and critically engaging with contemporary sociopolitical realities. These Lebanese improvisatory encounters represent a reclamation of political agency and a refusal of an inherited culture of sectarianism, which propagates—and is propagated by—intersectarian enmity and hostility in Lebanon. As such, improvisation in this context emerges as a powerful tool for surviving crisis and imagining a functional postsectarian society.

NOTES

I would like to thank the following individuals and institutions for making this publication possible: the Social Sciences and Humanities Research Council of Canada, the University of Alberta, and the University of Alberta Department of Music, for their financial support; Mazen Kerbaj, Sharif Sehnaoui, and Raed Yassin, for their unique insights and constant cooperation; Dr. Michael Frishkopf, Dr. Federico Spinetti, Dr. Regula Qureshi, and Dr. Mojtaba Mahdavi, for their incredible support throughout my master's research; and the volume editors, for their insightful critiques and welcome suggestions.

1. The official website of Irtijal is http://www.irtijal.org/. Here, it is important to note that although *irtijal* is the literal Arabic translation of *improvisation*, the former should be distinguished from the culture-specific term *taqsim*, which refers to a type of musical improvisation prevalent within the Arabic classical tradition.
2. Borgo, "Negotiating Freedom," 184.
3. Hourani, *History of the Arab Peoples*, 264.
4. Shiloah, *Music in the World of Islam*, 104–9.
5. Hourani, *History of the Arab Peoples*, 351.
6. Burkhalter, "Mapping Out the Sound Memory," para. 6.
7. Salibi, *House of Many Mansions*, 2–3.
8. Khalaf, *Lebanon's Predicament*, 118–19.
9. Makdisi and Sadaka, "Lebanese Civil War," 60–63, 71.
10. Burkhalter, "Mapping Out the Sound Memory," para. 11. Along with three other composers, the Rahbani Brothers (Assi and Mansour) are widely credited with creating a distinctly Lebanese musical style. Songs in the Lebanese style were short, employed the Lebanese dialect, and were characterized by the use of European instruments and Middle Eastern percussion instruments. Burkhalter, *Local Music Scenes*, 156.
11. Burkhalter, "Mapping Out the Sound Memory," paras. 7–10. Although Ziad Rahbani, Khalife, and el Haber were born into Christian families, they did not identify publicly with any religion. Their personal ideologies were strongly aligned with the pro-Palestinian leftist political parties that were based in West Beirut throughout the civil war.
12. Burkhalter, "Mapping Out the Sound Memory," paras. 7–10.
13. Kerbaj, "Infos"; and Kerbaj, "CV English."
14. The Lebanese National Higher Conservatory of Music remains the quintessential avenue for public (and affordable) music education in the country.
15. Burkhalter, "Thanks for Letting Me Hear."
16. Mazen Kerbaj, interview with the author, August 15, 2008.
17. Sharif Sehnaoui, interview with the author, June 5, 2008; and Sehnaoui, "Biography."
18. Unlike private universities in Lebanon that generally teach in English or French, the Lebanese University's primary language of instruction is Arabic.
19. Abdelnour, "Home."
20. Makdisi and Sadaka, "Lebanese Civil War," 69, 78; and Tabar, *Lebanon*, 5.
21. Haugbolle, "Memory of the Lebanese Civil War," 193.

22 On the culture of sectarianism, see Khattab et al., *Politics of Sectarianism*; on globalization and digitalization, see Burkhalter, "Multisited Avant-Gardes."
23 Frishkopf, "Introduction."
24 Burkhalter, *Local Music Scenes*, 12–15.
25 Burkhalter, "Mapping Out the Sound Memory," para. 5.
26 Burkhalter, "Multisited Avant-Gardes," 89–90.
27 Examples of Lebanese independent record labels include Those Kids Must Choke, Johnny Kafta (Kafta is Arabic for "beef kebab"), and Annihaya (Arabic for "the end").
28 Kerbaj, "Infos."
29 Examples of funding include grants provided by European and American institutions such as the Centre Culturel Français, the Goethe-Institut, the Swiss Arts Council Pro Helvetia, the American Embassy, and the Ford Foundation.
30 Sehnaoui, interview.
31 Raed Yassin, interview with the author, April 20, 2009.
32 Khattab et al., *Politics of Sectarianism*, 4–8.
33 Sehnaoui, interview.
34 Sehnaoui, interview.
35 A Trio, *A*, liner notes.
36 Khalaf, "Scares and Scars of War," 228–31.
37 Bailey, *Improvisation*, 83.
38 Kerbaj, interview, August 15, 2008.
39 Sehnaoui, interview.
40 Ricci, "Review—*Old and New Acoustics*."
41 Sehnaoui, interview. One may listen to excerpts from Sehnaoui's various recordings on SoundCloud at https://soundcloud.com/sharif-sehnaoui.
42 Wilson-Goldie, "Beirut Music Festival."
43 Burkhalter, "Thanks for Letting Me Hear"; and Burkhalter, "Mapping Out the Sound Memory."
44 El Kadi, "Satirical Illustrations," 5; see also Burkhalter, "Thanks for Letting Me Hear"; and Burkhalter, "Mapping Out the Sound Memory."
45 Hamilton, quoted in Al Maslakh, "Catalog MSLKH 04"; and Wuethrich, "Review—*The Adventures of Nabil Fawzi*."
46 Yassin, interview.
47 Yassin, interview.
48 Meyer, "Review—*Cedarhead*." For the recording, see Zerang et al., *Cedarhead*. *Darbekki* is the Lebanese term for a goblet drum that is widely used in the Middle East and North Africa.
49 Wilson-Goldie, "Beirut Music Festival." One may listen to excerpts from Yassin's various recordings on SoundCloud at https://soundcloud.com/raedyassin.
50 "Ya Habibi Ta'ala" is the name of a famous love song by Asmahan, a Syrian singer and film star who rose to prominence in the Arab world during the 1930s and 1940s.
51 Yassin, interview.
52 Burkhalter, "Thanks for Letting Me Hear."
53 Ferri, *Music during Wartime*.

54 Kerbaj, interview, August 15, 2008. On belliphonic sounds, see Daughtry, "Belliphonic Sounds and Indoctrinated Ears," 113.
55 Wilson-Goldie, "Beirut Music Festival." The track mentioned is on Al Maslakh, "Catalog MSLKH 01."
56 Mazen Kerbaj, interview with the author, January 20, 2009. One may listen to excerpts from Kerbaj's various recordings, including "Starry Night," on SoundCloud at https://soundcloud.com/mazenkerbaj.
57 Kerbaj, interview, January 20, 2009.
58 Kerbaj, "Talking To."
59 El Kadi, "Satirical Illustrations," 11.
60 Sehnaoui, interview.
61 Ang, *On Not Speaking Chinese*, quoted in Fischlin, Heble, and Lipsitz, *Fierce Urgency of Now*, 228; and Stanyek, "Transmissions of an Interculture," 113.
62 Yassin, interview.
63 Ayoub, "Lebanon between Religious Faith and Political Ideology," 242.
64 *Dabke* is a traditional line dance that has been passed down for generations among Arabs living in the mountainous areas of the Levantine region, including the Lebanese mountains.
65 As examples of music that has been forgotten, he provides obscure examples such as Mayyada, a boogie, rock 'n' roll, and jazz singer of the 1960s who sang in the Lebanese Arabic dialect, and Jacqueline, a singer from the 1980s who resembles today's sexy pop sensation Haifa Wehbe.
66 Yassin, interview.
67 Sehnaoui, interview.
68 Fischlin, Heble, and Lipsitz, *Fierce Urgency of Now*, 190.
69 Kerbaj, interview with the author, August 15, 2008.
70 Khalaf, "Scares and Scars of War," 222–23.
71 Kerbaj, interview, August 15, 2008.
72 The radio played an essential role in Lebanese citizens' daily lives during the civil war, and there were allegedly around two hundred local radio stations operating during that period. Each militia broadcast its own updates to listeners, usually concerning strategic moves, casualties, and road blockades. Burkhalter, "Mapping Out the Sound Memory."
73 Burkhalter, "Mapping Out the Sound Memory."
74 Yassin, interview. Within Lebanon's sectarian society, inquiring about one's ancestral city usually betrays a desire to uncover that person's sectarian affiliation and political views.
75 Haugbolle, "Memory of the Lebanese Civil War," 194–202.
76 Yassin, interview.
77 Kerbaj, "News."
78 Sfeir, "'The July War' at Théâtre Monnot."
79 Yassin, interview.
80 Yassin, interview.
81 Yassin, interview.
82 Khalaf, "Culture, Collective Memory," 277–78.

83 Khatib, *Lebanese Cinema*, 68.
84 According to Haugbolle, private memory is frequently communicated through cultural intimacy, defined as "the social and cultural language employed by a social group to make sense of its past and present, often in response to the misrepresenting generalizations of the nation-state." Haugbolle, "Memory of the Lebanese Civil War," 199.
85 Haugbolle, "Memory of the Lebanese Civil War," 197.

BIBLIOGRAPHY

Abdelnour, Christine. Home page. Christine Abdelnour Sehnaoui's website. Accessed March 15, 2016. http://christineabdelnoursehnaoui.jimdo.com/.
Ang, Ien. *On Not Speaking Chinese: Living between Asia and the West*. London: Routledge, 2001.
A Trio. *A*. La CDthèque, 2003, compact disc.
Ayoub, Mahmoud. "Lebanon between Religious Faith and Political Ideology." In *Peace for Lebanon? From War to Reconstruction*, edited by Deirdre Collings, 241–48. Boulder, CO: Lynne Rienner, 1994.
Bailey, Derek. *Improvisation: Its Nature and Practice in Music*. New York: Da Capo, 1993.
Borgo, David. "Negotiating Freedom: Values and Practices in Contemporary Improvised Music." *Black Music Research Journal* 22, no. 2 (2002): 165–88.
Burkhalter, Thomas. *Local Music Scenes and Globalization: Transnational Platforms in Beirut*. New York: Routledge, 2013.
Burkhalter, Thomas. "Mapping Out the Sound Memory of Beirut: A Survey of the Music of a War Generation." In *Itinéraires Esthétiques et Scènes Culturelles au Proche-Orient*, edited by Nicolas Puig and Franck Mermier, 103–25. Beirut: Presses de l'Institut Français du Proche-Orient, 2007. http://books.openedition.org/ifpo/550.
Burkhalter, Thomas. "Multisited Avant-Gardes or World Music 2.0? Musicians from Beirut and Beyond between Local Production and Euro-American Reception." In *The Arab Avant-Garde: Music, Politics, Modernity*, edited by Thomas Burkhalter, Kay Dickinson, and Benjamin Harbert, 89–118. Middletown, CT: Wesleyan University Press, 2013.
Burkhalter, Thomas. "Thanks for Letting Me Hear the War Again." *Norient*, July 31, 2006. http://norient.com/en/stories/2006war/.
Daughtry, Martin. "Belliphonic Sounds and Indoctrinated Ears: The Dynamics of Military Listening in Wartime Iraq." In *Pop When the World Falls Apart: Music in the Shadow of Doubt*, edited by Eric Weisbard, 111–44. Durham, NC: Duke University Press, 2012.
El Kadi, Rana. "Satirical Illustrations and Militant Improvisations: A Multimodal Social-Semiotic Analysis of Mazen Kerbaj's Wartime Art." *Popular Music and Society* 40, no. 2 (December 2015): 1–21.
Ferri, Leonardo. "Mazen Kerbaj Music during Wartime 2007." Video, 9:50. Uploaded September 12, 2007. https://youtu.be/9lcgou7kkdk.
Fischlin, Daniel, Ajay Heble, and George Lipsitz. *The Fierce Urgency of Now: Improvisation and the Ethics of Cocreation*. Durham, NC: Duke University Press, 2013.

Frishkopf, Michael. "Introduction: Music and Media in the Arab World and *Music and Media in the Arab World* as Music and Media in the Arab World: A Metadiscourse." In *Music and Media in the Arab World*, edited by Michael Frishkopf, 1–66. Cairo: American University in Cairo Press, 2010.

Haugbolle, Sune. "Public and Private Memory of the Lebanese Civil War." *Comparative Studies of South Asia, Africa and the Middle East* 25, no. 1 (2005): 191–203.

Hourani, Albert. *A History of the Arab Peoples*. Cambridge, MA: Belknap Press of Harvard University Press, 2010.

Kerbaj, Mazen. *Brt Vrt Zrt Krt*. Al Maslakh MSLKH 01, 2005, compact disc.

Kerbaj, Mazen. "CV English." Mazen Kerbaj's website. Accessed March 15, 2016. http://www.kerbaj.com/CVenglish.html.

Kerbaj, Mazen. "Infos." Mazen Kerbaj's website. Accessed March 15, 2016. http://www.kerbaj.com/infos.html.

Kerbaj, Mazen. "News." Mazen Kerbaj's website. Accessed March 15, 2016. http://www.kerbaj.com/news.html.

Kerbaj, Mazen. "Talking To: Mazen Kerbaj." *NOW*, August 2, 2007. Accessed March 15, 2016. https://now.mmedia.me/lb/en/interviews/talking_to_mazen_kerbaj.

Khalaf, Samir. "Culture, Collective Memory, and the Restoration of Civility." In *Peace for Lebanon? From War to Reconstruction*, edited by Deirdre Collings, 273–85. Boulder, CO: Lynne Rienner, 1994.

Khalaf, Samir. *Lebanon's Predicament*. New York: Columbia University Press, 1987.

Khalaf, Samir. "The Scares and Scars of War." In *Cultural Resistance: Global and Local Encounters in the Middle East*, 201–33. London: Saqi Books, 2001.

Khatib, Lina. *Lebanese Cinema: Imagining the Civil War and Beyond*. New York: I. B. Tauris, 2008.

Khattab, Lara, Shoghig Mikaelian, Jinan Al-Habbal, Bassel Salloukh, and Rabie Barakat. *The Politics of Sectarianism in Postwar Lebanon*. London: Pluto, 2015.

Makdisi, Samir, and Richard Sadaka. "The Lebanese Civil War, 1975–1990." In *Understanding Civil War: Evidence and Analysis*, vol. 2, *Europe, Central Asia, and Other Regions*, edited by Paul Collier and Nicholas Sambanis, 59–85. Washington, DC: World Bank, 2005.

Al Maslakh Records. "Catalog MSLKH 01—*Brt Vrt Zrt Krt*." Accessed March 10, 2016. http://www.almaslakh.org/catalog_mslkh01.php.

Al Maslakh Records. "Catalog MSLKH 04—*The Adventures of Nabil Fawzi*." Accessed March 15, 2016. http://www.almaslakh.org/catalog_mslkh04.php.

Meyer, Bill. "Review—*Cedarhead*." *Dusted Magazine*, July 11, 2007. http://www.dustedmagazine.com/reviews/3678.

Ricci, Massimo. "Review—*Old and New Acoustics*." *Touching Extremes*, December 4, 2011. https://touchingextremes.wordpress.com/2011/12/04/sharif-sehnaoui-old-and-new-acoustics/.

Salibi, Kamal. *A House of Many Mansions: The History of Lebanon Reconsidered*. New York: I. B. Tauris, 2003.

Sehnaoui, Sharif. "Biography." Sharif Sehnaoui's website. Accessed March 15, 2016. http://www.sharifsehnaoui.net/bio.htm.

Sehnaoui, Sharif. *Old and New Acoustics*. Al Maslakh MSLKH 11, 2010, compact disc.
Sfeir, Bechir. "'The July War' at Théâtre Monnot . . . Starring Grendizer Trio." *Al-Akhbar*, October 18, 2006. http://www.al-akhbar.com/node/160368.
Shiloah, Amnon. *Music in the World of Islam: A Socio-cultural Study*. Detroit, MI: Wayne State University Press, 1995.
Stanyek, Jason. "Transmissions of an Interculture: Pan-African Jazz and Intercultural Improvisation." In *The Other Side of Nowhere: Jazz, Improvisation, and Communities in Dialogue*, edited by Daniel Fischlin and Ajay Heble, 87–130. Middletown, CT: Wesleyan University Press, 2004.
Tabar, Paul. *Lebanon: A Country of Emigration and Immigration*. Cairo: American University in Cairo (Center for Migration and Refugee Studies), 2011. http://www.aucegypt.edu/GAPP/cmrs/reports/Documents/Tabar080711.pdf.
Wilson-Goldie, Kaelen. "Beirut Music Festival Gives Dissonance a Fair Hearing." *Daily Star*, July 8, 2005. http://www.dailystar.com.lb/Culture/Art/2005/Jul-08/95761-beirut-music-festival-gives-dissonance-a-fair-hearing.ashx.
Wuethrich, Matthew. "Review—*The Adventures of Nabil Fawzi*." *Dusted Magazine*, April 17, 2007. http://www.dustedmagazine.com/reviews/3505.
Zerang, Michael, Sharif Sehnaoui, Mazen Kerbaj, Raed Yassin, Christine (Abdelnour) Sehnaoui, Charbel Haber, Jassem Hindi, and Bechir Saade. *Cedarhead*. Al Maslakh MSLKH 06, 2006, compact disc.

EIGHT Street Concerts and Sexual Harassment in Post-Mubarak Egypt

Ṭarab *as Affective Politics*

DARCI SPRENGEL

In the two years following the 2011 revolution that toppled the thirty-year military dictatorship of Hosni Mubarak (r. 1981–2011), new forms of art and creative expression, including public theater, film, storytelling, graffiti, and music concerts, flourished in Egyptian public spaces.[1] Seeking to produce a new public culture, activists and artists from a variety of disciplines used the street as a stage for improvisatory practices and expressions. In so doing, they aimed to challenge state policies that had limited public gathering and expression and, in so doing, fulfill some of the goals of the 2011 revolution.[2]

One such undertaking was Mini Mobile Concerts (which I will abbreviate as MMC), founded shortly after the revolution by musician Ramez Ashraf in Alexandria, Egypt's second-largest city.[3] It consisted of small impromptu concerts of two to four musicians held in streets and squares throughout the city. Between 2011 and 2014, MMC staged about fifty such concerts featuring traditional Arab art music and "independent music," a genre encompassing a wide diversity of styles blending Arab musical aesthetics—including rhythms, tonalities, and ornamentation—with globally circulating musical genres such as jazz, rock, and electronic. Musicians experienced these concerts as forming community, calming anxiety, pacifying aggression, beautifying public space, breaking down "the barrier of fear," uplifting public feeling and consciousness, and overall supporting the goals of the 2011 revolution.[4] This revolution endeavored to institute civic and democratic rights, as well as end systemic inequity and poverty, high unemployment, police brutality, and corrupt governance.

Musicians in MMC aimed to transform their society by utilizing improvisatory practices in two ways. First, they used improvisation as a method for organizing concerts. Keeping their concerts small and unadvertised, and holding them in different public locations, served as a means to challenge the stasis in public culture and everyday life caused by the restrictions imposed in part by an authoritarian regime. Second, and more significantly, MMC's approach to performance centered on an improvised interactive process between performer and audience that ideally resulted in affective transformation. This approach has long been a central characteristic of musicking in the Arab world. Ṭarab, which is often simplified in English translation as "musical ecstasy," encompasses both a culture in which music is treated first and foremost as an affective practice and the name of a specific ecstatic state caused by music performance and listening. In the urban context, it has primarily been attributed (at least among middle- and upper-class Egyptians) to Arab art music (al-mūsīqa al-ʿarabīyyah), a genre associated with music connoisseurs that for at least the past half century has been performed live almost exclusively in private homes or at official concert venues.

Musicians' reworking of ṭarab culture through performing alternative "fusion" musical styles and engaging common Egyptian listeners toward revolutionary ends signals a departure from some historical understandings of ṭarab as strongly associated with Arab art music. I argue that the transformative work of MMC performances in the context of revolution indicates a politicization of ṭarab *culture* and what amounts more broadly to an emergent political form I call "affective politics." I define "affective politics" as the intentional utilization of the body's capacity to affect and be affected toward the destabilization or reification of specific power relations.[5] In the context of postrevolutionary Egypt, improvisatory street-music concerts enact affective politics by unsettling social boundaries, such as those between audience and performer, citizen and activist, man and woman. This subversion has the potential to achieve some goals of the 2011 revolution by building new social solidarities that form the basis of an alternative public culture. When successful, these concerts produce moments of lived social change under authoritarian conditions that repress more discursive forms of activism and social transformation.[6]

As an approach that treats musical experience as primarily affective, ṭarab culture foregrounds the relationship between music and the body through what is often oversimplified as a transformation of "emotion." The politicization of ṭarab culture, in which the listener's capacity to both affect and be affected by music is utilized toward realizing revolutionary goals, invites a rethinking of oppositional politics. Dominant approaches in Western social theory often conceptualize oppositional politics through liberal subjectivity, which treats political subjects as ideally rational, disembodied, engaged in critical debate, and affectively self-contained.[7] The liberal subject is built on a spurious Cartesian mind-body dualism, in which the mind is given primacy over the body, where emotions lie in a state of interiority.[8] Stemming in part from this dualism is a deep antipathy toward the idea of not fully being in control of the self. Reason is linked to control. Losing control is overwhelmingly gendered as feminine and racialized through its association with the "uncivilized" or "primitive."[9]

In addition to perpetuating dominant power relations, this model leaves many avenues for political participation undertheorized. For example, authoritarian regimes violently repress direct protest and discursive critique, resulting in self-censorship that to some social theorists may indicate complacent or apathetic populations. Likewise, in situations of gender- and sexuality-based violence, disembodiment is impossible, because the body serves as the very basis of such relations of inequality. Those toward whom violence is directed are usually situated as the irrational other against which the reasoned individual is defined. Those on the losing end of this power imbalance are thus robbed of their own claims to reason and find themselves instead arguing against superior contentions to know "what's good" for them or what their "true nature" is.[10]

Scholars, especially feminist and queer theorists, across a variety of disciplines have shown how the devaluing of the body and of emotion is involved in securing a hierarchy of some bodies (white, male, elite, Global North) over others (female, black and brown, poor, Global South). This chapter engages theories of affect emerging in the past several decades from feminist studies to avoid the false mind-body dualism that reifies these unequal relations of power. Encompassing more than emotion, affects are not self-contained or interior but instead emerge through encounter. They synthesize the body and the mind and thus involve reason and passion equally, posing them as a continuum.[11] Looking at both oppositional politics and musical improvisation through the lens of affect refocuses our attention on the ways each of these practices is embodied, encompassing both emotion and cognition. Whereas discursive models of oppositional politics privilege the persuasive agency of the (reasoned) speaker, an attention to affective politics, in contrast, allows one to focus on the solidarities that form through intersubjective deep listening. Such listening treats speaker and audience as equals; *both* contribute to a visceral affective exchange that emerges through encounter with the other.

Viewing improvisation as a form of affective politics, then, gets away from notions of the performer as genius and sole creator. In ṭarab culture, musical outcomes result from the unique affective interaction between performer and audience in each specific time and place. In MMC, this affective potential is used to form unlikely solidarities that are meaningful in the context of the postrevolutionary violence that had exacerbated social divisions in Egypt since the revolution of 2011. Addressing that context, this chapter demonstrates how losing control of the self, becoming vulnerable to experiencing the other, can be a sought-after ideal utilized toward revolutionary ends. Further, the emphasis in ṭarab culture on musical experience as intersubjective and affective predates and extends Western feminist interventions that have sought to unsettle the centrality of the disembodied rational subject in Western social theory. Signaling the emergence of a different kind of political engagement, my notion of affective politics rooted in ṭarab culture enables alternative ways of producing a more livable society *without* relying on traditional modes of political opposition that are so easily invalidated under unequal relations of power.[12]

Although MMC musicians strove for many social and political changes through their performances, I focus here on a single issue: sexual harassment. Sexual harassment is often treated as uniquely pervasive in Egypt. A 2013 UN study, for instance, reports that 99 percent of women in Egypt have experienced it.[13] It received heightened national and international attention when dozens of female protesters were brutally assaulted during the 2011 revolution and its aftermath. With some survivors bravely coming forward to publicly condemn it, sexual harassment became a central issue in defining a post-Mubarak Egyptian society, with larger implications for Egyptian conceptions of self, nation, and ethical citizenship. This essay examines how sexual harassment connects broad social changes to intimate daily practices. These changes involve state policing and policies toward its citizens, especially in terms of the regulation and disciplining of the body, which have had profound effects on daily life and the gender relations that order public space. I focus on one MMC event performed by a female musician to examine how improvisatory performance engages issues of gender, class, and sexuality, transforming them, in some instances, to produce what was understood to be a new public culture.[14]

Sexual harassment has likewise long been associated with certain racialized others in the West. The 2016 "sex attacks" in Germany, for instance, were overwhelmingly attributed to Arab refugees and men of "North African descent." Such discourses situate sexual harassment as a practice that originates in the Middle East and North Africa, one that is foreign to Germany and Europe. Major European government studies have shown, however, that sexual violence is a pervasive problem throughout Europe, with more than half of European women having experienced it.[15] The recent Me Too movement further demonstrates that harassment is not a phenomenon conveniently reducible to any culture, race, or religion. It is global in scope.[16] Discourses that attribute sexual harassment to certain men and not others homogenize and criminalize entire populations and are used to perpetuate and justify state violence, including racial profiling, the policing and deportation of Arab and Muslim immigrants, and Western economic and military intervention in the Middle East.[17] Hence, my analysis of sexual harassment at a particular moment when it was at the forefront of national debate in recent Egyptian history is not meant to suggest that it is a phenomenon unique to, or more pervasive in, Egypt. Instead, I show how one female musician used the specific cultural tools available to her to tackle its manifestation in a particular time and place.

Ṭarab beyond Arab Art Music

Musicians in MMC are part of what Egyptians refer to as the independent music scene.[18] Independent musicians are primarily male youth who rely on do-it-yourself methods such as free software and samples downloaded from the internet and low-budget studio recordings.[19] Generally speaking, they do not rely on the multinational music industry or state patronage, and the scene includes musicians who perform heavy metal, jazz, rock, electronic, and hip-hop as well as styles more heavily influenced by Arab art music, Nubian music, and musical fusions.

Many independent musicians have little or no institutional training. Instead, they often learn their instruments through watching YouTube videos and playing covers of their favorite songs. With many musicians joining bands after playing their instruments for only a few months, the independent music scene is primarily built on a culture of jamming in which young men, especially, get together with peers to experiment musically. In these jams, traditionally held in private homes or studios, musicians gather with friends for a night of collective improvisation that draws on eclectic musical languages and techniques.[20]

Though comprising musicians from diverse socioeconomic backgrounds, independent music is most commonly associated with middle-class youth, who have traditionally made up its primary audience. This association is due in part to its use of costly electrified instruments and equipment, occasional incorporation of English lyrics, frequent references to certain Western musical styles and genres, and the dominance of the band formation (drum kit, bass guitar, electric guitar, vocals) or slight variations thereof. The focus on collective forms of music making that decenter the individual is often cited by independent musicians as a reason for their relative lack of success in mainstream media channels, because both mainstream popular music and Arab art music have primarily focused on the individual singer (*muṭrib/ muṭribah*). Nonprofit cultural venues are the main sources of support for these groups, and, as with many independent music scenes, most independent musicians make little money from their musical endeavors.[21]

In MMC performances, independent musicians perform a combination of improvisations, precomposed works, and informal jams on city streets, sidewalks, and squares. A typical MMC performance is often organized only a few hours in advance. There is no advertising apart from a status update to MMC's official Facebook page as the concert is happening.[22] Concerts occur based on the available musicians and locations deemed appropriate for the musicians, their musical styles, and the time of performance. Performers adapt the genre of music they perform, choosing, for instance, to perform Arab art music instead of "oriental rock," depending on the neighborhood, the time of day, and the gender of the performers. Likewise, performers adjust individual songs/improvisations (in tempo, length, mode, volume, timbre, and so forth) according to their skills and mood, the time of day of performance, and the perceived mood or desires of the audience. That the music MMC musicians perform is time- and place-specific gets at the heart of its transformational potential.

Although much of what they perform can be considered improvisation, the nature and effect of MMC's specific set of practices are better understood through the concept of ṭarab culture because it emphasizes an approach to experiencing music that centers on affective transformation. Eminent ethnomusicologist A. J. Racy argues that in Arab Middle Eastern performance practice, as well as in the Arabic language, there is no standard term for "improvisation."[23] Instead of defining improvisation as distinct from precomposition, Racy focuses on the concept of ṭarab as fundamental to Middle Eastern performance practice, whether "precomposed" or "improvised." Ṭarab, which does not have an exact equivalent in English, is epitomized by "the merger between music and emotional transformation" and is commonly understood to describe ecstasy experienced as a result of musical performance. Ṭarab describes both a musical genre (Arab art music, or al-mūsīqa al-ʿarabīyyah) and the "extraordinary emotional, affective state

FIGURES 8.1–8.2 Sisters Sabrin el-Guindy on *qanūn* (plucked zither) and Safinaz el-Guindy on *ʿūd* (plucked lute) at a Mini Mobile Concert at eight in the morning in al-Raml Station, downtown Alexandria, June 2013. Courtesy of the photographer, Omar Adel.

evoked by the music." It manifests when engaged listeners experience sensations of intoxication or lose their sense of time.[24]

Beyond its ties to transcendent emotional states, ṭarab is also a *culture* that encompasses ways of thinking about and practicing music in which musical experience is primarily understood in terms of affective transformation for both audience and performer. Performance in ṭarab culture centers on musicians entering a state of ecstasy through the sonic exploration of pitch, rhythm, timbre, and so forth. They then confer their ecstatic state on their audience, whose verbal and expressive feedback during the performance heightens the performer's own ecstatic state and inspires the direction the musical performance will take.

During the performance, listeners perform a variety of affective responses, including altering their facial expression or posture as well as making gestures and/or vocal exclamations such as "ah!," "ya salam!" ("How marvelous"), and even phrases such as "Ḥatmawwitnā al-yūm?" ("Are you trying to kill us?"), which compliment the performer and allude to the listener's transformed state as a form of "pleasurable affliction."[25] Such expressions on the part of the listener "inspire the performer and enhance the effectiveness of the musical performance."[26] For example, a performer, when improvising *or* when performing the skeletal framework of a precomposed work (*laḥn*), may repeat a phrase several times; elongate certain pitches, syllables, or passages; modulate to a specific mode known for expressing a particular emotional state; improvise new phrases or sections (*ḥarakāt*); and the like, based on his or her mood, audience feedback, and what he or she feels will heighten the sense of collective ecstasy.

By focusing on the interactive process between audience and performer to explain not only performance practice but also improvisational and compositional techniques in the Arab Middle East, Racy takes a different approach than other scholars who have analyzed improvisation in the region.[27] For instance, Habib Hassan Touma as well as Bruno Nettl and Ronald Riddle focus on the relationships among various melodic modes (*maqāmāt*) as a way to define Arab improvisation.[28] By contrast, Racy argues that the creative process is considered time- and place-specific and thus privileges live, embodied interaction.[29] In contrast to common Western art-music compositional practices (for instance, where composers as self-contained geniuses isolate themselves from their audience in order to compose in a way that is highly introspective and creator focused), in ṭarab culture the composer treats the audience as an indispensable source of inspiration. By understanding MMC performances through the lens of ṭarab culture, I highlight the spontaneous interactive process involving both performer and nonperformer and elide the problematic dichotomy in music performance between "improvised" and "precomposed." A context-specific performance materializes based on the mood and desires of both audience and performer. Thus, each performance, even of a well-known work, is a result of their unique, improvised interaction in a particular time and place.[30] As will become clear, the goal of MMC performances is not only what is performed but the impact a performance will have on listeners and performers as a collective.[31]

In Arab art music, ṭarab is known to have profound effects on performers and listeners. In some more critical accounts, the concerts of singer Umm Kulthum, considered one of the most emotive and masterful musicians in modern Arab history, were described as "a drug that leads Arabs to linger in truancy" and were cited as a reason for the Arabs' defeat in the 1967 war.[32] Similarly, Racy reports that after especially moving ṭarab performances, people often give the music deep philosophical meanings. One listener in his study felt that "music was love in the broadest sense, love for one's wife, love for one's family, love for everybody."[33]

The affective potential of musical experience in ṭarab culture is deeply rooted in full-bodied, agentive listening that blurs the distinction between self and other. Drawing from composer Pauline Oliveros, ethnomusicologist Judith Becker calls this type of listening "deep listening," to account for how we "experience music with our skins, with our pulse rates, and with our body temperature." A full-bodied experience, it is a secular "trancing" that produces "feelings of transcendence or a sense of communion with a power beyond oneself."[34] Going "beyond oneself" is a central characteristic of experiencing ṭarab. Ṭarab is not simply an abstraction of internal emotional states but instead "the intersubjective processes of the 'mutual tuning-in relationship' itself" between performer and listeners.[35] In Racy's study, master musician Sabah Fakhri states, "I consider the audience to be me and myself to be the audience."[36] Other performers express the dissolution between self and other through a range of metaphors. The relationship between audience and performer is, for instance, akin to two lovers where sexual arousal (which Racy argues is a metaphor for artistic inspiration) in one partner induces a like response in the other. Or the audience and performer are like "two mirrors facing each other. The image, which stands for inspiration, appearing in one mirror is reflected by the other mirror, and in turn the reflection is reflected again back and forth."[37] In these contexts, ṭarab culture enacts conceptions of self that contrast sharply with European Enlightenment ideologies that stress autonomous rationality.[38] It also demonstrates a view of listening as an agentive action itself—a listening that is a "doing"—instead of a passive activity.[39]

Mini Mobile Concerts' approach to musical experience builds from longstanding approaches to music as deeply affective and meaningful in ṭarab culture. But MMC also reworks how ṭarab has traditionally been conceptualized in the region. In most music scholarship, and in more traditional conceptions of ṭarab as Arab art music, being emotionally transformed is contingent on the presence of *sammīʿah* ("listeners"), connoisseurs of Arab art music who are knowledgeable of the musical vocabulary of ṭarab, especially as it relates to the musical idioms of Arab art music, and of the appropriate behaviors that emotionally engaged listeners manifest.[40] Racy, for instance, reports that concerts by highly skilled musicians that were dominated by non-sammīʿah were converted into a "'sing-along,' 'clap-along' occasion" in which the music was kept on an emotionally superficial level.[41] In another instance, a performer of Arab art music claimed that "if there were more *sammīʿah* in the world there would be less evil and fewer wars," revealing the importance of certain types of listeners.[42] Additionally, by presenting a range of musical styles influenced especially by contemporary popular music, the music MMC musicians perform does not sit comfortably as ṭarab music, traditionally strongly associated with Arab art music, a style often viewed as synonymous with ṭarab itself.

By contrast, MMC musicians perform music in street locations where they aim to encounter a variety of listeners from diverse backgrounds who may not be knowledgeable of Arab art-musical language and techniques.[43] Given the waning of ṭarab culture and deep listening over the past several decades, listeners today are regarded to be more accustomed to genres, such as Arab pop music or rock, that are considered to be much less affectively charged. By bringing their diverse and "fusion" musical styles to the public street, many MMC musicians attempt to bridge the gap between dominant secular popular music and genres more strongly linked with full-bodied, or deep, listening practices. Many build their music from the rhythms, melodic modes, and styles of ornamentation found in Arab art music albeit mixed with elements not traditionally associated with ṭarab, such as distorted electric guitar. As part of navigating this new middle ground, musicians differed in the terms they used to describe the transformative potential of their practice. Some preferred less-localized terms, such as the English word *energy*, or *ṭarab lite*.

While remaining sensitive to the diverse language musicians used to describe their practices, I use the concept of ṭarab culture as an umbrella term to foreground the common ground among their various approaches: that, ideally, music should be profoundly affective in ways that dissolve hierarchical distinctions between self and other. It is the political potential subsumed in this dissolution that drove so many MMC musicians to perform in the street. While keeping in mind that these performances did not always realize their own egalitarian ideals, a topic I've explored elsewhere, I concentrate here on musicians' *desires* and lived *experiences* of both affecting others *and* being affected, here based on their own accounts of street performances.[44]

Ṭarab Culture and the Street

Perceived changes in listening practices, from deep to more superficial listening, point to broader social changes in public culture that MMC musicians engage in their ṭarab-lite style of music. Although ṭarab culture is sometimes treated as a timeless expression of urban musical culture in the Arab Middle East, the availability of it, or desire for it, is deeply intertwined with changing social, cultural, and political contexts. Throughout the nineteenth and twentieth centuries, listening was increasingly divested of its agentive dimensions, becoming diluted to passive receptivity as part of a process of creating what anthropologist Charles Hirschkind calls a "modern national auditory—an ear resonant with the tonalities of reason and progress."[45] Though stemming from a variety of factors and influences, this tendency has been facilitated by a general trend of increased government regulation and institutionalization of music's affective potential as a means of developing a "modern" Egyptian nation.[46] Owing to space constraints, I present an admittedly incomplete history here to give a general sense of how music performance and listening practices have changed, especially over the course of the past century. This history is necessary to understand how and why MMC's practices are experienced as revolutionary, producing a new public culture, in the present.

Before and at the beginning of the twentieth century, the *takht*, a small ensemble comprising four to six musicians each playing a different instrument—vocalist, violin, *qānūn* (plucked zither), *ʿūd* (lute), *riqq* (tambourine), and *nāy* (reed flute)—was the most popular urban performance ensemble. The relationship and balance among the instrumentalists, each adding their own timbre and improvisations, were envisaged to induce most effectively a state of ṭarab. The importance of the takht, however, began to decline after the 1920s, when the British-supported Egyptian monarchy was established, in favor of more "modern" musical aesthetics and performance practices.[47]

Owing to these changing performance aesthetics, the influence of Western art music, and the introduction of recording technology, the twentieth century heralded an increase in what ethnomusicologist Salwa el-Shawan calls "mediated transmission" between composers and performers.[48] By the 1940s, changing musical aesthetics, mediated by transcribers, conductors, and sound recordings, contributed to the alteration of what was traditionally understood to be musical sound, the decreased centrality of improvisatory practices, and the introduction of new norms of musician-audience interaction.[49] In the case of sound recording, for instance, instead of performing and composing through an interaction with the audience, as had been customary in ṭarab culture, performers were forced to adapt to the limitations of recording devices. According to Racy, "this [recording] equipment became the performer's indirect channel to his audience.... This meant the creation of a musical language meticulously designed and remodeled to suit the new medium."[50]

These changes in composition and performance practice were accompanied by state and social efforts to regulate the public and embodied nature of the arts. Although a common site of performance in the nineteenth century, the street became increasingly viewed as inappropriate for artistic performances and entertainment.[51] The Egyptian state, for instance, even before the British occupation of Egypt beginning in 1892, had long viewed public spaces as dangerous sites where those structurally excluded from positions of power could challenge government control.[52] Whereas male street performance was restricted out of fear that it promoted "disorderliness" later in the twentieth century, female entertainers were criminalized first owing to the female body's heightened affective potential. In her study of contemporary working-class female entertainers, anthropologist Karin van Nieuwkerk argues that female entertainers have traditionally been considered shameful in Egypt because of the notion of the female body as primarily "sexual" whereas the male body is viewed as "productive."[53] As sexualized bodies, women who entertain, whether through singing, playing an instrument, or dancing, are often considered morally suspect for using the female power of seduction to make a living. The female body's power to affect—to cause sexual arousal in others—rendered it dangerous to the existing social order.

In short, the arts became increasingly institutionalized and regulated through classed and gendered discourses of "morality" for women, or "hygiene" and "order" for men.[54] Ultimately, the removal of the arts from daily life amounted to a form of affective management in which improvised interactive exchanges between performers and audiences were increasingly limited and separated—especially along class lines. This affective management of public culture, which was closely tied to the regulation of public space and the body, was considered fundamental to forming a modern Egyptian nation and solidifying the power of the state.

These processes continued after the Egyptian military overthrew the British-supported Egyptian monarchy in 1952. The newly independent Egyptian state founded the Ministry of Culture, which sought to centralize the arts and use them to define a sovereign nation independent of colonial powers. By the 1970s, performers were required to pass government exams and obtain certification to perform at state-run venues or sell their work commercially; the state, however, only supported artists whose work conformed to its particular brand of nationalism.⁵⁵ There was a concerted effort, for example, on the part of government officials and cultural elites to patronize large orchestras (*firqāt*) (including a conductor, a chorus instead of a solo vocalist, and large instrument sections) that could "compete" with European ensembles. Street and more intimate public performances were moved to large concert halls, where performances began to follow the norms associated with Western symphony orchestras, in which the audience was required to remain silent. Such changes amounted to attempts to regulate, restrict, and in some cases eliminate the improvisatory interaction between audience and performer.⁵⁶

In the 1970s, the state initiated new neoliberal economic policies (*al-infitāḥ*) that aligned Egypt more closely with the West, increased foreign investment and development catered to the needs of the middle and upper classes, and reduced state welfare for low-income Egyptians.⁵⁷ This neoliberal turn reoriented culture toward consumerism, with official cultural production centralized in either multinational corporations or the state's patronage. As the Egyptian music industry became multinational, it prioritized the new Arab pop genre, characterized by three- to five-minute songs that were associated with superficial instead of deep listening.⁵⁸ Hence, ṭarab, as an ecstatic mode of full-bodied listening and affective engagement through music, further waned in availability and popularity in the 1970s. Many Egyptian youth who championed independent music around the time of the 2011 revolution considered themselves and their music to be independent from this multinational music industry, which they believed promoted a consumer lifestyle instead of social critique, and independent from the state, which, since the 1980s, has remained the largest patron of noncommercial arts in Egypt.⁵⁹

Along with the increased centralization and regulation of the arts, emergency laws and the repressive control of public spaces in the second half of the twentieth century made non-state-sanctioned music performance in public increasingly risky. Through "security" campaigns, the Mubarak regime further politicized the street as a social space. As government services for poor and working-class neighborhoods began to disappear following Egypt's 1970s neoliberal shift, services were replaced by nonstate organizations such as the Muslim Brotherhood. The state sought to curb the influence and power of such groups, using the enforcement of emergency laws and state violence to control especially working-class men in various spaces, such as streets, mosques, and local markets.⁶⁰ These laws dictated that civilians could be detained without reason and for an unlimited period of time, and they criminalized unauthorized public gatherings.[61] Security forces were legally granted extensive powers to stop, search, question, and detain individuals suspected of threatening order and security. By the 1990s, emergency laws meant to diminish the power of nonstate organizations had been normalized.

Acts of violence and domination of public space were repeated and patterned over the course of thirty years during the Mubarak regime, which used fear as a means of control. Though many state policies targeted men in working-class neighborhoods, they were not the only victims of these policies—the atmosphere of fear created by the state was enough to influence the behavior of those whose communities were not specifically targeted. Police worked in uniform as well as in civilian clothes, and it was widely known that in addition to the official police, there existed a large network of undercover informants. Anthropologist Sherine Hafez maintains that through state violence, civilians were instilled with a sense of "randomness and unreliability" so that it was "this potential for random violence—more than the act of violence itself—that promoted fear and uncertainty among Egyptians."[62]

Whereas men, and working-class men in particular, were considered the primary targets of police repression, women also felt its effects owing in part to its impact on gender relations. Some scholars contend that working-class masculinity, which values men who are brave, tough, assertive, prideful, and powerful, has been humiliated by years of government repression. Repression results in an "injured masculinity" that working-class men negotiate through attempts to control public spaces by enforcing a "moral order." Enforcing moral order can include monitoring women's behavior and attire in public through gossip, exclusion, and harassment.[63] By problematically demonizing working-class men as the sole or primary perpetrators, such studies do not do enough to interrogate middle-class and elite discourses, reinforcing trends that attribute sexual harassment only to certain deviant "others." Other scholars working outside the Egyptian context have demonstrated that militarism generally increases violence against women, with the military being a major site where male bodies are gendered through discipline, violence, and aggression.[64] The Egyptian military is one of the most powerful institutions in Egypt, and there is compulsory military service lasting one to three years for all men between the ages of eighteen and thirty.[65] Historian Hanan Hammad has shown, however, that sexual harassment in Egypt is not a new phenomenon but has historically risen during moments of drastic change, such as in response to industrialization and urban migration throughout the nineteenth and twentieth centuries. Through these changes, women increasingly played more prominent roles in public life, including by working in factories or going to school. Hammad concludes that sexual harassment is an expression of rising class and gender tensions during rapid periods of transformation, with disenfranchised males using it as a means to impose dominance.[66] In short, and regardless of the cause, public space was also understood to be a controlled environment for many women.[67]

Hence, a militarized public atmosphere of fear, which Egyptian activists refer to as "the barrier of fear," was the only environment many youth in the country had ever known. Many involved in the independent music scene grew up in a public culture in which the state endorsed only certain art forms, and as the Mubarak regime became more involved in a "politics of security," those not under government patronage could easily be suspected of engaging in criminal activity or of challenging the regime.[68] The Mubarak years, then, normalized state domination of urban public space and control over what would become mainstream arts. The atmosphere of fear that Mubarak's government fostered discouraged both male and female musicians in the independent music scene from attempting to perform music in the street for fear of arrest, imprisonment, and/or harassment.

Ṭarab as Social Change

This public atmosphere characterized by fear and paranoia dramatically changed during the initial eighteen days of protest in 2011, when independent musicians joined millions of protesters in Cairo and Alexandria by spontaneously performing music in public space for the first time in living memory. The revolution's festive public culture helped infuse public space with new affects: it temporarily transformed the street from a site of government dominance and fear to an artistic space of unity, hope, and potential.[69] Independent musicians, such as guitarist Ramy Essam, helped facilitate this affective transformation by improvising melodies to accompany and lead protest chants. Protesters reported that the presence of music during the protests helped them unite and endure the long days and nights spent in public spaces.[70] This period indeed marked one of the periods of drastic change identified by Hammad, when both women and men were highly visible and active in public space in ways unprecedented in living memory.

During the political and social turmoil in the years that followed, however, the unity experienced in public space did not continue.[71] Differing ideas about who and what should replace Mubarak's deeply entrenched military dictatorship pitted citizens against each other, fueling social animosities that sometimes escalated into violence. Between 2011 and 2014 especially, there was a stark increase in reports of sexual harassment and assault, including organized gang rapes, of women in public places.[72] Many women and men organized to combat this violence, creating nonprofit organizations and squads of antiharassment volunteers to monitor protests. It was common knowledge among activists that the perpetrators were paid by the regime to punish female protesters.[73] Police often did not intervene to protect women and, especially during political protests, were sometimes the perpetrators themselves with the intention of deterring political activism.[74] These attacks also increased animosity between different social classes as the perpetrators were assumed to be from the working class.[75] After two years of deeply polarizing politics and economic instability, a military regime closely resembling that of Mubarak returned to power in 2013. This "new" military regime, headed by military-general-turned-president Abdel-Fattah El-Sisi, exacerbated the repressive policies of its predecessor. It recriminalized public protest in 2013 and imprisoned tens of thousands it accused of challenging the regime, including the leaders of the 2011 revolution.[76]

In this precarious atmosphere, street performances continued in order to maintain the revolutionary "spirit" and perpetuate the "ongoing revolution" (*al-thowrah al-mustamirrah*).[77] Responding to the belief that the 2011 revolution had failed, Ramy Essam claimed, "The closest weapon we have in our hands now is art.... Of course I want the people back in the streets chanting against the system, but our best option now is art."[78] That the arts, and not traditional political protest, represented the "best option" indicates a strategic shift. For some Egyptian activists, direct protest was no longer tenable since it was only fueling social animosity and again being met with severe repression. Discursive critique and protest became embedded in a relationship of "cruel optimism":[79] the more activists protested in these conventional ways, the more they were harassed, imprisoned, or killed, reinscribing the very barrier of fear they sought to dismantle. In this context, artistic projects such as MMC gained traction as a more effective way to continue the revolution by utilizing spontaneity, improvisation, and affective exchange to evade the polarizing stigma of political activism and repression by the authorities.

In part because traditional politics had "failed," MMC musicians maintained that they were *not* political activists. Instead, they were artists interested only in promoting creative expression and beauty in public. One MMC musician told me, "We are not trying to take a political stance. As soon as you bring politics into it, everyone is divided.... Our aim is to get people out of their homes and involve them in culture. Uniting the people around culture is the most important thing. That we have music in the street like this now is more powerful than politics."[80] The notion that live music in the street is "more powerful than politics" indicates the desire for something *beyond* normative political discourse and gets at the heart of MMC's affective potential. In the midst of a highly politicized environment when social animosity was at its peak, live music in the street allowed strangers to engage each other in new ways as performer and audience.[81]

Many MMC musicians viewed the lack of opportunities to experience this affective relationship in public prior to the revolution as problematic. According to one, "people in the street are always angry and frustrated and on the verge of fighting. There is nothing beautiful in the street to calm them, all they see is ugliness and all they hear is noise."[82] For this musician, the people most likely to act aggressively were those who were "starved" of culture and exposed only to musical genres associated with superficial listening, such as Arab pop music.[83] Since the lack of the arts in daily life contributed to a tense public atmosphere, many MMC musicians believed that the performance of independent music in public spaces could produce its opposite through the intersubjective affective transformation of those who experienced it.

One example of this change was recounted to me by Yasmine El Baramawy, an ʿūd (lute) player and women's rights activist, who performed improvisations (*irtigālāt*) and her own compositions alone at several MMC concerts. El Baramawy survived a violent sexual assault during a protest in November 2012. Going on national television to tell her story, she became the face of activism against sexual violence. Speaking to me in 2013, she recounted how she had only had positive experiences performing music in the street with MMC. Before one MMC concert that was set to begin late at night, El Baramawy waited in the car while the men set up the equipment: "I didn't feel comfortable waiting outside the car because people were making comments and giving me looks." Once she started performing, however, the same people's attitudes toward her changed: "They listened to my music and congratulated me on my performance. After that I stood in the street and even smoked a cigarette in the middle of them without any problem."[84]

These actions of a female, middle-class musician performing live music impromptu in the street challenge some state social structures that had ordered public space. For female musicians, their positions as citizens in a state-controlled public environment *and* as females in relation to men situated them within multiple social structures that complicated their ability to perform in the street. Hence, the women performing in MMC challenged not only political taboos but also what some in society considered acceptable behavior for women.

Through affective exchange, El Baramawy believes she was able to challenge these social structures without repercussions. When the audience heard her perform, she claims they were emotionally transformed in a way that altered both her and her audience's behavior in socially meaningful ways, especially in terms of gender norms. Although she played timidly at first, reflecting her unease in what she felt was a hostile atmosphere, her exploration of the sonic potential of her instrument altered her emotional state. As her audience showed more interest in and enthusiasm for her performance, El Baramawy was encouraged to take more risks in her playing. Her choice of mode, rhythm, timbre, and volume strayed more dramatically from her initial, more timid phrases, both reflecting and contributing to an atmospheric change. Through this process she was able to "let go" and open herself up emotionally, even if it meant losing control and unconsciously contorting her face, which she told me is of special concern for women because it can suggest sexual arousal. Although as an independent musician El Baramawy uses a musical language that extends beyond only Arab art music, her performance reanimated some central elements of ṭarab culture: the musical experience began with the performer's altered emotional state resulting from her sonic exploration of pitch, rhythm, timbre, and so on. This altered state was conferred on the audience, whose expressive feedback then heightened the performer's own state of ecstasy. El Baramawy believes she was not harassed during or after her performance owing to this affective exchange. It allowed both her and her audience to view and experience the other differently.

That she played the ʿūd made this performance particularly conducive to affective exchange. The ʿūd is often referred to as *amīr al-ṭarab*, "the prince of ecstasy," for its particularly affective sound quality. It is an instrument traditionally associated with Arab art music and central to the traditional takht ensemble. Additionally, by presenting soloists or ensembles consisting of only two to four musicians, MMC concerts, regardless of the instrumentation, resemble in some ways the intimacy and potential collection of "sound timbres" of the takht.[85] Small ensembles facilitate a unique balance between each of the instruments, and they allow more personalized spontaneous interaction with the audience without a mediator. Although not all of the independent musical styles featured in MMC are in and of themselves associated with ṭarab, small ensembles are believed to be more conducive to producing an intimate public atmosphere filled with affective charge, regardless of genre or instrumentation.

By performing music in an intimate, undetermined way that invited deep listening, El Baramawy made herself vulnerable. Vulnerability involves being receptive to the potential of being affected by others.[86] Vulnerably shedding the boundedness of the self, the performer is receptive to the moods and desires of the audience. The audience's spontaneous verbal and gestural feedback not only inspires the direction of the performance but also illustrates how music "gets into the skin" through full-bodied (embodied) listening. Listeners, in this case the men in the street, were likewise made vulnerable, unselfconsciously contributing ecstatic words, sounds, and gestures to El Baramawy's performance. As Racy notes of public performances, listeners' improvised ecstatic gestures, and the affects to which they are attached, are contagious.[87] Performer and audience contribute to how the music performance unfolds and to the composition of the atmosphere, which all in attendance collectively experience. Through the circulation of affect, atmosphere "literally gets into the individual."[88] It shapes feeling in such a way that it becomes shared sentiment, or public feeling, opening new possibilities for the experience of subjectivity.[89] Receiving such affective communication from her audience altered El Baramawy's state of being in her own body—she no longer felt afraid to sit alone, at night, in the street.

Not all MMC performances produced such a positive affective exchange. Rarely, for instance, some audience members hurled objects and insults at the performers. Insults often attempted to highlight the imagined middle-class or elite background of the performer in a way that indicated that they were understood to be out-of-touch or culturally a "Westerner." These assumptions were exacerbated, in part, by some musicians performing Western classical music or other genres, such as jazz, that are associated with the foreign or elite. Musicians also sometimes entered isolated, intimate communities and were treated with suspicion as outsiders. These moments were likewise an affective exchange produced by improvised and ecstatic gestures. But they amounted to a rejection rather than an open vulnerability to the other, and they reinforced social divisions. By placing audience and performer on equal footing, musical experience in ṭarab culture, and affective politics more broadly, always run the risk of affectively "failing" as the performers alone do not control or dictate the course of performance.[90] This produces both its limitations and its potential. The absence of a singular agentive force or guarantee of positive affective exchange increases the power, akin almost to an otherworldly experience, of experiencing those performances that *do* affect in desired ways.

In the example of El Baramawy's performance, a shared affective experience transformed the public atmosphere from one of distrust, fear, and hostility to one of comfort and even solidarity as the audience praised the performer. Similar to Racy's interlocutor who claimed that ṭarab "was love in the broadest sense," El Baramawy told me that because both performer and listener were transformed through the other's actions, her performance revealed the shared humanity of those at the concert: "When you perform music you are not seen as a piece of meat, but as a human being. They can no longer deny your humanity."[91] Feelings of "shared humanity" illustrate the profound potential of improvisatory music culture to dissolve the distinction between self and other. The affective performance in this instance worked to desexualize the female body, challenging the traditional association of female performers with seduction and shame. As a result of her audience's appreciation for her music, El Baramawy was able to change her own behavior in public. She initially feared that her audience might consider smoking a cigarette to be a social taboo. Smoking is traditionally considered unfeminine, and, especially in certain neighborhoods and in the presence of unknown men, it could be seen as inviting unwanted attention or serve as justification for enforcing "moral order."[92] Her ability to smoke a cigarette in front of strangers indicates more broadly that she experienced her own embodiment differently, transforming her and her audience's behaviors; she commented, "The revolution gave us endless possibilities, particularly in the realms of expression. . . . I believe it is our role as artists to help promote this type of expression, because, sometimes, all it takes is one song to change a person's mind from doing something bad, to hopefully doing something good."[93] In this way, MMC musicians extended the principles of ṭarab culture beyond only transforming individual moods, emotions, and behaviors. They viewed musical experience as having the potential to incite broader social and cultural changes, forming a new public culture in line with the goals of the 2011 revolution.

Ṭarab as Affective Politics

The way Egyptian musicians in MMC reanimated core principles of ṭarab culture to transform precarious social conditions was an example of how improvisatory site-specific practices can form the basis for a new kind of politics. This affective politics unsettles the disembodied, rational, liberal subject that has been central to notions of both the musical genius and the political activist in Western thought: improvisation as a form of affective politics is an embodied practice that has the potential to act on the world. Focusing on listening, instead of performing or composing, gives equal weight to performer and audience. It is the mutually contingent "tuning-in" between them that forms the political potential of musical experience, whether spontaneously produced or precomposed.

Affective politics, by producing messages conveyed through music that are *felt* by the listener, can be especially valuable under conditions of unequal power, whether between women and men or between civilians and a dictator.[94] El Baramawy used her embodiment and that of her audience in ways that are persuasive beyond reasoned speech. Reasoned speech, to be taken as reasoned, necessitates a certain affective containment, a disembodiment and objectivity that are often precluded for survivors of gender-based violence: it is the survivor's *body* that forms the basis for this experience of violence. Likewise, the body's potential to affect and be affected can be especially productive under authoritarian regimes that violently suppress the modes of persuasion, solidarity building, and political participation that traditionally characterize grassroots organizing and oppositional politics. By changing the way people feel together with strangers in public, MMC musicians directly challenged—and successfully limited—the state's power to rule through imposing fear and producing animosity between citizens. Musicians in MMC used their improvisational approach to turn some aspects of the randomness and unreliability that produced a barrier of fear under an authoritarian regime into a transformative force productive toward their own revolutionary goals. Speaking of Portugal's own dictatorial past, ethnomusicologist Ellen Gray argues that from a "habitus of dictatorship," "small affective worlds" emerge in which tremendously powerful symbolic relations, and the affects they generate, are condensed into small gestures.[95] Similarly, the social exchange facilitated by MMC's improvisatory music practice was an affective world. When successful, it facilitated meaningful communication "without the distancing mediation of speech" that could so easily contribute to social animosity or be subject to state repression.[96]

The alternative public culture MMC built attempted to reinvigorate public interest in and direct experience of the social unity that initially brought down the rule of Hosni Mubarak. It was deep, intersubjective listening with diverse others—not just with fellow musical connoisseurs—in the street that brought down the barrier of fear, producing instead a sense of public safety, even when differences were sustained. Deep listening, available regularly in public for ordinary Egyptians, was crucial in the context of the 2011 revolution: it is not the presence of music that "reduces wars" but the presence of certain types of *listeners*. This is a type of listening, foundational in ṭarab culture, that invites the affective capacity of "the other." Although each MMC concert ran the risk of reinforcing boundaries and producing negative affects, that this type of contingent listening could also temporarily transform the relations between men and women as well as the atmosphere of fear in public space held tremendous potential. Even if a single concert is unlikely to transform an entire social environment, MMC musicians still momentarily produced the world they imagined could exist. It was an experiential model of politics that was felt and realized in the present.

Although MMC stopped its activities by 2015 owing to increasing state repression, in a political and social environment marked by great uncertainty and resounding disappointments from the Egyptian revolution's "failure," it is important to recognize small gestures as having great potential to resonate in unexpected and often-unquantifiable ways. Otherwise, we risk viewing repressive systems as totalizing, and communities, or entire populations, as apathetic. As anthropologist Sondra Hale argues in her discussion of the Arab revolutions, we must account for the "unintended consequences" of "failure" that allow people to explore new territory, even if only in thought.[97] New structures of feeling and "small affective worlds" are an important part of these unintended consequences. The politicization of ṭarab culture in the "ongoing revolution" reveals how a small affective world can have great importance through its potential to spark new thoughts, cultures, and modes of politics that imagine a way forward in the aftermath of crisis and systemic repression.

NOTES

I thank Yasmine El Baramawy, Ramez Ashraf, the violinist, Omar Adel, Alex Rodriguez, Eric Schmidt, Chris Nickell, Helen Rizzo, Timothy D. Taylor, A. J. Racy, and the anonymous reviewers.

1 See *Ahram Online*, "Downtown Contemporary Arts Festival"; and Montasser, "Year of El-Fan Midan." Note that for Arabic transliteration, I generally follow guidelines set by the *International Journal of Middle East Studies*. Exceptions include expressions or words more commonly expressed in conversation in Egyptian Colloquial Arabic. In that case, I use the spelling that better expresses Egyptian pronunciation, such as using *g* instead of *j* for the letter jeem, or "mazika" for "mūsīqa." For people's names, I use a simplified transliteration without diacritics. For public figures, I use the spelling commonly used in Egypt-based English-language media, such as *Ahram Online*. For musicians, I use the English spelling they told me to use or that they use on their social media profiles.

2   Some critics prefer the word *uprising* over *revolution* because it accounts for the protest's "failure" to permanently unseat military rule. See Hale, "New Middle East Insurrections." I have chosen to use the word *revolution*, however, because it (*al-thowra*) is the term used by this essay's interlocutors. See also El Chazli, "Sur les sentiers."

3   The founder named "Mini Mobile Concerts" in English. The use of English further situates this project as emerging from educated middle-class Egyptians.

4   I conducted approximately twenty interviews with MMC musicians between 2012 and 2014 in addition to several interviews with founder Ramez Ashraf over the same period. This piece was originally written in 2014, before MMC and other postrevolutionary public arts projects ceased owing to increased state repression. I have decided to keep some sections in the original present tense to maintain a sense of the profound optimism and transformative energy of the revolutionary moment in which it was written.

5   Although *affect* is notoriously difficult to define, I consider it a kind of empathic "force" or "potential" that circulates in and between bodies and environments. Gregg and Seigworth, *Affect Theory Reader*. Beyond connecting individuals to each other, affect dissolves the distinction between people and their environments, producing "atmosphere." Brennan, *Transmission of Affect*, 6. They account for the way the body's capacity to affect and be affected is social, and such affective capacities circulate socially in ways that inform behavior, feeling, and cognition. Clough and Halley, *Affective Turn*, 2. By traversing bodies and spaces, affect dissolves reductive distinctions between "inside" and "outside." This dissolution has implications for how we understand conceptions of self and other. Since we are moved by forces that exceed ourselves, we can no longer understand the self as bounded or as the sole cause of its own experience. I use the concept of affect to account for how and why musical experience is understood to move certain bodies in particular ways.

6   For my purposes here, I take discursive forms of politics to involve naming what is wrong, such as by spreading awareness of injustice, making demands, and/or engaging in reasoned critique. Affective politics, in contrast, involves experiencing in the present the alternative world one imagines, even if only momentarily.

7   For example, see Habermas, *Structural Transformation*; and Warner, *Publics and Counterpublics*.

8   Lutz and Abu-Lughod, *Language and the Politics of Emotion*.

9   On the association between loss of control and the feminine, see Becker, *Deep Listeners*, 13. On the loss of control as "primitive," see Goodwin, Jasper, and Polletta, "Why Emotions Matter," 2.

10 Warner, *Publics and Counterpublics*, 51–54.

11 Hardt, "Foreword," ix–x.

12 Scholars, including Jürgen Habermas, Fredric Jameson, and David Harvey, working across a variety of disciplines on the Global North, have lamented the supposed end of oppositional politics under contemporary conditions variously called *late capitalism*, *postmodernism*, or *neoliberal capitalism*. The improvisatory practices emerging in the wake of the 2011 revolution challenge the hopelessness of these theories since they materialized despite Egypt's 1970s shift to neoliberal policies. On alternative ways of engaging the political, see also Lauren Berlant's concept of the "post–public sphere public" in *Cruel Optimism*, 223.

13 Schultz, "99 Percent of Women."
14 Owing to space constraints, I am unable to give a full account of the complex ways class and gender are working in and through MMC's work. Although MMC performances are transformative for women in some ways, in other ways they reify gender and class boundaries. Whereas male musicians have performed throughout the city, female musicians have performed concerts only in downtown Alexandria. Among most of my interlocutors in the independent music scene, "faraway" neighborhoods were associated with the working class and were believed to be too dangerous for women. I analyze some of these class politics in Sprengel, "'More Powerful than Politics.'"
15 See, for instance, European Union Agency for Fundamental Rights, "Violence against Women."
16 Rizzo, "Who Is to Blame . . . ?"
17 Abu-Lughod, *Do Muslim Women Need Saving?*; and Abdelmonem et al., "The 'Taharrush' Connection."
18 Musicians often use the English word *independent*, but also the Arabic term *mustaqill*, or denote the scene by saying *al-bandāt al-mustaqilla*, "independent bands."
19 At the time of writing (in 2014), there are a handful of active female performers, including Dina al-Wedidi, Sherine Amr, Nancy Mounir, Maryam Saleh, Youssra al-Hawary, Shereen Abdo, and Maii Walid. These women are a minority, however, relative to the number of male performers active in the scene.
20 These jams are strikingly similar to A. J. Racy's *jalsah* (*Making Music*, 51–58); however, they comprise musicians who excel at different musical traditions. Despite the diversity of traditions, the musical language, techniques, and performance practices characteristic of Arab art music—such as the style of ornamentation, technique of call-and-response between performers, and approach to expounding various melodic modes (*maqāmāt*)—are often the most dominant.
21 Rizk, "Stories from Egypt's Music Industry," 114–15. Being outside of the channels of mainstream media and major government-run arts institutions has, however, allowed musicians in this scene to offer alternative viewpoints in their music.
22 "Mini Mobile Concert—Mazikā fī al-Shariʿ," Facebook page, https://www.facebook.com/MiniMobileConcert?fref=ts. This page features photographs, videos, event notifications, and discussion of Mini Mobile Concerts.
23 Racy, "Improvisation." Within youth independent subcultures, some terminological standardization appears emergent. Most musicians I spoke to used the English word *improvisation*, arabicized the word *to jam* (*hanjayyam al-nahārda*), and/or used the non-music-specific Arabic word *al-irtigāl*.
24 Racy, *Making Music*, 5–6.
25 Racy, *Making Music*, 132–33.
26 Racy, "Musical Aesthetics," 392.
27 Racy, "Improvisation."
28 See Touma, "Maqam Phenomenon"; and Nettl and Riddle, "Taqsim Nahawand."
29 Racy, "Improvisation." Although privileging embodied interaction, ṭarab can also be induced through mediation, such as through sound recordings; see Shannon, *Among the Jasmine Trees*; Danielson, *"Voice of Egypt"*; el-Shawan, "Traditional Arab Music Ensembles"; and el-Shawan, "Role of Mediators."

30. Racy, "Why Do They Improvise?"
31. I build from Racy's approach to understanding the relationship between improvisation and composition by referring to MMC's musical practices in relation to ṭarab culture rather than simply improvisation. As previously stated, MMC musicians perform precomposed works, improvisations (in the style of Arab art music, or *taqāsīm*), and informal jams (in the style of independent music) in public spaces. Thus, not all the music performed in MMC is spontaneously composed. What is improvised, however, is the interactive exchange between performer and audience as it occurs in each time and place. This exchange directly influences how an MMC musician performs a work, whether "precomposed" or "improvised," and it also determines what works they will perform. I use the concept of ṭarab culture to better account for this particular approach to music performance that privileges these improvised interactions with the audience as fundamental to both composition and performance.
32. Sahhab, *Difāʿan ʿan al-Ughnīyah al-ʿArabīyah*, 19.
33. Racy, *Making Music*, 53.
34. Becker, *Deep Listeners*, 6, 2.
35. Shannon, *Among the Jasmine Trees*, 170.
36. Quoted in Racy, *Making Music*, 131.
37. Racy, *Making Music*, 131.
38. Shannon, *Among the Jasmine Trees*, 9.
39. Listening is understood to be so agentive that some religious accounts treat it as the primary sensory activity related to moral conduct. See Hirschkind, *Ethical Soundscape*.
40. Racy, *Making Music*; and Danielson, "Voice of Egypt."
41. Racy, *Making Music*, 58.
42. Racy, *Making Music*, 53.
43. Yet, as Jonathan Shannon has found, even "uncultivated" listeners, who do not understand melodic modes, or in some cases even song lyrics, and who comprise the majority of listeners in many contemporary Arab societies today, are still able to experience ṭarab. Shannon, *Among the Jasmine Trees*, 169.
44. See Sprengel, "'More Powerful than Politics.'"
45. Hirschkind, *Ethical Soundscape*, 41–42.
46. See also Nieuwkerk, *"A Trade like Any Other."*
47. As discussed by Racy in "Music in Nineteenth-Century Egypt."
48. El-Shawan, "Role of Mediators."
49. El-Shawan, "Traditional Arab Music Ensembles."
50. Racy, "Musical Change," 145.
51. By the twenty-first century, the street became the domain of the working-class as the middle class and elites had more access to institutionalized music education and state-run performance venues. Nieuwkerk, *"A Trade like Any Other."* Thus, although beyond the scope of this chapter, class remains an important analytic category in dealing with independent music and its spaces of performance.
52. Bayat, "'Street,'" 11.
53. See also Nieuwkerk, *"A Trade like Any Other."*
54. Nieuwkerk, *"A Trade like Any Other,"* 32–38.

55 Winegar, *Creative Reckonings*, 137–74; and Winegar and Pahwa, "Culture, State and Revolution."
56 El-Shawan, "Traditional Arab Music Ensembles," 281.
57 Ismail, *Political Life in Cairo's New Quarters*; and Sharp, "Urbanism and the Arab Uprisings."
58 Frishkopf, *Music and Media*; and Danielson, *"Voice of Egypt."* In "New Nightingales of the Nile: Popular Music in Egypt since the 1970s," Danielson argues, however, that Arab pop singers in live performance sometimes evoke ṭarab in their audiences.
59 See also Winegar, *Creative Reckonings*.
60 Ghannam, "Meanings and Feelings," 34. See also Ghannam, *Remaking the Modern*.
61 Egyptian Organization for Human Rights, "Itiqal al-Siyasi."
62 Hafez, "No Longer a Bargain," 39.
63 Ismail, *Political Life in Cairo's New Quarters*, xliv. Others argue that the lack of employment opportunities and increased poverty have delayed marriage for many men who are unable to afford it, thus producing a generation of sex-deprived male youth. Amar, "Turning the Gendered Politics." For detailed studies of working-class masculinity, see el-Messiri, *Ibn al-Balad*; and Ghannam, *Live and Die*.
64 Hafez, "Bodies That Protest"; Peach, *Women at War*; Enloe, *Maneuvers*; Shalhoub-Kevorkian, *Militarization and Violence*; and Marshall, "Connection between Militarism and Violence."
65 Exemptions can be granted if the conscript has medical issues, is an only son, has dual citizenship, or supports his parents.
66 Hammad likewise demonstrates that in periods of rapid change, laws protecting women in public are typically slow to catch up. Media portrayals and court decisions from the nineteenth and twentieth centuries indicate, for instance, that sexual harassment at the time was considered "amusing" or "good" for women and at worst a "bad habit." Lower-class and rural women were the most affected. Hammad, "Sexual Harassment in Egypt," 45–48.
67 Egyptian women have no singular or universal experience of public space. The extent to which a woman's behavior or movements are monitored or controlled are highly contingent on her particular family, neighborhood, marital status, whether or not she has children, and so on. It is highly variable and often changes throughout a woman's lifetime. See also Ghannam, *Remaking the Modern*.
68 Ismail, *Political Life in Cairo's New Quarters*, 97.
69 Ghannam, "Space and Resistance."
70 Many Egyptians have expressed in the media and to me in interviews that independent musicians helped facilitate this affective transformation. See, for example, Lynskey, "Ramy Essam."
71 For example, Egyptians were divided on the legitimacy of the first presidential election, on the ratification of a new constitution, on the political and ideological makeup of the Egyptian parliament, and the like. These divisions resulted in continued protests and social unrest following the initial protests of January and February 2011.
72 Kholaif, "Sexual Harassment Taints Egypt's Euphoria."
73 Radwan, "How Egyptian Women Took Back the Street"; Hafez, "Bodies That Protest"; and Abaza, "Cairo Dairy."

74 Hammad, "Sexual Harassment in Egypt," 55–57.
75 Amar, "Turning the Gendered Politics."
76 Al Jazeera, "Sisi"; and BBC, "Court Confirms."
77 For more on street art in 2011, see Winegar and Pahwa, "Culture, State and Revolution."
78 Quoted in Rollins, "Singer from 'The Square.'"
79 Literary scholar and cultural theorist Lauren Berlant defines cruel optimism as relations wherein "the object that draws your attachment actively impedes the aim that brought you to it initially." Berlant, *Cruel Optimism*, 1.
80 Interview with the author, March 28, 2013.
81 For more on the power relations involved in desires to avoid politics, see Sprengel, "'More Powerful than Politics.'"
82 Interview with the author, December 13, 2013.
83 One musician viewed public art as a basic necessity: "Culture is important. It's like food. It is a part of people's lives. But to the government it was something extra, it did nothing to promote it or make it available to regular people. So for decades we just starved" (personal communication, March 20, 2013).
84 Interview with the author, March 18, 2013.
85 Racy, *Making Music*, 77.
86 Butler and Athanasiou, *Dispossession*, 158.
87 Racy, *Making Music*, 64.
88 Brennan, *Transmission of Affect*, 1.
89 Gray, *Fado Resounding*, 137.
90 See, for example, Racy, *Making Music*, 58.
91 Interview with the author, March 18, 2013.
92 Nieuwkerk, *"A Trade like Any Other."* Whether smoking is considered a taboo for women is highly dependent on a variety of factors, including age, marital status, class, education, neighborhood, and so on. It is not uniformly condemned or considered unfeminine in Egyptian society. In this particular instance, however, El Baramawy had initially felt that smoking would be inappropriate.
93 Quoted in El-Nabawi, "Itinerant Music Show Spreads Peace."
94 See also Racy, *Making Music*, 216–17.
95 Gray, *Fado Resounding*, 130.
96 Berlant, *Cruel Optimism*, 224.
97 Hale, "New Middle East Insurrections."

BIBLIOGRAPHY

Abaza, Mona. "Cairo Dairy: Space-Wars, Public Visibility and the Transformation of Public Space in Post-revolutionary Egypt." In *Public Space, Media Space*, edited by Chris Berry, Janet Harbord, and Rachel Moore, 88–109. London: Palgrave Macmillan, 2013.

Abdelmonem, Angie, Rahma Esther Bavelaar, N. Elisa Wynne-Hughes, and Susana Galán. "The 'Taharrush' Connection: Xenophobia, Islamophobia, and Sexual Violence in Germany and Beyond." *Jadaliyya*, March 1, 2016. https://www

.jadaliyya.com/Details/33036/The-%60Taharrush%60-Connection-Xenophobia, -Islamophobia,-and-Sexual-Violence-in-Germany-and-Beyond.

Abu-Lughod, Lila. *Do Muslim Women Need Saving?* Cambridge, MA: Harvard University Press, 2013.

Ahram Online. "Downtown Contemporary Arts Festival (D-CAF) Saturates Cairo Streets." February 23, 2013. http://english.ahram.org.eg/NewsContent/5/35/65373/Arts-Culture/Stage-Street/Downtown-Contemporary-Arts-Festival-DCAF-saturates.aspx.

Amar, Paul. "Turning the Gendered Politics of the Security State Inside Out? Charging the Police with Sexual Harassment in Egypt." *International Feminist Journal of Politics* 13, no. 3 (2011): 299–328.

Bayat, Asef. "The 'Street' and the Politics of Dissent in the Arab World." *Middle East Report* 226 (2003): 10–17.

BBC. "Court Confirms Egypt Muslim Brotherhood Death Sentences." BBC, June 21, 2014. http://www.bbc.com/news/world-middle-east-27952321.

Becker, Judith. *Deep Listeners: Music, Emotion, and Trancing.* Indianapolis: Indiana University Press, 2004.

Berlant, Lauren. *Cruel Optimism.* Durham, NC: Duke University Press, 2011.

Brennan, Teresa. *The Transmission of Affect.* Ithaca, NY: Cornell University Press, 2004.

Butler, Judith, and Athena Athanasiou. *Dispossession: The Performative in the Political.* New York: Polity, 2013.

El Chazli, Youssef. "Sur les sentiers de la révolution." *Revue française de science politique* 5, no. 62 (2012): 843–65.

Clough, Patricia, and Jean Halley, eds. *The Affective Turn: Theorizing the Social.* Durham, NC: Duke University Press, 2007.

Danielson, Virginia. "New Nightingales of the Nile: Popular Music in Egypt since the 1970s." *Popular Music* 15, no. 3 (1996): 299–312.

Danielson, Virginia. *"The Voice of Egypt": Umm Kulthum, Arabic Song, and Egyptian Society in the Twentieth Century.* Chicago: University of Chicago Press, 1998.

Egyptian Organization for Human Rights. *Al-ʿItiqāl al-Siyāsī, Siyāsa al-Bāb al-Mughlaq, wa al-ʿItiqāl al-Jināʾī: Siyāsat al-Bāb al-Dawār* [Political detention, closed-door policy, and criminal detention: The revolving door policy]. Cairo: Egyptian Organization for Human Rights, 2003.

Enloe, Cynthia. *Maneuvers: The International Politics of Militarizing Women's Lives.* Berkeley: University of California Press, 2000.

European Union Agency for Fundamental Rights. "Violence against Women: An EU-Wide Survey." Luxembourg: Publications Office of the European Union, 2015. https://fra.europa.eu/sites/default/files/fra_uploads/fra-2014-vaw-survey-main-results-apr14_en.pdf.

Frishkopf, Michael. *Music and Media in the Arab World.* Cairo: American University in Cairo Press, 2010.

Ghannam, Farha. *Live and Die like a Man: Gender Dynamics in Urban Egypt.* Stanford, CA: Stanford University Press, 2013.

Ghannam, Farha. "Meanings and Feelings: Local Interpretations of the Use of Violence in the Egyptian Revolution." *American Ethnologist* 39, no. 1 (2012): 32–36.

Ghannam, Farha. *Remaking the Modern: Space, Relocation, and the Politics of Identity in a Global Cairo*. Berkeley: University of California Press, 2002.

Ghannam, Farha. "Space and Resistance." *The Immanent Frame* (blog), February 8, 2011. http://blogs.ssrc.org/tif/2011/02/08/space-and-resistance/.

Goodwin, Jeff, James M. Jasper, and Francesca Polletta. "Why Emotions Matter." In *Passionate Politics: Emotions and Social Movements*, edited by Jeff Goodwin, James M. Jasper, and Francesca Polletta, 1–24. Chicago: University of Chicago Press, 2001.

Gray, Lila Ellen. *Fado Resounding: Affective Politics and Urban Life*. Durham, NC: Duke University Press, 2013.

Gregg, Melissa, and Gregory Seigworth. *The Affect Theory Reader*. Durham, NC: Duke University Press, 2010.

Habermas, Jürgen. *The Structural Transformation of the Public Sphere: An Inquiry into a Category of Bourgeois Society*. Cambridge, MA: MIT Press, 1991.

Hafez, Sherine. "Bodies That Protest: The Girl in the Blue Bra, Sexuality, and State Violence in Revolutionary Egypt." *Signs* 40, no. 1 (2014): 20–28.

Hafez, Sherine. "No Longer a Bargain: Women, Masculinity, and the Egyptian Uprising." *American Ethnologist* 39, no. 1 (2012): 37–42.

Hale, Sondra. "The New Middle East Insurrections and Other Subversions of the Modernist Frame." *Journal of Middle East Women's Studies* 10, no. 3 (2014): 40–61.

Hammad, Hanan. "Sexual Harassment in Egypt: An Old Plague in a New Revolutionary Order." *Gender* 1 (2017): 44–63.

Hardt, Michael. "Foreword: What Affects Are Good For." In *The Affective Turn: Theorizing the Social*, edited by Patricia Clough and Jean Halley, ix–xiii. Durham, NC: Duke University Press, 2007.

Hirschkind, Charles. *The Ethical Soundscape: Cassette Sermons and Islamic Counterpublics*. New York: Columbia University Press, 2006.

Ismail, Salwa. *Political Life in Cairo's New Quarters: Encountering the Everyday State*. Minneapolis: University of Minnesota Press, 2006.

Al Jazeera. "Sisi: Right to Protest Harms Egyptian Economy." *Al Jazeera*, January 21, 2015. http://www.aljazeera.com/humanrights/2015/01/sisi-right-protest-harms-egyptian-economy-201512174011670123.html.

Kholaif, Dahlia. "Sexual Harassment Taints Egypt's Euphoria." *Al Jazeera*, July 6, 2013. http://m.aljazeera.com/story/20137617131125427.

Lutz, Catherine A., and Lila Abu-Lughod, eds. *Language and the Politics of Emotion*. Cambridge: Cambridge University Press, 1990.

Lynskey, Dorian. "Ramy Essam—the Voice of the Egyptian Uprising." *Guardian*, July 19, 2011. http://www.theguardian.com/music/2011/jul/19/ramy-essam-egypt-uprising-interview.

Marshall, Lucinda. "The Connection between Militarism and Violence against Women." In *Beyond Borders: Thinking Critically about Global Issues*, edited by Paula S. Rothenberg, 307–10. New York: Worth, 2005.

Messiri, Sawsan el-. *Ibn al-Balad: A Concept of Egyptian Identity*. Leiden: E. J. Brill, 1987.

"Mini Mobile Concert—Mazikā fī al-Shariʿ." Facebook page. Accessed July 25, 2019. https://www.facebook.com/MiniMobileConcert?fref=ts.

Montasser, Farah. "A Year of El-Fan Midan in Egypt." *Ahram Online*, April 10, 2012. http://english.ahram.org.eg/NewsContent/5/0/38785/Arts—Culture/0/A-year-of-ElFan-Midan-in-Egypt.aspx.

Nabawi, Maha el-. "Itinerant Music Show Spreads Peace in Alexandria's Streets." *Egypt Independent*, August 19, 2014. http://www.egyptindependent.com//news/itinerant-music-show-spreads-peace-alexandria-s-streets.

Nettl, Bruno, and Ronald Riddle. "Taqsim Nahawand: A Study of Sixteen Performances by Jihad Racy." *Yearbook of the International Folk Music Council* 5 (1973): 11–50.

Nieuwkerk, Karin van. *"A Trade like Any Other": Female Singers and Dancers in Egypt*. Austin: University of Texas Press, 1995.

Peach, Lucinda J. *Women at War: The Ethics of Women in Combat*. Bloomington: Indiana Center on Global Change and World Peace, 1993.

Racy, A. J. "Improvisation, Ecstasy, and Performance Dynamics in Arabic Music." In *The Course of Performance: Studies in the World of Musical Improvisation*, edited by Bruno Nettl and Melinda Russell, 95–112. Chicago: University of Chicago Press, 1998.

Racy, A. J. *Making Music in the Arab World: The Culture and Artistry of Ṭarab*. Cambridge: Cambridge University Press, 2003.

Racy, A. J. "Musical Aesthetics in Present-Day Cairo." *Ethnomusicology* 26, no. 3 (1982): 391–406.

Racy, A. J. "Musical Change and Commercial Recording in Egypt." PhD diss., University of Illinois at Urbana-Champaign, 1977.

Racy, A. J. "Music in Nineteenth-Century Egypt: An Historical Sketch." *Ethnomusicology* 5 (1983): 157–79.

Racy, A. J. "Sound and Society: The Takht Music of Early-Twentieth Century Cairo." *Selected Reports in Ethnomusicology* 7 (1988): 140–58.

Racy, A. J. "Why Do They Improvise? Reflections on Meaning and Experience." In *Musical Improvisation: Art, Education, and Society*, edited by Gabriel Solis and Bruno Nettl, 313–22. Urbana: University of Illinois Press, 2009.

Radwan, Noha. "How Egyptian Women Took Back the Street between Two 'Black Wednesdays': A First Person Account." *Jadaliyya*, February 20, 2011. http://www.jadaliyya.com/Details/23716.

Rizk, Nagla. "Stories from Egypt's Music Industry: De Facto Commons as Alternatives to Copyright." In *Access to Knowledge in Egypt: New Research on Intellectual Property, Innovation and Development*, edited by Nagla Rizk and Lea Shaver, 92–133. London: Bloomsbury, 2010.

Rizzo, Helen. "Who Is to Blame for Sexual Harassment? Understanding the Intersection of Toxic Masculinity, Racialization and Social Class in Sexual Harassment Discourses in Egypt and Beyond." Presentation organized by the NVIC (Netherlands-Flemish Institute in Cairo), Egypt, November 16, 2017.

Rollins, Tom. "Singer from 'The Square' in Shadows of Egypt's Crackdown." *al-Monitor*, January 21, 2014. http://www.al-monitor.com/pulse/originals/2014/01/tahrir-movie-egypt-ramy-singer.html.

Sahhab, Ilyas. *Difāʿan ʿan al-Ughnīyah al-ʿArabīyah* [In defense of Arabic song]. Beirut: al-Muʾassasah al-ʿArabīyah lil-Dirāsāt wa al-Nashr, 1980.

Schultz, Colin. "In Egypt, 99 Percent of Women Have Been Sexually Harassed." *Smithsonian*, June 13, 2014. http://www.smithsonianmag.com/smart-news/egypt-99-women-have-been-sexually-harassed-180951726/.

Shalhoub-Kevorkian, Nadera. *Militarization and Violence against Women in Conflict Zones in the Middle East: A Palestinian Case-Study*. Cambridge: Cambridge University Press, 2009.

Shannon, Jonathan Holt. *Among the Jasmine Trees: Music and Modernity in Contemporary Syria*. Middletown, CT: Wesleyan University Press, 2006.

Sharp, Deen. "Urbanism and the Arab Uprisings: Downtown Cairo and the Fall of Mubarak." *Jadaliyya*, August 6, 2012. http://www.jadaliyya.com/Details/26808/.

Shawan, Salwa el-. "The Role of Mediators in the Transmission of Al-Musiḳa al-'Arabiyyah in Twentieth Century Cairo." *Yearbook for Traditional Music* 14 (1982): 55–74.

Shawan, Salwa el-. "Traditional Arab Music Ensembles in Egypt since 1967: 'The Continuity of Tradition within a Contemporary Framework?'" *Ethnomusicology* 28, no. 2 (1984): 271–88.

Sprengel, Darci. "'More Powerful than Politics': Affective Magic in the DIY Musical Activism after Egypt's 2011 Revolution." *Popular Music* 38, no. 1 (2019): 54–72.

Touma, Habib Hassan. "The Maqam Phenomenon: An Improvisation Technique in the Music of the Middle East." *Ethnomusicology* 15, no. 1 (1971): 38–48.

Warner, Michael. *Publics and Counterpublics*. New York: Zone, 2002.

Winegar, Jessica. *Creative Reckonings: The Politics of Art and Culture in Contemporary Egypt*. Stanford, CA: Stanford University Press, 2006.

Winegar, Jessica, and Sonali Pahwa. "Culture, State and Revolution." *Middle East Report* 42 (2012). http://www.merip.org/mer/mer263/culture-state-revolution.

NINE Improvisation, Grounded Humanity, and Witnessing in Palestine

An Interview with Al-Mada's Odeh Turjman and Reem Abdul Hadi

DANIEL FISCHLIN

> As for the birds,
> don't they know that this is not the time for singing?
> Here they are, singing
> as usual,
> twittering melodies you do not understand.
> Maybe they echo the refrain:
> nothing equals
> one more hour with you.
> —MOURID BARGHOUTI, "Midnight"

Musical improvisation is a form of witnessing, holding on to the moment as it occurs. The reality of the witness, as any improviser will tell you, is being present in the fragility of time passing. Vulnerability is an aspect of the urgency that music brings to that which always disappears. We are in this moment but once, and what we do in that moment always has the potential to transform—or not. Improvisatory cocreation resonates with the potential ethics of listening, of acting, of engaging in any given moment that addresses the knife's edge of being here and now. How we embody impermanence is a question every improvisation asks.

Listening and learning ground the witness, as do the reciprocal exchanges that arise from encounters. Improvisation, making it new through dialogue and interchange, respecting that there is something to be shared and learned—all are active in witnessing. Who is really witnessing whom?

What lies in the melody you don't understand? Who sings the refrain that tells us that nothing can equal this *one chance we have to be together—"nothing equals one more hour" spent with you*? How do we persist together through song and sound? How does musical resonance translate into sympathy and empathy?

I'm in Ramallah in early April 2014 with John McLaughlin's band the 4th Dimension—Ranjit Barot, Gary Husband, and Étienne M'Bappé. Also there, among others, are Ina Behrend (John's wife), who has an academic formation in anthropology and Indology (South Asian studies), as well as NGO experience in India and Pakistan; Deeyah Khan, a two-time Emmy Award–winning Norwegian filmmaker and musician; and Reem Abdul Hadi and Odeh Turjman, cofounders of Al-Mada, the Palestinian community-facing music center in Ramallah whose work we are here to witness and support. Al-Mada is active in the refugee camps throughout the occupied West Bank, using improvised musical encounters as a way to address trauma, oppression, and alienation; to give voice to the marginalized (especially women and children); to build solidarity; and to address the realities of aggrieved peoples who have been displaced for five generations—turned into refugees as hundreds of Palestinian towns and villages have been either depopulated, destroyed, or resettled.

In this site of sustained crisis and suffering, Al-Mada struggles to address the precarity and trauma of everyday life through improvisatory music techniques. Abdul Hadi puts it as follows:

> Our frustration with the status quo and the way in which "development" has been implemented led to the creation of Al Mada Association for Arts-Based Community Development.... More than 90 percent of Palestinians, mainly youth and children, suffer from depression, frustration, anxiety, and post-traumatic stress disorder because of the Israeli occupation. That's precisely why we tend to use expressive arts therapies, specifically music therapy and arts education, to advance self-expression, inclusion, healing, social justice, and advocacy through our work with Palestinian communities. We seek to bring a sense of joy and relief from what is often a very stressful life in Palestine—and we support change that comes from within communities, through their own members, resources, capacities, and diversities. The arts provide a space and a platform where individuals can express, create, and heal: they are a powerful tool to advocate for concerns and rights.

In such a scenario, improvisation becomes a critical means for accessing shared experiences of trauma and developing resilience, since Al-Mada clinicians and animators are often faced with communities in which access to musical instruments and training has been severely limited. Turjman discusses the effects of the Second Intifada (2000–2005), noting:

> We used to do workshops in schools for traumatized children. At the time, shelling was going on. The feeling in the school was glum.... But we managed to continue in spite of the ongoing crisis. And when we were working with children, I realized—because I work in improvisation and composition—that we had to let them improvise and compose. When they composed, what they came up with was all they talked about: the difficult situations they were facing. It was very serious what they were speaking to, and as musicians we could not handle it. They opened up, and as a musician you didn't know how to respond ethically and appropriately to what they were saying. These were serious problems, and this is when we thought to use maybe this kind of combination of something in music and expression and improvisation.

What does it mean to make, teach, and use improvised sounds in spaces where your existence and nonexistence, simultaneously, define you—where erasure, through strategies of occupation, containment, restriction, and humiliation, is deeply at odds with other realities found in solidarity, community, creation, and resilience?

Erasure is discursively as well as structurally violent, and it has deadly consequences. In Palestine it is a form of ongoing crisis. Sound is a form of voicing that counters erasure, one that allows ideas to be given voice, to travel, to manifest beyond walls, beyond borders. In 2016 an Israeli parliamentarian argued against Palestine's existence because of the lack of the letter *p* in Arabic.[1] That year also saw Google Maps severely criticized for enacting a form of ethnic cleansing by excluding Palestine from its supposedly standard-setting geo-software.[2] Further, in 2017 Israeli ministers supported a proposed new law "that would downgrade Arabic as an official language and which states that the right to self-determination in Israel 'is unique to the Jewish people,' despite the country's sizeable non-Jewish minority."[3] Al-Mada's work within these prejudicial contexts is extraordinarily courageous, using music to address crisis, trauma, and erasure via the cocreative dialogue and agency it enables.

FIGURE 9.1 John McLaughlin and the 4th Dimension, solidarity concert program cover, produced by Al-Mada.

John's band is playing a solidarity concert, his second, in the cultural palace at Ramallah at the end of an extended tour of India and Asia. Deeyah and I are here at the invitation of John and Ina to witness their encounters in the refugee camps and to tell what we can of Al-Mada's struggle to use music to address an impossible, unsustainable situation for Palestinian communities facing cascading cycles of violence. John and Ina had become involved with Al-Mada in 2010 after John received a lifetime achievement award at the Jazzahead Festival in Germany for his extraordinary contributions to music. As Ina tells it, "we were looking in 2010 for an organization to donate some prize money, which John had been awarded from Germany, [and] we wanted to give it to an organization [that] works with women, children and mainly through music therapy.... That's how we funded Al-Mada."

After donating all the prize money from the award, John, along with long-time musical friend and collaborator Zakir Hussain, played a 2012 solidarity concert supported by UNICEF and UNRWA (United Nations Relief and Works Agency for Palestine Refugees in the Near East) and featuring Remember

Shakti—a group that included the late U. Srinivas (mandolin), V. Selvaganesh (kanjira), and Shankar Mahadevan (voice).⁴ As reported by *This Week in Palestine*, all "funds raised by the concert will be used directly to implement collaborative programmes between Al-Mada and UNRWA. Al-Mada has worked with UNRWA as a key partner since the establishment of the music therapy center in 2009. Through a series of child protection and psychosocial programmes, Al-Mada has trained more than 100 UNRWA staff from the health department, under the supervision of Dr. Umaiyeh Khammash, director of the department." The solidarity concert was seen as "a symbol of Palestine's enduring social, cultural, and political relevance. The concert can and should act as an indication that heavily policed borders can neither isolate a culture from the world nor prevent the cultures of the world from engaging with it."⁵

Al-Mada does the impossible. It imagines a world without borders brought together by the arts—especially music—in one of the most policed, contentious, violent places on the planet. The Arabic term *Al Mada*, "taken literally, means no borders—it describes an infinity of space and possibility."⁶ Borders have long been a critical fact of life for Palestinians, not only an affront to geographic realities tied to family and community identity, but also an ongoing source of stress and misery occasioned by how borders generate displacement, exile, myriad checkpoints that must be passed to access formerly easily accessed lands, among others—and so the choice of Al-Mada as the name for the organization is no small symbolic gesture.

There is a long, painful history of Palestinian struggles with borders, as Mourid Barghouti reminds us in his memoir of returning to Palestine with his son Tamim:

> The Palestinian forced to become a refugee, to migrate, and to go into exile from his homeland in the sixty years since the Nakba [the catastrophe] of 1948, or the forty since the June 1967 War, suffers miseries trying to obtain a document by which he will be recognized at borders. He suffers miseries trying to obtain a passport from another state because he is stateless and has to go through Kafkaesque interrogations before being granted an entry visa to any place in the world, even the Arab states. The Palestinian is forbidden to enter his own country by land, sea, or air, even in a coffin. It is not a matter of romantic attachment to a place but of eternal exclusion from it. The Palestinian stripped of an original identity is a palm tree broken in the middle.⁷

Today, borders, segregation, and exclusion are everywhere in the Palestinian imaginary. Palestine is a place where territorial incursions, the continued

FIGURE 9.2 West Bank signage prohibiting cross-cultural contact.

progress of illegal settlements, arbitrarily designated zones and checkpoints, a planned 650-kilometer wall already some 440 kilometers long, and numerous limited roadways and access points define space and time. For Palestinians in Ramallah working in Jerusalem, this means running a gauntlet of checkpoints, stops, and quotidian obstacles in which regular humiliations and arbitrary impositions occur. For Israelis contemplating entering the West Bank, severe warnings are posted by Israel at entry points to areas controlled by the Palestinian Authority suggesting that crossing these borders is illegal and life threatening.

The signs marking entrances to the West Bank and Gaza have become a rallying point for Palestinian and Israeli activists. Both groups understand that finding sustainable solutions to the crisis will occur only by building bridges into each other's communities, not by segregating them through walls, fear, or legal structures that make it difficult, if not impossible, to enter into the other's space—let alone into meaningful dialogue—in a peaceful manner.[8]

Reem Abdul Hadi explains that these ominous red signs are everywhere: "As you may know, we're divided into three areas: Area A being main cities under the Palestinian Authority; Area B being under joint administration between the Palestinian Authority and the Israeli administration; and Area C consisting of Palestinian areas under full control of the Israelis." She goes on to say that "you can find these signs in the checkpoints at Nablus, Ramallah, Bethlehem, Jericho, Jenin, Tulkarem, Hebron, and so forth, and one can easily say that they can be found in each main Palestinian city." On another day, Abdul Hadi confides that Palestinian ID cards are more valuable than credit or debit cards or money, as without them stateless people become even more invisible and disempowered. So, segregation is alive and well here, and the oldest principle for resolving human differences—encounter in public spaces to eat, love, make music, argue, and so forth—has been abdicated.

According to UNRWA, the barriers take a psychosocial toll throughout the region, particularly on the West Bank ID holders living on the Jerusalem side of the Barrier, who "face acute hardship and [a] pressure on their households [that] can be intolerable. Most West Bank ID holders cite the Barrier and its associated gate and permit regime as a main source of stress in their lives. The Barrier and its associated measures such as permits and checkpoints cause stress by dramatically reducing the economic opportunities and access to services such as health and education in East Jerusalem. West Bank ID holders are also more vulnerable to harassment at checkpoints due to their precarious residency situation." Moreover, "the psychosocial situation of West Bank ID holders isolated on the Jerusalem side of the Barrier has deteriorated substantially due to the pressures of daily life resulting from their precarious residency situation and inability to access services. 95 per cent of West Bank ID holder households reported a decline in the emotional well-being of adults since the completion of the Barrier. Of these households, 92 per cent reported a similar deterioration in the well-being of their children."[9]

Music, famously, has the power to traverse walls, to bridge linguistic differences, and to resolve tension and dissonance peacefully. I'm reminded of the early modern poet Fulke Greville, who envisages the futile attempt to build a wall around a flock of birds. And of course, when it comes to walls and music, there's that nagging biblical reference to Joshua and his army of Israelite trumpeters who blow down the walls of Jericho as they begin their conquest of Canaan (Joshua 6:1–27), which, as historical ironies would have it, encompassed the current Occupied Territories (including Gaza). Musical resonance transports, travels, and traverses . . . and not only walls. Resonance and its correspondence in listening unleash intense intimacies that link people—ears being the sympathetic organs that transform sound into affect and then action.

If music in biblical times had the power to bring down walls, what powers might it possess in the here and now? I think of the 2016 concert in the Jules Ferry center beside the "Jungle" in Calais, where thousands of refugees were housed, led by Catalan musician Jordi Savall. Savall's musical intervention on behalf of Syrian refugees culminated in an unexpected, improvised convergence of his international group of musicians (from Syria, Turkey, Bulgaria, Greece, and Israel) with refugee Ishmael Afghan and his *dambura* (also known as the *dombura* or *danbura*, an Afghani folk instrument especially popular among the northern Tajiks and the Hazaras). Connections are made, and music transforms isolation and exile, however momentarily, into community and home—absence and erasure into presence and affect.[10]

Responsibility, moral courage, and directed actions to resist the spread of violence and alienation that imposes deeply perverse notions of being human need to be proliferated—and improvisation is a key tool in this proliferation if only because it is so vitally connected to cocreative agency. The risk of improvisation is listening to the other with whom you are called on to harmonize, or at the very least to dialogue, no matter what your differences. What strategies of reconciliation arise from this listening, this risking to listen as a starting point for cocreation?

Izzeldin Abuelaish, the Palestinian doctor who lost three children in 2009 during the Israeli invasion of Gaza, tells of Raffah, a daughter who survived the shelling, writing a poem to Aya, a daughter who died: "Where has the beautiful light gone . . . Where have you disappeared Aya?" Raffah asks. This question—"Where has the beautiful light gone?"—urgently needs addressing in order to move beyond cycles of hate, oppression, and violence.[11]

Dr. Abuelaish dedicates his book *I Shall Not Hate* "to children everywhere. / Their only weapons are love and hope." How do we restore creation and world-making to this space where love and hope resonate with the potential to renew failed and failing world systems? How can we learn from sites of difference that use improvisation to attempt at least a partial answer to this question? The more time I spent in the refugee camps with Al-Mada's animators, the more these were the questions that resonated, and the more evidence I saw of the power of music to transform conflict, stress, and despair, however fleetingly, into something radically different.

As I travel through the West Bank, the contradictions are everywhere. Janos, a Croatian-Hungarian taxi driver, tells me that without the "crazy politics here," he would not have work—he's neither Palestinian nor Israeli, and this allows him to cross borders and checkpoints with minimal hassle. A politico-economic refugee from Croatia, Janos shuttles packages between Jordan, the West Bank, and Jerusalem, and he speaks Croatian, Russian, English, and Hungarian. He says his favorite place to holiday is in Gaza because, in spite of the poverty, it is so beautiful, the people so welcoming. Achmed, another driver, says Ramallah is safer than Jerusalem—and he lives in Jerusalem but is Arab. He takes me through a checkpoint into the West Bank where the Israel Defense Force guard is a young girl. They wave at each other and smile. Just beyond the verdant green fields we are leaving behind is the brutalist architecture of the checkpoint: all razor wire, concrete blocks, towers, and sandbags. Palestinian workers, all men, are forming a bleak line in the dust and garbage. It is clearly going to be a very long day for them.

Achmed is incredibly courteous to all as we pass; his window is down, and he seems to know a lot of people, exclaiming a word I will hear often: *habibi* حبيبي (male)/*habibti* حبيبتى (female), meaning "my beloved, my dear." *Insha'Allah* إن شاء الله ("God willing") is also a word I hear constantly, an expression that is the Arabic source of the related Spanish exclamation *ojalá*, itself a deeply layered expression of hope for the future, of desiring that something good will come to pass. Out of the corner of my eye as we're driving along the grotesque wall that separates Israel from the West Bank, I spot yet another contradiction: a young man has run up the wall with a ladder and is scampering up and over the barbed wire with acrobatic agility. I'm told the wall is constantly being circumvented along its length—as one witty Palestinian tells me, it's a good daily workout for the many compelled to traverse it to shop, work, get to medical appointments, and visit family.

And yet the various forms of systemic exile and exclusion I witness are overwhelming and deeply disturbing in contrast to the warmth and courtesy I experience. David A. McDonald's discussion of political activist and intifada protest singer Kamal Khalil takes note of how Khalil "has spent a lifetime struggling for the right to return to his ancestral village in the West Bank. Growing up on the socially dispossessed periphery of the Jordanian nationscape, Kamal developed a profound sense of exilic nationalism realized in his performances of Palestinian protest songs. Such songs brought forth in the minds of his audience alternative aesthetic realities in which the Palestinian nation could be celebrated, mourned or otherwise performed from within foreign state regimes."[12] So music in Khalil's context is, yet again, a force at work countering ghettoization and segregation. It is Khalil's choice to make music serve this purpose, thus unleashing the transformative aesthetics music potentiates.

The contemporary prohibitions and humiliations that dehumanize, frighten, and separate populations are radically at odds with conductor Daniel Barenboim's observation, in conversation with literary and cultural critic Edward W. Said, that "if conflicts are one day to be solved [in the Middle East], they are only going to be solved by contact between the warring parties. . . . I believe that in cultural matters—with literature and, even better, with music, because it doesn't have to do with explicit ideas—if we foster this kind of a contact, it can only help people feel nearer to each other, and this is all."[13] This is, indeed, *all*. Hope persists, and many in the region continue to believe that sonic contacts rooted in cocreative expression do indeed produce constructive ways of forging (improvising) relations that address difference and dissonance nonviolently. Hope turns silence into sound, or as graffiti I see on a wall in the West Bank says, "No more silent consent or loud indifference." Music gives hope agency, makes it more active than aspirational. Sound transforms indifference into agency and, by extension, into the potential for resilience and resistance.

Al-Mada's defining principles lie in music as a source of human solidarity, an expression of our vulnerable and contingent relation to each other that is in constant need of renewal and sustenance. Its creative potential liberates and sustains spaces that counter state definitions of "space and possibility." Al-Mada reshapes the highly regulated spaces of the Occupied Territories via arts-based expression in which communities can self-define. The organization "was launched in 2009 having one single clear message—that community development is only measurable by the quality of people's lives. Hence the project title 'arts for life' which underscores that art is not a luxury, but an essential element of everyday life—only the arts can produce a space for truly free expression."[14]

Al-Mada's mission arose out of the particular circumstances, energies, and qualities manifest in cofounders Abdul Hadi and Turjman. Abdul Hadi has an exceptional breadth of NGO experiences (including work with the World Health Organization), and Turjman, Abdul Hadi's husband, is an internationally respected musician, composer, educator, and community organizer: "the first person to initiate, design, develop and implement music education programs in Palestinian schools. He has trained hundreds of teachers and helped in developing music education resource materials for primary education."[15] Turjman directed the Music Department at the Ministry of Culture for three years after serving as director of the Palestinian National Music Committee affiliated with UNESCO. A founder of the influential

Palestinian music group Sabreen, he also played a key role in establishing the Edward Said National Conservatory of Music, founded in 1993.[16]

Abdul Hadi and Turjman serve as Al-Mada's executive and artistic directors and have played a key role in how the center defines its vision: "Al Mada believes in the dignity and worth of every individual and the communities we serve. Our vision is a Palestine where music and the arts are at the heart of a culturally vibrant and healthy community life. We work on the basis that everyone contributes towards making social changes and that the power of art can be used to achieve truly sustainable development if individuals are enabled to contribute to the shaping of their societies. Communication, integrity, innovation, respect and diversity are the core values, which inform every aspect of our work."[17] Indeed, their remarkable initiatives are part of a turn to music as a way out of the "no way" that is the crisis in the Occupied Territories. Like Ramzi Hussein Aburedwan, a classically trained Palestinian violist, who has "created musical programs in ten locations, including three in refugee camps in Lebanon," with a "vision of freedom through music that had reached thousands of Palestinian kids," Al-Mada locates its activities in conflicted sites where poverty and violence are rampant, causing significant trauma for Palestinian communities throughout the region.[18] In *Children of the Stone: The Power of Music in a Hard Land*, Sandy Tolan describes Aburedwan's work with the Al Kamandjati music school in Ramallah, arguing that there is a "growing movement of nonviolent resistance, new ways of thinking across the Israeli-Palestinian divide, the challenge of confronting religious extremism, the potential of music to protect and heal traumatized children, . . . and above all, the transformative power of music in a land of brutality, beauty, and confinement."[19] Reclaiming and disseminating Palestinian culture, as with the spring 2016 opening (ironically empty of exhibits) of the Palestinian Museum in Birzeit, is a critical component in their struggle to survive. Creating a space, sonic or otherwise, in which people can share their stories is a vital component not only in retaining identity but also in bridging difference, fostering mutual respect, and healing.

So with the 4th Dimension listening keenly to what we're all hearing as the Al-Mada animators take us from musical encounter to encounter, day after day we're shepherded by UNRWA and the Al-Mada team from refugee camp to refugee camp—from Qalandia (between Ramallah and Jerusalem) to Ein as-Sulṭān in Jericho. John's entire band, Deeyah, and I are introduced as observers and taken through multiple musical situations where improvisation is the key element, the one thing all people in the room—most of whom are not musicians or have never touched a musical instrument—can use to share information with each other.

At each camp we meet with one or two groups of people with whom Al-Mada has been working, using improvised musical games and encounters to prompt community dialogues that respond to the improvisations. Everywhere we go we find circles of people, mostly women and children, improvising music and reflecting on why doing so matters. Grabbing the time to do this is clearly no small matter, and there is an urgency and an edginess in the rooms where these events happen that generates a very focused energy. There's shyness and a sense of ceremony too in how this group of famous musicians encounters the residents of the refugee camps—but the band members' expansive humility combined with the grace and hospitality they're shown quickly makes for warmly shared encounters. At a school for boys that has painful depictions of imprisonment, torture, and suffering in the classrooms and hallways, John spots a soccer ball and spontaneously initiates a game in the dusty yard, to the amusement of all. All around us is barbed wire—we're just minutes away from the infamous barrier wall that scars the landscape—and spontaneous laughter is still possible. I'm struck by how familiar the scenes are to other improvised musical encounters I've experienced—especially in how quickly cocreative improvised musicking can turn adversarial, difficult situations into laughter and displays of resilience; tensions and dissonances into dialogues.

In one camp, an elderly woman arrives late to the session, upset and clearly agitated. Despite the heat, she is in full *jilbāb* (a long, loosely fitting outer garment worn by some Muslim women) and enters the small room we've gathered in—with peeling plaster and children's drawings pasted to the walls—eager to engage. In minutes she is singing with the other participants, hands uplifted, clearly transported by the opportunity to make music in spite of the earlier upset. She looks me straight in the eye and smiles. Her eyes are bright blue and weathered. She has clearly not had an easy life, and she quickly hides her uncovered hands when she spots me looking at them. I am the stranger here, and whatever the differences, the music connects us. This experience is repeated day after day as the remarkable team from Al-Mada negotiates camp after camp with an array of encounters that includes young schoolboys singing self-composed songs together; a group of multilingual teenage girls from one camp who improvise sounds, before a profoundly disturbing discussion of their efforts to combat sexual violence

FIGURE 9.3 Women's Programme Center, Amari Camp: encounter with Al-Mada, John McLaughlin, the 4th Dimension, Ina Behrend, and UNRWA.

in the camps; and a women's center where improvised music serves as an expression of the assembled women's shared struggles in the camps.

At the women's center, children play, instruments are scattered on the ground, and the members of the 4th Dimension listen attentively to the musical exchanges, laughing and remarking on how deftly Al-Mada music therapist and animator Buran Sa'ada handles the group. I am reminded that the band consists of some of the greatest fusion players on the planet, and that John's early explorations of world music led to Shakti: a brilliant illumination of what a musical intercultural encounter might look like yet still a prescient example of how musical exchanges of this kind produce radically beautiful new forms. As a path to interchange and hybrid forms of expression, improvisatory music is at the core of what all these players do, and you can see that they are moved by what they see and hear. Fusion, whatever baggage the word carries, integrates, after all, and is wildly at odds with the politics of segregation.

Early in the trip, I spend an afternoon speaking with Turjman, sitting in a small courtyard behind the Al-Mada offices sipping Arabic coffee from small porcelain cups. The pungent aroma of dark tobacco is in the air, and the busy sounds of Ramallah traffic intermix with the muezzins' ethereal *adhan* (the call to prayers that occurs five times a day). The word *adhan*, I'm told, derives from *adhina* أَذِنَ, meaning "to listen, hear, be informed"—precisely what I'm doing with Turjman as he patiently shares his thoughts on the significance of music in the fraught circumstances all Palestinians face. He tells me that the lemon tree in the courtyard behind Al-Mada's offices was destroyed by snow this year, as were the grapevines, when some thirty centimeters fell and brought Ramallah to a standstill. He is resigned when he tells me this—he's seen far worse destruction, as when his house was flattened by an Israeli air strike during the First Intifada. We speak for almost five hours on our first encounter, as if we've known each other for many years: "Peace is not a process," he says. "It is either *now*, or it is not real." Turjman's serene insight skewers the politics that bureaucratize and defer peace in the here and now where lemon trees die and roosters crow and vast orchards of olive trees have been razed to provide sight lines for snipers. Tony, another Palestinian I meet who takes pity on my ignorance, tells me late in the trip that scholastic arguments around religious difference annoy him—to each their own. He ignores the sound of the muezzins because he is Christian and secular and because while music here may be the salvation of prayer for some, not everyone is listening in the same way. His message is clear: don't reduce Palestinians to simplistic stereotypes about religion, identity, or ideology.

Underlying what Turjman tells me are crucial considerations from the 2013 report of the special rapporteur in the field of cultural rights: "The Right to Freedom of Artistic Expression and Creativity," authored by Farida Shaheed.[20] Shaheed's analysis of the challenges to artistic freedoms includes the following concerns:

> 35. Artists, like journalists and human rights defenders, are at particular risk as their work depends on visibly engaging people in the public domain. Through their expressions and creations, artists often question our lives, perceptions of ourselves and others, world visions, power relations, human nature and taboos, eliciting emotional as well as intellectual responses.
>
> 36. Artistic expression and creativity may entail the re-appropriation of symbols, whether national (flags, national anthems), religious (figures, symbols, venues), or social/economical (a certain brand for example), as part of a response to the narratives promoted by states, religious institutions or economic powers. States, religions, corporate companies and social groups also use art to propagate their ideas and promote their interests, including concepts of right and wrong to create homogeneity of belief and behaviour. In most cases, restrictions on artistic freedoms reflect a desire to promote a world vision or narrative "while simultaneously blocking all others."[21]

FIGURE 9.4 Street art in the West Bank. Mapped on a wall, a path forward through learning and books.

Palestinians have had to struggle against remarkable odds to sustain communities and cultural identity. Ibtisam Ilzghayyer, director of the Ghirass Cultural Center in Bethlehem, reminds readers,

> [When we] started the center, we wanted to educate children about Palestinian culture, Palestinian music, Palestinian poetry. We have famous poets like Mahmoud Darwish, but it was forbidden for us to read from them or read other Palestinian writers.... We couldn't have Palestinian flags, political symbols, anything considered propaganda for a Palestinian state.... With these restrictions in mind, one of our first goals at the center was to provide a sense of Palestinian culture to children. We wanted the center to be inclusive, so we didn't allow any religious symbols or symbols of any specific political parties in the center.... In the center, I tried to make students thinkers before fighters.[22]

The importance of these sentiments to the future of the region, in like-minded community centers and schools—like Al Kamandjati, Ghirass, and Al-Mada—that have sprung up in Palestine, cannot be underestimated. And everywhere I see evidence that the kind of community education and experience provided by these groups matters profoundly to the people they engage with.

Turjman understands well the valences that music carries as a significant conduit of identity and affect, and the need to engage people—his

FIGURE 9.5 One wall, two jails. Another form of wall just beyond the Qalandia checkpoint between Ramallah and Jerusalem.

people—through the arts as a way of providing alternative narratives closely tied to cultural survival. Palestinian music, as Moslih Kanaaneh argues, is a special case that is "the cumulative outcome of the dialectical relationship between a long intrinsic tradition and a long history of occupation and subjugation to foreign rule. The influence of surrounding cultures and music traditions on Palestinian music has also been marked by cultural intrusion resulting from the asymmetrical power relation between Palestine and its neighboring cultures and countries."[23]

Turjman's leadership in Palestinian musical communities was at the core of the drive to institute (in 1993) the Edward Said National Conservatory of Music, which now has branches in Ramallah, Jerusalem, Bethlehem, Nablus, and Gaza City (and over a thousand students enrolled). Al-Mada continues the work of establishing spaces where education and creative expression can enable agency and resistant alternatives to power asymmetries. Turjman explains that one of the core missions of Al-Mada is to give voice to a dispossessed younger generation:

> For young people living in this situation it is a crisis because this is a time when you build your own identity and culture, but at the same time you do not have the environment to support those activities because of the contradictory and conflicting environment that deprives you of access and identity. You are a Palestinian, but you do not have a state. You are living in a state that does not recognize you as a citizen, so you do not

know where you belong. You have the sense from your family and so on that, yes, I am a Palestinian, I belong to this culture. But the other institutional realities and allocation of resources do not support your belonging in any way. So this Al Mada youth project . . . was aimed at young people to help them express what it means to be Palestinian, to capture the situation in their own voices.

He also tells me that in first working with children in the refugee camps, it became apparent that improvisation allowed them to confront traumatic experiences in ways that nothing else could, and that initially the musicians doing the work had no idea how deep the improvisations could go in allowing the trauma to speak. A concrete example of this sort of work is evident in the 2013 Al-Mada–produced album *I Love Life*, which includes songs sung by children

> about children's rights and touch[es] on the themes of equality, the right to life, protection from child labour, and safety from conflict. The album was recorded and edited in Al-Mada's state-of-the-art recording studio by a team of professional musicians and technicians and a group of eight Palestinian children aged 8–12. 2000 copies of the CD were printed and 1000 of them were distributed to kindergartens and schools across the occupied Palestinian Territories in partnership with the Ministry of Education, UNRWA, and ANERA [American Near East Refugee Aid]. Our goal is to increase the number of children who have access to this CD in Palestine and to make it available regionally and in the diaspora, as well.[24]

The fifth song from the album states, "I love life, I love people / I hate all war / Can anyone tell me / Why so many people have to die?" These words echo the daily experience of people throughout Palestine who, like Gazan fisherman Jamal Bakr, experience violence as part of the fabric of everyday life: "Every single day, I hear that someone got shot at. Every single day, I expect to be killed. Whenever I leave my home in the morning, I'm not sure I will get home alive. That's what it's like to be a fisherman in Gaza. . . . The soldiers often shoot for no reason at all."[25]

Our group of observers meets primarily with youth and women, the audience most open to engaging with Al-Mada's group of therapists. In one encounter at the Women's Programme Center at the Amari Camp, an obviously talented young mother wearing traditional dress shows remarkable ability on the percussion instruments she has chosen to play from a pile of instruments in the middle of the room. The band immediately sits up and takes notice, and both Gary Husband and Ranjit Barot, no percussion slouches themselves, break into broad smiles at how skillfully she plays. She is offered an instrument to take home but emphatically refuses the gift. She tells us, while putting her hands around her throat, that her husband would not put up with it—and she laughs saying that she practices on the pots and pans in her kitchen . . . regardless.

Who needs a drum when the world offers so many surfaces that can be played?

Coda: Improvising Balloons in the Ein as-Sulṭān Refugee Camp

In Jericho, a group of teenage girls gather to make music based on images they draw during the workshop. There's a large image of a beautiful tree on one wall, and one of a bird on another wall. These images are startlingly at odds with these multilingual young women trapped between their aspirations—to become actors, reporters, academics—and their circumstances as refugees surviving sexual violence in their own homes, trying to build solidarity groups that work with young women in other camps, and dealing with their own statelessness and the ever-present potential for state violence.

More so, the tree image is at odds with what we have witnessed on the way to Jericho, with hectares of olive orchards razed to stumps below the settlements encroaching on the arid Bedouin lands and the tin bidonvilles and shantytowns beneath them. I'm told the orchards are now stump yards because they were deemed a threat to national security and because their removal provides clearer firing lines from the illegal settlements into the Occupied Territories. And yes, we've seen images of this form of ecocide elsewhere, on walls, the art countering the erasure and memoricide that the occupation entails.[26]

Yet as soon as the improvised music starts, the solidarity I've heard in language becomes palpable. There are more smiles and dialogue. One of the Al-Mada therapists throws balloons in the air, and the women dance to the music while randomly bumping the balloons across the room. The balloons are a small joy whose uplift connects and carries us all. The moment is over fast, but it is transformative. The simple exchange is followed, as part of Al-Mada's methodology connecting activity to talk and critique, by a therapist-led discussion on improvisation and the importance of art as an expressive force that builds and sustains community.

FIGURE 9.6 The razing of the olive orchards depicted in a student painting in Ramallah. "Israeli authorities have uprooted over 800,000 Palestinian olive trees since 1967, the equivalent to razing all of the 24,000 trees in New York's central park 33 times" (*Mondoweiss*, "Since 1967 Israel Has Razed").

Ein as-Sulṭān camp is Palestine's smallest refugee camp. Nestled at the foot of the Mount of Temptation, just outside the historic city of Jericho, the camp's current population is about two thousand people. Established in 1948, the camp once hosted twenty thousand refugees, but the vast majority were forced to flee to Jordan during the hostilities of the 1967 war—its residents' origins can be traced to Jaffa, Ar Ramla city, Bir al-Sabi', and their surrounding villages, in addition to Gaza city. Many of those who remain once relied on employment in Israel to make ends meet, but when the occupation intensified during the Second Intifada (2000–2005), most lost their jobs because of the severe movement restrictions that were imposed. Today, poor socioeconomic conditions, inadequate basic infrastructure such as roads and sewers, and severe water shortages, all compounded by the Israeli occupation, cause tremendous hardship for the refugees, who continue to be largely dependent on food rations and other forms of international aid. As part of the Al-Mada visit, a small group of us are lucky enough to attend a series of workshops in Ein as-Sulṭān and to meet with a number of women's groups working in concert with Al-Mada. Contrary to the stereotypical images of stone-throwing terrorists found in most mass media, the Palestinian women we meet are thoughtful, playful, and articulate in their desire for justice and respect achieved through nonviolent means.[27]

The more I listen to these women, the more I think of Ignacio Ellacuría, the Salvadoran Jesuit, assassinated in 1989, who argued that "it is the oppressed who discovers the oppressor," suggesting, as Martha Nandorfy and I argue, that "the true reality of the oppressor can only be seen from the point of view of the oppressed."[28] Ellacuría's observation inverts received wisdom on who knows what and what kinds of knowledge are traditionally given value. If one dares cross what the Portuguese sociologist Boaventura de Sousa Santos calls the abyssal line separating visible knowledge systems from invisible, marginalized ones, then the knowledge of the oppressed, like the knowledge of improvisatory practices, becomes a compelling way to connect across the divides that alienate.[29] This, to me at least, is a profound form of knowledge, palpable in Ein as-Sulṭān, that remains to be discovered elsewhere.

The improvised music I hear in Palestine in humble cinder-block buildings has no commodity value, no obvious commercial value—no presence, except for its fleeting appearance in passing encounters. Yet it matters and has tremendous, immediate value. Like the balloons bouncing randomly in this simple classroom, such music is fragile and evanescent, but somehow aloft, powerful and resonant in unexpected ways. It expresses a grounded humanity that lies at the core of what it means to be in contingent relation to others, respectful of how powerful the cocreative impulses at the heart of improvisatory practices can be in the face of violent, dysfunctional realities.

At the end of the session at the Woman's Programme Centre in the Amari refugee camp, a very shy older woman who has clearly been moved by the proceedings discreetly shuffles around the room, giving all the visitors handmade keychains of the Palestinian flag, painstakingly crafted out of cheap beads and carried in a tattered plastic bag. She says our visit is a gift, but I'm not so sure. Each of us is approached, greeted, and thanked before we receive the keychain: a simple gesture of friendship and appreciation, but one also highly emblematic of that key to improvisatory doing—the use of what is at hand to create, and to do so in ways that connect us at a basic level of human understanding. Yet again, we see women as an enduring, constant force for social justice.

The gift is telling: it symbolizes keys to imaginary spaces we have yet to inhabit; it speaks of access, trust, humble acts of making—the keychain has no keys yet, and there are keys to be placed on it for doors yet to be opened. As I have learned, keys are an important symbol in the West Bank of the right to return after the "ethnic cleansing"—described at length by Israeli historian Ilan Pappe—of the 1948 Nakba that saw the forced displacement of hundreds of thousands of Palestinians from their homes.[30] Giving and hospitality, listening and responding, the capacity to turn impoverished material circumstances into a reminder of our interconnected, grounded humanity—there's grace and connection, history and circumstance, in the giving.

I look around, and we, the visitors, are all in the same plight.

None of us have anything to give her in return . . . except perhaps to learn what her gesture can teach us, to listen to her invitation for reciprocal engagement, for respect, for our ability to connect in ways that make us real to each other no matter our differences.

Everyone in the room I speak with acknowledges that music changes how we witness each other's presence.

Might this be what "improvising community into being" means in these circumstances? Might this gift of life also be a gift of love, of the potential we collectively embody? Khaled Juma, a Palestinian poet from Gaza, wrote the following lyrics, set to music by Turjman and sung by children:

> The thing about people is
> wherever we are, we're all alike.
> Look at me and my friends,
> with all our clever bodies—
> hands with quick fingers,
> eyelashes that even help us
> shield our eyes from the dust.
> Our mouths make words,
> our ears catch sounds,
> our brains can think
> so we all know.
> The whole wide world
> is what we love.[31]

The word *passion* in English, in its earliest sense, meant to suffer and to endure, a meaning that did not shift to its more current sense of powerful emotion until centuries later. One scant syllable separates *passion* from *compassion*, the latter intending sympathy and empathy, the capacity to be *together* in the face of suffering, to imagine another's circumstances and be moved to action by them.

Is it too much to ask that people of goodwill find ways to improvise this *being together* from common ground, and in the public commons we share? Might this be the way forward in bringing social justice and artistic expression together in response to crisis and its aftermath, in response to the contingent relations without which community and coexistence are impossible? Improvisation in this context implies a choice to be made, an action to be taken, and emptiness of form from which an ethics of doing emerges.

The inner mounting flame that gives birth to poetry and sound turns us all toward life. The "wide world . . . we love" is what we must improvise daily in the unfolding necessity of the unpredictable everyday. If the poet can turn sand into rain, and the musician light into sound, is it too much to believe that these powers can foster, sustain, and harmonize an underlying, grounded humanity?

Let's give the last word to John McLaughlin—who spoke in conversations with his friend Daniel Barenboim about being profoundly moved by the plight of Palestinians. And indeed, his improvisatory engagement with Al-Mada is a form of both witnessing and taking action that brings our humanity into focus. At a press conference I attended that preceded the solidarity concert in Ramallah, he mused, "If we can do small things, then small things count. What are we going to do about what we see?"

"Change That Comes from Within"

These interviews occurred in April 2014 and represent accurate information at that moment. Much has changed with regard to Al-Mada since then.[32]

DANIEL FISCHLIN: *I know you and Al-Mada's cofounder, Odeh Turjman, have worked very hard to make the Al-Mada center happen. So, Reem, could you talk a bit about the genesis of Al-Mada, how the idea came into being for both of you? I know Odeh has his musical background: he's been very active both as a prominent musician and composer and also as one of the founding members of the Edward Said National Conservatory of Music, and as his partner, you're part of the journey. But to go from an idea to a fully functioning center like this is many steps, and I know you played a very crucial role. So maybe tell us your history with Al-Mada in your own words.*

REEM ABDUL HADI: In 2001, during the Second Intifada, Odeh was involved in a program called "Childhood Testimony," which partners with Palestinian schools to provide psychosocial support to students who have suffered a variety of traumatic events as a result of the Israeli occupation. The program brought together young students and gave them the chance to use music as a tool to explore creatively their personal challenges, problems, and other issues of importance in their lives and communities. These young students were asked to talk about issues that have impacted their lives in order to later develop musical compositions based on these same issues or topics. During one of the interventions, fifteen-year-old female students chose "unity" as a topic of discussion. The word for "unity" in Arabic is the same as the word for "loneliness"—وحدة (pronounced wa-hə-dah). Only one girl in the class, however, understood the word in the latter sense. The topic—loneliness—triggered strong emotional responses and reactions among the students, and the discussion suddenly shifted toward their relationships with their bodies, society, families, friends, and parents, which required different forms of psychological relief intervention. Odeh, as a young musician at the time, had to focus on music making, as it was difficult to deal with these issues on his own, without any kind of psychological or therapeutic support and little training in the link between music and therapy. The whole process was frustrating for both Odeh and the students, as these issues required more attention, and therapy was very much needed. The power of music and the way in which it managed to trigger these emotions and allow students to express feelings openly, creatively, and freely made us consider combining music with psychology. This idea nevertheless remained dormant and unrealized for quite some time.

Our son Tareq, who was five years old at the time, had persistent and noticeable speech and sound difficulties. He couldn't pronounce the letters *s* and *z* properly and had difficulty saying particular consonants and letters. He was very much bullied and made fun of at school because of his speech impediment, so we took him to a speech pathologist. His therapist helped him with different techniques, and after months of practice, he was finally able to say the letter *s*. This, however, did not resolve the speech problem. What came as a complete surprise, though, was Tareq's ability to articulate and pronounce letters correctly only when singing. Odeh kept encouraging him to sing more, and record songs, and in no time his speech problem was gone. This is when we realized the importance of incorporating music into speech and language therapy, or, to put it differently, to incorporate music therapy in addressing children with speech disorders.

When I was working as a program analyst at the United Nations Development Program, I was responsible for different portfolios, including health (a psychosocial intervention program), education, and gender. My experiences made me question the concept of "sustainable development under occupation" and pushed me to examine the ways in which it could be revised and redefined to suit our context in the Occupied Territories. All of these accumulated experiences and interactions enabled us to develop a project called "Bring Us Our Voices Back," which acknowledged the role of music in making a difference, or, in other words, in creating a platform for healing to take place. Soon, though, we were confronted with another problem—the dilemma of whether or not the name of the project reflected our reality, particularly in a colonial setting where all dissenting voices had been silenced. The question that kept running through my mind is the following: Who's going to bring us [Palestinians] back our voices? The occupation? The international community? Those who are complicit in taking them away? This is where the dilemma seemed to arise—especially with respect to Palestinian agency and marginalized narratives. Our frustration with the status quo and the way in which "development" has been implemented led to the creation of Al-Mada Association for Arts-Based Community Development.

DANIEL FISCHLIN: *And you were expecting it to be difficult?*

REEM ABDUL HADI: Palestinian nongovernmental organizations face a myriad of challenges when operating in Jerusalem. Setting up an NGO or a nonprofit organization can be an extremely lengthy, bureaucratic, and time-consuming process. Israel has partially succeeded in isolating Jerusalem from most West Bank cities with its policy of barring Palestinians from those cities from entering Jerusalem. It is true that Jerusalemites suffer from a lack of basic services, but they can still access the West Bank city of Ramallah. Despite several challenges, we were able to acquire limited funding from a German NGO that believed in our mission and purpose. There was, however, no salary for the post of director, so I decided to volunteer for the position in order to keep the place running. I loved everything about this place. We designed everything from scratch.

DANIEL FISCHLIN: *It sounds like from the start you had a very clear vision.*

REEM ABDUL HADI: Yes, everything was in place from day one. I knew what needed to be done and how to execute it. I also knew that it would *not* be easy: it was a relatively new field for me, but one that has really piqued my interest and that has become a medium of ongoing inspiration, whatever the difficulties. We started in 2009. Odeh at the time was a member of the Palestinian National Music Council and the director of the National Music Committee. We were both thinking about whom to approach first. Dr. Umaiyeh Khammash—the chief of the UNRWA health program in the

West Bank—was the first name that came to mind, mainly because of his human rights work.

DANIEL FISCHLIN: *So very prominent in the national music community . . . (referring to Odeh).*

REEM ABDUL HADI: Yes, and he's very modest . . .

DANIEL FISCHLIN: *. . . considering how with Sabreen he was such a force in the context of the group's focus "on the development of the Palestinian modern song, reflecting the humanitarian and cultural reality in general, and the suffering endured from the political situation in particular."* [33]

REEM ABDUL HADI: Yes, and he has also received numerous awards for his music composition and production. He won first prize for best musical composition—competing among thirty-six other films selected for an international documentary film festival. Music therapy is a new and rising field or discipline, and thus does not have an established agenda, which means it can be tailored according to local needs, particularly as issues may change slightly according to the specific contexts out of which they emerge. Al-Mada, for instance, has always been trying to provide a safe space and environment for those who have suffered physical, mental, or emotional trauma. Hence, it was important to use a familiar language, or type of music, to meet the social and political needs of Palestinians—taking into account that Palestinians are not homogeneous but are differentiated with respect to socio-economic, cultural, and political conditions. Finding music therapists was another challenge that required more effort on our end, but after months of research, three Palestinian music therapists joined our team.

DANIEL FISCHLIN: *And did you already have the space in Ramallah?*

REEM ABDUL HADI: Yes. It was empty, actually. We used to rent chairs from a nearby store, because of the lack of funds. Projects have a lifetime of several months, sometimes several years, but they all eventually end, and this is where the problem lies. Especially at the beginning, it takes time to establish new concepts, build, and accumulate the expertise necessary to deliver projects on time and within the set budget, but these projects are mostly tied to a timeline. This issue of sustainability, in my opinion, is the main problem of development and the cause of many failed development projects. Simply put, progress is not something that can be quantitatively measured by conventional metrics, especially in a situation as complex and challenging as what we face in Palestine.

So, yes, now we had the space, and we were both working there in two different capacities, in conformity with the rules and regulations for operating a not-for-profit NGO. At the end of the day, we are just employees. Just to clarify: a nonprofit organization's board of directors is the one responsible for hiring and firing the executive director. The employment relationship, like anywhere else, is based on a contract of employment. I have been basically working full-time for free, despite the fact that I'm scheduled to work part-time, while Odeh has been working as a consultant, paid by the day—only if there is a particular project being developed, such as training sessions, and the like. This situation has been challenging for us, let alone the fact that music therapy in and of itself is not a popular concept.

We live in a particular social and political situation. I therefore understand why Palestinians in Gaza—who have been living in an "open-air prison" for years now, without electricity, running water, medical supplies, or sanitation—don't find the idea of music therapy very appealing. But they have been exposed to traumatic events and experiences, and psychological intervention and support are very much needed in the same way that water and electricity are needed. These all form part of a continuum of rights needed to address the conditions of oppression under which they live. We had a session where one of the counselors burst into tears. He was imprisoned by Israeli authorities, tortured during interrogation, and subjected to different sorts of psychological pressure. The stress was later on projected onto his own family. Prolonged untreated post-traumatic stress disorder can only contribute to other psychological ailments that are deeply felt far beyond the confines of the prison or facility where torture occurs.

DANIEL FISCHLIN: *One of the things I was going to ask was about some of the cases that stand out in your mind, where you've seen the kind of interaction that's provided by Al-Mada making a difference, because part of the story means that people want to hear concrete examples, and it is certainly what those of us who have been here over the past days have seen on a daily basis. You are unique in that you are doing something in one of the most conflicted zones on the planet—and you are using music when dealing with the occupation and the walls and the constant threat of violence, let alone the violence itself. So I was going to ask on behalf of the people who will be reading this that you give some examples that stand out. So, this man, who was training to* be a therapist himself, or who is already a therapist, was feeling tremendous shame about the pains he was feeling, and also projecting that onto his own family. In that situation, the therapy helped him, but we've seen over the past few days a lot of kids of different ages—only women really, except for the boys at the school. Are there maybe a few other cases that stand out in your mind?

REEM ABDUL HADI: Disruptive and aggressive behaviors are common among children, but one of the boys was very hyperactive, labeled as violent, and had serious temper tantrums regularly. He also had a terrible time staying focused during class and constantly fought with his classmates and teachers. But during the music sessions, he was very much engaged and started singing. He had a beautiful voice, and luckily enough one of the counselors who had been previously introduced to music therapy was present in the room and tried to encourage him; the music therapist was there as well. And in no time, he went from the most "hated" to the best singer of the school. His academic performance improved significantly, which came as a complete surprise for everyone involved. The problem is that music and the arts are often neglected in our schools and tend to be seen as less important.

DANIEL FISCHLIN: *Not so different from what is happening elsewhere (as in Canada), really. We call them the fifth-wheel classes—the extra things that, so the argument goes, you don't really need because they have no ostensible value to the bureaucrats and politicians, who don't understand the breadth of what makes us fully human.*

REEM ABDUL HADI: Exactly. Schools tend to place more and more emphasis on math and sciences, neglecting other equally important subjects, which is exactly why we are currently working with the Palestinian Ministry of Education to encourage alternative forms of education, precisely giving more attention to more inclusive notions of education. Including art and music in the curriculum is a first step in that direction, with an emphasis on the interactive nature of these subjects. This is especially true with shy, introverted, and somewhat-withdrawn children. We dealt with a similar case in one of our interventions, and through interactive music activities, we were able to identify the child's condition, and the reason why he was reluctant to speak with others.

There is another story of a thirteen-year-old girl who was sexually abused. As you may know, children who experience rape or sexual abuse are more likely to show negative outcomes that carry forward into adult life, with ongoing problems with self-identity, social skills, confidence, and academic motivation, as well as serious learning and adjustment problems, including severe depression, aggressive behavior, and peer difficulties—which was exactly the case here. The counselor gave her a guitar, and she started playing loud music, without saying a word. She managed to let her anger out by breaking a couple of strings, so the counselor gave her another instrument and asked her to write a song. This exercise helped her to express her feelings and work through some difficult times. Surprisingly, she was more upset with her father, as he not only blamed her for being raped but also failed to take any sort of action against her rapist. She found this to be a lot worse than the assault itself. So we were dealing with two traumas—one from the present, and one from the past, as she was still living with her father. We had to establish some priorities.

DANIEL FISCHLIN: *Plus, on top of that she's having to lie to her father about where she's going to get help . . .*

REEM ABDUL HADI: Exactly. But then of course the father got involved. Sometimes it is difficult to pinpoint where the problem actually lies, because it is not a physical injury, but once you know where to start, you can take it from there. That is why this exercise was helpful and why music and the sense of improvising a response that was true to her experience played such a key role in making this intervention work.

Another story comes to mind—a six-year-old child, diagnosed with blood cancer. His mother is a holder of a Jerusalem ID, while his dad is a West Banker. I don't know if you are aware of this, but Jerusalem ID holders must live in Jerusalem, or else their residency is revoked, and of course, as I mentioned earlier, Palestinians from the West Bank cannot enter Jerusalem. So this was already a complicated situation to begin with. The only hospital specializing in treating this type of cancer is located in Jerusalem, so the mother had to take the child there, while the father had to stay at home and take care of the kids. Usually, or in most cases, it is the other way around. The ensuing family tensions appear to have led to domestic violence, and the mother just didn't know what to do.

DANIEL FISCHLIN: *An incredibly stressful situation . . .*

REEM ABDUL HADI: Yes, so her son got treated but had to go back for follow-up appointments. We met with him when he was eleven, and by that time he was still undergoing treatment and was experiencing bed-wetting. This, however, was not related to the cancer diagnosis, and it also had nothing to do with his liver, kidney, or urinary system.

DANIEL FISCHLIN: *Bed-wetting is often related to stress: it's a reaction to stress, so music therapy would have given him some tools for handling the stress?*

REEM ABDUL HADI: Exactly. But a further problem we have is that many people are reluctant to see a therapist or to approach community centers such as ours. Three women refused to speak to the media and tell their stories. One of them said, "My husband doesn't know I come to the center, and he would probably recognize my voice." Another woman is also not allowed to come here, so she pretends to be participating in sewing classes instead, as her mother-in-law has to have control over everything.

DANIEL FISCHLIN: *That's one thing that we noticed with the first group of women on Tuesday. They were very direct with us afterward. We asked one, "Does your husband allow you to come?" and she made this physical gesture of being choked. A lot of them were saying, "We have an hour, maybe, once a week that we can call our own." So the lack of free time is a huge problem, and it's obviously gender based.*

REEM ABDUL HADI: I had a conversation with the woman you're talking about in particular. I offered her free percussion lessons, and she said, "Are you kidding me? I always play music on kitchen pots and pans."

DANIEL FISCHLIN: *The women we saw yesterday, the two groups, both very clearly understood that the music, being together in a room, doing what they were doing, creates its own momentum and force and community—and the younger girls were especially vocal about it. They were very precise, and they saw it as a way of being in solidarity together and then also creating momentum to generate solidarity with other kids in other camps, which was very striking. It's not like an argument for them: that it's valuable or not. They understand, and they were clear that what they were doing with the improvised musical activities, even if it seemed silly, stands in for something else that is important.*

So, they played a game where they had all these hoops on the floor, and when the music stopped, they had to jump into the hoop. It was amazing, because as it got down to fewer and fewer girls, they became more interested in surviving themselves as opposed to the whole group surviving, and then they were very critical of each other for having gone in that direction, rather than having stayed together as a community. They totally got it, and it was amazing to see: you don't have to sell it, the idea of music therapy, to them—and it's not a therapy. I don't think they're seeing it that way; it's an activity that allows them to express another part of their lives.

One of the questions I really wanted to ask you had to do with that more general sense of the philosophy of using music—and art, whether it's music or not—to generate community, and the kinds of things that you've observed and think that you would say about that now. How you would frame that way of being in the world and that functional use of music and the functional use of art in community settings, especially in conflict, in terms of addressing reconciliation, and also the gender biases that create enormous stress in patriarchal communities. You've been doing this for several years now and have reached a certain stage of experience—in seeing how the program is working. You have trained people to go out into the field. You're facing challenges, for sure, but I also think there's been a sense that at heart what you're doing is the right thing to be doing, and there are reasons why that's the case. I was trying to get at what those reasons are: we've talked about transformations, the power to transform reality, the power to diagnose things that are hidden. So what is your sense now, with the experience that you've had?

REEM ABDUL HADI: With music therapy, or psychotherapy, there has been a kind of taboo that is, however, quickly changing as we adapt to different ways of coping with an ever-changing world of the occupation. But there is still a widespread view that those who go to therapists are "crazy," "ill," or "insane," and so people fear the stigma around that label.

DANIEL FISCHLIN: *In English it's the same. It feels like* therapy *is a clumsy word that medicalizes healing situations that are exceptionally complex . . .*

REEM ABDUL HADI: I know, but it is important to recognize that there are different types of therapy, such as speech therapy, physiotherapy, and so forth. The word *therapy* in Arabic translates to *al-ilage* العلاج (pronounced al-a-ee-laaj), which means "treatment"—and it is a contested term. Al-Mada uses what is known as "expressive arts therapy" in our work and interventions. Increasingly popular as an alternative to traditional psychological counseling and therapy interventions, and used around the world in diverse contexts, this umbrella term defines a form of therapy that actively uses the creative arts, including but not limited to music, drama, movement, and drawing/painting. It allows individuals or groups to examine the body, feelings, emotions, and thought processes in an open and integrated way to encourage growth, development, and healing with the support of a trained facilitator/counselor, and it can be used in psychology, education, organizational development, and community work. It differs from traditional arts expression in that the creative process is far more important than the final product. It also differs from many traditional forms of psychological counseling or interventions that rely on talk therapy as the primary form of healing.

DANIEL FISCHLIN: *Yes, I've seen that study actually. Depression.*

REEM ABDUL HADI: Depression is fundamentally about the suppression of energy, which eventually takes its toll in physical terms. More than 90 percent of Palestinians, mainly youth and children, suffer from depression, frustration, anxiety, and post-traumatic stress disorder because of the Israeli occupation. That's precisely why we tend to use expressive arts therapies, specifically music therapy and arts education, to advance self-expression, inclusion, healing, social justice, and advocacy through our work with Palestinian communities. We seek to bring a sense of joy and relief from what is often a very stressful life in Palestine—and we support change that comes from within communities, through their own members, resources, capacities, and diversities. The arts provide a space and a platform where individuals can express, create, and heal: they are a powerful tool to advocate for concerns and rights.

Hence, advocacy represents another important component of our work. You cannot heal or make a difference without solidarity. We need to keep advocating for the Palestinian cause, despite financial constraints. We provide support to Palestinian refugees, the displaced, the oppressed, and violated children, youth, women, and those who work in the areas of child protection, early childhood development, inclusive learning for children with disabilities, and psychosocial support services in, but not limited to, schools and refugee camps.

The Grammy-winning jazz-fusion guitarist and songwriter John McLaughlin's first solidarity concert represented a milestone in the short history of Al-Mada. John and his wife, Ina Behrend, believed in Al-Mada's endeavor to use music as a tool for healing, in the necessity of providing the highest-quality child protection to Palestine's refugee population, and in the importance of placing the Palestinian cause on the international agenda. I believe that personal success stories are very important and are connected to the kind of direct action that John and Ina have taken. These can actually have more impact than all the symbolic gestures and existing UN resolutions that have been violated countless times. Support is very much appreciated, but we need to deliver concrete results on the ground. All these symbolic gestures tend unintentionally to maintain the status quo instead of challenging it, while issues remain unresolved.

DANIEL FISCHLIN: *Namely, Jerusalem, borders, refugees, water, and settlements.*

REEM ABDUL HADI: "For My Identity, I Sing!" is another success story. It is a unique cultural and arts education initiative targeting youth in Palestine. The program brings together young people without formal arts training and gives them the chance to use the arts, and especially music, as a tool to creatively explore their identity, personal challenges, problems, and other issues of importance in their lives and their communities. Participating youth meet weekly with professional musicians who train them in basic principles of musical elements, technique, and composition. There are also workshops on writing, movement, theater, and other creative processes. During this period, Palestinian youth are asked to choose issues that impact their lives and begin to explore the chosen topics through the creative processes, incorporating elements of music therapy to help them fully express themselves.

Musicians work with the youth to develop original music compositions based on these issues. These original songs are then recorded and presented to the community through online platforms and public performances. Youth are also trained in elements of advocacy, and the songs themselves become advocacy tools to talk about and increase popular awareness around youth problems and issues. The first stage of the program was an eighteen-month-long project that started in 2013 and worked with two hundred youth in East Jerusalem, aged between fourteen and seventeen. The participants came from diverse backgrounds, helping to bridge the separation that has been imposed on Palestinians as a result of occupation, the apartheid wall, displacement, and social division. Listening to personal stories and experiences can have a profound sentimental effect and make an impact. It's not abstract because it personalizes the issues and empowers people to act. Music and performance are hugely important tools for creating agency for people living under such a grievous situation.

DANIEL FISCHLIN: *There is a lot of hidden suffering, because it's like the police who use phone books to batter people because it doesn't bruise them—you don't* see the bruises. Tony, a member of the incredible UNRWA staff I've met with, was saying that in Gaza they regularly and arbitrarily decide not to let in fuel trucks, and this causes ongoing frustrations because of the consequent power outages, and this affects the predictability of day-to-day life for families, for hospitals, for schools, and so forth.

REEM ABDUL HADI: Few people are aware that electricity in Gaza is a luxury.

DANIEL FISCHLIN: Yes, so if there's no power, you can't get around, and nobody hears about it because the blockade, any blockade on that scale, is not news. Only the people on the ground experience that. I think that's sort of a metaphor for the bigger scenario, of what you were saying before, of Palestine being just this little dot, and people don't really tune in, but there are millions of people experiencing this. So I think it's amazing having John. I just saw, by the way, that Ina sent out an email: there's an Associated Press story on Yahoo about the concert last night. I read it quickly, and it was very direct in a way . . . but beautiful without being politicized in the normal way. But the message is getting through, and the message is associated with a man who has a lot of integrity, who is very respected. Although I did hear from Ina yesterday that after the last solidarity concert they got a lot of emails, from Israelis, I guess, saying, "I used to like you John McLaughlin, but we're not going to listen to you anymore, because of what you did."

It's part of the problem, that kind of ad hominem attitude—it's been normalized even though it is prejudicial and ignorant of the historical truth of what is happening here. But the interesting thing is that the music, it transforms people, it gets people away from that kind of logic and gets them into a different way of thinking about it. That humanizes it, that gives it a face, and that's the problem, right? It's how to get the story out, how to make the story more widely disseminated and change those stereotypes that are so brutal and will never lead to meaningful solutions. The way, you know what you were saying about how the Irish visitor was thinking, that *you're the violent ones, that* you're *the source of the violence, and here you are throwing stones against tanks* . . . and Tony was saying that there's at least one Palestinian a day who's shot by a sniper and killed throughout the territories. And those stories, too, disappear, or are contained and not widely disseminated.

REEM ABDUL HADI: Under the terms of the 1993 Oslo peace accords, over 60 percent of the occupied Palestinian territory in the West Bank remains under full Israeli military and administrative control. Here, in what is known as Area C, Israel restricts Palestinians' access to land and resources by instituting systemic segregation, forcibly evicting and displacing Palestinian residents, demolishing civilian property, and expanding Israeli settlements, severely constraining the living space and development opportunities of Palestinian communities. Settlers have also carried out dozens of attacks on Palestinians or their property. Who's going to protect them? And the peace process has been stalled for quite some time now.

The question that I always try to look at is whether you can actually have negotiations in a situation of unequal power like the one between the Palestinians and the Israelis; in my opinion, it's simply an illusion of equivalence between the occupier and the occupied. How can you possibly accept that? I'm aware of the fact that Al-Mada can't do much—it's a small organization with limited resources—but we're trying our best to do what we can with what we have. Odeh and I are not rich, and we're not trying to make a living out of this—we don't even have a car—but we are both unwilling to abandon things we have invested our time, effort, and energy in, especially when it comes to serving our community. Education is very important for us. I worry about my children's future.

"In Their Own Voices"

DANIEL FISCHLIN: *Odeh, can you tell me where you come from, and how you came to music, and where your family is from, and just a little bit about your own history.*

ODEH TURJMAN: My interest in music started as a child. I do not know how it came that I was always attentive to the sounds of music. My parents realized my interest, and my father bought me a small accordion. I never "learned" music in the traditional European sense, up until now. Improvisation was my way through music all through my life, even my professional life. I tried when I got older to learn to read music. I had a few lessons, but I didn't continue it. It would be difficult, at this age, to change how I perceive and relate to music.

DANIEL FISCHLIN: *When you say* improvisation, *what do you mean by that? Research we've done through the International Institute for Critical Studies in Improvisation (IICSI) has found that* improvisation, *not surprisingly, means very different things to different people. What does it mean for you?*

ODEH TURJMAN: Mostly, I start with repeating things that I like. I hear a nice melody, and I try to copy it. But most of the improvisation I've done, in a professional sense, has been through my experiences with Sabreen.

DANIEL FISCHLIN: *When you founded Sabreen, did the band create its music through improvisation?*

ODEH TURJMAN: Partly... It was a new form of music, a fusion between Arabic and Western music traditions. The compositions were mainly the work of Said Murad, the composer, oud player, and percussionist who was mostly writing the melodies for Sabreen. But improvisation was a fundamental part of the music.

DANIEL FISCHLIN: *Isn't that the basis of maqam? You know, scale work? You play through different sounds within a certain framework, but you are always trying to find a way?*

ODEH TURJMAN: There are two types of improvisation. Within a certain maqam, for me, it doesn't become an improvisation. It's called improvisation because it's not a definitive, fixed melody played. But even that melody becomes normal. Effectively, you learn it—and yet you call it improvisation.

DANIEL FISCHLIN: *Like some kinds of jazz.*

ODEH TURJMAN: Improvisation in the sense that you have not played it straight before; it comes out spontaneously in different forms.

DANIEL FISCHLIN: *You think that coming to music through improvisation changed the way you deal with other musicians—as opposed to, say, more classical formation or more classical ways of learning music?*

ODEH TURJMAN: Yes, absolutely. There are many barriers that exist. If you play certain kinds of music, and you play with other musicians who have their own formations and styles, it becomes a challenge to play together. But if you both improvise, regardless of the content of the music you are working with, then you have something in common.

DANIEL FISCHLIN: *Do you think there is meaning, like a social meaning, to improvisation beyond just the music? Or is it something in the music itself?*

ODEH TURJMAN: If you mean by social that what I learn comes from culture, of course, every music you learn is through your own environment, your own context, and your exposure to other cultures and so on. As a result, it has this personal component that depends on how you as an individual put these different things together.

DANIEL FISCHLIN: *Close listening to the sounds around you, let alone the sounds you yourself are making, is a really important concept for improvisers. You have to always be listening. But listening, we've found in the IICSI research group, is very much context based and culturally determined. What does listening mean to you?*

ODEH TURJMAN: Listening is interpretation. You do not listen directly. When I listen to music, when I listen to you talking, I am interpreting through subjective experience what you are saying. And this is the same in music. If I have educated myself in different styles and different cultures, then I have the capacity to understand through my own interpretation what this *might* mean. Other than that, it becomes meaningless. Music has no meaning outside of your own interpretation. Otherwise, it becomes noise. And that is what happens within certain cultures when an individual is exposed to certain musics that they have never heard before. The music is unreadable from within the frame of that person's listening experience. Some people just close their ears and cannot listen. You have to educate yourself in any new music to which you're exposed and then start appreciating it.

DANIEL FISCHLIN: *Here at Al-Mada and in the work you do in the refugee camps throughout the West Bank, you use a lot of improvisatory techniques to get people to make music. Could you talk about some of the ways in which your work here at Al-Mada uses improvisation specifically?*

ODEH TURJMAN: Improvisation in therapy plays two roles. The first thing is that it is extremely important as a form of personal expression. If you play certain sounds, they are also a general, recognizable expression for the culture, for the society, and so on. But the key is that in improvisation you create your own personal expression within that larger cultural context.

The second is that we work in therapy with people who are not musicians. If you start with something that requires musical skills, then you create immediate barriers. The people in the sessions we lead will feel that they don't have the competency to express, and so you hinder the process of self-expression as a way of getting at trauma and anger and all the emotions we deal with regularly. But with improvisation, as Al-Mada animators and therapists present it, there is nothing special or specific required other than a willingness to follow the improvisatory structures we introduce. You most emphatically do not have to be a musician or have musical skills in order to have a meaningful experience in the contexts in which we work. Participants can express themselves freely through improvisation, and they like it and find that it is not all that difficult. Improvisation for somebody who is not a musician involves playing with sounds, and inevitably improvisers are drawn to some of those sounds. But perhaps for a professional musician, you come and listen to those same sounds, and maybe you end up covering your ears and say this is noise, not music. Al-Mada music therapists are trained to listen to improvisation in a different way because the purpose is to help expression, to help healing, to address crisis and frustration and anger, and not to develop musical skills in the conventional sense of what that might mean.

DANIEL FISCHLIN: Healing *is such an important word. How do you see improvisation in relation to healing? What is the concept behind how Al-Mada uses music and improvisation to heal? What have you seen happen when using improvisation in this process?*

ODEH TURJMAN: There are many people here who on the individual level have had traumatic experiences—like people who have been unfairly jailed and who do not like to talk about their experiences. Sometimes when you are in prison, you have to give the impression that you are brave or courageous when in fact you are frightened and struggling to survive. You may survive the experience, but on a personal level deep inside, the trauma remains, and you pay an ongoing price that is often unexpressed. And yet expression is what happens in the Al-Mada music workshops, where for the first time people are given the opportunity to articulate things they usually don't like to share with other people or make known about themselves.

DANIEL FISCHLIN: *Is there a transition that happens from expressing pain to releasing it—or finding some measure of joy, or finding some sort of resolution? Do you see that kind of transition happening in the improvised musical work Al-Mada does?*

ODEH TURJMAN: Yes. The fact that you can let deep hurt out in front of other people through music is a big change. Because everybody tends to think,

"It is my personal story, and I would rather not share it with others." Since Al-Mada usually works with group therapy situations, participants find out that there are other people who have also gone through the same things they have gone through. It makes it easier that you are part of something, that you are expressing pain openly. You are not shy anymore. The pain does not go away always because it's deep memory pain. But if you don't find a way to express it, it can become something that can hold you back and prevent you from moving forward. This is why the trauma we address is so difficult to overcome and music is such an important aspect of accessing these deep memories that can take hold of, if not destroy lives.

DANIEL FISCHLIN: *How do you think musical notes express pain? How does it translate into sound?*

ODEH TURJMAN: I think you need to understand this from Al-Mada therapists' point of view: part of their training is to look for the intensity of the sound made by specific players in a group, what type of instrument a participant picks, how she deals with it. Sometimes you invite a group to improvise, and people hesitate. Our therapists are trained in psychology, and they try to link what is going on in the music with the psychology of what is going on in the sounds. And sometimes they ask participants, "Why did you choose this sound? What do you like about this?" as a way to make connections between the sounds and the feelings being expressed. I remember one time I was doing a workshop with a group of girls in music expression. I usually put the instruments in a circle, and they choose whichever they prefer. And one girl did not choose an instrument. I asked her why. And she said, "I like the guitar." So, I said, "Why didn't you pick the guitar?" She said, "Because my brother taught me the guitar. He was a guitar player, and he was shot by the Israeli soldiers. And since that time, I have never touched the guitar." I said, "Would you just like to see?" And she picked it up and started playing.

DANIEL FISCHLIN: *That is a powerful example...*

ODEH TURJMAN: You expect participants to be excited about things in these sessions and can't ever anticipate the specific contexts that contribute to why someone can or can't play in these situations.

DANIEL FISCHLIN: *...That the instrument would have so much symbolic connection to her brother. She loves it, but she doesn't want to touch it.*

ODEH TURJMAN: So, yes, this is a very upsetting example, among many others we've encountered, of how powerful these connections between sound and feeling are. The principle at Al-Mada is to sustain being in the local community, keep talking to people, keep bringing them in the door, keep seeding the idea that music can lead to ways of addressing deep trauma and crisis, so that it goes further out into the community. We feel that all these things are important if you want to deploy the process of music therapy in such a challenging context, especially as it is a new concept here in Palestine. It is only about fifty years old all over the world. Yet what we found when we did our research was that it was part of the Oriental tradition, including people like the philosopher and jurist Al-Farabi (c. 872 CE to between 14 December 950 and 12 January 951 CE), whose treatise *Meanings of the Intellect* dealt with music therapy and the therapeutic effects of music, the Persian polymath Al-Razi (854 CE–925 CE), and Ibn Sina (Avicenna; 980–1037 CE). Ibn Sina was a famous doctor over a thousand years ago who used music therapy in the Damascus hospital. He wrote books about music and medicine—which maqam is to be used to generate what mood or for what temperament, in what specific medical circumstances, and so forth. And then two, three hundred years ago, it all but disappeared before we saw it reappear in the West about fifty years ago.

DANIEL FISCHLIN: *We are here in Ramallah, the West Bank, in a very specific Palestinian political context, and often, in Canada, we barely get your side of the story, your lived experience. How does being in this political context defined by the ongoing crisis of occupation, illegal settlements, and violence change how people make music? What happens when you connect music to this specific context of struggle and oppression?*

ODEH TURJMAN: Maybe it would be good to answer this by talking about the Sabreen experience. In the 1970s the cultural influence of music was greater, and there was a very active music life prior to the occupation; mostly Western music with electric guitars. All of that—so very detached from the local political reality. With Sabreen we each left the various groups to which we belonged and decided to do something for us as Palestinians to express ourselves, and our lived experience of this reality. And it made a big difference because in this context the music becomes a life for you in the sense that it is an opportunity to express how you feel and how you think from within the culture that is experiencing what you just described. It became, in other words, a way of life, and not just music detached from cultural context.

DANIEL FISCHLIN: *So it gave you . . . ?*

ODEH TURJMAN: As a human, you now have a tool at your disposal to express yourself. You usually don't have this because of other things that suppress or make it difficult to have voice. It is a powerful thing to discover how music activates this form of community and identity.

DANIEL FISCHLIN: *It connects to the heart . . . ?*

ODEH TURJMAN: You feel that when you make music in this form, you can remove boundaries and relate to other people no matter who they are.

DANIEL FISCHLIN: *There are people that would say that it's a myth that music can cross cultural boundaries, that it has transcendent powers, and so forth. There is a more cynical way of looking at music, as just a commodity.*

ODEH TURJMAN: As we discussed earlier, I don't believe that music is universal, in the sense that every listener has limits defined by that person's history and context and culture. But the fact is that *every* culture has music. So music, like improvisation, is universal in this sense: it is part of the world. It's everywhere. Now, to be sure, it has its own instruments and meanings for each culture. This is why the more you are exposed to other cultures, the more you find new tools to communicate, new perspectives. One of the things we worked on in Sabreen was that it was not enough to say you are Palestinian. It is not enough if I make good music to be defined by that kind of a limitation. "The world *must* sympathize with me." We did *not* have this attitude. We said, instead, we need to be professional musicians, to make professional music, and the world will respect us for our music, not for being Palestinian. Part of what we did involved listening to different kinds of music—jazz, classical—to expose ourselves very deliberately to different types of music, all styles from many different cultures. Otherwise, what Sabreen did would have been perceived as just a form of folk music, and that was a limitation we did not want. We wanted to be heard by more than just our own community.

DANIEL FISCHLIN: *When I listen to Sabreen, I can hear many different styles synthesizing and finding their own unique expression. And it is very powerful for that reason. Shocking, but in a good way. I've been listening a lot to Le Trio Joubran, an amazing band of Palestinian brothers who play traditional*

Palestinian music on the oud. And some of the things that they do as a trio are astonishing, where you just go, "Oh my God! Where did that sound come from?" They're all the same instruments, but it is like sound magic. And I had the same feeling when listening to Sabreen; the sense of sound coming out of nowhere and finding you somehow.

ODEH TURJMAN: You have to experiment with sounds, and this is what we did. You have to discover new sounds. This is part of what makes music special, whether it's Sabreen or any other band. And you get there through improvisation and experimentation: "Let's try this . . . let's try that."

DANIEL FISCHLIN: *So can we go back to your history? As a young boy, you were drawn to music, and your parents saw that.*

ODEH TURJMAN: With a small instrument. I don't know how my interest in music started. One day with my small accordion I started trying to imitate the tunes, to play them myself, because there were no music schools, there was no place to learn music. So I had to learn on my own. I was experimenting on this instrument, trying to play back the melodies and songs I liked. And then, little by little, I started to watch the groups I liked; to observe how they played their instruments. So mostly through observation. And then I started a group actually, as a teenager, a music group. We were playing mostly Western pop music and sometimes Arabic pop, but pop music. That was all through my own trial and error. I didn't have anybody to teach me.

DANIEL FISCHLIN: *Why do you think music became part of who you are?*

ODEH TURJMAN: I don't remember at that time what was the drive. Maybe I'm not a social person, and music, for me, was a way of expressing myself and spending time with something I enjoyed. I don't know. Maybe. At another point it helped me to connect, to make friends through the music groups. It created a life for me.

DANIEL FISCHLIN: *. . . which sounds so much like Al-Mada and how it uses music to create other forms of connection.*

ODEH TURJMAN: Really. I didn't have the chance to acquire a formal music education because it wasn't available at the time. And going abroad for me was a problem for different reasons. I like to see now that even for people who don't have the money, music is accessible for all—that you can express yourself through music without being a professional musician. What I have been deprived of, I like that other people can have. I mean, I had the chance to have music, but it was a difficult way to get here.

DANIEL FISCHLIN: *It always starts that way. My mother was a concert pianist and a woman who gave up her career to have six children. One year my father bought her a classical guitar as a birthday present. She had no interest in playing the guitar. But my father said to all the kids, "Nobody is allowed to touch this guitar. It's your mother's." It sat there for a long time. Nobody touched it. I would look at it, and I wanted to play it. And I couldn't play it. The minute it moved he would see that it had been moved. So, what I did was find a way: a neighbor who had a guitar. I would go to his house. Eventually one day my father caught me playing the guitar at home, and it was like, I knew how to play. He was furious, but I think there was also maybe a strategy to get me playing. So, yes, music always seems to start in funny ways with obstacles to be overcome and various challenges including the social and political contexts in which it is being made.*

ODEH TURJMAN: As long as you were doing something that was not threatening here, the authorities didn't directly interfere, unless, of course, you started writing and performing songs that were directly provocative and political. So we didn't. Not because we were afraid of being arrested. Our concern was how to make the music and choose lyrics that had human content that everyone could relate to. We were appealing to our common humanity, and I think this made a big difference because people tended to relate to the lyrics, which didn't only talk about Palestinians.

DANIEL FISCHLIN: *Okay, so how did Al-Mada come into the picture?*

ODEH TURJMAN: I left Sabreen in 1993, and I began teaching in schools.

DANIEL FISCHLIN: *What were you teaching?*

ODEH TURJMAN: Music. But remember, I was not a teacher by profession. Being a professional musician, I thought teaching would be easy for me to do. And I was shocked to learn that being a professional musician is not enough to teach music properly. And yet I was stuck with the children. What to do? How to reach them and be effective? Then I applied for a British

Council scholarship for music, and they accepted my application, which led to my studying music education in Reading.

DANIEL FISCHLIN: *How many years were you at Reading?*

ODEH TURJMAN: One year. It was a master's. I came back to the school I was teaching at before with fresh ideas. And then I worked for the Ministry of Culture, as director of the Music Department for three years. And then I contacted Sabreen. I said, "I have an idea for music education. We can do it differently. We do not have music teachers at school. We do not have a music curriculum." And we managed to find a way [for] the Ministry of Education to link up with a donor who was interested in starting a music education program. We started the program on a national level here, training teachers and developing curriculum.

DANIEL FISCHLIN: *So that was with Sabreen?*

ODEH TURJMAN: Yes. This was in 1998–99, and the program is still going strong, and has been very successful. We have curricula for grades 1 through 4. We have about 130 music teachers, and at least now there is a program in the schools that formerly didn't have anything to offer.

DANIEL FISCHLIN: *Are you still involved in this?*

ODEH TURJMAN: Now only as a consultant. I worked full-time for this program for seven to eight years, and at the same time, in the early 2000s, it was the period of the Second Intifada (2000–2005). We used to do workshops in schools for traumatized children. At the time, shelling was going on. The feeling in the school was glum. . . . But we managed to continue in spite of the ongoing crisis. And when we were working with children, I realized—because I work in improvisation and composition—that we had to let them improvise and compose. When they composed, what they came up with was all they talked about: the difficult situations they were facing. It was very serious what they were speaking to, and as musicians we could not handle it. They opened up, and as a musician you didn't know how to respond ethically and appropriately to what they were saying. These were serious problems, and this is when we thought to use maybe this kind of combination of something in music and expression and improvisation. We had to know something about psychology and how to deal with deeply traumatized children when something came up in the music the youth were producing. This is where the idea for Al-Mada came from; combining psychology and music for traumatized children. We started with music therapy as the focus at Al-Mada, as a community outreach and development program with music therapy at its core, because I believed this is something that we need here, especially given the long-term impact of the ongoing crisis. From what I saw and experienced, there are a lot of ways in which music can be dangerous in a situation like ours. You think, "Improvisation, nice. Composition, wow!" But when you work with children who have experienced severe traumas, using music composition and improvisation can create problems—however unintentionally.

DANIEL FISCHLIN: *Can you explain that? Can you give me some examples?*

ODEH TURJMAN: A girl, for instance, started doing the music program, and she was talking about where the music comes from. She has terrifying nightmares. Every night. She imagines herself as an Israeli soldier in an airplane and bombing her own family. This is a nightmare she typically has, and she tries to express herself. I did not know what to do. How can you comfort her? Thirteen, fourteen, fifteen years old . . . and I felt helpless. So this was something. And many experienced similar things to this, which we, as musicians, could not handle. You think it is a positive thing. Improvisation opens up things, but psychologically what it opens up needs to be addressed, which the music alone does not necessarily do. Somebody had to help her learn how to deal with what she was experiencing and what the music had opened up in her.

DANIEL FISCHLIN: *So, how did you deal with that? To move from the music that helps open things up to helping to reconcile the youth with their experiences. What did you do?*

ODEH TURJMAN: Once we realized how serious the reactions were to the musical situations we were creating we added a psychologist to our team. It was this combination—of a musician and a psychologist—trying to have dialogue and see how to diagnose and respond effectively that we settled on. But to be sure, with Al-Mada, we started with the music therapy because I initially thought this approach implicitly combined both.

DANIEL FISCHLIN: *What does Al-Mada (المدى) mean?*[34]

ODEH TURJMAN: *Al-Mada* means "horizon," like space.

DANIEL FISCHLIN: *Why did you pick that name?*

ODEH TURJMAN: We thought we wanted to have initiatives that were not confined to any one thing.

DANIEL FISCHLIN: *In Arabic does it have a sense of hope? Hoping?*

ODEH TURJMAN: Yes, it has a sense of hope; not boundaries, but doing whatever you can do, achieving your potential. Al-Mada is more about moving beyond whatever boundaries are in your way; how to overcome difficult challenges with new approaches. I think music therapy is beneficial in releasing some of those aspirations. It was definitely needed.

DANIEL FISCHLIN: *So, what have you seen in terms of the practical, material benefits of Al-Mada's programs?*

ODEH TURJMAN: When you asked me earlier about institutionalization, when we were starting, we tried to look for organizations that already had structure so that if you worked with them you had less trouble doing so. Since then we've had many partnerships with other NGOs and like-minded organizations pretty much since the beginning of the program. We also have a partnership with the Ministry of Education and a little component with the Ministry of Health. All of these have good infrastructures. The heaviest work was done with children and women—but it also included hundreds of social workers and counselors. We developed the program bit by bit. We started with an introductory course, and then we developed advanced training that included coaching in the field. I think it reached a total of about 120 hours of training with the goal being to establish a full team of trainers—a core team that helps to train people. Those people now themselves feel confident enough to do the music therapy we deploy throughout the West Bank. And improvisation is a key component of that work.

DANIEL FISCHLIN: *Is that program written out? Is there a handbook or guide how to do that?*

ODEH TURJMAN: We developed a music therapy manual that we consider to be an open manual, and we use it to train fieldworkers. They give us feedback, and we try to improve the manual based on their experiences and examples from the field.

DANIEL FISCHLIN: *Do you have meetings where the animators come together and discuss specific issues, like the girl who was having that terrible dream? And how do you resolve that?*

ODEH TURJMAN: Yes, that type of meeting occurs with a music therapist who deals with the support issues. She goes and visits animators in the field, supervises what they do, and gives them counsel. And then they come back here to discuss cases that are challenging, what they think, and what she thinks. If they have difficulties, she gives support, and often that occurs in group interactions.

DANIEL FISCHLIN: *You spoke of the Second Intifada, which began in 2000, and I wanted to ask you what the effect of that was on the musical community in Palestine and the Occupied Territories. Is there a connection? Is there something to be said about how the community was impacted and reacted? How people created art?*

ODEH TURJMAN: You know, in certain situations you try to maintain things, but it's inevitable in a crisis like that that you will be greatly affected. To be able to perform this kind of work, you need to have safe places. So things did not stop, but it became very difficult to do this work at a time when it was so needed. And this was also what happened in the First Intifada, which lasted from 1987 to 1993.

DANIEL FISCHLIN: *In Canada we have a lot of problems in big cities with venues shutting down. It is increasingly difficult to do different kinds of music in spaces. The economics are very bad because space is so expensive.*

ODEH TURJMAN: Cultural activities are the first things they cut.

DANIEL FISCHLIN: *Also, you are being policed. Experimentalists, people who make noise, seem to always invoke a threat. The noise seems to call for a response, and it tends to be negative. In my city, Guelph, we have created an organization called Silence, which is an ironic title for a space where we make noise.*

ODEH TURJMAN: Silence the language?

DANIEL FISCHLIN: *Exactly. A group of musicians bought a building about the size of Al-Mada where we are doing this kind of work, and we are inviting musicians to present and experiment. And we are finding that musicians from Toronto, a much bigger city, are coming to Silence to play because the venues in that very large urban center are shutting down. Do you have the same problem here, in terms of public spaces where you can perform things as a musician easily?*

ODEH TURJMAN: Now it is much easier because the Palestinian Authority has increased the availability of new event spaces. But prior to the establishment of the Palestinian Authority, there were very few places that were available for events. One of them was El-Hakawati Theatre [the Palestinian National Theatre situated in East Jerusalem]. Because it is a Palestinian theater in East Jerusalem, they have to get permission to mount events from the Israeli occupation authorities based on all sorts of criteria: what kind of concert, who's performing, and so on. Sometimes the authorities come just an hour or a few minutes before a concert, and they say, "By military order, it's closed. Everybody go home." Sometimes they close a space for weeks or months. For years one university tried establishing an arts academy, but they were never given permission.

DANIEL FISCHLIN: *And why was that?*

ODEH TURJMAN: They never say.

DANIEL FISCHLIN: *They do not say why, but why do you think?*

ODEH TURJMAN: Because of culture . . .

DANIEL FISCHLIN: *Because culture is so dangerous?*

ODEH TURJMAN: We have a stronger identity because we sing. Culture is identity. And the whole struggle, especially in Jerusalem, is about identity. You know, normally a city like Jerusalem should be open to all kinds of identities, but unfortunately it has become a place for one identity eliminating the other. And identity, you cannot get rid of it. This is the nature of humans, how we are. You are Palestinian, Canadian. You cannot get rid of it. Why should you turn identity into a source of conflict? But the Israelis are trying to turn Jerusalem into a Jewish city. And the Palestinians are saying that they are part of both the history and the present reality of Jerusalem. It's about identity, culture, and who has the right to live—to be here. It's not just about a thing on the surface. When they prohibit a musical performance or a theater play, what they are actually prohibiting is not the performance itself but the potential of maintaining and developing the Palestinian identity in this place, in this city. It seems as if it's something small, no performance. But actually it's the possibility of maintaining your cultural activity and presence in this city.

DANIEL FISCHLIN: *Solidarity is an important word in terms of music because musicians know each other, they recognize and listen to each other, and there's a solidarity that comes out of playing together or even just listening to somebody whom you respect as a musician. This is something tangible and real that happens in music. Do you see the work of Al-Mada in terms of building solidarity beyond what's going on here? One of the things IICSI is interested in is reaching out and finding ways to be helpful, without any sense of patronizing. What would make a difference in terms of action that is in solidarity with you?*

ODEH TURJMAN: Like we discussed—the more you give to understand the other, to be informed, the more you see that we are not that much different, and this sense of reciprocity is an important aspect of musical learning across cultures. I think there are many things that can work both ways. Usually here, because of the difficult situation that makes it difficult for donors to support our work, you get the impression that the West is helping, and you know, as musicians, that this is not necessarily the case. It really has to be a two-way thing here where we can all contribute to looking at the situation in an equal way and then see how we can support and contribute to each other's cause and future development.

DANIEL FISCHLIN: *One of the most frustrating things about that work that I have done in Cuba has been that we cannot bring Afro-Cuban musicians to Canada because they are restricted from travel. And it's not Cuba that is restricting them. It is Canada that won't let them in. They are seen as poor, Black, and potential defectors, as opposed to valuable cultural emissaries from whom we have a lot to learn. And that is even with people who sign documents that say, "We will take full responsibility for their costs while they are in Canada." Even with that they won't get in. So it has been very frustrating. What are the challenges Al-Mada faces now?*

ODEH TURJMAN: Like everybody, the finances. We don't have the resources that we need to develop the program the way we want and need to.

DANIEL FISCHLIN: *How many people work at Al-Mada all together?*

ODEH TURJMAN: Fourteen or so volunteers ... so a small group with only two therapists to address so many needs in the community. We are actively looking for a partner or partners that can collaborate with us in the music therapy aspect of things, as that requires significant skills and training.

DANIEL FISCHLIN: *I found out about you through John McLaughlin because when I interviewed him two years ago, the first thing he told me about was Al-Mada. How did John find you, or how did you find him?*

ODEH TURJMAN: In 2010 John donated his entire cash prize from the Jazzahead Festival in Germany to support Al-Mada's music therapy center in Ramallah, the first of its kind in Palestine. Then in 2012 John came to Palestine with Remember Shakti for the first solidarity concert by major international artists.

DANIEL FISCHLIN: *So it was their idea to come to Ramallah?*

ODEH TURJMAN: Yes. He was very interested and supportive, and the money he donated allowed us to work with children with disabilities. At that time, Al-Mada was also running another project called "For My Identity, I Sing!" That project was based on the idea that through music you can talk about identity, and it then becomes something personal and directly experienced and therefore matters a great deal to participants. So this project involved mainly Palestinian youth—both boys and girls, mostly from schools in Jerusalem, to give them opportunities through music to express their difficulties; what they are facing on a daily basis in Jerusalem. For a young person living in Jerusalem identity is a problem.

DANIEL FISCHLIN: *Maybe explain that more fully.*

ODEH TURJMAN: You know that as a Palestinian you do *not* have a nationality—like a Palestinian passport? You do *not* have an Israeli passport either. All you have is a travel document; an Israeli ID as a resident but not as a citizen. You are living in a community where you are not recognized as a Palestinian but at the same time not as an Israeli. So who are you?

DANIEL FISCHLIN: *So do you consider yourself stateless, then? It's a tricky question, I know.*

ODEH TURJMAN: Psychologically, you have a state, and you know what state. But on the ground, yes, you are legally stateless. For young people living in this situation it is a crisis because this is a time when you build your own identity and culture, but at the same time you do not have the environment to support those activities because of the contradictory and conflicting environment that deprives you of access and identity. You are a Palestinian, but you do not have a state. You are living in a state that does not recognize you as a citizen, so you do not know where you belong. You have the sense from your family and so on that, yes, I am a Palestinian, I belong to this culture. But the other institutional realities and allocation of resources do not support your belonging in any way. So this Al-Mada youth project, "For My Identity, I Sing!" was aimed at young people to help them express what it means to be Palestinian, to capture the situation in their own voices.

DANIEL FISCHLIN: *How are you working with the young people? What are some of the things you are doing to make the project happen?*

ODEH TURJMAN: I think what is interesting is that most of them did not have any experience in music before. They are not singers or musicians. They are generally young people, and the project is how to create music for people who have generally been deprived of the education you need to do that. We have eight songs on the CD composed by different groups. They wrote the lyrics; they composed the melodies. This month they are having a performance for their families to show them what they have created.

DANIEL FISCHLIN: *Has Al-Mada used radio as a tool to diffuse some of things that are being created here?*

ODEH TURJMAN: Yes, we have, both radio and television. There have been interviews with the youth also. We have another campaign going with another training course for social media. So we have another group of youth working on social media to promote the campaign and share songs with other youth.

DANIEL FISCHLIN: *And how are you finding the lyrics of the songs they are writing are about?*

ODEH TURJMAN: Mainly about the impact of the current situation on their lives. So one lyric, for example, states, "I like life without the wall . . ." Another song starts with a story: "Once I was walking and I saw a child crying and I asked him, 'Who are you? Where are you?'" Another lyric is about what Jerusalem means, how in the Old City the Israeli occupation is doing its best to forcibly evacuate Palestinians from their houses in whatever way possible. And now we have, like, neighbors living beside each other but antagonistic—not in harmony. What I've noticed is that in the process of developing the lyrics and the songs, each group ends up in a very different place from where they started.

DANIEL FISCHLIN: *Can you explain for people who do not know the situation in East Jerusalem what it is like on the ground there? What it means to be Palestinian living in East Jerusalem?*

ODEH TURJMAN: Essentially, when you see that your neighbor is somebody forced on you and is protected by the Israeli police, that some of them get the house and part of the land next to the house, they don't care for it because it is so fundamentally unfair.

DANIEL FISCHLIN: *And that is in the lyrics?*

ODEH TURJMAN: One of these is in the lyrics. In Jerusalem before 1948, Jews, Muslims, and Christians were living together, and there was not a problem. I do *not* think the problem is religion. I don't think the problem is having Jewish, Muslim, or Christian neighbors. It's a problem created by using force to change the demographics of the city, to make it a Jewish city. So that if you are a Christian or a Muslim or an atheist or whatever, you feel like you do not belong here because you are a minority and are isolated. I think this is the painful thing, and I'm happy that these children are able to express their perceptions about injustice in music.

DANIEL FISCHLIN: *How many kids are involved in the project?*

ODEH TURJMAN: More than 150. This is the core group, but we work with others.

DANIEL FISCHLIN: *And then you break them up into smaller groups?*

ODEH TURJMAN: They work in groups because they come from several schools. So they come together in the concert and in rehearsals. They are given basic training to connect also through social media to see what each other have done and to share ideas.

DANIEL FISCHLIN: *That really worked? And then they can self-affirm by seeing each other doing and sharing what they have done?*

ODEH TURJMAN: Sometimes they have different examples. Because living in, for example, one part of Jerusalem or in any number of other cities in the West Bank, half or all of one neighborhood may have been taken over. Living elsewhere may be quite different, and these differences are important to share, and they come through in the musical work that the different groups are creating. So the music is also an important way of sharing information about how people live.

DANIEL FISCHLIN: *And what is the condition, then, for Palestinians who live in East Jerusalem in terms of their relationship or connection to Ramallah? For example, can they travel easily here?*

ODEH TURJMAN: It depends on what you mean by "easily." They have to get across checkpoints, and it is not easy. Sometimes you can spend hours. The problem is that people from the West Bank are not allowed to visit Jerusalem. You have to request a permit, and it is very difficult to get. So people who want to pray at the Al-Aqsa Mosque in Old Jerusalem, for example, cannot. We have many children here in Ramallah who have never visited Jerusalem—it's five, ten minutes from Ramallah—and they do not know Jerusalem. So we now have this program, and we have performances next Friday, and they are in schools in Jerusalem. But the youth do not have permits to go to Jerusalem. Because of the separation wall built by the Israeli occupation, they became outsiders, but they still undertake part of their education in the system that disadvantages them. And if they want to perform or attend the concert, they have to request permission. They have not gotten permission yet. And we do not know if this group will perform yet.

DANIEL FISCHLIN: *So you were part of the committee that established what is now known as the Edward Said National Conservatory of Music?*

ODEH TURJMAN: Yes, I was on the advisory committee in 1995. In discussions, I proposed the idea that education has to include improvisation and composition for children. And there was opposition because they said composition for children is a tough thing. That you only do this when you reach a certain age. I said, for me, this is not the way. If you do not learn these things when you are a kid, it becomes extremely difficult to do it, especially improvisation, when you come up through this formal stream with all its restrictions and conventions. And this is what happens with most musicians. They cannot break free from the tradition they have learned, because "How can I compete with whatever I have learned?" But when you're exposed to these ideas from the beginning, you don't perceive it this way. It becomes a natural part of the development of children. They improvise everything, after all. Why not music? They learn language through improvisation. They do not learn it at school. At school, they learn to read and write.

DANIEL FISCHLIN: *At the conservatory, did they institute a stream where people were improvising?*

ODEH TURJMAN: No. It is very difficult to include improvisation and composition in music education. It is easier to take a ready-made model to drive a successful curriculum. But to build something, to respond to specific needs and ideas we had for the children, many of which involved improvisation, means hard work. How do you build a system that includes improvisation and composition? Nobody has done it this way, so we had to create it from scratch. It was risky because as you know improvisation is understudied and often misunderstood.

DANIEL FISCHLIN: *That's one of the problems with improvisation as a practice—because you have to engage with risk, with unpredictability. And yet at the same time you are engaging with something that any composer of structure relies on, but they do not necessarily acknowledge that because the outcome is always set, and all the hidden play of improvisation to arrive at structure remains invisible.*

ODEH TURJMAN: And you might not be happy with the outcome because someone else might not consider it music, but this is how music develops: becoming a good composer often requires breaking the rules that came before. And yet, afterward, the rule-breaking music becomes tradition.

DANIEL FISCHLIN: *So much has changed since we got into the concept of music as having to be reproducible in the same way all the time, and performances always having this notion of the performer's repeating what has been recorded* on the disc. And then the concert is about reproducing, when it should it be the other way around.

ODEH TURJMAN: Yes, of course, why should I live the life that somebody else has lived, do something that somebody else has done? Bach, Beethoven, they lived their lives, and they produced what they liked to do, what they wanted to hear. But what about me . . . or you? Why should I be a copy of anybody, no matter how great he or she is?

DANIEL FISCHLIN: *And the structures that allowed them to create the music, Bach in Leipzig and having all the court and church support. Imagine Bach in Palestine, or living in Jerusalem and working in Ramallah.*

ODEH TURJMAN: Like I said before, everyone wants Palestinians to be a copy of somebody else, and they promote role models we're supposed to imitate at the expense of our own identity and expression. Whether in music or religion they tell you that this is the model that you should be—that you should imitate. You try, but you cannot. Everybody has originality, and one of the ways to unlock that is through improvisation. Every human being is unique. You have this uniqueness that you cannot, and should not, struggle against—you cannot be like anybody else. You simply cannot be.

NOTES

I am indebted to many people for their help with this project: David Hutton, the Canadian deputy director of UNRWA Operations (Programmes), and Dr. Umaiyeh Khammash, chief of the UNRWA Field Health Programme, were exceptionally generous with time and information during the visit. Tony Bero of UNRWA, Nadeen Khoury and Mahmoud Awad of Al-Mada, and many of their colleagues provided superb hospitality and support as the trip unfolded. Reem Abdul Hadi, Odeh Turjman, Hala Turjman, Ina Behrend, Deeyah Khan, Martha Nandorfy, Eric Porter, Jessica Notwell, Brian Lefresne, and the amazing staff at the International Institute for Critical Studies in Improvisation were all instrumental in facilitating this work—and I offer sincere thanks to them all. I'd especially like to thank Jess Notwell for her outstanding work on the ground in Palestine in the last stages of completing this work; Eric Porter for his uncanny ability to see the order of things where it is only dimly outlined; and Brian Lefresne for his unstinting diligence on this file over four years.

1 Kershner, "No 'P' in Arabic."
2 Cresci, "Google Maps."
3 Beaumont, "Israeli Ministers."

4   In the same year, Hussain refused to play a concert in Tel Aviv (along with, among others, Cassandra Wilson, Bruce Springsteen, Coldplay, and U2) after receiving a letter from the Indian Campaign for the Academic and Cultural Boycott of Israel, which acknowledged his contact with Al-Mada:

We are aware that in February 2012, the Palestinian Al Mada Association for Arts-Based Community Development, in partnership with the United Nations Relief and Works Agency for Palestine Refugees in the Near East (UNRWA) and UNICEF, hosted you together with the group Remember Shakti in Ramallah. You played free of charge in the knowledge that the event was a solidarity concert and a fundraising event to develop music therapy programs for Palestinian refugee children. In addition to your music, this is what we admire you for. So please don't let your wonderful music be used to legitimize home demolitions, illegal raids, the use of white phosphorous, political and child imprisonments, racist marriage bans, piracy and execution in international waters, collective punishment, Occupation, checkpoints, roadblocks, and the bombing and closing of educational institutions. If you cancel your performance in Israel, you will also be encouraging other artists to follow your lead. And your fans all over the world will know you stand for justice and an end to apartheid. ("Zakir Hussain Won't Drum")

5   *This Week in Palestine*, "Solidarity Concert in Palestine."
6   Al-Mada, "Solidarity Concert."
7   Barghouti, *I Was Born There*, 81.
8   One practice (of Israeli activists) has been to replace the prohibitions on these signs with the following message: "Civilian Zone: No entry to the army. This road leads to Palestinian settlements. Israeli civilians do not need to be afraid. Come and visit Palestinian settlements. Refuse to be enemies." *Mondoweiss*, "Israeli Activists."
9   UNRWA, "West Bank."
10 Music is not the only place where solidarity of this sort erupts. Kate Shuttleworth, in "The Israelis and Palestinians Who Work Together in Peace," describes spaces in the Israel/Palestine matrix where working and learning together lead to a measure of reconciliation and understanding: hospitals, schools, and start-ups in which intercultural collaboration occurs are far from the norm but provide a starting point for imagining nonviolent, incremental solutions to the conflict. This essay describes similar musical ventures where cocreation in shared musical spaces imagines similar reconciliatory gestures.
11 Abuelaish, *I Shall Not Hate*, 192.
12 McDonald, *My Voice Is My Weapon*, 21.
13 Barenboim and Said, *Parallels and Paradoxes*, 11.
14 Al-Mada, "Solidarity Concert."
15 Al-Mada, "Odeh Turjman."
16 Sabreen was "formed in 1980 with a vision focused on the development of the Palestinian modern song, reflecting the humanitarian and cultural reality in general, and the suffering endured from the political situation in particular." Sabreen Association for Artistic Development, "Sabreen." For more on Abdul Hadi and Turjman, see

Al-Mada, "Reem Abdul Hadi"; Al-Mada, "Odeh Turjman"; and Edward Said National Conservatory of Music, "History."

17 Al-Mada, "Mission and Vision."
18 Tolan, *Children of the Stone*, xxiii
19 Tolan, *Children of the Stone*, xxv.
20 "The Human Rights Council, through resolution 10/23 decided to establish, for a period of three years, a new special procedure entitled 'independent expert in the field of cultural rights.' The mandate was extended in 2012 for a period of three years, conferring to the current mandate holder the status of Special Rapporteur in the field of cultural rights (resolution 19/6). This mandate was further extended in 2015 for a period of three years through resolution 28/9 of 10 April." United Nations Human Rights Office of the High Commissioner, "Special Rapporteur."
21 Shaheed, "Report of the Special Rapporteur," 8–9.
22 Quoted in Malek and Hoke, *Palestine Speaks*, 29–30.
23 Kanaaneh, "Introduction," 3.
24 Al-Mada, "CDs Production: I Love Life."
25 Quoted in Malek and Hoke, *Palestine Speaks*, 179.
26 As a Canadian, I am also keenly aware of the infamous Canada Park, a seven-hundred-hectare area just northwest of Jerusalem that extends into the West Bank. The park was created in the aftermath of the 1967 Six-Day War and saw three Palestinian villages (Imwas, Yalo, and Beit Nuba) razed. Two thousand inhabitants were forcibly removed from the land currently used for the park and denied access to it, in defiance of the fourth Geneva Convention that clearly terms such actions war crimes. Funded by, among others, the Jewish National Fund (JNF) of Canada, the city of Ottawa, and Temple Beth Sholom (Montreal), the site is a painful reminder of erasures and injustices inflicted on Palestinians, all the more so given that the road into the park is named after former Canadian prime minister John Diefenbaker, who officially opened it in 1975, some twelve years after he left office (see "Canada Park"; and Larson, "Is the City of Ottawa Linked"). This annexation and afforestation project are clearly part of a larger strategy of land grabs and settlement incursions that have increasingly placed pressure on the autonomy of the West Bank. Music plays a small role in this history: in 2014 Independent Jewish Voices—Canada initiated a petition calling on Nikki Yanofsky, a young Canadian jazz singer, to cancel her performances on behalf of the JNF, stating, "While the JNF/KKL markets itself as an environmental organization, its purpose has always been to acquire Palestinian land to be held exclusively for Jews around the world, and covers the sites of depopulated and demolished Palestinian villages with forests and parks. JNF/KKL is a large landowner in Israel, owning 13% of the land, and having a large influence over 93% of all state lands, which are nationalized for the Jewish people. Israel's Attorney General, the United Nations Committee on Economic, Social and Cultural Rights, and the U.S. State Department have found that JNF/KKL systematically discriminates against Palestinian citizens of Israel, who amount to 20% of the population." Independent Jewish Voices—Canada, "Support Equal Rights."
27 For more, see the Applied Research Institute Jerusalem, "'Ein as Sultan Camp Profile"; and UNRWA, "Ein el-Sultan Camp."

28 Fischlin and Nandorfy, *Eduardo Galeano*, 73.
29 Santos outlines the meaning of this concept at the beginning of his essay "Beyond Abyssal Thinking: From Global Lines to Ecologies of Knowledge," arguing, "Modern Western thinking is an abyssal thinking. It consists of a system of visible and invisible distinctions, the invisible ones being the foundation of the visible ones. The invisible distinctions are established through radical lines that divide social reality into two realms, the realm of 'this side of the line' and the realm of 'the other side of the line.' The division is such that 'the other side of the line' vanishes as reality, becomes nonexistent, and is indeed produced as nonexistent. Nonexistent means not existing in any relevant or comprehensible way" (45). Crossing over the abyssal line that separates visible from invisible forms of knowledge, as one does in the highly policed realities of the West Bank, is a cogent reminder of the ecologies of knowledge that oppression conceals.
30 Pappe, *The Ethnic Cleansing of Palestine*.
31 "The Body," Song 8 from *I Love Life*.
32 For further information about the organization, consult their Facebook page (https://www.facebook.com/pg/Al-Mada-Association-for-Arts-Based-Community-Development-176579815694601/about/) or their website (http://al-mada.ps/).
33 See Sabreen Association for Artistic Development, "Sabreen."
34 "The name Al-Mada evokes the sense that the power of music is universal, eliminating barriers. It reaches us, no matter who or where we are. Whether it makes us dance or sing along, or evokes tears or laughter, music always touches us in ways nothing else can." Al-Mada, "About."

BIBLIOGRAPHY

Abuelaish, Izzeldin. *I Shall Not Hate*. London: Bloomsbury, 2011.
Applied Research Institute Jerusalem. "'Ein as Sultan Camp Profile." 2012. http://vprofile.arij.org/jericho/pdfs/vprofile/'Ein%20as%20Sultan_En_FINAL.pdf.
Barenboim, Daniel, and Edward W. Said. *Parallels and Paradoxes: Explorations in Music and Society*. New York: Vintage Books, 2004.
Barghouti, Mourid. *I Was Born There, I Was Born Here*. Translated by Humphrey Davies. New York: Walker, 2011.
Barghouti, Mourid. *Midnight and Other Poems*. Translated by Radwa Ashour. Todmorden, UK: Arc, 2008.
Beaumont, Peter. "Israeli Ministers Back Proposed Law Demoting Arabic Language." *Guardian*, May 8, 2017. https://www.theguardian.com/world/2017/may/07/israeli-ministers-back-proposed-law-demoting-arabic-language.
"Canada Park." Wikipedia. Last edited March 5, 2019. https://en.wikipedia.org/wiki/Canada_Park.
Cresci, Elena. "Google Maps Accused of Deleting Palestine—but the Truth Is More Complicated." *Guardian*, August 10, 2016. https://www.theguardian.com/technology/2016/aug/10/google-maps-accused-remove-palestine.

Edward Said National Conservatory of Music. "History." Birzeit University. Accessed June 29, 2016. http://ncm.birzeit.edu/en/history.

Fischlin, Daniel, and Martha Nandorfy. *Eduardo Galeano: Through the Looking Glass*. Montreal: Black Rose Books, 2002.

Independent Jewish Voices—Canada. "Support Equal Rights by Cancelling Your Gigs for the Discriminatory Jewish National Fund (JNF)." Change.org. Accessed June 29, 2016. https://www.change.org/p/nikki-yanofsky-support-equal-rights-by-cancelling-your-gigs-for-the-discriminatory-jewish-national-fund-jnf.

Kanaaneh, Moslih. "Introduction: Do Palestinian Musicians Play Music or Politics?" In *Palestinian Music and Song: Expression and Resistance since 1900*, edited by Moslih Kanaaneh, Stig-Magnus Thorsén, Heather Bursheh, and David A. McDonald, 1–11. Bloomington: Indiana University Press, 2013.

Kershner, Isabel. "No 'P' in Arabic Means No Palestine, Israeli Lawmaker Says." *New York Times*, February 11, 2016. http://www.nytimes.com/2016/02/12/world/middleeast/israel-anat-berko-palestine.html.

Larson, Peter. "Is the City of Ottawa Linked to a 50 Year Old War Crime in Palestine? Perhaps . . ." *Canada Talks Israel-Palestine*, January 2, 2015. https://canadatalksisraelpalestine.ca/2015/01/02/is-the-city-of-ottawa-linked-to-a-50-year-old-war-crime-in-palestine-perhaps/.

Al-Mada. "About." Facebook page. Accessed July 8, 2019. https://www.facebook.com/pg/Al-Mada-Association-for-Arts-Based-Community-Development-176579815694601/about/.

Al-Mada. "CDs Production: I Love Life." Accessed July 8, 2019. https://al-mada.ps/cds-production-2/.

Al-Mada. "Home." Facebook page. Accessed July 8, 2019. https://www.facebook.com/Al-Mada-176579815694601/.

Al-Mada. "Home Page." Accessed July 8, 2019. http://al-mada.ps/.

Al-Mada. *I Love Life*. Composed by Odeh Turjman, lyrics by Khaled Juma. Al-Mada Recording Studio, 2013, compact disc. http://al-mada.ps/?page_id=129.

Al-Mada. "Mission and Vision." Accessed June 29, 2016. http://al-mada.ps/?page_id=56.

Al-Mada. "Odeh Turjman." Accessed June 29, 2016. http://al-mada.ps/?pirenko_team_member=odeh-turjman.

Al-Mada. "Reem Abdul Hadi." Accessed June 29, 2016. http://al-mada.ps/?pirenko_team_member=john-doe.

Al-Mada. "Solidarity Concert: John McLaughlin, Zakir Hussain and Remember Shakti." Program booklet produced in Ramallah, 2012.

Malek, Cate, and Mateo Hoke, eds. *Palestine Speaks: Narratives of Life under the Occupation*. San Francisco: McSweeney's Books, 2014.

McDonald, David A. *My Voice Is My Weapon: Music, Nationalism, and the Poetics of Palestinian Resistance*. Durham, NC: Duke University Press, 2013.

Mondoweiss. "Israeli Activists Hit Signs That Segregate and Promote Fear of Palestinians." July 14, 2013. http://mondoweiss.net/2013/07/israeli-activists-hit-signs-that-promote-fear-of-palestinians-in-west-bank/.

Mondoweiss. "Since 1967 Israel Has Razed over 800,000 Palestinian Olive Trees." October 10, 2013. http://mondoweiss.net/2013/10/palestinian-equivalent-destroying/.

Pappe, Ilan. *The Ethnic Cleansing of Palestine*. London: Oneworld, 2006.

Sabreen Association for Artistic Development. "Sabreen." Accessed June 29, 2016. http://www.sabreen.org/about_sabreen.html.

Santos, Boaventura de Sousa. "Beyond Abyssal Thinking: From Global Lines to Ecologies of Knowledge." *Review* 30, no. 1 (2007): 45–89.

Shaheed, Farida. "Report of the Special Rapporteur in the Field of Cultural Rights: The Right to Freedom of Artistic Expression and Creativity." Human Rights Council, United Nations General Assembly, Twenty-Third Session, Agenda Item 3, 2013. Accessed July 8, 2019. https://www.refworld.org/docid/51b9a3d04.html.

Shuttleworth, Kate. "The Israelis and Palestinians Who Work Together in Peace." *Guardian*, July 11, 2016. https://www.theguardian.com/world/2016/jul/11/israel-jews-arabs-palestinians-work-together-peace.

This Week in Palestine. "Solidarity Concert in Palestine." No. 166 (February 2012). http://archive.thisweekinpalestine.com/details.php?id=3627&ed=203&edid=203.

Tolan, Sandy. *Children of the Stone: The Power of Music in a Hard Land*. New York: Bloomsbury, 2015.

United Nations Human Rights Office of the High Commissioner. "Special Rapporteur in the Field of Cultural Rights." Accessed June 29, 2016. http://www.ohchr.org/EN/Issues/CulturalRights/Pages/SRCulturalRightsIndex.aspx.

UNRWA (United Nations Relief and Works Agency for Palestine Refugees in the Near East). "Ein el-Sultan Camp." Accessed June 29, 2016. https://www.unrwa.org/where-we-work/west-bank/ein-el-sultan-camp.

UNRWA (United Nations Relief and Works Agency for Palestine Refugees in the Near East). "West Bank I.D. Holders Stranded on the 'Jerusalem' Side of the Barrier." UNRWA West Bank ID Holder Fact Sheet. January 1, 2013. http://www.unrwa.org/resources/reports/west-bank-id-holders-stranded-%E2%80%9Cjerusalem%E2%80%9D-side-barrier.

"Zakir Hussain Won't Drum for Apartheid." *Palestine Israel One Country: Say NO to Apartheid* (blog), April 29, 2013. https://refrainplayingisrael.wordpress.com/2013/04/29/zakir-hussain-wont-drum-for-apartheid/.

TEN *Silsulim* (Improvised "Curls") in the Vocal Performance of Israeli Popular Music

Identity, Power, and Politics

MOSHE MORAD

Improvising "Curls" and Fighting for Recognition

During a 2012 conference on popular Israeli music and the role of the media in fostering and promoting it, a heated debate erupted between two of the participants, Tomer Sagis and Yossi Gispan.[1] Sagis, an advocate of *shirey eretz Israel* ("songs of the land of Israel"), argued for the preservation and promotion of "original Israeli/Hebrew music."[2] In his opinion, this music did not get enough exposure on Israeli radio, compared to the popular, yet foreign and "inferior," as he implied, *muzika mizraḥit* (Oriental music).[3] This enraged Gispan, the most prolific lyricist of muzika mizraḥit, or, as it is called today, using a milder and more "politically correct" term, *muzika yam-tichonit* (Mediterranean music).[4] He responded to Sagis, "Enough of your arrogance and trying to seclude us in the ghetto. We are Israeli just like you are, and our music is Israeli just like yours. I was born here and my parents came over from Yemen. Your parents came from Eastern Europe. Stop calling our music muzika mizraḥit, or yam-tichonit, as opposed to *your* music which is 'Israeli.' I suggest a new name for our genre—*muzika isra-elit mesulselet* ['curled' Israeli music]." Gispan's suggested new term emphasizes the unique and essential musical feature of the genre—an improvised, "curled" melismatic way of singing.

Muzika mizraḥit evolved in Israel among Jewish immigrants from the Muslim world, specifically from the Middle East, North Africa, and Yemen (collectively called Mizraḥim, Orientals). A key site of its development was the poor southern *sh'chunot* (neighborhoods) of Tel Aviv, especially Sh'chunat Hatikva ("the neighborhood of hope," an ironic name for Tel Aviv's poorest and most troubled neighborhood, at the time associated with poverty, misery, and crime). The emergent musical genre drew from the rich cultural heritage of Mizrahi Jews, and soon began functioning as a vehicle for cultural resistance to the tendency of acculturation and assimilation into the hegemonic ("Ashkenazi European") culture, while, as I will show in this essay, providing at a later stage a pathway into this culture. The music also served as a basis for the creation of the new collective identity of the underprivileged coming from different countries in the Muslim world—the Mizrahim.

Eliezer Moshe Finegold explains that the European Jews' prejudices against "Oriental Jews" led to the creation of a pan-Oriental social, political, and cultural identity and that muzika mizrahit is the musical expression of this collective identity.[5] Since the massive influx of immigrants from Islamic countries (mainly from the Maghreb, Yemen, and the Middle East) in the 1950s, they had been collectively regarded by the Ashkenazi/European Jews, already established residents in young Israel, as Mizrahim, and they soon identified themselves with this collective identity. This invented "pan-Oriental identity" was intensified in the Ashkenazi Israeli psyche and culture by Orientalist stigmas viewing their places of origin as "sensual, mysterious, tempting, primitive, lacking sense, and dangerous."[6] Edwin Seroussi claims that the quick adoption of this distinctive collective identity (*Mizrahiyut*, "Orientality") came as a counterreaction to the "formal" labeling of Jews of North African and Middle Eastern descent as *adot ha'mizrah* (the communities of the Orient) by the media and the establishment, then dominated by Ashkenazi Jews, while the Ashkenazi Jews were not labeled "the communities of the Occident."[7]

In his response to Sagis, Gispan joined other mizrahit/Mediterranean music artists who had fiercely demanded to be tagged as Israeli rather than Mizrahi. This acrimonious controversy over the term used for a musical genre is not just semantic, since "musical genres are contested sites in which people negotiate their identities and territorial claims."[8] This West-versus-East, Ashkenazi-versus-Sephardi, European-versus-Arabic, or even "white-against-black" music war has been going on for more than half a century in Israel, and continues to acquire new expressions, in spite of continuous institutional and national attempts at integration and assimilation.[9] A muzika mizrahit singer and composer told me of "the Ashkenazi attempt to 'straighten our curls,' tame us savages, lock us in an organized frame of European-style music and kill our spirit of 'curling' and improvising."[10]

Gispan's term *mesulselet* ("curled," the adjectival form of the noun *silsulim*, "curls") remains accurate in present-day Israel. Many other distinguishing features of muzika mizraḥit, such as its production (once considered cheaply and poorly produced), arrangements, distribution, and even poor media exposure, have diminished over time, but the vocal improvisation technique known as silsulim remains the distinctive characteristic of the genre. More than any other genre distinction, popular Israeli vocal music nowadays is clearly divided into two defined kinds—mesulselet ("curled") and non-mesulselet ("noncurled"). As Gispan's refusal of ghettoization indicates, this is not just an aesthetic and stylistic division but reflects a social divide in Israeli society, one in which a musical practice closely tied to Arab-style vocal and instrumental improvisation plays a critical role.

The struggle of the mizraḥit/yam-tichonit artists and producers to become part of the Israeli mainstream has succeeded in spite of the ongoing accusation of media bias. Still, silsulim, even when performed on prime-time TV or in music arenas, bear a heavy symbolic, semantic, psychological, social, and political load. The musical genre characterized by improvised vocal "curls," which started on the edge of society as "cassette music," has gradually gained acceptance but has also been seen, pejoratively, as invading the Israeli musical mainstream. Silsulim has become in modern Israel a strong signifier of ethnicity, power, and resistance—and the most conspicuous symbol of Israeli culture wars and of the enduring divide between Sephardic and Ashkenazi Israelis.

In what follows I describe the musical phenomenon, explain its cultural and social sources while attending to the politics-laden debates about it, provide a brief historical background of its evolution and crossover from the margins to the mainstream of Israeli popular music, and show how it has become a significant force in the Israeli music industry, shifting the dominant vocal musicscape from European/syllabic to Middle Eastern/improvised and melismatic.

Silsulim and *Mawwal* Sensitivity: Emotional Intuitive Improvisation as a Way of Vocal Production and Expression

Muzika mizraḥit/yam-tichonit blends Middle Eastern, Greek, and Turkish melodies with Western pop. It is typically performed on Western instruments and adheres to Western pop harmony and structure, but it also includes the flavoring of Middle Eastern and Balkan instruments (*oud, bouzouki, darbukka*), typical melismatic-style singing (silsulim), and sections of nonrhythmic vocal or instrumental improvisation (*mawwal* and *taqsim*, respectively).

Whereas the genre's production styles and the music business and media approach toward it have become closer to the "Western" Israeli mainstream, its typical vocal production and expression technique, silsulim, remains the one strong and very clear distinction between Israeli "Western" music and Israeli Mediterranean music, a distinction at the center of Israeli music politics. *Lesalsel* (the verb, "to curl"), or *silsulim* (the plural noun), indicates a melismatic style of singing in which the singer "twirls" around the pitch, "bending" the note in microtonality—up and down—and demonstrating virtuosity by prolonging the tones and producing improvised elaborate ornamentations on one syllable.

Interestingly, and probably not incidentally, the choice of the word *silsulim* as a metaphor for this particular melismatic vocal expression is also related to a typical visual feature of Mizraḥim. Many Israelis of Yemenite, North African, and Middle Eastern origin have curly hair (*mesulsal*). The general aesthetic perception in 1970s Israel was that "straight hair" was more European and therefore more beautiful, especially for women, and many Mizraḥi women with naturally curly hair used to straighten their hair.[11] Furthermore, curly hair was considered "wild" and "untended," whereas straight (or straightened) hair was considered neat, looked-after, and aesthetically pleasing. I even remember my secondary school teacher commenting, "Hase'ar shelach lo mesudar" ("Your hair is untended") to a Yemenite-Jewish classmate who had very curly hair. Hebrew is a gendered language, and *muzika* (music) is a feminine form—hence the phrase is *muzika mesulselet* (using the feminine form of *mesulsal*). The expression *mesulselet* for both the music and a curly-haired woman, then, holds descriptive and symbolic meaning.

Silsulim-style singing incorporates more than an occasional vibrato or episodes of ornamentation and is reflected in the vocal performance throughout.[12] Silsulim is embedded in the aesthetic character of muzika mizraḥit, derived as it is from the *maqam* sensitivity (maqam, literally "place" in Arabic, the system of spatial-tonal melodic modes in traditional Arabic music), but expressed differently when applied to Western non-maqam music. Silsulim can reach heights of ecstasy, especially in the opening and the closing parts of the song but also during breaks of ecstatic pitches in the middle of the piece, where the audience cheers a particularly impressive curled vocal improvisation. These elaborate free-rhythm silsulim parts, usually in the opening of a song, are called in muzika mizraḥit discourse *mawwal* (*mawwalim* in the plural, an Arabic-Hebrew portmanteau applying the Hebrew plural ending to the Arabic word), a term taken from maqam music.

The mawwal in Arabic maqam music is a highly ornamented improvised vocal form, "an intricate improvisation . . . with which a singer opens a vocal performance . . . [and] focuses the singer and the audience on the modes used in the piece." It is improvised yet consists of "carefully placed vocal spirals and twists."[13] Silsulim is a hybrid form that incorporates maqam sensibility within non-maqam music. El'ad, a twenty-five-year-old singer and aficionado of muzika mizraḥit, describes this improvised-yet-carefully-placed duality in silsulim: "When I 'mesalsel' [curl] I invent [improvise], I never do exactly the same kind of 'silsul.' I let my soul wander freely, but still this invention, or wandering, has to be accurate in its feeling and tones [tonality] to touch the people's [listeners'] hearts."[14]

This kind of invention/improvisation was dismissed as "primitive" by the hegemonic European music establishment in Israel's early days. In my youth I heard expressions such as "not clean," "ugly," "not professional," and "sounds like [it is] out of tune" from my classical music teachers regarding both Arabic and Oriental/Mediterranean vocal performance, and especially in relation to its intricate microtonality. These commentators' traditional European doctrine advocated accurate pitch and tempo "as written," and they considered improvisation or extemporization inferior. This corresponds with the way improvisation was regarded by early twentieth-century musicologists, who associated it with nonprofessional "primitive" musical performers: "The primitive act of music-making, existing from the moment the untutored individual obeys the impulse to relieve his feelings by bursting into song. Accordingly, therefore, amongst all primitive peoples' musical composition consists of extemporization subsequently memorized."[15]

According to Habib Hassan Touma, mawwal singing goes back to the ninth century, during the era of the caliph Hārūn ar-Rashīd, when it was described in connection with the working class. The text of the mawwal sections of the song is in colloquial Arabic, even if the rest is in poetic literary Arabic.[16] Both the nonrhythmic *layali* (improvised introduction) and the following mawwal present the particular maqam (mode) of the song, and its "characteristic emotional content." The mawwal's melodic line "dispenses with any division into measures, and the tone levels and phases characteristic of the maqām are . . . realized, with the highest phase clearly defining the climax of the entire piece."[17]

Whereas in most Western types of music improvisation is considered the opposite of composition, in Eastern music traditions this is not the case. This different approach is the key factor in understanding mawwal (vocal) and taqsim (instrumental) sensibilities. In an essay about improvisation in Iranian classical music, Laudan Nooshin discusses the creative process, challenges the "paradigmatic positioning of 'improvisation' and 'composition' in a largely oppositional relationship," and explains that prior to the twentieth century there was no equivalent in Iranian music to "the Western concept of improvisation," since "creativity in performance was simply an accepted part of a tradition in which no distinction was made between the roles of composer and performer." Nooshin mentions that already in 1974 Bruno Nettl suggested viewing improvisation and composition as "a continuum of creative practice" rather than as oppositional categories.[18] Such a perspective is certainly necessary for understanding mawwal sensitivity. This different approach toward improvisation in the Eastern musical world (as being a continuum of composition) versus the Western musical world (as being the opposite of composition), and the traditional high regard for creative improvisation in the East, as opposed to the traditional Western dismissal of improvisation as "primitive," "untutored," and "impulsive,"[19] is mirrored in the mesulselet/Mizraḥi (Eastern) versus non-mesulselet/Ashkenazi (Western) aesthetico-political conflict in Israeli music.

The connection to religion adds another dimension to this sensitivity, and to the creative and spiritual role of the performer of the mawwal. According to Touma, mawwal singing derives from, and is strongly related to, the Muslim call for prayer and its "richly embellished melodic passage," and the reading of the Koran, which "not infrequently... involves a complete maqām presentation." During the pauses in the reading, "the faithful burst into spontaneous applause, especially when an excellent Koran reader, by modulating to neighboring maqām rows or by abruptly finishing a melodic passage on a high tone, manages to heighten the inner tension of the listeners until they have no choice but to release it with exclamations praising God."[20] Likewise, silsulim are strongly influenced by the cantillation (the ritual chanting of readings from the Hebrew Bible in synagogue services) of the Torah in Sephardic and Yemenite synagogues, and in the traditional singing of prayers and *piyyutim*, Jewish liturgical chants, in the Sephardic tradition.[21] In the Sephardic tradition, the cantillation makes use of the maqam system and sensitivity.[22] Sephardic piyyutim are even categorized according to the relevant maqam used in each piyyut.[23]

Almog Behar discusses this phenomenon in a blog post titled "Umm Kulthum in the Synagogue."[24] This rather controversial title illustrates the Jewish adoption of popular secular Arabic melodies (including the songs of Egyptian singer Umm Kulthum) to serve Hebrew prayer and liturgy texts.[25] The cultural connection between Islam and Sephardic Judaism is both fascinating and controversial. According to Amy Horowitz, the mawwal symbolizes "the story in which Jews from Islamic countries carried Umm Kulthum's music to their new home in Israel."[26]

What is "improvised" and what is not in silsulim? How does the production of silsulim and their creativity relate to what is traditionally called improvisation in Western music? Does this style merely consist of an improvised embellishment on certain notes, or does it represent a more complete affective musical ordering? R. Cohen, a twenty-one-year-old soldier and singer from a family originating in Morocco, provides a detailed description of what happens to the singer during a silsulim session:

> I cannot sing yavesh ["dry," meaning "straight"], without doing silsulim. It just doesn't seem right to me. It is not natural. It is singing from the brain, not from the heart. When I sing from the brain, I can do it "dry," but when it's from the heart, it has to be mesulsal.
>
> Is it improvised? Of course. Each tone and each silsul is different—it is coming from my gut, my intuition. [It's] not planned, and it's improvised on the spur of the moment. When I intend to start a song or end it with a long mawwal, I know only the starting point [initial pitch], and I know where I want to reach at the end [final pitch]. I don't even know when I want to reach the end of the mawwal. All the rest is improvised, not a planned improvisation, like maybe you have in rock or jazz, but an emotional, intuitive improvisation. . . .
>
> It is difficult to describe the process, but it also has to do with technical matters and with changing circumstances—like how much air you have left in your lungs or how much inspiration you take [absorb] from the musicians and from the audience. For example, if they cheer in the middle of a mawwal, it encourages me to continue and even climb to higher notes.
>
> I would say it is an emotional improvisation that comes from within, and only uses your technical ability, but to do it right you have to have all gates wide open at the time—first, of course, your voice, throat, and vocal technique have to be at their best.
>
> You also have to be very musical and with "roots." [*Roots* meaning a maqam sensitivity from Arabic music heard at home and from syna-

gogue cantillation.] Technically, you have to be able to hit the right notes, not only the long ones, but also all the small ones [microtones] on the way. You also have to be totally open to hear and feel the musicians and the audience, as the mawwal should react to what they project, and last [but not least]—you have to have your heart wide open, to let the feeling from inside lead you all along the way.[27]

Cohen's words not only describe the process of silsulim production and mastery but shed light on the emotional aspect of silsulim, in his words, "an emotional, intuitive improvisation." It is emotional when produced but also, just as importantly, when consumed by the audience.

During a radio program I presented about the late blind Iraqi-Jewish *qanoon* (zither) player Abraham Salman, I interviewed David Regev Za'arur, a young Israeli qanoon player, the great-grandson of Yosef Za'arur, one of Iraq's greatest qanoon players from the 1940s and 1950s. David Regev Za'arur is dedicated to the research, collection, and preservation of authentic Iraqi maqam music recordings. We were listening to a live recording of Salman playing Taqsim Rast. The piece was studded with audience cries of approval switching from "bravo" to "Allah" and "ya ruhi" (my soul). Za'arur explained: "The members in the audience differentiate between a 'technical' improvisation and an 'emotional' one, in their cries of approval—if they call 'bravo,' it is in a praise of a particularly virtuoso/technical performance, and if they call 'Allah' or 'ya ruhi,' it is in response to a particularly strong emotional playing/singing."[28] The European "bravo" is used in connection with technical virtuosity, whereas the Arabic spiritual expressions "Allah" (God, God) and "ya ruhi" (my soul) are saved for moments of spiritual and emotional elation in the music. A similar sensitivity exists within the silsulim audience, where technical silsulim are appreciated, but not as much as those that bear a particular emotional expression. On various occasions, I heard muzika mizrahit specialists differentiating between *technika* (technique) and *regesh* (feeling) when critiquing or instructing vocalists about silsulim.

Zohar Argov (1955–1987) and Zehava Ben (b. 1968) are the two iconic protagonists of silsulim, setting the tone for a whole new generation of *mesalselim* ("curlers," that is, performers of silsulim). Both were born into poor families and led difficult lives.[29] During his short life, and in the years that followed, Argov became a role model for silsulim singers, and even today the best compliment any singer performing silsulim can receive is "You remind me of Zohar Argov." Musician Yigal Hared says about Argov, "It was so natural with him. At the end of the line he would add Oriental variations [silsulim]. This was his trademark. It became a model that other singers copy. Others that tried did not succeed in doing the silsulim like him."[30]

Horowitz describes a performance by Argov in the 1982 Festival Ha-Zemer Ve-hapizmon Besignon Adot Hamizraḥ ("the festival of popular music songs in the style of the communities of the Orient"), the first attempt to incorporate (but still distinguish) muzika mizraḥit in Israeli public-service TV, the only television channel operating then, and perhaps the first time powerful silsulim were heard on Israeli TV: "A slender Yemenite in a tight-fitting Western suit appears at stage left. He walks to the microphone and fills the hall with a single, clear, piercing tone. The sound shoots out from a deep well somewhere between his heart and gut. It streams through his throat and nose, lips and cheeks, like unexpected rain winding down the interior crevices of a desert canyon. It is neither a cry not a roar, but evokes both feelings."[31]

While the Mizraḥim in the audience identified with Argov's performance, one could see the culture shock on the faces of many Ashkenazim in the audience. In spite of the "Western suit," the Western orchestra, and the choreographed production, Argov's "untamed" voice demonstrated the connection of silsulim to political struggle. "Argov's audience identified with his voice, which resonated with their struggles. The political took on the contours of the aesthetic. Yemenite composer/guitarist Yigal Hared noted, 'He would start a phrase of muwwal; it was like a charge forward in battle.'"[32]

Israeli ethnomusicologist and composer Avraham Eilam-Amzallag uses the word *power* to describe Argov's vocal performance of the song performed in the festival, "Ha'perah Be'gani" ("The Flower in My Garden"): "The direct and authentic way in which Zohar sings that song and puts the *muwwal* into it gives the song an enormous power, even though its melody is simple."[33] The word power (*koaḥ* in Hebrew) is frequently used in the discourse of silsulim and muzika mizraḥit: *shira im koaḥ* ("powerful singing") does not necessarily indicate the level of volume or even intensity but a strong affective power deriving from the emotional charge and the quality of the silsulim.[34]

Zehava Ben learned Argov's mawwal techniques from pirated cassettes but was also influenced by Egyptian diva Umm Kulthum, whom she had heard at home. Ben's silsulim style was different from Argov's. Describing Ben's interpretation of Argov's song "Ha'perah Be'gani," Horowitz writes, "Unlike Argov's hungry and piercing *muwwal*, Zehava Ben's opening improvisation . . . engulfed the listener in a sonic moment that unfolded slowly

FIGURE 10.1 Zohar Argov, album cover. Courtesy of Reuveni Bros.

like a garden flower that is the song's central metaphor.... Ben's *muwwal* charted an emotional territory through which ensuing song lyrics could be contextualized. Sadness and hope were woven into the carefully executed melisma, as if to catch and comfort the weary listeners between the notes of their daily struggle."[35]

"Like a Charge Forward in Battle": Silsulim as Resistance and the Politics of Muzika Mizraḥit

The political struggle of the Mizraḥi Jews against discrimination started in the early 1970s with the creation of the Israeli Black Panthers movement. This struggle has since been a significant force in Israeli internal politics, culminating with the formation in 1984 of Shas, a popular religious Sephardi

FIGURE 10.2 Zehava Ben, album cover. Courtesy of NMC United Entertainment Ltd.

party that has become influential in Israeli politics. Historically music has played an effective role in such movements and social phenomena, helping the marginalized to regain pride and to combat fear and anger.[36] According to Motti Regev and Edwin Seroussi, muzika mizraḥit "emerged as the result of a particular sociopolitical conjuncture in which public expressions of a pan-mizraḥi Jewish culture began to emerge in Israel," and furthermore has become "a major expression of a profound process of social change that has affected Mizraḥi Israelis since the 1970s."[37] The genre's emergence and popularity were part of the social uprising of Sephardic Israelis "lifting up their heads," politically, socially, and culturally. In fact, one could say that muzika mizraḥit remains the soundtrack of this ongoing social conflict and, as argued in this chapter, makes a political, as well as an aesthetic, statement. Furthermore, as described earlier in relation to Zohar Argov's performance ("He would start a phrase of muwwal; it was like a charge forward in battle"), the silsulim improvisational component of the music provides both the performers and the audience with an aesthetico-political agency, individual as well as collective.

Ahuva Carmeli, born in the early 1950s and living since in Kerem Ha'teimanim (the Yemenites' quarter) in Tel Aviv, told me, "I remember that we used to listen to muzika mizraḥit in the neighborhood, not only as a matter of taste but also as a kind of psychological reassurance, comfort, security, for people who were discriminated [against] by the Ashkenazim [European Jews]. It gave us pride and security. My son was once arrested during a demonstration of Ha'panterim [the Black Panthers] and told me how [muzika mizraḥit] cassettes helped them in prison to regain their pride and strength, and not to feel so humiliated and threatened by the prison guards."[38]

Until the late 1990s nationwide radio and other media outlets in Israel, which according to muzika mizraḥit advocates were dominated by the hegemony of European culture, gave very little airtime to the genre in spite of its street-level popularity (cassette stalls, weddings, nightclubs, and so forth). In fact, since the establishment of Israel's main public-service radio stations (the IBA and Galei Zahal, the military radio station), and later the IBA's TV channel, the culture of the Sephardic Jews had been marginalized, considered either inferior or "ethnic" (and so confined to "ethnic" programs, such as the festival described above).[39]

Horowitz claims that "the pan-ethnic music Mizraḥi musicians created from the 1970s through the 1990s was both unabsorbable and unaccommodative; the language, arrangements, vocal lines [silsulim], distribution, and audience all placed it outside mainstream channels."[40] The exclusion from the mainstream was, however, due not only to its musical characteristics but also to its social status. The mainstream music industry avoided signing and producing muzika mizraḥit artists in spite of the genre's street popularity, and a phantom music industry flourished, based on cassette sales (and later CDs), mainly in market stalls.

This situation changed during the 1990s when the already-popular-at-street-level genre was welcomed, albeit with reservations, into the arms of the Israeli mainstream music industry and media. The change came with the emergence of local radio stations and commercial TV channels, some of which embraced the popular genre in order to appeal to its growing audience, and as an answer and counterreaction to the "European elitism" of the public-service broadcasters. The music industry followed. In 1998, in my role as the managing director of Israel's leading record company NMC, I decided to sign top muzika mizraḥit artist Zehava Ben. Up until then the major record companies had ignored the genre, as it was considered "inferior and it was managed and controlled by unprofessional crooks and mafiosos, with no respect for signed contracts, royalties or the industry rules."[41] I was aware of the difficulties an established company would encounter in dealing with artists and managers who were used to cash payments and handshake agreements but thought it was time to sign to the label a prominent muzika mizraḥit artist, produce a high-standard album, and provide the marketing tools of a major company. I would say it was a commercial decision influenced by ideology. This was the first time a hard-core Mizraḥi artist was signed to a major record label, and the decision proved commercially viable and indeed changed the attitude of the other major labels, which followed suit.

The shift in terminology from *muzika mizraḥit* (Oriental music) to *muzika yam-tichonit* (Mediterranean music) gathered momentum in the early 1990s. The transformation in musical representation was the result of the infiltration of pop and rock crossover elements in the production and instrumentation; less use of heavy and long taqsim nonrhythmic sections; and more use of an organized Western pop structure, together with a higher standard of computerized studio production. "The music became lighter, more European-friendly, less deep and Arabic. More Greek than Turkish," explains Morris, a mizraḥit aficionado and collector since the early 1970s.[42] But the main catalyst of the terminological switch was economic (marketing), social, and even politically driven. According to Regev and Seroussi, "the evolution of labels used to refer to this music is revealing of this change in the eyes of the musiqa misraḥit producers themselves. They stopped referring to it as musiqa misraḥit yisraelit and began calling it musiqa yam tikhonit, in order to differentiate it from 'other' musics, particularly Arab music. By adopting this strategy, they avoided the tendency of European Israelis to confuse them with the Arabs, whom they resembled in musical tastes and other aspects of culture."[43] Whereas I agree with Regev and Seroussi about the role of the genre's producers and managers in instilling and commercializing the new term, I argue that the media and the audience also played an important role in the switch from *mizraḥit* to *yam-tichonit*. The reason given by Regev and Seroussi, to differentiate the music and its audience from the Arabs, although not officially stated, was a sociopsychological catalyst in this transition. The escalation of violence and terrorist attacks following the eruption of the First Intifada (the Palestinian uprising) in 1987 added to the hostility toward Arabs in Israel, and to the wish of muzika mizraḥit artists to disassociate themselves from Arab culture, especially when the "European" Israeli mainstream started accepting them.

"The Music of the Enemy"

Indeed the ongoing Arab-Israeli conflict has affected the role and status of muzika mizraḥit in more ways than one. The cultural proximity between Arabs and Sephardic Jews from the Arab world fueled some of the bigotry that the Sephardic Jews suffered. I clearly remember a comment of an elderly Polish-Jewish woman living in my childhood neighborhood about her Iraqi-Jewish neighbors, when the music of Umm Kulthum blared out their window on a Saturday morning: "Not only do they [the neighbors] look like Arabs, they sound like Arabs. Listen to this awful Arabic music. The people we are fighting. Not only are we surrounded by them, but we have them among us." Old-generation Ashkenazi-versus-Sephardic bigotry as such would hardly be expressed in contemporary Israel, but it does reflect the musical alliance between Arabs and Sephardic Jews, and the ongoing musical and cultural rupture between Sephardic and Ashkenazi Jews in Israel.

The cultural alliance of muzika mizraḥit with Arabic music takes on an even more complex nature when one looks at Israeli politics, affected both by internal social issues and by the Arab-Israeli conflict. Election polls since the early 1980s show a strong tendency among Mizraḥi voters toward allegiance to right-wing parties. Many of the official polls and statistics, however, are based on the voting results of towns with a large percentage of Mizraḥim from low socioeconomic levels, and not Mizraḥim in general. The general perception in the media and among researchers indicates a preference among Mizraḥim for Likud (the right-wing party) and hawkishness in their political views toward the Palestinian-Israeli conflict.[44] It may seem paradoxical that a population of low socioeconomic status supports the neoliberal right wing, but this long-term support started, and continues, as a vote of protest against the Labor Party and the "socialist Ashkenazi elite," and the way it has treated the Mizraḥim. Many even attribute the transfer of power in 1977 from the Labor Party to Menachem Begin and the Likud to the Black Panthers movement and the Mizraḥi uprising. Smadar Lavie claims, "It was during the right-wing Israeli regimes that Mizraḥi culture, as long as it avoided connecting its own Arabness with that of the Palestinians, began to embark on a renaissance."[45]

The de-arabization of Mizraḥi Jews, begun during the Labor Party rule in the early 1970s, made them "'Israelized,' [and] alienated from their own cultural roots."[46] The yam-tichonization of muzika mizraḥit in the 1990s was yet another step in this de-arabization and Israelization process. The use of the term *yam-tichonit*, rather than *mizraḥit*, brings the genre geographically and culturally closer to the Mediterranean shore of Israel, and distances it from the diasporic Orient and the surrounding Arab world. Yet, the term still differentiates it from "Israeli music," and it is therefore debated by Gispan and many of his colleagues. This complex of cultural alliance, transculturation, politics, and terminology shows in fact how muzika mizraḥit/yam-tichonit was throughout its history affected by, shaped by, and stigmatized by two main political and sociocultural conflicts taking place in Israel: the Sephardic-Ashkenazi and the Arab-Jewish.

Silsulim in Present-Day Israeli Broadcast Media

In spite of the huge popularity of muzika yam-tichonit these days, the genre's musicians and producers still complain of discrimination and marginalization in the Israeli media. Objective surveys show they are right. A survey carried out by the internet portal *Walla News* in 2013, based on data from Media Forest, the leading airplay-monitoring company in Israel, showed that barely 16 percent of the music played on the nationwide stations can be defined as mizraḥit/yam-tichonit.[47] The most popular nationwide music station in Israel, the military-run Galgalatz, which has a nearly 30 percent listenership according to recent media surveys, is constantly attacked by the mizraḥit/yam-tichonit sector for not giving them the amount of playtime they deserve according to their popularity, and further excluding them from the station's playlist system, which selects each week the songs that will get priority and extensive airplay. In a wave of protest against the "whiteness" of Galgalatz's playlist, seen as being "anti-Mizraḥit," in July 2012, some Mizraḥit artists, including the very popular Dudu Aharon, threatened to set up a protest tent outside the station's headquarters. Their claim resonated with, and raised again, the old and ongoing ethnic prejudice issue titled in the media as *hashed ha'adati* ("the ethnic demon"), which keeps "popping out" every so often.

In a 2012 article by Asaf Nevo in the *Mako* online news portal, titled "The Conspiracy of Silence of Muzika Mizraḥit in Galgalatz," some of the genre's leaders "who were not afraid to speak their mind," according to Nevo, expressed bitter accusations against the station's music policy, which, they claim, strongly reflected a social and financial bias.[48] Avihu Medina, one of the most reputable muzika mizraḥit composers, says, "What happens in Galgalatz disgusts me. Muzika mizraḥit is 80 percent of what is heard in live shows in Israel. . . . They let a few soldiers do what they want in a national radio station."[49] The main argument in Nevo's article is that the musical editors of the station play songs according to their personal tastes and not according to "the people's taste," a claim often repeated in the ongoing struggle of mizraḥit/yam-tichonit artists and managers against the Israeli media.

In November 2015 the claims against Galgalatz gained a powerful new voice. The minister of culture, Miri Regev, launched an attack against the military station, saying that they should play more local music, with particular emphasis on muzika mizraḥit. Regev "expressed the desire to change the nature of the station, with the aim of 'creating cultural justice.'"[50] This involvement enraged the minister of defense, who is in charge of the popular military radio station. Still, Regev, herself of Mizraḥi origin, insisted her agenda is to support Mizraḥi culture in Israel and fix the "historic injustice."

The counterargument heard from radio music editors is that the exclusion of many mizraḥit/yam-tichonit popular songs from the programming is due to their low standards of production and lyrics, whereas "high-quality" muzika mizraḥit does find its way in. This argument reflects the development of "elitist Oriental" music by artists who use silsulim and maqam sensitivities in a musically sophisticated manner; their songs have meaningful texts (including poetry), are considered better arranged and produced, and are embraced by the cultural establishment and considered hip among trendsetters and the cool audiences, yet are still defined as ethnic.[51]

In opposition to the lack of airplay on the nationwide radio stations, and as a response to it, there is a popular dedicated local muzika yam-tichonit radio station called Lev Ha'medina ("The heart of the country," hinting at both its central location in Rishon Le'zion, broadcasting to the country's central region, and its repertoire—"the people's music"), as well as numerous online radio stations playing Mediterranean music. On Reshet Gimmel, the nationwide public-service Hebrew-music-only station, there are programs nowadays dedicated to muzika yam-tichonit. Advocates of the genre welcome the increase in airplay but object to the ghettoization that runs through the history of muzika mizraḥit in the Israeli media. "The ghetto is much bigger now and more comfortable, but it is still a ghetto," a muzika mizraḥit producer (who asked to remain anonymous) told me.[52]

Things, however, have changed drastically in recent years on commercial TV. The two operating commercial channels have given the power to the voting audience in popular TV music contests. As in many other countries, the global phenomenon of TV singing contests has hit Israel, with programs such as *A Star Is Born*, *The X Factor*, and *The Voice* dominating commercial TV and gaining high viewing figures. These programs expose and fuel the new stage of the muzika mizraḥit conflict in Israel, which has turned into a simplified dichotomic "mesulselet versus non-mesulselet" music war, and has been brought into everyone's living rooms. Watching the competitors and listening to the voices featured in these programs, one can see and hear a clear distinction between the two kinds of vocal performances. Owing to the blending of visual features among third- and fourth-generation Israelis as a result of mixed marriages, what used to be a primary visual differentiation between Mizraḥi/Sephardic (dark-skinned) and Ashkenazi (light-skinned) singers has now transformed into a sonic differentiation between mesalselim and non-mesalselim.

Put bluntly, the performers in these shows can be easily divided into two groups, which nowadays indicate an ethnic origin to a lesser extent, but mainly a social status and a musical sensitivity. In conversations with twenty-four viewers of *The Voice*, aged sixteen to twenty-five (May 2015), I asked my interviewees to describe and categorize each competitor in three different episodes of the program into two distinctive objective categories of their choice (not according to their subjective quality or appeal to the viewer).[53] Most of them divided the competitors into two categories: "mesalselim" and "lo mesalselim" (non-mesalselim). In these conversations the vocal distinction between mesalselim and non-mesalselim was used much more than the ethnic one between Mizraḥim and Ashkenazim. Furthermore, when musicians and music industry executives were asked to categorize the competitors objectively, they almost exclusively used the distinction between mesalselim and non-mesalselim as well.

The non-mesalselim in these programs usually have a US/European style of performance with pop-, rock-, or folk-type vocals and mannerisms. Most of them choose to perform Hebrew or English-language pop and rock songs. The mesalselim in the contests sing mostly in Hebrew, but sometimes in Arabic. They usually (but not always) interpret mizraḥit/yam-tichonit hits. Some of the mesalselim male competitors wear a *kipa* (skullcap), indicating they are religious or *masorti* ("traditional," that is, "lightweight" religious). The distinction between mesalselim and non-mesalselim was especially evident in a popular TV music contest program called Music School where the competitors were children, many of whom were third- and even fourth-generation Israelis, with hardly any visible ethnic distinctions. Still, when they started singing, the silsulim sensitivity of some of them was immediately evident and powerful. This division between mesalselim and non-mesalselim is also embedded in the Israeli TV music contest programs' agenda, when even its mentors/judges are clearly chosen and divided into these two categories. In the case of the program I used as a test case, the mentors/judges were Sarit Hadad and Shlomi Shabbat, two yam-tichonit music stars, known for their silsulim, and Aviv Geffen and Mosh Ben

Ari—two "non-mesalselim" rockers. Geffen and Ben Ari are guitar-oriented singer-songwriters, and their music corresponds with Anglo-American folk and rock.[54]

Geffen kept "teasing" the mesalselim mentors about their "provinciality" with comments like, "You play in weddings, and wherever you are invited," and so forth. Likewise, successful competitors who were clearly mesalselim were usually selected by the yam-tichonit mentors and ignored (and sometimes snubbed) by Geffen, whereas rockers and folk-style singers (mostly singing in English) were picked up by Geffen and Ben Ari. Geffen's derogatory approach to silsulim expresses the opinion of those who look down at the genre, describing it as "cheap," "primitive," and "whiny." I heard such expressions from a wide range of people in Israeli society, from older European Jews to musicians, music critics, and musicologists. In many cases the use of "whining" carries a double meaning—ridiculing the melismatic singing but also the protest against discrimination in society and in the media.[55] In contemporary Israel these elitist, arrogant, and condescending views are strongly challenged by "the public," that is, the numerous SMS votes given in response to impressive silsulim in the TV music contests.[56]

In spite of the genre's immense popularity, the sociopolitical tension associated with it is still present, dividing Israeli popular music (and society) into two clear groups marked by a stigmatized technique of vocal production, silsulim. Issues of discrimination, inferiority and superiority, and even what some of the genre's performers and producers call "racism" are still at the forefront of Israeli popular music politics.

Epilogue: Silsulim—a Bridge for Peace?

I first wrote this epilogue in 2014 between siren alerts and rockets booming over my office in Tel Aviv, with enormous destruction and suffering only sixty kilometers away, in Gaza, in the midst of yet another bloody episode in the ongoing Israeli-Palestinian conflict that has yet to be resolved. Horowitz pertinently asks, "Under which conditions do people accept or reject each other's (or their own) music, and how does that rejection/acceptance map onto political affiliations across the line of conflict?" She answers, "People create both aesthetic genres and political boundaries, and each realm influences the other."[57] This chapter has focused on the role of muzika mizraḥit and silsulim sensitivity in the internal politics and conflicts of Israeli society. But what about the BIG conflict, the Israeli-Arab one, and more specifically the Israeli-Palestinian one? Can muzika mizraḥit and its silsulim sensitivity unite Israeli Jews and Arabs, creating a cultural bridge between the disputants in the Arab-Israeli conflict? Does Israeli muzika mizraḥit appeal to the neighboring Arab societies, just as Arabic music appeals to, and has infiltrated into the culture of, Jews from Islamic countries (in a reversal of the "Umm Kulthum in the synagogue" phenomenon described earlier)?

The close musical contact between Muslims and Jews in the Arab world is a result of times when Jews and Muslims lived side by side in the Arab countries. Israeli muzika mizraḥit was born into the ongoing Israel-Palestine conflict; however, it is popular not only among Arabs living in Israel but also among those in neighboring countries, especially Palestinians in the West Bank and Gaza. This phenomenon creates a paradoxical cultural reality where the same Israeli silsulim artists are popular both among the Palestinians and among the Israeli soldiers confronting them. Zehava Ben has performed in the Palestinian cities Nablus and Jericho in the West Bank, following the Israeli withdrawal from Gaza in 2005. In an interview with the Arab website El Arabi'ya quoted on *Walla News*, she commented, "I am not a politician, and I am not interested in politics, but I always try in my own way to strengthen the coexistence between Palestinians and Israelis."[58] Not only are classic silsulim vocalists Zehava Ben and Zohar Argov popular among Palestinians, but so are young mesalselim stars such as Sarit Hadad, Omer Adam, Ofer Levy, and Etti Levy.[59]

Avihu Medina tells of a Palestinian pirate CD manufacturer in Hebron who duplicates Israeli Mediterranean-music CDs and distributes them all over the West Bank. He attributes Palestinians' strong attraction to muzika mesulselet to the "Westernization" of Palestinians and Israelis, and to the fact that both are relatively young nations. Musically, Medina claims, young Palestinians' musical tastes are closer to Israeli muzika mizraḥit and its hybrid nature, than to "classical" maqam music from Arab countries such as Egypt, Iraq, and Syria.[60]

In an article published after the Israeli withdrawal from Gaza in 2005, titled "Hebrew Songs Making a Comeback in Gaza," Yasser Baraka describes the popularity of muzika mizraḥit in Gaza, especially among older Gazans who used to work in Israel before the Second Intifada. A taxi driver in Gaza City who listens in his car to Israeli cassettes told Baraka about his first encounter with muzika mizraḥit: "We were in a taxi heading to Haifa to the factory we worked at. The driver was Jewish and listened to Zehava Ben. Her voice and music were very oriental, and I've liked Hebrew music ever since." Another Gazan, a tailor who used to work in an Israeli sewing factory, explains, "I know that most of the Israeli singers we listen to [muzika mizraḥit] originally came from Arab countries like Morocco, Iraq, and even Yemen.... Some of them were brought up just like us, which explains their oriental tone."⁶¹ A music store owner in Gaza City told Baraka that he used to sell a thousand Israeli music cassettes a month following the signing of the Oslo peace accords in 1994.

Still, politics has had its effect on the popularity of Israeli muzika mizraḥit in Palestine, if not on the cultural affiliation. Whereas the signing of the Oslo peace accords made Israeli "curled" music more accessible and popular in Gaza and the Palestinian territories in the West Bank, the next round of violence, with the outbreak of the Second Intifada in 2000 and the Israeli invasion of Gaza, brought a decline in the consumption of Israeli music by Palestinians. As Baraka writes, "it was hard for the fans of Hebrew songs to put these songs on the shelf, but listening to them in public reminded Palestinians of their oppressors." He quotes Khader Abbas, a psychology professor at Al-Azhar University in Gaza, who claims that the rise in religious zeal in Gaza contributed to this decline in popularity. The rise in nationalism and the Islamic resistance movement drove people to consume Koran recitals and nationalist songs, and the secular "corrupting" music of the enemy was rejected. Just as some Israelis used to denounce muzika mizraḥit (and the Arabic music listened to by Jews from Arab countries) as "the music of the enemy," Palestinians were told to avoid listening to Israeli music because it is akin to "consorting with the enemy."⁶² Hence, somewhat ironically, muzika mizraḥit, music born out of a conflict (between Mizraḥim and Ashkenazim), has been depicted by both opposing sides—the anti-Mizraḥit Israelis and anti-Israeli Palestinians—as "the music of the enemy."

Following the Israeli withdrawal from Gaza in 2005, Israeli silsulim cassettes were put up on the shelves again and heard in Gaza's taxis again. Baraka ended his 2005 "comeback" article, published a few months after the disengagement, with an optimistic quote from a Gazan music store owner: "I've already made some phone calls to bring new albums from Israel." This euphoria didn't last long, and soon new rounds of violence erupted. Thanks to the internet, Palestinians who wish to hear their favorite muzika mizraḥit artists can do so, but the music albums and live performances of Israeli singers in Gaza and the West Bank will have to wait for better days.

NOTES

1 Sagis and Gispan participated in a panel in the conference addressing the role of the public radio service in fostering and promoting popular music in Israel. The conference was organized by ACUM (Society of Authors, Composers and Music Publishers

in Israel) and the Israel Broadcasting Authority (IBA) and took place in Bet Hayotser hall in Tel Aviv, on December 26, 2012.

2   This is a debatable term that generally refers to nostalgic patriotic songs, considered by aficionados like Sagis to be "the true Israeli music," even though many of them were created by composers and lyricists who immigrated from Eastern Europe and were strongly influenced by their Eastern European musical heritage.

3   The literal translation of *Mizraḥi* (male)/*Mizraḥit* (female) in Hebrew is "Eastern." *Muzika mizraḥit* is generally translated as "Oriental music," and it is even used in a hebraized version as *Orientali* (male) and *Orientalit* (female). In Israel the term *Oriental* is generally used to refer to the Near East, that is, the Middle Eastern and Arab cultures. Other Asian music, such as music of the Far East, is not broadly called Oriental in Israel. In this chapter I will mostly use the Hebrew term *Mizraḥi* rather than *Oriental* to avoid confusion with the US/European use of *Oriental* as an outdated and somewhat-pejorative synonym for *Asian*, or as a reference to various Western projections onto the East.

4   In the terms *Mizraḥit* and *Yam-Tichonit*, the *ḥ* and *ch* are pronounced by most Israelis as /χ/ phonetically, but Mizraḥi Jews pronounce, more correctly, the *ḥ* in *Mizraḥi* as a guttural /ħ/, and the *ch* in Tichonit as a /χ/.

5   Finegold, *Musika Mizrahit*, 6.

6   Levy, "Towards a Politics of Identity."

7   Seroussi, "Yam Tikhoniyut." This can perhaps be compared to other pejorative terms reappropriated by marginalized social groups as an act of protest, such as *nigger* or *queer*.

8   Horowitz, *Mediterranean Israeli Music*, 161. Singer Haim Moshe claims that his music, labeled Oriental, is in fact "the new, authentic, Israeli expression." Quoted in Horowitz, *Mediterranean Israeli Music*, 161. Israeli authenticity in general, and Israeli musical authenticity in particular, is a disputed concept, owing to the country being so young and multicultural, so it is easy to support or dispute such a paradoxical claim (can "new" be authentic?). As Horowitz notes, "this renewal subverts the previous 'new Israeli authenticity' formulated by Eastern and Central European immigrants, whose own search for national identity and authenticity privileged European styles and embellished these with Middle Eastern, and particularly Yemenite, elements" (161).

9   "White-against-black": Mizraḥi Israelis tend to have a darker skin than Ashkenazi/European Israelis. A strong skin-color prejudice prevailed in the 1950s and 1960s in Israel, following the waves of immigration of the "dark-skinned" Mizraḥim. I clearly remember during my childhood and youth the derogatory Yiddish term *schwartzes* (blacks), or even *schwartze hayes* (black beasts), being used by European Jews in reference to Mizraḥi Jews.

10 Personal communication, 2015. All personal communication quotes are taken from interviews/conversations with performers and audience members in Israel in preparation for radio programs and my current research project concerning muzika mizraḥit. Most of them have asked to remain anonymous.

11 Ahuva Carmeli, personal communication, 2013.

12 The use of the term *ornamentation* can be misleading as it indicates a Western perspective, according to which a note is supposed to be straight on a stable pitch, and any deliberate variants on the pitch are seen as ornamentation rather than as an in-

tegral part of the way it should be performed according to the *maqam* sensibility of Arabic music.

13 Horowitz, *Mediterranean Israeli Music*, 86. In Arabic music the mawwal usually follows an improvised solo vocal free-time introduction called *layali* (Touma, *Music of the Arabs*, 97), but in Israeli *silsulim* terminology, the umbrella term *mawwal* is also used to describe an improvised nonrhythmic vocal part reminiscent of the layali.
14 El'ad, personal communication, 2015.
15 Colles, "Extemporization."
16 Touma, *Music of the Arabs*, 97.
17 Touma, *Music of the Arabs*, 96, 97.
18 Nooshin, "Improvisation as 'Other,'" 242, 244, 254.
19 Colles, "Extemporization."
20 Touma, *Music of the Arabs*, 158, 155. This audience reaction to an elaborate improvisation is a global phenomenon, and the reaction to the Koran reading described by Touma can be compared to that of a jazz or rock audience after an impressive solo.
21 Horowitz, *Mediterranean Israeli Music*, 98–99.
22 Kligman, *Maqam and Liturgy*.
23 See references to this phenomenon on various websites, such as Sephardic Hazzanut Project, http://www.sephardichazzanut.com/; and Atar Hapiyyut Ve'hatfila, the website of the Piyyut and the Prayer, http://www.piyut.org.il/.
24 Behar, "Umm Kulthum."
25 Umm Kulthum was admired all over the Arab world, including, of course, by Jews from the Arab world and their descendants in Israel, despite her switch to patriotic Egyptian and therefore anti-Israeli songs during the Six-Day War and the Egyptian-Israeli conflict.
26 Horowitz, *Mediterranean Israeli Music*, 147.
27 R. Cohen, personal communication, 2015.
28 David Regev Za'arur, personal communication, July 18, 2014, during a radio session.
29 Argov was born to a poor family of Yemenite origin, became addicted to drugs, went in and out of rehabilitation and prison, and in 1987 committed suicide in prison. Ben was born to a Moroccan Jewish family who lived in a poor neighborhood in the southern desert city of Beer Sheva.
30 Quoted in Horowitz, *Mediterranean Israeli Music*, 100.
31 Horowitz, *Mediterranean Israeli Music*, 86.
32 Horowitz, *Mediterranean Israeli Music*, 100.
33 Eilam-Amzallag, "Musikat Ha'kasetot," 34–35, quoted in Horowitz, *Mediterranean Israeli Music*, 98.
34 Horowitz notes that in the first years of muzika mizraḥit the aesthetic and emotional power of silsulim vocal production was particularly prominent in light of the "thinness" and impoverishment of the early arrangements. Horowitz, *Mediterranean Israeli Music*, 97.
35 Horowitz, *Mediterranean Israeli Music*, 135–38.
36 Morad, "Music of the Underdog."
37 Regev and Seroussi, *Popular Music*, 233, 191.
38 Ahuva Carmeli, personal communication, 2013.

39 In the 1980s the only Israeli TV channel (public service) presented a weekly music chart program titled *Lahit Ba'rosh* (A hit at the top) with live performances by top Israeli pop artists (I was the presenter of this program in its first years, between 1984 and 1990). When episodes of this cult program were rebroadcast a few years ago on a commercial TV channel supporting muzika mizraḥit, a rather cynical subtitle was added at the end of one of the repeated episodes, reading, "Zohar Argov was never invited to perform in Lahit Ba'rosh," indicating that Israeli TV in the 1980s was biased against the popular muzika mizraḥit artists.
40 Horowitz, *Mediterranean Israeli Music*, 157–59.
41 Personal communication, 2015 (with a veteran record company executive who wishes to remain anonymous).
42 Morris, personal communication, 2015.
43 Regev and Seroussi, *Popular Music*, 234. Note that these authors use a different system of transliterating the Hebrew terms.
44 Weissbrod, *Israeli Identity*, 197.
45 Lavie, *Wrapped in the Flag*, 57.
46 Regev and Seroussi, *Popular Music*, 233.
47 Walla Culture Editorial Board, "Bekoshi 16%."
48 Nevo, "Kesher."
49 Nevo, "Kesher."
50 Stern, "Miri Regev."
51 Levy, "Towards a Politics of Identity." See also, for example, well-known Israeli musicians Shlomo Bar, Amir Benayun, Dikla, Shai Tsabari, and recently Liron Amram.
52 Personal communication, 2015.
53 Ten were high school students, six university students, and eight soldiers on leave.
54 In the most recent *The Voice* competition (Series no. 5, Summer 2019), two artists strongly identified as mesalselim—Nasreen Qadri, an Arab-Israeli female star, and veteran singer Shlomi Shabbat, both known for their elaborate and expressive silsulim—were chosen as the mentors representing the "silsulim section" of the competition.
55 Other expressions of subtler criticism I heard on silsulim were from musicologists who see the genre as inferior to Western music, yet "emotional," "exotically interesting," and "inspiring." This Orientalist approach may be similar to the approach of old-school European musicologists to Romani music.
56 In an article published in August 2019, music journalist Ben Shalev writes about a new trend/tendency among some Israeli mainstream pop vocalists (which are not identified as mesalselim) to use "super softened" Yam Tichonit–style silsulim in their singing. He mentions, in particular, Idan Raichel, who, he claims, started this trend. Shalev calls this a "pasteurized silsul" and "an interesting and regretful mutation," and argues that it mainly reflects Raichel's sharp commercial instincts and deep understanding of the current musical preferences of "the local ear." Shalev, "Mihu Ha'Muzika'i." I agree with Shalev pinpointing this recent trend; however, the "Raichel silsul," as he calls it, is a pure stylistic element used only at certain instants in the singing and far from the deep elaborate silsulim which form an essential characteristic of the vocal performance in muzika mizraḥit and yam-tichonit. I disagree with his prediction that "the

Raichel silsul will push out of the way the meditteranean silsul and will become the official Israeli silsul."

57 Horowitz, *Mediterranean Israeli Music*, 163.
58 Ben, "Zehava Ben."
59 Gibor, "Hivtachtem Yona." Sarit Hadad, the most popular Mediterranean music star in Israel in recent years (mentioned earlier as the silsulim-oriented mentor in the TV program *The Voice*), went to perform in Jordan in 1997 disguised as a Palestinian singer.
60 Gibor, "Hivtachtem Yona." This may be the case in popular music; however, there is a rich Palestinian tradition of maqam folk and art music.
61 Baraka, "Hebrew Songs."
62 Baraka, "Hebrew Songs."

BIBLIOGRAPHY

Baraka, Yasser. "Hebrew Songs Making a Comeback in Gaza." *Common Ground News Service*, September 12, 2005. http://www.commongroundnews.org/article.php?id =974&lan=en&sid=0&sp=0&isNew=0.

Behar, Almog. "Umm Kulthum Be'veit Ha'knesset" [Umm Kulthum in the synagogue]. *Almog Behar* (blog), September 29, 2009. https://almogbehar.wordpress.com/2009 /09/29/.

Ben, Zehava. "Zehava Ben Rotza Lashir Be'Aza Uve'Beirut" [Zehava Ben wants to sing in Gaza and in Beirut], by Nir Yahav. *Walla News*, March 30, 2008.

Colles, H. C. "Extemporization." In *Grove's Dictionary of Music and Musicians*, 3rd ed., edited by H. C. Colles, vol. 2, 184–86. London: Macmillan, 1935.

Eilam-Amzallag, Avraham. "Musikat Ha'kasetot—Lo Musika Mizraḥit" [Cassette music—not Oriental music]. *Musika* 9 (1987): 28–35.

Finegold, Eliezer Moshe. *Musika Mizrahit—from the Margins to the Mainstream*. Cambridge, MA: Harvard Judaica Collection, Harvard College, 1996.

Gibor, Asaf. "Hivtachtem Yona, Kibalnu Omer Adam" [You promised a dove, we received Omer Adam]. *NRG*, September 22, 2013. http://www.nrg.co.il/online/47 /ART2/507/871.html.

Horowitz, Amy. *Mediterranean Israeli Music and the Politics of the Aesthetic*. Detroit, MI: Wayne State University Press, 2010.

Kligman, Mark L. *Maqam and Liturgy: Ritual, Music, and Aesthetics of Syrian Jews in Brooklyn*. Detroit, MI: Wayne State University Press, 2009.

Lavie, Smadar. *Wrapped in the Flag of Israel: Mizraḥi Single Mothers and Bureaucratic Torture*. Oxford: Berghahn Books, 2014.

Levy, André. "Likrat Politica Shel Zehuyot" [Towards a politics of identity]. *Panim: Quarterly for Society, Culture, and Education* 10 (1999). https://www.itu.org.il/ ?CategoryID=570&ArticleID=1786.

Morad, Moshe. "Music of the Underdog: Sociological and Musical Similarities between Muzika Mizraḥit and Salsa." In *Returning to Babel: Jewish Latin American*

Experiences, Representations, and Identity, edited by Amalia Ran and Jean Axelard Cahanm, 121–42. Leiden: Brill, 2011.

Nevo, Asaf. "Kesher Hashtika Shel Hamuzika Hamizraḥit BeGalgalatz" [The conspiracy of silence of muzika mizraḥit in Galgalatz]. *Mako*, July 22, 2012. http://www.mako.co.il/music-news/local-taverna/Article-05a1045e67ea831006.htm.

Nooshin, Laudan. "Improvisation as 'Other': Creativity, Knowledge and Power—the Case of Iranian Classical Music." *Journal of the Royal Musical Association* 128 (2003): 242–96.

Regev, Motti, and Edwin Seroussi. *Popular Music and National Culture in Israel*. Berkeley: University of California Press, 2004.

Seroussi, Edwin. "Yam Tikhoniyut: Transformations in Mediterraneanism in Israeli Music." In *Mediterranean Mosaic: Popular Music and Global Sounds*, edited by Goffredo Plastino, 179–98. New York: Routledge, 2003.

Shalev, Ben. "Mihu Ha'Muzika'i She'ma'alim Et Ha'Muzika Ha'Mizraḥit Ha'Shorshit?" [Who is the musician who eliminates rootsy muzika mizraḥit?] *Haaretz*, August 14, 2019. https://www.haaretz.co.il/gallery/music/selective-hearing/.premium-1.7683296.

Stern, Itay. "Miri Regev Trying to Change Army Radio's Tune." *Haaretz*, November 3, 2015. http://www.haaretz.com/israel-news/.premium-1.683887.

Touma, Habib Hassan. *The Music of the Arabs*. Portland, OR: Amadeus, 1996.

Walla Culture Editorial Board. "Bekoshi 16% Me'hashirim Baradio Ha'artzi—Mizraḥit" [Hardly 16 percent from the songs on national radio—Mizraḥit]. *Walla News*, September 3, 2013. http://e.walla.co.il/?w=/272/2675319.

Weissbrod, Lilly. *Israeli Identity: In Search of a Successor to the Pioneer, Tsabar and Settler*. 2002. Abingdon, UK: Routledge, 2013.

ELEVEN Three Moments in *Kī Hōʻalu* (Hawaiian Slack Key Guitar)

Improvising as a Kanaka Maoli *(Native Hawaiian) Adaptive Strategy*

KEVIN FELLEZS

Kī hōʻalu, or Hawaiian slack key guitar, is a fingerpicking acoustic guitar folk music tradition that emerged from the *paniolo* culture of Hawaiʻi in the mid-nineteenth century. *Paniolo* is a Hawaiian-language term denoting "Hawaiian cowboy"; derived from the Spanish word *español*, the term indicates the significant role Mexican vaqueros played in the formation of a recognizably Kanaka Maoli (native or indigenous Hawaiian) guitar tradition.[1] In this essay, I think through a series of questions regarding the role of improvisation in slack key by Kanaka Maoli musicians in performative as well as musical terms. In speaking of Native Hawaiian performativity, I recall Laura R. Graham and H. Glenn Penny's observation that "performances of indigeneity ... are contextually situated embodied speech and action ... anchored in past performances, local traditions, and ideologies. At the same time, they are always creative and forward looking, infused with expected outcomes."[2] While sympathetic to their definition, I want to extend their conceptual framing by thinking about performances of indigeneity that have either resulted from or resulted in *unexpected* outcomes. The three moments in Hawaiian slack key guitar history I detail in this essay will help think through Kanaka Maoli responses to the unexpected and the key role of the improvisatory in those responses, which are rooted in Kanaka Maoli indigeneity.

Conventional musical analysis asks, How does improvisation shape the music? Performative improvisation, as I am calling it here, is more concerned with questions such as, How can we think of the jumble of histories that came together to produce slack key as improvisatory? How might the various strategies adopted by slack key guitarists at various moments in the tradition's history be heard as improvisations, as unrehearsed yet thoughtful responses by Kanaka Maoli guitarists to non-Hawaiian, colonial interests, which were often in conflict with Native Hawaiian concerns, such as those mobilized by Christian missionaries, US imperialism, and the global music industry? How might we think of Hawaiian guitarists as masters of improvisation when acting as agents of change in the face of these powerful interests that have tried to corral and constrain Hawaiians while also profiting from their creative labor?

In this regard, indigenous Hawaiian guitarists have acted as agents of preservation as well as transformation in both social and musical senses, as I describe below. The decidedly mixed success of Native Hawaiian guitarists in raising slack key's visibility both inside and outside of Hawai'i has proven double-edged. The recognition of its value as an indigenous Hawaiian tradition, and of Hawaiian guitarists as guardians of an invaluable musical tradition, initially took place in the 1970s, a time when Hawaiian culture was felt to be at a nadir, which sparked an outburst of activities dubbed the Second Hawaiian Renaissance.[3] At that time, slack key was seen as one of Native Hawaiians' cherished musical traditions that exemplified in its *nahenahe* (sweet, gentle) aesthetic the core Hawaiian values of *aloha* (love, welcome) and generosity.

Yet criticisms of the deleterious effects of slack key's formation as a commercial genre and circulation within the marketplace, particularly since the 1990s, link it to a long history of commodification of Hawaiian culture (or what is taken to be Hawaiian culture), especially its music.[4] With its dominance as a visible Hawaiian musical export—slack key is far less popular at home in Hawai'i than other Hawaiian musical idioms—critics have more recently questioned the place and value of Hawaiian slack key guitar within Kanaka Maoli culture. These moments, I argue, highlight issues of the improvisatory within Hawaiian slack key as an adaptive strategy in which unforeseen circumstances force unrehearsed, immediate responses. Musicians' responses are, as detailed below, grounded in a musical aesthetic in which a commitment to spontaneity and a willingness to take calculated risks, shaped by a traditional pedagogical practice based on active listening sans explicit instruction, become articulated as both musical and social practice. As Daniel Fischlin, Ajay Heble, and George Lipsitz argue, "Improvised musicking is a critical form of agency, of embodied potential that is inseparable from other social practices that call upon us to be purposeful agents of our cocreated, lived reality."[5] Likewise, the three moments highlighted in this essay will illuminate the ways in which the meanings of musical improvisation extend outward from Native Hawaiian musicians' musicking as a performative and social practice with resonances beyond the musical.

The first moment is concerned with the early history and origin narrative of kī hōʻalu, which will afford us the chance to think about improvisation as indigenization, by which I mean the creative (re)use of materials by indigenous populations that resists prior determination of uses or the "intentionality" of materials. This redefines appropriation, for instance, by suggesting that Hawaiians appropriated the Spanish guitar in order to sing songs proscribed by Christian missionaries, who decried Hawaiian song as pagan, licentious, or trivial. This history speaks to the ways in which musical improvisation articulates broader social processes.

The second moment occurs during the Hawaiian Renaissance of the 1970s with the revival of slack key, along with a number of cultural practices, including use of the Hawaiian language, revealing improvisation as a process of renewal, meaning the active and acknowledged "(re)inventing" of tradition by indigenous tradition bearers confronting more than a century of efforts to eradicate Kanaka Maoli and their culture. This revitalization of Hawaiian culture and identity came on the heels of the post–World War II era in which Hawaiʻi became one of the most militarized areas in the world—a feat obscured by the higher visibility of the islands' number-one industry, tourism, which is predicated on notions of the Hawaiian Islands as a "tropical paradise." As a primary industry in the Hawaiian Islands, the US military presence complicates Kanaka Maoli self-determination efforts, particularly those seeking an autonomous solution external to US jurisprudence.[6] Importantly, the musicians of the Hawaiian Renaissance of the late 1960s and 1970s helped shape the continuing struggle for Kanaka Maoli self-determination in the public sphere, including the world beyond Hawaiʻi.

The third moment involves the Grammy Awards, in which slack key's domination of the Best Hawaiian Music Album category raised questions in the Hawaiian music community about whether or not slack key was truly representative of Kanaka Maoli culture. Improvisation, in this instance, can be thought of as the often ill-fitting accommodations Kanaka Maoli have been forced to negotiate under unequal power relationships with, first, colonial and, subsequently, US military and transnational corporate power. In this light, improvisation as accommodation may appear overdetermined by its relationship with corporatist logics. While accommodation may appear too much like unprincipled compromise, it is important to remember that these guitarists have labored at the shallow end of the music industry, reaping little material benefit. Theirs is not the tale of unearned plenitude but, rather, another instance of Kanaka Maoli culture bearers being caught in the gap between indigenous priorities and capitalist prerogatives. What, for instance, might we make of the fact that almost all of the guitarists mentioned in this chapter have relied on nonmusical day jobs?

I would like to suggest other possibilities that accommodation provides—*to accommodate* is to provide comfort, or, as the *Merriam-Webster Dictionary* defines the term, "to provide with something desired, needed, or suited," and "to make fit, suitable"—definitions that seem less concerned with avoiding compromise and more concerned with working with others toward "desired, needed, or suited" goals.[7] As my initial hesitancy to use *accommodation* indicates, this moment may also serve as a cautionary tale of unintended consequences, which is always a risk in improvisation.

Each moment involves improvising—not in the sense of performing a completely spontaneous composition or unleashing unrestricted, uninhibited expression but in the sense of adjusting to a momentary finger flub that proves fortuitous (the first moment, with its series of historical happenstance), extemporizing on a melodic line (the second moment, with its active resuscitation of older musical aesthetics), or allowing for another musician's phrasing to dictate the flow or rhythmic emphasis in a given performance (the third moment, in which Hawaiian slack key guitarists become involved with powerful music industry interests).

These three moments also serve notice against the idea that the "moments of improvisation" I detail here are merely case studies exploring a widely distributed sense of just what, exactly, improvisation entails in terms of performance, aesthetics, and politics. In contrast to the urge to draw universalist ideals from particularized improvisatory practices, I mean to draw out the implications of rooting slack key's improvisatory moments within Native Hawaiian acoustemologies, to borrow Steven Feld's generative portmanteau, in which "local conditions of acoustic sensation, knowledge, and imagination embodied in the culturally particular sense of place" are enacted, articulated, and performed by slack key guitarists.[8]

By drawing on the notion of acoustemology, I understand Kanaka Maoli improvisation as emerging out of a culturally specific set of practices originating from a particular place, namely, Hawai'i, and articulating a particularly Hawaiian perspective. My argument is that the sense of Hawaiian-ness attributed to Hawaiian slack key guitar musicking rests on an improvisatory sensibility promoted by traditional Hawaiian pedagogical practice (detailed below) in which guitarists' articulations spring from an acoustemology shaped by living in a land of waterfalls, waves, and volcanoes. Slack key musicking is steeped in a landscape in which patterns and cyclic structures include built-in unpredictability capable of dramatically shifting geographies and recalibrating humans' place within them.

Additionally, the nahenahe (sweet, gentle) aesthetic not only enables guitarists to sound out specific wind patterns or evoke significant sites such as the Hiʻilawe waterfalls in the Waipiʻo Valley on the island of Hawaiʻi but also helps them articulate an underlying mischievous impulse that is part of Native Hawaiian sensibilities, preventing nahenahe from becoming saccharine or anodyne. Slack key's deceptively "soft" orientation is more properly thought of as elastic and flexible, allowing Hawaiian guitarists to absorb or deflect foreign elements, gauging nonindigenous elements as either innovative or invasive. In this light, we can hear that performances of slack key are not completely planned, but they are not without an internal logic, either, while slack key's deceptively simple forms make infinite variations available. Again, improvisation in this sense is not restricted to the musical but can be thought of as a set of social practices.

As Daniel Fischlin and Eric Porter point out in the introduction to this collection, improvised vernacular musics fill a contradictory space. On one hand, musical improvisation can be seen as the acts of agentive subalterns in negotiating, even challenging, hegemonic standards of musical evaluation and aesthetics. By extension, I posit that Hawaiian guitarists and their musicking have enacted improvisational logics that transcend the musical as a result of being raised in a social world in which improvisational approaches reflect, express, and partially constitute a social order in which creativity can be mobilized in the moment to deal with, for example, geological as well as political changes.

On the other hand, improvisational skill does not *necessarily* mitigate the downsides of participation with, in the case of Hawaiʻi, the settler-colonialists' desire to incorporate subaltern communities into their social order, which is also nimbly improvisational as, to continue with this example, it is through the commodification of indigenous cultural productions within capitalist structures of exploitation that settler-colonialist interests accrue surplus value from the labor of subaltern culture bearers. Improvisation as both a methodology and a technology manages to cut both ways.

Throughout this chapter, I aim to demonstrate that improvising Hawaiian musicians articulate social relations as much as they display instrumental prowess. Recognizing that instrumental can mean both a *musical instrument* and the *instrumentalizing* of social relations gives additional support to the ways in which Hawaiian guitarists have enacted an improvisational approach that is both musical in a strict aesthetic sense and social in a broader context. The linkages from the musical to the social, from the musical performance to the politically performative, can be heard in the intentional aesthetic pursuit of Hawaiian musical values as well as in their (mis)interpretation by non-Hawaiian listeners, even those sympathetic to Hawaiian concerns and sensibilities.

The nahenahe aesthetic orientation, for instance, is often limited by non-Hawaiian misinterpretation. The "sweet, gentle" sounds of slack key guitar can be misheard as mollifying, even acquiescing to, Kanaka Maoli exploitation rather than as resisting or protesting, as calculated by indigenous Hawaiian musicians and audiences. It is within this gap between non-Hawaiian interpretation and Native Hawaiian intention that the limits of slack key improvisation may be heard (and these were played out publicly in the third moment).

The politics of Kanaka Maoli improvisation are complicated further by its basis in Native Hawaiian pedagogical practices, which rest on a pragmatic yet nonexplicit and intuitive approach. Slack key's traditional method of transmission is best described as an aural tradition in which improvisational possibilities—and, just as important, their limits, such as the borders between kī hōʻalu and other Hawaiian musical expressions—are conveyed solely through musical sound. Native Hawaiian master guitarists such as Charles Philip "Gabby" Pahinui and Raymond Kane followed an older *paʻa ka waha* ("shut your mouth") school of aural transmission. The four pillars of traditional Hawaiian pedagogy stress performativity and require unquestioning silence of students: *nānā ka maka*, see with your eyes; *hoʻolohe ka pepeiao*, hear with your ears; *paʻa ka waha*, shut your mouth; *hana ka lima*, use your hands. When Pahinui was asked what a beginning guitarist desirous of learning Hawaiian slack key guitar should first go about accomplishing, he responded, "I would think, first, Hawaiʻi style is, you listen but don't ask question. Never ask question."[9]

Finally, I do not mean that improvisation, or improvising, should be used casually, or merely as a metaphor. As an *adaptive*—rather than solely disruptive—strategy, kī hōʻalu improvisation indicates the open-ended and often-unspoken or implicit nature of Kanaka Maoli resistance, as its teaching methods suggest. Even the most talented student with the most astute ears will introduce variations—"mistakes" in other traditions—that are not exactly innovations, at least at the student level, but continually transform kī hōʻalu as part of its very definition. The three moments in kī hōʻalu history I detail in this chapter reveal the ways in which improvising has always been, and continues to be, a vital yet complicated Kanaka Maoli strategy of survival, resistance, and renewal.

The Song of the Paniolo

Much of early slack key history remains obscured because of a historical lack of interest in a rural Hawai'i that had been transformed by imported ranching and plantation culture. Early non-Hawaiian observers painted the erasure of indigenous Hawaiians and their culture in poignantly nostalgic colors that obscured their investment in the very ranch and plantation cultures displacing Native Hawaiians and erasing their culture and way of life. These early writers figured Hawaiian land as virginal and underdeveloped, on which they were bringing a much-needed civilizing project to bear. It served their interests to construct Kanaka Maoli traditions not only as disappearing but also as untouched by outside influences, thus rendering a rural, hybrid, and vibrantly contemporaneous Kanaka Maoli musical practice such as kī hō'alu invisible.

Slack key guitar history, then, can be heard as a series of performative improvisations shaped by Kanaka Maoli attempts to sustain their ways of life in the face of imperialism, resource extraction for settler-colonial interests, and external religious and political ideologies that, if not rendering them completely invisible in their own land, attempted to trap them in amber depictions of a disappearing culture, unfit for modernity. Kanaka Maoli and their culture survived by relying on indigenous ways of improvising provided by an indigenous culture produced by working *with*, rather than against, the natural world around them, a world of potentially cataclysmic volcanoes, seasonal surf patterns, and always-shifting winds overseen by fickle gods and goddesses—a habitual practice of creating meaningful lives out of circumstances for which previous experience neither fully accounted nor wholly prepared them, though tracked meticulously for millennia. This long-standing practice of improvising within forms as foundational to Native Hawaiian epistemology and cultural formation was transferred to the adoption of the guitar by Hawaiian musicians and shapes my idea of indigenization as improvisatory practice.

As mentioned, the slack key aesthetic aspires to nahenahe, soft and sweet, expression and therefore avoids abrasion except for the gently mocking. Indeed, slack key guitarists enjoy the slightly naughty or mischievous, which keeps slack key from becoming overly precious or cloying despite its emphasis on nahenahe. For example, a number of songs on a landmark recording, *Pure Gabby*, by renowned Kanaka Maoli musician Gabby Pahinui, are openly sexual in nature. A verse from "Nanea Ko Maka I Ka Le'ale'a" is translated in the liner notes as "I get inside your mu'umu'u [dress] / To the shiny window / Here I am, long-nosed / The opening gets the large member," leaving little to the imagination or esoteric *kaona* (hidden) readings.[10]

There are various theories concerning the origin of the guitar in Hawai'i, though an advertisement in 1782 for a musical performance featuring a number performed on a guitar indicates that the instrument was already familiar to Hawaiians a mere four years after their first encounter with Europeans.[11] By 1840 there are advertisements for the sale of the instrument in Honolulu newspapers. Still, the debate about the initial person or persons who introduced the six-stringed instrument to the islands remains unsettled.

A significant event in early kī hō'alu history was the arrival of Mexican vaqueros and the introduction of their cowboy and ranch culture to Hawai'i in the early 1830s. On February 22, 1793, cattle were first introduced to Hawai'i as a gift from British admiral George Vancouver to King Kamehameha I. Initially, Kanaka Maoli were both excited by and apprehensive of these *pua'a pipi* (beef pigs). Because Vancouver had experienced numerous losses to his original gift, which was reduced by the hardships of sea travel to a mere four cows, two ewes, and a ram, Vancouver requested that a *kapu* (taboo) be placed on the killing of the cattle and advised Kamehameha I to build an enclosure for them. Built from shaped rock, the Pa Nui (Big Pen) is still in evidence today in the area around Honalo, Hawai'i. The cattle, however, were not contained. As little as eleven years later, the cattle had multiplied into large herds of feral animals that were dangerous to the native flora and fauna, occasionally killing humans.[12]

In 1830 King Kamehameha III sent an official of his court to Mexico. While visiting there, the court official observed a rodeo and was impressed by the cattle-handling skills displayed by the Mexican vaqueros. Convinced the vaqueros were the answer to Hawai'i's cattle problem, the official arranged for their hire on the island of Hawai'i, settling them primarily in the area around Waimea. The Parker Ranch, now one of the oldest and largest cattle ranches in the United States, was established there in 1847 as part of an already established ranching culture initiated "four decades before The Alamo [1836], a generous eighty years before the great cattle drives along the Chisolm [*sic*] and other trails [post–US Civil War, 1865], and fully 140-plus years before the Taylor Grazing Act [1934]."[13] By 1859 the *Honolulu Pacific Commercial Advertiser* announced that "the imported cowboys [Mexican vaqueros] have disappeared and in their place has sprung up a class of Hawaiian mountaineers, equally skilled as horsemen as their foreign predecessors."[14]

Along with their knowledge of horse riding and cattle handling, the vaqueros brought their music and their guitars. In the evenings, after working out in the pastures, paniolo listened to the vaqueros playing their music around the campfires. A common performance practice called for two Mexican guitarists performing together with one guitarist playing the lead melody and the other providing a bass line and harmonic accompaniment. When the vaqueros returned to Mexico, some of them left their guitars with their paniolo companions, who began integrating the instrument into their native songs and rhythms. There is a strong possibility of musical exchanges between vaqueros and paniolo occurring throughout the period, as some Mexicans remained in Hawai'i, a number of whom may have been guitarists.

The lack of widespread knowledge about kī hōʻalu at one time fueled speculation that Hawaiian guitarists' use of nonstandard tunings in kī hōʻalu was the happy result of mistakes in tuning the instrument, but the dominance of major tonalities in the most common open tunings used by kī hōʻalu musicians is reflective of Hawaiian musical sensibilities, indicating a systematic adaptive approach to integrating the guitar into Hawaiian musical culture. Moreover, Hawaiian musicians' seemingly offhand informality, even casualness, is the result of a particular musical aesthetic and cultural orientation in which apparent effortlessness, even carelessness, is valued and not simply the result of a natural correspondence between the "pleasantness of the Hawaiian Islands" and the "benevolence of her people." That is, kī hōʻalu is a learned craft reflective of a particular cultural aesthetic, not an ethnic essence expressing itself as an easygoing pleasantness.[15] Thus, Spanish instrumentation, Mexican performance practices, and Hawaiian musical forms and aesthetics—a history of performative improvisations—would merge in the creation of kī hōʻalu.[16]

Owing to Protestant missionaries' proscriptions of Kanaka Maoli religious and cultural practices such as *hula* (dance) and *mele* (chant) as pagan, uncivilized, and morally degenerate, along with their enactment of measures to eradicate Kanaka Maoli culture, by the end of the nineteenth century slack key guitarists no longer performed the music publicly as such, guardedly passing its secrets down exclusively among *ʻohana* (family).

Indeed, it wasn't until 1946, when Pahinui recorded "Hiʻilawe," that a commercial kī hōʻalu recording was widely available. Until that time, while Hawaiian steel guitar and *ʻukulele* musicians had circulated Hawaiian music around the world, kī hōʻalu had remained largely in Hawai'i, performed at family *lūʻau* (feast) and other private functions, and had not entered the music industry as a commercial genre. Still, kī hōʻalu recordings, including those by Pahinui, appeared as B-sides on 78 and 45 rpm singles, meaning these recordings were not promoted by their record labels nor were they played on Hawaiian radio.[17] Tellingly, a recording produced in 1961 that is now considered a definitive recording for modern slack key guitar, *Pure Gabby* (Hula Records, 1978), was withheld from release for seventeen years owing to record companies' assumption that the buying public was disinterested in exclusively slack key guitar recordings.

Sharing and Selling

The development of kī hōʻalu as a commercial genre and Hawaiians' strategic involvement with the music industry to share their musical traditions demonstrates the ways in which Native Hawaiian improvisation is articulated through a sharing rather than a hoarding sensibility, a mark of a Kanaka Maoli ethos of generosity, which was distorted by various nonindigenous interests such as the tourism industry to portray Native Hawaiian culture as readily accessible. Yet, in the second moment, which we now consider, Kanaka Maoli began reaching outward in order to not simply resuscitate but invigorate their cultural heritage, highlighting Native Hawaiian improvisational practices as an inclusive, as opposed to insular, set of performativities. Though striking a devil's bargain by participating in the global music market, Hawaiian musicians calculated their exploitation against a growing sense of slack key's obsolescence, especially in Hawaiʻi.

By the 1960s, kī hōʻalu's role as accompaniment to hula or other forms of Hawaiian music had become primarily a thing of the past. Importantly, Hawaiian music scholar Elizabeth Tatar insists that "of the Hawaiian music types considered traditional—chants, hymn-like songs and *hula* songs—[each] evolved in the 20th century to their present status as traditional musical styles because of tourism's cumulative influences. Each was shaped by the Hawaiian musical community in response to the changing tastes of the US mainland tourist. Indeed, tourism has been a major influence on the development of Hawaiian music in the 20th century, and its effects on musical performance continue unabated."[18]

Kī hōʻalu continued to survive below the radar of the tourist industry for the most part, hidden away within various ʻohana as guitarists jealously guarded their music from outsiders, including Kanaka Maoli outside of their particular ʻohana. Scholars such as Noenoe K. Silva and Jonathan Kay Kamakawiwoʻole Osorio have documented how a long history of efforts by European and American elites to efface the vitality of Hawaiian culture for political and capital gain simultaneously elided the political and cultural opposition of Native Hawaiians.[19] The result was a narrative of Hawaiian cultural loss that obscured the ways in which Hawaiian cultural traditions managed to survive.

Kī hōʻalu "disappeared" as Hawaiian cultural producers moved their art and folkways underground to avoid continual harassment by colonial authorities and the zealous proscriptions of missionaries.[20] But living connections to traditional Hawaiian culture were disappearing in the 1970s and, along with them, the knowledge of the old ways, the traditions, and the songs. As much as these practices safeguarded kī hōʻalu, the insularity of these musicians began to choke off the musical tradition they were invested in preserving. So, the circumstances that had spawned a particular set of performative improvisations to preserve slack key had shifted, requiring Native Hawaiian musicians to improvise anew.

As noted Native Hawaiian musician Keola Beamer asserted, "I'm old enough to remember when we all thought slack key would die. There were many reasons for that. One of them was that our *kupuna* [elders] had lost so much: their land, their religious system, their sense of place in the universe. The last thing they wanted to lose was their music, so tunings became very cultish and protected. The irony was that by way of holding the secrets too close, this art form was actually dying, suffocating because the information wasn't being communicated."[21] Drawing on non-Hawaiian music, Beamer's inventive variations on traditional and original themes mirror the broader improvisational ethos of shared reciprocity in Kanaka Maoli culture. His slack key recordings are virtuosic examples of fingerpicking acoustic guitar musicking that argue convincingly for the tradition's continuing vitality and flexibility and provide a rationale for serious aesthetic engagement. He is not the only slack key artist to engage this ethos. We can hear this same willingness to incorporate non-Hawaiian musical aesthetics in the work of earlier guitarists such as Gabby Pahinui, drawing on jazz, and Raymond Kane, anchoring his music with overt Spanish influences. As part of the 1970s Hawaiian Renaissance, Beamer was explicit about this broader approach to slack key. Yet for all his transcultural borrowings, Beamer performs, as Pahinui and Kane were widely acknowledged to have performed, unquestionably identifiable "Native Hawaiian music"—another sign of Native Hawaiians' performative sense of cultural reciprocity and the depth of Hawaiians' acoustemological sounding out of their sense of emplaced belonging.

Improvising creative new ways to reach out beyond the ʻohana, Beamer published the first slack key guitar method book in 1973, fomenting no small controversy. He survived the criticisms largely because he hails from a family whose musical roots can be traced for hundreds of years as elite Hawaiian musicians and defended his publishing of Native Hawaiian cultural "secrets" in terms of Kanaka Maoli traditions of generosity.

Throughout the 1970s, other young Hawaiian musicians also began researching and revitalizing Hawaiian music culture at a time when many thought that much of traditional Hawaiian music had disappeared, along with the catastrophic decimation of the Hawaiian people, or had been so thoroughly corrupted by consumerist interests that it appeared forever severed from traditional Hawaiian aesthetics and concerns. In response, young Hawaiian musicians began not only learning older styles of Hawaiian music but also invigorating the music with a number of innovations, including the merging of traditional and modern instrumentation and the unapologetic use of modern recording technologies. They also began drawing on outside influences, adding wider improvisational latitude beyond the melodic obbligatos dictated by the subordination of the guitarist to the vocalist and dancer in traditional Hawaiian music, borrowing, for example, from contemporaneous rock's expressive lead guitar styles.

They also sang in the Hawaiian language, effectively making their music less attractive to tourists and challenging the influence of the tourist market in the commercial music arena. Singing in Hawaiian was a political act, a counter against attempts to eradicate Hawaiian language codified in the 1896 passage of the Republic of Hawaii constitution, which made English the official language and the sole language of schools, effectively banning the Hawaiian language. As Kay Akindes points out in her study of Sudden Rush, a contemporary *na mele paleoleo* (rap) group, "muting the Hawaiian language and imposing the language of the colonizer was a means of controlling the minds of the colonized"—and Hawaiian Renaissance musicians literally challenged the muting of their mother tongue.[22]

But as kī hō'alu became known as instrumental guitar music (as detailed in the next section), it evaded the politics of language use and entered the public imaginary as the "soft, inviting sounds" of Hawai'i, allowing musicians to perform it, and audiences to appreciate it, without knowledge of the Hawaiian language or culture.[23] There is nothing new about this practice—a survey of popular music trends from the early twentieth century to the contemporary moment quickly reveals a series of relevant antecedents. Traveling around the globe in the Hawaiian music craze of the early twentieth century, Hawaiian sounds such as the lap steel guitar were appropriated by Nashville musicians, while the 'ukulele soon appeared in music that did not attempt to link to Hawaiian music at all, a practice continued by contemporary Hawai'i-born musicians such as Jake Shimabukuro.[24]

Kī hōʻalu's role as accompaniment to hula or other forms of Hawaiian music is primarily a thing of the past, though slack key artists occasionally feature a hula dancer on a song or two in concert (the guitarist remains the main attraction, inverting the historical relationship between music and dance in traditional Hawaiian culture). You can hear it, if faintly, embedded within arrangements of popular Hawaiian music on recordings from the post–World War II period as well as within the work of current Hawaiian artists such as vocalist Raiatea Helm, who recorded a duet album with Beamer (*Keola Beamer and Raiatea*, Mountain Apple Records, 2010). But the overwhelming proliferation of solo guitar recordings since the 1990s has increasingly framed kī hōʻalu as a soloist's art—a profitable transformation that came at a price, as the final moment reveals.

Accommodating Natives

I mean to play on the two possible meanings with this section title. On one hand, we might read the title as "making room for Hawaiians" in the world market or among the heritage-culture industrial complex.[25] On the other hand, we can read the title as noting the ways in which Native Hawaiian musicians have made their music culture fit with, or suitable to, vested interests dependent on shaping Hawaiian musicking into commodities while attempting to retain some sense of Kanaka Maoli imprimatur. Both involve improvisational skills in the sense of producing something for which there is no precedent. As I note earlier, working to "make fit [or] suitable" to outside dictates may necessitate compromise, but the fundamental orientation of Native Hawaiian performativities takes place within a sphere of reciprocal generosity. The question remains, though: What role might improvisation have played in the increased visibility yet diminished status in Hawaiʻi, at least for a time, of slack key musicians? I return to this question at the end of this section.

On February 13, 2005, the first Grammy for Best Hawaiian Music Album was awarded to *haole* (literally, "foreigner" but used to mark whites) guitarist Charles Brotman for his role as the producer of the compilation album *Slack Key Guitar, Volume 2* (Palm, 2004). The recording featured a field of ten guitarists, eight of whom were Native Hawaiian, but because Grammy regulations dictate that awards for compilation recordings are given to the producers, not the individual musicians, Brotman became the winner of the first Hawaiian Grammy despite being relatively unknown as a Hawaiian music guitarist at the time.

Less than a month later, the *Honolulu Star-Bulletin* ran an article that described the other nominees (Keali'i Reichel, the musical group Hoʻokena, the Brothers Cazimero, Amy Hanaiali'i Gilliom)—all of whom claim Hawaiian lineage and enjoy higher-profile careers than Brotman in the Hawaiian Islands—fielding calls of "outrage from friends, fans and family in Hawaii over the fact that Brotman is not Hawaiian."[26] During this time, Lilikalā Kameʻeleihiwa, director of the University of Hawai'i's Kamakakuokalani Center for Hawaiian Studies and noted Kanaka Maoli scholar and activist, argued in an on-air interview with a local television news reporter that Brotman's Grammy win was yet another instance of the commodified appropriation of Hawaiian music and culture by non–Kanaka Maoli that profited non–Native Hawaiian interests.

Grammy trustee Keith Olsen, who lives on Kaua'i, drafted the winning proposal for the Best Hawaiian Music Album category. Yet in the wake of Brotman's win—and as slack key recordings came to dominate the Grammys—Hawaiian musicians began clamoring for recognition of other Hawaiian musical traditions. Olsen responded, "The chances of expanding the [Hawaiian Grammy] within the next five years is [*sic*] slim to none, because there were so few submissions. We can't be like the Hokus [Nā Hōkū Hanohano, the local Hawaiian music awards given by the Hawai'i Academy of Recording Arts]. We have space for one [award]. And if they don't support it, we'll have space for none." Despite the active public discussions over the newly established award throughout 2004 and 2005, only twenty albums were submitted for consideration. Olsen argued that the small number of entries proved that the Hawaiian music community didn't fully support the new category, adding, "The Grammys don't operate on aloha time."[27]

Olsen's evocation of aloha time registered music industry leaders' frustrations with Hawaiian infighting over the definition of "Hawaiian music" that was a proxy war over economic leverage in the small Hawaiian music market and that had stalled the approval of a Hawaiian Grammy for two decades.[28] "Aloha time" refers to the allegedly poor time management skills of the Native Hawaiian that demonstrated the indigenous population to be unfit for colonial labor or capable of self-regulation. It was a way of impugning Kanaka Maoli who were able to escape demeaning plantation labor by disappearing into the hills, or onto whaling ships, as lazy and unfit to be members of modern society. Similarly to European colonization of the Americas, in which indigenous populations either died or escaped into the "wilderness," not only were nonnative laborers encouraged to immigrate, but stereotypes about Kanaka Maoli were offered as a legitimating rationalization of their subaltern status and eventual "tragic disappearance."

Because concepts such as aloha time figure Kanaka Maoli as a naive people with a natural disposition toward languid indulgence, plantation owners and their political allies mobilized its representative and rhetorical power to justify their claims to a "natural" dominance over Native Hawaiians. Indeed, the idea that Hawai'i is a multicultural paradise was built on the backs of immigrant plantation and ranch workers, who arrived in tandem with aggressive attempts by missionaries and their descendants to eradicate Kanaka Maoli culture. As Lisa Kahaleole Hall points out, "the most widespread American mythology about contemporary and historical Hawai'i revolves around the vision of the melting pot, a multicultural paradise where elements from every group combine into a rich whole that all can share.... The pleasure of this vision erases a violent, coercive, and tragic history. The multiplicity of races and cultures in contemporary Hawai'i was born in the attempt by plantation owners to divide and conquer their workforce."[29] The resistance of Kanaka Maoli to exploitive labor conditions led to the importation of, in Hawai'i's case, Asian laborers, primarily Japanese, Chinese, and Filipino. Many Locals (non-Native Hawaiians born and raised in Hawai'i) can trace their roots to Hawai'i plantation workers imported to perform work that neither Native Hawaiians nor white Americans could be induced to do, arriving in successive but overlapping waves from Portugal, Japan, China, the Philippines, and Puerto Rico, beginning in the eighteenth century. This history, including US militarization of the Hawaiian Islands, disappears owing to the tourist and hospitality industry's interests in promoting Hawai'i as a multicultural paradise, an exotic but welcoming destination for tourists.

This history of misrepresentations, appropriations, and dispossessions would reemerge in the controversies unleashed by the Grammy Award for Best Hawaiian Music Album. The impetus to lobby for the creation of a new category was largely economic. The debates surrounding the Hawaiian Grammy categorization, however, focused on Native Hawaiian cultural meanings and aesthetic values rather than increased marketing budgets or the upscaling of media interest, a silence that served to further obscure the material stakes at play. In the end, Grammy regulations specified that eligible recordings were required to feature the Hawaiian language on "more than half" of any vocals on a given recording, though instrumental recordings were acceptable, a stipulation that would prove to be a growing point of contention. Whatever their personal thoughts about the final agreement, at least at the outset, everyone involved claimed publicly that any individual's victory was secondary to the fact that "Hawaiian music" was going to be the ultimate victor.

Hawaiian slack key guitar recordings dominated the Grammy for Best Hawaiian Music Album throughout its seven-year history (note that the debates that led up to the establishment of the Hawaiian Grammy took longer). Before the arguments about slack key's place in Hawaiian music fomented by the Grammy Award, kī hōʻalu remained linked to ideas regarding precontact Hawaiian music culture, despite its hybrid roots. George Lewis, writing about the 1970s Hawaiian Renaissance movement, noted as late as 1991, "Many of the new songs also used musical forms that were associated with *native tradition*—from the chants of early Hawaii to *the song stylings of the slack-key guitarists*."[30] Most Hawaiians—and I use the term here as simply shorthand for "any individual who is living somewhere on the Hawaiian Islands"—would have found the idea of questioning slack key's Hawaiian cultural bona fides laughably inarguable prior to 2005.

In a recent conversation, Brotman conveyed a larger sense of the Hawaiian community that saw his Grammy win as a collective win for Hawaiian musicians: "To think that with this Grammy, it's come right back here to this [Kamuela] community, right back to the birthplace of kī hōʻalu, just like a full circle—it's an amazing thing. If there really is a controversy, it only exists because people were misinformed about the CD and didn't know anything about the music, the musicians, the recording, the Grammy voting process. It really is about the music, after all."[31]

For six years of the award's seven-year history, producer and musician Daniel Ho took home a Grammy statue. While raised in Hawaiʻi, Ho has not lived there since the late 1980s, leaving Oahu after his high school graduation to study in Los Angeles, California, at the Grove School of Music. Although Ho is a talented multi-instrumentalist, three of his six Grammy wins were as a producer of recordings featuring slack key guitar performances culled from a weekly Hawaiian concert series that slack key guitarist George Kahumoku directs at the Napili Beach Resort on Maui. In 2007 producer, slack key guitarist, and five-time Grammy nominee Milton Lau confessed, "The funny part is, [slack key guitarists are] the black sheep of the music industry on the island. We're not at all the most popular form of music at home, in terms of airplay. So all the island guys who get the publicity are pretty angry with us because they keep getting upstaged."[32]

But the attitude of "Hawaiian music wins no matter who takes home the trophy" ended when the first performers to claim a Hawaiian Grammy *as performing artists* were California-based Tia Carrere and Ho for their 2009 duo effort, *'Ikena*. As Ho and slack key continued to win Hawaiian Grammys, some observers in Hawai'i became openly dismissive of slack key, pointing to the fact that the slack key recordings avoided the "foreign-language problem" Hawaiian-language singers encountered within the English-dominant US music market despite the fact that every Grammy-winning slack key recording contained Hawaiian language vocals. Additionally, as critic Nate Chinen neatly observes, "wariness about slack key probably has to do with how it has been commercialized by mainlanders, from the guitarist Ry Cooder, who recorded with [Gabby] Pahinui in the 1970s, to the new age pianist George Winston, whose Dancing Cat label began releasing slack-key albums in the '80s and still sponsors national tours."[33]

Tatar's assertion (quoted above) regarding the relationship between tourism and Hawaiian music is exemplified by pianist George Winston's decision to popularize kī hō'alu as a result of a vacation in Hawai'i. Better known for his pastoral piano work than his affiliation with Hawaiian music culture, Winston happened to hear kī hō'alu while vacationing in Hawai'i and was immediately enthralled. On returning to California, he persuaded his label, Windham Hill, to allow him to distribute slack key guitar records under his own private label, Dancing Cat, located in the seaside town of Santa Cruz, well known for its California brand of laid-back beach culture. Dancing Cat recordings enabled kī hō'alu musicians to move beyond Hawai'i, as the label's distribution networks and promotional influence exceeded those of the music industry in Hawai'i. Dancing Cat's catalog is also significant, containing the final recordings for many of the guitarists of Pahinui's generation, such as Raymond Kane and Sonny Chillingworth, produced in settings that recognized and honored their achievements, for audiences otherwise unfamiliar with Hawaiian music culture.

Underlining the ways in which non-Hawaiians have sometimes had an outsized influence on Hawaiian music, a Dancing Cat web page reads, "Historically, most recordings have included slack key guitar only as accompaniment in a group setting. On Dancing Cat Records' Hawaiian Slack Key Guitar Masters Series, producer George Winston *brings the solo guitar to the forefront*, showcasing the stylings of some of the best players in the Islands."[34] Transforming slack key from an ensemble to a solo voice echoed earlier displacements of Kanaka Maoli cultural imperatives in Hawaiian music, giving way to the interests of a non-Hawaiian music market.

Yet Dancing Cat also provided a significant node in kī hō'alu's recent resurgence, building on the efforts of Hawaiian musicians such as Gabby

Pahinui, Peter Moon, and Keola Beamer during the Hawaiian Renaissance of the 1970s. Besides recording and distributing their recordings beyond Hawai'i, Winston provided a national and international platform for kī hō'alu musicians by using his position to organize tours for them in the continental United States, Europe, and Japan. Thanks to his efforts, kī hō'alu, which had remained largely an oral tradition even after the Hawaiian Renaissance, was transformed into a global commercial popular music genre—a Hawaiian variation of a "world music" fingerstyle guitar tradition within the global marketplace, notable because it was their slack key guitar skills rather than, say, their singing abilities in Hawaiian that were being recognized and valued by large non-Hawaiian audiences.

To return to the award controversy, Hawaiian critics, musicians, and fans disappointed by Grammy results began to insist that the fundamental distinction between Hawaiian music and all other musical traditions was the use of the Hawaiian language. Instrumental music such as kī hō'alu, they argued, while wonderfully expressive of Hawaiian values and certainly part of a multitextured Hawaiian musical culture, was unable to as fully or as powerfully articulate Hawaiian-ness as could Hawaiian-language verse, reversing long-held beliefs regarding kī hō'alu's place in "traditional" Hawaiian music.

In 2011, the final year the Hawaiian Grammy was awarded, Tia Carrere's winning recording featured all-Hawaiian-language vocals on every track.[35] No matter that Carrere sang arrangements based on Western concert music chestnuts such as Johannes Brahms's "Lullaby" and Giacomo Puccini's "O mio babbino caro" rather than repertoire more readily recognized as Hawaiian. More pertinently, Carrere's recording was far less popular in Hawai'i than perennial bridesmaid vocalist Amy Hanaiali'i's nominated recording, *Amy Hanaiali'i and Slack Key Masters of Hawai'i*. In the end, Native Hawaiian and Local artists "born, raised, and stayed" in Hawai'i, such as Raiatea Helm, the Brothers Cazimero, and Amy Hanaiali'i, who are far more popular in Hawai'i than Carrere, Ho, or any of the slack key guitarists, never won a Grammy for Best Hawaiian Music Album. Aloha time, it seems, doesn't just make Kanaka Maoli late to the show—it almost completely disappears them from the stage, as well.

I want to return now to the question regarding the role of improvisation in this bittersweet tale. In answering, I want to recall my cautionary note that improvisation is not always productive in the ways improvisers might hope for and that unintended consequences will sometimes win out—those "unexpected outcomes" I alluded to at the beginning of this essay. In this case, Ho and, to a lesser extent, Brotman were capable improvisers in the extramusical social sense I have been discussing throughout this essay. While musicians based in Hawaiʻi naively thought the Grammys would reflect the Hawaiian music scene, Ho understood that the Grammys represented the larger music industry and operated according to their own, rather than Kanaka Maoli, dictates. A significant outcome often left out of this story, particularly by those who wish to disparage Hoʻs participation, is that many Hawaiian musicians benefited from being associated with Hoʻs production work. George Kahumoku, Jeff Peterson, Sonny Lim, and other slack key artists were featured on the albums Ho produced and have been able to use their status as Grammy awardees to further their musical endeavors. In fairness to Ho, many of the other Hawaiian musicians will often promote themselves as Grammy nominees, particularly when addressing non-Hawaiian audiences. In this sense, all of these guitarists, Grammy winners or not, are improvising—using fresh approaches to circumstances they had not envisioned or encountered before and, similar to their musical precursors in other historical moments, accommodating themselves to sometimes-ignoble circumstances in order to assure the continuance of a Kanaka Maoli musical tradition.

Improvising Kanaka Maoli Indigeneity

Kanaka Maoli guitarists have used the performative improvising I outline throughout this essay as an adaptive strategy in confronting colonialism, US imperialism and militarism, and global corporatist capitalism by maintaining a central core of Native Hawaiian aesthetic ideals such as nahenahe around which any number of non–Kanaka Maoli elements—jazz, rock, reggae, hip-hop—might intermingle while remaining identifiably Hawaiian.[36] Kī hōʻalu is the aural expression of Kanaka Maoli musicality, a sounding presence against all efforts to remove and silence Kanaka Maoli. The uneasy relationship between Hawaiian music—and I include the history of that term, which has covered a lot of music in the past that most listeners today would agree is *not* Native Hawaiian music—and the music industry is double-edged. On one hand, it has offered many Kanaka Maoli musicians the opportunity to travel beyond Hawaiʻi, to be recognized and even gain mass-audience popularity. On the other hand, it has transformed Hawaiian music in ways that have not always benefited Kanaka Maoli or their culture. The pointed reactions to the dominance of slack key, for example, in the short-lived Grammy for Best Hawaiian Music Album demonstrate the limits of improvisational acuity. Improvisation, in short, provides no guarantees.

The performative improvisations within Hawaiian slack key guitar are the result of a Kanaka Maoli acoustemology, a sensibility rooted in the sounds or aural phenomena of a particular place that is not limited to the sounds created by humans but is, in fact, the relationship between humans and the environment in which they are embedded. Performative improvisation is a function of human soundings, both musical and nonmusical, produced out of specific geographic spaces and sound environments that are the result of interactions with the wider, nonhuman world. Understanding this dynamic grounds slack key not only in the nahenahe aesthetic but also in the ways in which Native Hawaiians have dealt with settler colonialism and global capitalism with aloha, capacious generosity, and infinite flexibility.

The Hawaiian landscape has been altered over the past three centuries, transforming the relationship of Kanaka Maoli to their homelands, which is articulated musically through the changing nature of their slack key guitar tradition. Performative improvisation still holds the key to the continuation of Hawaiian cultural and material existence or, even more important, their flourishing in a land that has not been altered for their benefit or according to their desires. Yet Native Hawaiians remain, maintaining a living presence and connection to the land, despite a history of "unsettling" and attempts to disappear their way of life. Committed to regaining self-determination and political autonomy, Kanaka Maoli are abetted by a legacy of improvisational strategies conceived within a Hawaiian acoustemology that continues to celebrate aloha, reciprocal generosity, and inclusivity through a nahenahe aesthetic.

The improvisatory bedrock on which kī hōʻalu rests was brought home by a story from Yuki "Alani" Yamauchi, a Japanese guitarist who studied under Raymond Kane under the older paʻa ka waha method.[37] The second day of his lessons took place at a performance in which he was to accompany Kane. When Yamauchi asked what they would be playing, Kane simply said, "Watch me and listen up!" Yamauchi quickly learned to never ask about anything—tunings, song lists, lyrics—and Kane would eventually give detailed explanations but only when he decided to explicitly disclose information. Yamauchi knew he had won approval when Kane began suggesting him for gigs Kane was unable to accept, and they would eventually record a number of albums together.

Native Hawaiian musician Brother Noland, writing in *The Hawaiian Survival Handbook*, notes that "'the lessons of aloha' . . . foreground practices of 'adjusting, adapting, blending, and being aware' of others, whether they be the inhabitants of the reef or the locals of an unfamiliar neighborhood."[38] Improvisation in kī hōʻalu is rooted in a Native Hawaiian acoustemology in which an acknowledgment of humanity's emplacement within the so-called natural world requires openness to the moment. Brother Noland also reminds us of improvisation's accommodation to and with others, including its unexpected outcomes as exemplified by, on the one hand, the Grammy Awards debacle and, on the other, Yamauchi's receipt of the Ki Ho'alu Foundation Legacy Award in 2014, an open acknowledgment of a non–Kanaka Maoli's legitimacy and authority within the tradition. Equally significant is slack key's transmission through an embodied pedagogical approach in which patient yet active listening is encouraged, rooting as well as routing Kanaka Maoli resilience in the face of always-changing circumstances. In these ways, Hawaiian slack key guitarists' improvisatory approaches embody and articulate the enduring power of Kanaka Maoli performative indigeneity.

NOTES

1 I will be using *Kanaka Maoli, native Hawaiian, indigenous Hawaiian*, and *Hawaiian* interchangeably throughout the text. I am following J. Kēhaulani Kauanui's usage in *Hawaiian Blood: Colonialism and the Politics of Sovereignty and Indigeneity*. Kauanui cites, in turn, Queen Lili'uokalani's use of the simple term *Hawaiian* to denote indigenous Hawaiians (xii). I am also following Noelani Goodyear-Ka'ōpua, Ikaika Hussey, and Erin Kahunawaika'ala Wright's usage of *Kanaka Maoli* to indicate nonspecific plural usage of the term. They, in turn, cite Hawaiian language experts No'eau Warner and Noenoe K. Silva. There are other terms such as *Kanaka 'Ōiwi* (People of the Bone), among others, but I will not be using them in this essay. As with all Hawaiian terms, any errors are entirely mine. The Mexican vaqueros were likely called *paniolo*, rather than *Mexicans* or *vaqueros*, because they spoke Spanish.
2 Graham and Penny, *Performing Indigeneity*, 2.
3 The First Hawaiian Renaissance is credited to King David Kalākaua (1836–1891), who revived the hula and surfing and also sanctioned the guitar and *'ukulele* by incorporating the instruments into his 1886 Silver Jubilee celebrations.
4 See Haunani-Kay Trask's "'Lovely Hula Hands': Corporate Tourism and the Prostitution of Hawaiian Culture," in her collection *From a Native Daughter: Colonialism and Sovereignty in Hawai'i*, for a critique of Hawaiian cultural appropriation. See also Christine Skwiot's excellent transatlantic-transpacific study of the relationship among the United States, Cuba, and Hawai'i, *The Purposes of Paradise: U.S. Tourism and Empire in Cuba and Hawai'i*, for a detailed analysis of the histories of use of tourism by the US political class to drive imperial dreams in Cuba and Hawai'i, leading to a number of failed attempts for the former and the eventual illegal annexation of the latter. See also Diamond, *American Aloha*; Desmond, *Staging Tourism*; and Picard and Wood, *Tourism, Ethnicity, and the State*. For a succinct history of the uses of Hawai'i in continental US American popular music, see Garrett, "Sounds of Paradise."

5   Fischlin, Heble, and Lipsitz, *Fierce Urgency of Now*, xv.
6   See Ferguson and Turnbull, *Oh, Say, Can You See?*; and Shigematsu and Camacho, *Militarized Currents*.
7   *Merriam-Webster Dictionary* online, accessed July 13, 2019, https://www.merriam-webster.com/.
8   Feld, "Waterfalls of Song," 91.
9   From an interview in the film *Slack Key and Other Notes*, directed by Ron Jacobs.
10 Dave Guard, liner notes to *Pure Gabby*. Kaona enjoys a long history in Hawaiian *mele* in which plural, even multiple, readings are available to the astute listener. The practice remains an essential element in mele and Hawaiian music broadly. There was also a tradition of *mele maʻi*, or genital or procreative chants, which were composed primarily for the firstborn child and celebrated the genitals, which were considered the life-giving parts of the human body. Needless to say, Christian missionaries found the practice reprehensible and prohibited it. The practice has survived as a historical rather than contemporary practice.
11 Tatar, "Slack Key Guitar," 351. Captain James C. Cook's first landing in Hawaiʻi was in January 1778.
12 See Slatta, Auld, and Melrose, "Kona." There were additional shipments of cattle subsequent to Vancouver's initial gift.
13 Starrs, "Millennial Hawaiian Paniolo," quoted in Slatta, Auld, and Melrose, "Kona."
14 Slatta, Auld, and Melrose, "Kona," 8. In 1908 paniolo Ikua Purdy became the world champion in the steer-roping competition in Wyoming. He was elected posthumously to the National Rodeo Hall of Fame in 1999.
15 This is an argument Rona Tamiko Halualani charts in the chapter "Abstract Nativism," particularly pages 9–26. She describes the ways in which Hawaiians were also figured as savage primitives. These two sides of colonial misrepresentation have been somewhat displaced by the "soft" representation of Hawaiians as an open and giving people through the workings of the tourist industry, serving the tourist trade as well as US national interests.
16 A wonderful example is provided by Auntie Alice Nāmakelua and her performance of "Paniolo Slack-Key" on her recording *Kuʻuleialohapoinaʻole*.
17 Tatar, "Slack Key Guitar," 359.
18 Tatar, *Strains of Change*, 2.
19 See Silva, *Aloha Betrayed*; and Osorio, *Dismembering Lāhui*.
20 See Dancing Cat Records, *A Brief History of Hawaiian Slack Key Guitar (Kī Hōʻalu)*.
21 This quote is from Beamer's comments about the song "Lei ʻAwapuhi," in the liner notes to his recording *Moeʻuhane Kīkā: Tales of the Dream Guitar*.
22 Akindes, "Sudden Rush," 82. The emergence of Hawaiian language classes and total immersion schools occurred during this period.
23 For an investigation of the relationship between Hawaiian language and musical meanings as performed in the Kamehameha Schools on Oʻahu, see Szego, "Singing Hawaiian."
24 Such non-Hawaiian ʻukulele music was revived for a brief moment in the 1970s by Tiny Tim (Herbert Khaury), whose 1968 recording of "Tiptoe through the Tulips" was a top-twenty hit. Besides Shimabukuro, masterful ʻukulele artists such as James Hill perform a repertoire that includes Michael Jackson and Radiohead in addition to

original work that alludes more to North American folk and bluegrass antecedents. For a fascinating history of the Hawaiian lap steel guitar and its circulation outside of Hawai'i, see Troutman, *Kīkā Kila*.

25 See Desmond, *Staging Tourism*; Diamond, *American Aloha*; and Skwiot, *Purposes of Paradise*.
26 Ryan, "Local Grammy Controversy."
27 All Olsen quotes are from Chang, "What Happened at the Grammys?"
28 Chang, "What Happened at the Grammys?"
29 Hall, "'Hawaiian at Heart,'" 406.
30 George Lewis, "Storm Blowing from Paradise," 63, emphasis added.
31 Brotman, interview with the author, October 16, 2012.
32 Quoted in Berger, "Nominees Talk Story."
33 Chinen, "Dear Grammy."
34 The Dancing Cat website has been redesigned since and this text no longer exists. A similarly worded rationale for the solo guitar recordings, however, can be found here (as of July 2019): https://www.dancingcat.com/liner-notes-masters-volume-1. The new wording does not alter my suggestion that Dancing Cat has had an impact on slack key priorities, at least in the realm of recordings.
35 Thirty other categories were eliminated, including contemporary folk, traditional folk, Native American, polka, zydeco, and Cajun. The Hawaiian, Native American, polka, zydeco, and Cajun categories were all replaced by a single American roots music award, now called the Grammy for Best Regional Roots Music Album. Besides the Grammys and the Nā Hōkū Hanohano awards, there are the Hawaii Music Awards, the Ka Leo Hano Awards, and the Hawaiian Music Hall of Fame and Museum awards, all based in Hawai'i.
36 Sudden Rush's cover of Pahinui's version of "Hi'ilawe," which they sample as part of their track, is a notable example of this cross-genre and cross-historical invigoration of Hawaiian slack key guitar.
37 Yamauchi's nickname, 'alani, meaning "orange" in Hawaiian, was given to him by Kane in response to Yamauchi's love of the orange fruit. Yamauchi spells it without the 'okina.
38 Quoted in Lyons and Tengan, "Introduction," 545.

BIBLIOGRAPHY

Akindes, Fay Yokomizo. "Sudden Rush: Na Mele Paleoleo (Hawaiian Rap) as Liberatory Discourse." *Discourse* 23, no. 1 (Winter 2001): 82–98.
Beamer, Keola. *Moe'uhane Kīkā: Tales of the Dream Guitar*. Dancing Cat, 1995, CD.
Beamer, Keola. *Moe'uhane Kīkā: Tales of the Dream Guitar*. Dancing Cat, 1995, liner notes. Accessed July 13, 2019. https://www.dancingcat.com/liner-notes-dream-guitar.
Beamer, Keola, and Raiatea Helm. *Keola Beamer and Raiatea*. Mountain Apple Records, 2010, CD.
Berger, John. "Nominees Talk Story." *Honolulu Star-Bulletin*, February 11, 2007. http://archives.starbulletin.com/2007/02/11/features/story02.html.

Brotman, Charles, prod. *Slack Key Guitar, Volume 2.* Palm, 2004, CD.
Chang, Heidi. "What Happened at the Grammys?" *Honolulu Magazine*, May 2005. http://www.honolulumagazine.com/Honolulu-Magazine/May-2005/What-Happened-at-the-Grammys/.
Chinen, Nate. "Dear Grammy, Is It Hawaiian Enough?" *New York Times*, February 4, 2011. http://www.nytimes.com/2011/02/06/arts/music/06danielho.html.
Dancing Cat Records. *A Brief History of Hawaiian Slack Key Guitar (Ki Ho'Alu).* Santa Cruz, CA: Dancing Cat Records. Accessed July 13, 2019. https://www.dancingcat.com/section-1-history.
Desmond, Jane C. *Staging Tourism: Bodies on Display from Waikiki to Sea World.* Chicago: University of Chicago Press, 1999.
Diamond, Heather A. *American Aloha: Cultural Tourism and the Negotiation of Tradition.* Honolulu: University of Hawai'i Press, 2008.
Feld, Steven. "Waterfalls of Song: An Acoustemology of Place Resounding in Bosavi, New Guinea." In *Senses of Place*, edited by Steven Feld and Keith H. Basso, 91–136. Santa Fe, NM: School of American Research Press, 1996.
Ferguson, Kathy E., and Phyllis Turnbull, eds. *Oh, Say, Can You See? The Semiotics of the Military in Hawai'i.* Minneapolis: University of Minnesota Press, 1998.
Fischlin, Daniel, Ajay Heble, and George Lipsitz. *The Fierce Urgency of Now: Improvisation, Rights, and the Ethics of Cocreation.* Durham, NC: Duke University Press, 2013.
Garrett, Charles Hiroshi. "Sounds of Paradise: Hawai'i and the American Musical Imagination." In *Struggling to Define a Nation: American Music and the Twentieth Century*, 165–214. Berkeley: University of California Press, 2008.
Graham, Laura R., and H. Glenn Penny, eds. *Performing Indigeneity: Global Histories and Contemporary Experiences.* Lincoln: University of Nebraska Press, 2014.
Guard, Dave. Liner notes to *Pure Gabby*, by Charles Philip "Gabby" Pahinui. Hula Records, CDHS-567, originally released in 1978, CD.
Hall, Lisa Kahaleole. "'Hawaiian at Heart' and Other Fictions." *Contemporary Pacific* 17, no. 2 (2005): 404–13.
Halualani, Rona Tamiko. "Abstract Nativism." In *In the Name of Hawaiians: Native Identities and Cultural Politics*, 1–37. Minneapolis: University of Minnesota Press, 2002.
Ho, Daniel, prod. *'Ikena.* Daniel Ho Productions, 2009, CD.
Jacobs, Ron, dir. *Slack Key and Other Notes.* Honolulu: *Hawaii Observer-*Videololo 2-Foodland-Hawaiian Airlines, producers, 1977.
Kauanui, J. Kēhaulani. *Hawaiian Blood: Colonialism and the Politics of Sovereignty and Indigeneity.* Durham, NC: Duke University Press, 2008.
Lewis, George. "Storm Blowing from Paradise: Social Protest and Oppositional Ideology in Popular Hawaiian Music." *Popular Music* 10, no. 1 (January 1991): 53–67.
Lyons, Paul, and Ty P. Kāwika Tengan. "Introduction: Pacific Currents." In "Pacific Currents." Spec. issue, *American Quarterly* 67, no. 3 (September 2015): 545–73.
Namakelua, Auntie Alice. *Ku'uleialohapoina'ole.* Hula Records, 1974, LP.
Osorio, Jonathan Kay Kamakawiwo'ole. *Dismembering Lāhui: A History of the Hawaiian Nation to 1887.* Honolulu: University of Hawai'i Press, 2002.
Pahinui, Charles Philip "Gabby." *Pure Gabby.* Hula Records, CDHS-567, originally released in 1978, CD.

Picard, Michel, and Robert E. Wood, eds. *Tourism, Ethnicity, and the State in Asian and Pacific Societies*. Honolulu: University of Hawai'i Press, 1997.

Ryan, Tim. "Local Grammy Controversy Strikes Sour Note." *Honolulu Star-Bulletin*, March 17, 2005.

Shigematsu, Setsu, and Keith L. Camacho, eds. *Militarized Currents: Toward a Decolonized Future in Asia and the Pacific*. Minneapolis: University of Minnesota Press, 2010.

Silva, Noenoe K. *Aloha Betrayed: Native Hawaiian Resistance to American Colonialism*. Durham, NC: Duke University Press, 2004.

Skwiot, Christine. *The Purposes of Paradise: U.S. Tourism and Empire in Cuba and Hawai'i*. Philadelphia: University of Pennsylvania Press, 2010.

Slatta, Richard W., Ku'ulani Auld, and Maile Melrose. "Kona: Cradle of Hawai'i's Paniolo." *Montana: The Magazine of Western History* (Summer 2004): 1–19.

Starrs, Paul F. "The Millennial Hawaiian Paniolo." *Rangelands* 22 (October 2000): 25.

Szego, C. K. "Singing Hawaiian and the Aesthetics of (In)Comprehensibility." In *Global Pop, Local Language*, edited by Harris M. Berger and Michael Thomas Carroll, 291–328. Jackson: University Press of Mississippi, 2003.

Tatar, Elizabeth. "Slack Key Guitar." In *Hawaiian Music and Musicians: An Encyclopedic History*, rev. ed., edited by George S. Kanahele and John Berger, 351–59. Honolulu: Mutual, 2012.

Tatar, Elizabeth. *Strains of Change: The Impact of Tourism on Hawaiian Music*. Bishop Museum Special Publication 78. Honolulu: Bishop Museum Press, 1987.

Trask, Haunani-Kay. *From a Native Daughter: Colonialism and Sovereignty in Hawai'i*. Honolulu: University of Hawai'i Press, 1999.

Troutman, John W. *Kīkā Kila: How the Hawaiian Steel Guitar Changed the Sound of Modern Music*. Chapel Hill: University of North Carolina Press, 2016.

TWELVE From Prepeace to Postconflict

The Ethics of (Non)Listening and Cocreation in a Divided Society

SARA RAMSHAW AND PAUL STAPLETON

> Listen!
> Follow the sound.
> Do not let it escape.
> Pursue *it* and not the spiderly threads of illusion.
> Wait.
> Let the sound come . . .
> —EDWIN PRÉVOST, *No Sound Is Innocent*

Following the signing of the Belfast (or Good Friday) Agreement in 1998, Northern Ireland (NI) has been well marketed internationally as an unqualified success in transitional justice.[1] And yet the jurisdiction continues to be in crisis.[2] On July 3, 2014, the two main Unionist parties in NI walked out of talks at the Stormont Parliament building in protest over the Parades Commission's decision to ban Orangemen from marching near a Republican area of North Belfast on July 12, 2014.[3] This was not the first time NI politicians have walked out on critical discussions—and it would not be the last.[4] More recently, on January 9, 2017, Deputy First Minister Martin McGuinness (Sinn Féin) resigned in protest over First Minister Arlene Foster's (Democratic Unionist Party, DUP) alleged involvement in the Renewable Heat Incentive scandal, as well as in response to DUP and Sinn Féin divisions over ongoing cultural and legacy issues. McGuinness's resignation resulted in the collapse of the NI Assembly on January 26, which in turn triggered a snap NI Assembly election on March 2, 2017. Following this election, discussions on the formation of a new executive have remained at an impasse. This situation has been further complicated by uncertainty around Brexit as well as the recent result of the snap UK general election on June 8, 2017, which has seen the DUP enter into a confidence-and-supply relationship with the United Kingdom's Conservative Party, all of which has the potential to undermine key principles of the Good Friday Agreement.[5] What these events illustrate is that, driven by a *refusal to listen*, both to those on the other side of the sectarian divide and to those who are outside of or who reject placement within this duality, NI currently finds itself in what architect and academic Ruth Morrow calls a "hazy phase," one that is better described as prepeace than postconflict.[6] Prepeace in this context does not signify a return to the unrelenting violent sectarian conflict prominent during the period of NI history known as the Troubles.[7] It does, however, connote a peace *without* reconciliation, or a continued conflict that is, at least for the time being, primarily nonviolent—albeit still *unproductive*—in nature.[8]

From the outset, we must clarify that this is *not* an analysis of the current political or legal situation in NI, nor a discussion of the continued conflict in the region.[9] Instead, we wish to focus on the concept of *(non)listening* as it applies to improvised music and life in NI.[10] Living in a divided society, and through sustained social, political, and religious conflict, has encouraged perhaps a different type of listening, one that, at times, can necessitate a (non)listening to sectarian subtexts. Listening, in this context, is not just about the sense of hearing. Rather, it is multisensory and, more importantly, collaboratively enacted by a broad range of human and nonhuman actors. Thus, our focus will be on the social and dialogic nature of improvisation and the way the active listening skills promoted by musical improvisation may reveal different forms of social relations.[11] In doing so, we ask: How might improvisation promote openness to narratives outside those commonly portrayed as dominant in NI, potentially teaching us when to listen and when it is just as productive not to?

Our chapter draws heavily on the words and works of improvising musicians in Belfast, exploring the specific listening skills of these musicians and audiences. We also make extensive use of the work of Marcel Cobussen and Nanette Nielsen in their book *Music and Ethics* (2012), which informs our primary argument that attentive (non)listening, as an ethical practice that endeavors to both listen and *not* listen to the voices and sounds of the "other," may actually be a productive skill to nurture and encourage in a society enduringly beset by division and conflict.[12] Moving from the ethics of improvisation to that of cocreation, we thereby propose a reimagining of an alternative future for NI, a "playing for keeps" in which being-with-others might challenge or resist sustained unproductive crisis.[13] In the process, we aim to reveal how improvisatory practices in NI simultaneously upset or complicate conventional notions of improvisation as a homogeneous form of cocreative endeavor.

Improvised Musics in Belfast: A Brief Account

Improvised music in Belfast primarily clusters around festivals and ad hoc events featuring free jazz and experimental music, as well as noise and DIY electronic music.[14] Not unlike in other cities of a similar size, most of these activities receive limited financial support (public or otherwise), are often of a grassroots nature, and generally take place on the margins of the city's musical terrain.[15] Yet improvisation has been present in the sonic landscape of the island of Ireland for some time.

Improvisation has long played a role in Irish traditional music (trad), where tunes and songs are preserved through their continual reinvention. An example of the explicit use of improvisation in trad is found in the work of Dublin-born fiddle player and composer Tommy Potts (1912–1988). Potts was known for performing extended solo improvisations based on traditional tunes that were often rendered nearly unrecognizable. Potts's unique performance style has been described as challenging "the communal social nature of the dance-music tradition by breaking in a seemingly erratic manner what up to his time (and interestingly, since his time also) were musical taboos."[16] Despite such subversion, Potts continues to be celebrated by many contemporary trad musicians and scholars both as "the epitome of tradition, on the one hand, and as the epitome of innovation, on the other."[17]

Although cross-fertilization between the jazz and trad scenes is a relatively recent phenomenon in Ireland, Potts's improvisational innovation was concurrent with the emergence of Irish jazz. As it happens, NI was central to this activity, with music critic George Kerr claiming in a 2003 article on jazz in Belfast that "the first band to play jazz anywhere on these Islands was the Ken Smylie band in Belfast in 1951."[18] Kerr goes on to mention key NI players in the early days of Irish jazz, including trombonist Jimmy Compton, cornetist Billy Hopkins, the Rodney Foster band, the Apex Jazz Band, and others. He also highlights the role of UTV, a commercial television broadcaster in NI, which ran the "highly successful" *White Line* series in 1970 featuring a modern jazz quintet led by pianist Billy White. Perhaps most significant to current improvisatory musical activities in Belfast, as Kerr highlights, was the contribution of Brian Carson, founder and current director of Moving on Music, who in the 1980s "began bringing the best of post-bop outfits from London and New York and started to attract young audiences that hadn't been seen since the '60s."[19] Notable artists brought in for Moving on Music concerts in Belfast include Ornette Coleman, the Sun Ra Arkestra, Derek Bailey, Max Eastley and David Toop, Han Bennink, Peter Brötzmann and Paal Nilsson-Love, and Sidsel Endresen and Jan Bang. Carson continues to play a significant role in the promotion of experimental and improvised music in Belfast through curating performances by international and local musicians as part of annual events such as Belfast Festival at Queen's, Cathedral Quarter Arts Festival, and Moving on Music's Brilliant Corners jazz festival.[20] The Brian Irvine Ensemble and Bourne/Davis/Kane are two examples of local improvising groups who have been frequently supported by Moving on Music and have received critical acclaim on the international circuit.

The performance of jazz in NI shares many musical characteristics with that in other parts of the world, such as instrumentation (e.g., drum kit, double bass, piano, saxophones), rhythmic devices (syncopation, polyrhythms), and extended use of improvisation. There are, however, unique social factors that mediate this local practice, resulting in distinctive "social aesthetics."[21] Through performance, musicians and their audiences in NI mobilize new social relations that offer an alternative to the institutionally supported sectarian dichotomy that still looms over local cultural policy and everyday life.

In recent years local musicians in Belfast can be found improvising in a variety of other periodic or one-off events. These performances are often distinct in style and atmosphere from the more widely promoted events described above, offering improvised musics that have little or nothing to do with a jazz aesthetic. Notable examples over the past decade include Barry Cullen's "listen . . . ," a monthly evening at the old Four in Hand bar (and later as an ad hoc event at the Menagerie) of DJs, DIY noise music, and live visuals; Pretty Circus happenings, promoted by Ciaran Sherry, which include eclectic cabaret-style events mixing hip-hop, experimental music, alternative pop, and live art upstairs at the Front Page bar; John McGurgan and Pawet Bignell's Vibic Sexy Time weekly open improv jam session at the Black Box's Green Room, often showcasing musicians with a strong roots and blues feel; and the recent Round Buttons Square Tones five-day event featuring performances and talks mixing the visual and sonic arts, curated by Min Kim and Barry Cullen in collaboration with the art gallery and project space PS^2. The diversity of improvisational musical events in Belfast continues to increase in recent years; many of the above activities, however, have proven to be unsustainable as regular events. As the city continues to see rapid changes following the formal end of hostilities in 1998, the gentrification of Belfast's social spaces has not always benefited more challenging and questioning forms of music making.

Perhaps most idiosyncratic to Belfast is the diverse program of music presented by the Sonic Arts Research Centre (SARC), including the Sonorities Festival Belfast. This interdisciplinary research center unites internationally recognized experts in the fields of music composition and performance, musicology, digital signal processing, human-computer interaction, and auditory perception.[22] It features regular concerts by international and local improvising musicians who explore the intersection of music performance with new technological developments. This work includes networked music performances (musicians improvising together across different geographic locations), biosensor musical interfaces, real-time notation systems, collaborative sound sculptures, and human-machine improvisation systems. An example of the last is composer and trombonist George Lewis's use of a "creative machine"–driven "interactive (acoustic) piano" in a human+machine+human trio with bassist Barry Guy in a 2007 concert in SARC's Sonic Lab. Guy commented on this experience in a postconcert discussion: "So it's a three-way conversation . . . adding up the information, analyzing it, anticipating—all of these things happen in real-time improvisation anyway. I'm kind of thrown into the middle of it, and you make the best of that situation because that's the life that we're in as improvisers, which is to try and make the story add up, and be surprised."[23] Guy's remarks reveal an interesting tension that is common in the types of technologically mediated musical activities taking place at SARC: it is necessary to try and sink or swim in such situations, to listen to the conversation as it unfolds, to take risks, to be open to the possibility of surprise. There is also the unspoken possibility of failure, which in such uncharted territories is a frequent reality.

It is clear from our discussions with local promoters and musicians that, despite its wealth of improvised music (both historical and contemporary), Belfast has failed so far to produce a cohesive music improvisation scene. The reasons for this are many, and it is questionable whether such a unified scene is desirable in a cultural context where difference is overshadowed by two dominant conflicting political identities. Yet, in this current state of contingency, it is Belfast's ability to continue to promote international acts and develop individual local innovation that may be instructive with regard to its ongoing unproductive political situation.

The Ethics of Improvisation, or the "Good" Improviser

Drawing on the work of Emmanuel Levinas, the late French philosopher Jacques Derrida equates ethics with hospitality and otherness, with the notion or act of being hospitable to the other, to the stranger or foreigner.[24] For Derrida, hospitality (and ethics) can only be understood in a double sense.[25] On the one hand, absolute hospitality (what Derrida also terms "*The* law" or "the Law") requires unqualified generosity and open doors/borders to *all* visitors.[26] This unconditional welcoming of the unpredictable other involves a certain level of *risk* for there is always a chance that the stranger/foreigner/trespasser/other will destroy everything and even murder the hospitable host.[27] Ethics as absolute hospitality is thus possible only when certitude is abandoned, when risks are taken.[28] This absolute hospitality, however, is constrained by conditional "laws," such as those in place to protect all-welcoming hosts from unsavory guests who wish to steal from or even kill them.[29] Ethics as hospitality thereby entails an openness to the unexpected ("*The* law") but also constraints on this unpredictability ("laws," the legal system).[30]

Improvisation shares with ethics (as hospitality) an impossible openness to the unpredictable and uncertain other (the Law).[31] To be recognized *as* improvisation, it must obey certain preexistent structures or "laws." "You gotta improvise on *somethin'*," says Charles Mingus.[32] That said, improvisation simultaneously involves a pushing beyond the known and predictable, without guarantee or certainty. As such, it chances failure. The ethical improviser must thus embrace failure and error as a source of learning, and the most accomplished improvisers turn unexpected problems into (musical) opportunities.[33]

Improvisation and Ethical Listening

The unconditionally hospitable attitude described above, as that which creates a space for ethics to happen, can be achieved, according to Cobussen and Nielsen, only through "an open *listening* attitude, an openness towards other voices and the voices of others."[34] Drawing on Derrida's distinction above between the Law and the laws of hospitality, attentive listening involves a constant negotiation between recognition of the preexistent and discovery of the unknown.[35] Listening with respect, openness, and responsiveness necessarily enables the listener to meet otherness *as* otherness, without the need to reduce it to "the order of the same."[36] It involves an ethical commitment and responsibility to, and interaction with, all that surrounds us: persons, the environment, and the sounds of daily life.[37] Attentive or deep listening demands attunement not only to the singularity of the situation but also to the context and community within which music is made. From such listening can spring compassion and understanding.[38] Improvisational music is very much in tune with attentive listening. As noted above, it relies on certain laws of music to be recognized as improvisation. Yet, at the same time, it must transgress these laws in a gesture toward the unknown other, toward voices and sounds typically silenced in music and society.[39] Attentive listening in improvised music thus does not merely sound surprise in relation to auditory sounds.[40] It also forces us to think otherwise in terms of our *social* relationships and "customary frameworks of assumption."[41]

Applied to the improvised musics scene in Belfast, the ethical importance of attentive listening is evidenced, for instance, in a performance of the AMM at the Crescent Arts Centre on Saturday, September 7, 1996 (to a crowd of about fifty people).[42] It was the group's first performance in Ireland, and Moving on Music Festival organizer Brian Carson was praised by Mairtín Crawford of *Fortnight* for "bringing a slice of difference to Belfast." In a review of the performance, Crawford described AMM as producing sounds that "seem to come from another dimension."[43] His analysis of the performance is a telling example of ethical listening and deserves extended recitation:

> Totally improvised the music veers from cacophony to silence where the audience is almost straining to hear the piano's faint notes which hang in the air with Rowe's masterful evocations of sound, plaintive, disturbing and ethereally beautiful. Prévost's drumming was nothing short of outstanding, ranging from carefully offbeat strokes to full out assaults, though eyebrows were raised when he removed his cymbals and began to play them with a bow! Pianist Tilbury also surprised the crowd when he rose from his seat and began to pluck the strings with his fingers.
>
> This was however a sign of the sheer intensity of the performance, with each musician working off each other and as the playing went on it was clear that AMM knew exactly what they were doing. There was no slavish hierarchy of rhythm to soloist—rather a collective assemblage of elements of sound, texture, atmosphere and silence creating mutating tones of sound. As much about creating atmosphere as making music the audience soon felt themselves becoming part of the performance—the opening of a can of beer was an atonal accompaniment to the drums, a

sneeze a wisp of radio static, and a shrill siren of a fire engine as it sped past the Crescent became a somewhat suitable finale.

After moments of silence the band looked at each other and one by one left the stage leaving a totally engaged, if at times somewhat bewildered crowd to decide it was over and give the band the applause they so richly deserved.[44]

The openness of the audience to these sounds of difference in a city that, at the time, was predominantly intolerant of difference in the social, political, cultural, and religious spheres points to the potential of attentive listening, as promoted through improvised music, as an ethical tool for transgressing established identities in a polarized society.

Steve Davis (of Bourne/Davis/Kane), a NI-based percussionist and regular participant at Moving on Music gigs, adds to the above account his memories of this event: "The music was quiet, unnerving, and extreme. This was the first and only time I saw this group. I had never heard improvised music like this. They took their time and let the music unfold very slowly. The music had drama and never revealed itself until it needed to. This moved and inspired me."[45] If ethics calls for attentive listening, one that "compels us to listen to others and to otherness—to the unfamiliarity of certain sound worlds, to the unheard sounds of our environment," then the audience's reception to the other-dimensional AMM performance in Belfast undoubtedly constitutes an ethical encounter, or ethics of encounter, that demanded, even if for just a few hours, an acceptance or appreciation of otherness and difference.[46]

One further example of a musical event requiring attentive or ethical listening to difference and otherness, which took place, once again, at the Crescent Arts Centre in Belfast, was the concert by Collective 4tet, comprising Heinz Geisser (drums), Mark Hennen (piano), Jeff Hoyer (trombone), and William Parker (bass), on May 15, 1997. In the liner notes of the live recording of the concert, the music was likened by reviewer George Kerr to "impromptu" poetry by the beloved Seamus Heaney, a massive accolade for any outsider to NI.[47] Davis, again in attendance, reflects on this Collective 4tet performance: "A great band that chattered, banged, crashed, screamed, and had a strange swing that seemed to flow and stop on a dime. I practised for days after this gig trying to tap into what they had going on, it was amazing!"[48] Although this particular concert clearly had inspiring results, such intensely passionate openness and exploration is not void of potentially disastrous consequences. Expressing the risk and danger involved in any ethical listening, Kerr goes on to write: "At times the quartet seem to be on the knife-edge of success and failure—often flirting with either side of the divide. The attentive capacity audience seems to add danger to the moment and the cathartic experience forces the players into a fiery freedom of texture, intensity and higher levels of creativity."[49] Creativity requires risk, and it is the ability to bravely listen to what is often unheard, or what has yet to be heard, that allows improvising musicians to turn danger into imagination.

The Ethics of (Non)Listening in NI

While the performance of the AMM in Belfast in 1996 was employed above as an example of attentive or ethical listening, AMM guitarist Keith Rowe has spoken about the (ethical) possibilities of nonlistening:

> The act of NOT listening is very important, preferring juxtaposition to confabulation, disturbing the congruity and avoiding Pavlovian laminates.
> Non listening for me is about the intensification of the edge, or frame. This might be seen as an attempt to limit certain aspects of encroachment of the external environment, and it's always been a part of my musical makeup. I'm very aware that it's almost heretical to praise not listening, but nevertheless I feel there is a place for it.[50]

Nonlistening, according to Cobussen and Nielsen, involves "deliberately not paying attention to the performance of your fellow musician in order to arrive at an aesthetically satisfying result; consciously obstructing the possibility of letting yourself be influenced by the other's input and/or by (certain) memories."[51] While nonlistening has the potential to undermine ethics as hospitality, it may also conversely "*deepen* an aural ethics": "At any given moment in a performance, the improviser makes musical choices in relation to what the others are doing—choices that might radically alter the orientation of the piece. The ability to respond in an appropriate manner to constantly changing musical events is an attainment that any improviser has to learn. She/he constantly has to make decisions regarding what to play and when to play it, thereby also inevitably eliciting responses from the co-musicians."[52] Accordingly, musicians share responsibility not just for their own actions but also for the way these decisions may affect others and the piece of music as a whole—and this response-ability has not only a musical but also a *social* (and resistant) component.[53]

The ethical potential of (non)listening is of particular relevance in the context of a divided society such as NI. Musical improvisation in Belfast happens *in spite of* this division, finding sustenance in the spaces in-between. Some residents of Belfast are deeply unhappy choosing between nationalism and unionism, instead preferring to develop alternative or more nuanced forms of cultural identity. Rather than seeking to create a unity between two polarized dominant narratives, improvisation promotes multivocality through celebrating (in)difference (to the sociopolitical status quo). Again, it is therefore important to know when to listen and when not to listen.

As a specific example of how the ethics of (non)listening, as that which can occur in improvisatory practices, gets construed in the wider social practices of NI, the Listening Project, a partnership between the British Broadcasting Corporation (BBC) and the British Library, visited Derry/Londonderry, NI, in 2015 to explore the issue of whether cultural characteristics can shape the ways in which people listen to others (or otherness).[54] Speaking with Brian McGilloway, host Fi Glover comments on the "certain ease" with which people in NI talk with one another and inquires about a "level of companionship" that she has not experienced otherwise, at least not in the United Kingdom.[55] In response to the query, McGilloway speaks of the "strong sense of language" that inhabitants of NI have, especially the strong sense of other meanings in language. He cites the name of the interview location, Derry/Londonderry, as a striking example. The name designates not only a place or location but also a particular political, or even cultural, affiliation.[56] McGilloway stresses the expertise those in NI have at distinguishing the natural meaning of words from their subtext. Citing Heaney's famous lines, "Whatever you say, say nothing," he explains that although one thing may be said, underneath a completely different meaning may be coming across.[57] This is why, McGilloway says, NI people are extremely skilled at listening in the sense of picking up on hidden meaning and understanding the damage that words can do. So many different sides exist in the story of NI, and yet everyone has their own story. McGilloway stresses that, in many ways, "everyone's story is the same," notwithstanding the side one was or is on. He focuses on the "huge group of people in the middle" of the Troubles, who, regardless of the side, lost so much.

The ethics of (non)listening in musical improvisation entails individual responsibility both for decisions made during a performance and for the final sonic outcomes.[58] How, then, might this assist in rethinking the individual character of not only ethical behavior but also collective responsibility, or the subordination of individuality to a supposed unified collective or community founded on preestablished rules, premises, and goals, which can have extremely detrimental effects on a society founded on division and intolerance?[59] Conversely, how might the situation in NI problematize the ethics of (non)listening by making visible the strategic or coded aspects of listening?

"Playing with Others": Cocreation in a Divided Society

Oft lauded as the expression of individual freedom, improvised creativity actually sits *between* individuality and collectivity, or constitutes a *being-with* of the singular and the general/plural.[60] Musicians, in short, always *play-with*—play with *others*. This is true not only for ensembles but also for soloists, who are "constantly connected to other human beings, other musicians, other entities, either diachromatically, by pursuing a certain tradition, or synochronically, by playing the same instrument, in the same style or in the same venues."[61] For French philosopher Jean-Luc Nancy, existence is fundamentally social and relational in nature, as he explains in *Being Singular Plural*: "Being cannot *be* anything but being-with-one-another."[62] And later in the same book, he writes, "Existence *is with*: otherwise nothing exists."[63] Elsewhere, drawing on the philosophical work of Martin Buber, Stapleton has argued that "identities are shaped not through internal contemplation, but rather through our relations between ourselves and others."[64] In this sense, the being-with of the singular and the general/plural does not pit the individual against the community, whether musical or otherwise.[65] Instead, the *with* signals connection and community, while simultaneously gesturing toward a distancing or rupture as between individuals in a community, and between individuals and a community.[66] Existence, therefore, is not just social; it is also *ethical*, giving space to a plurality of singularities and voices.

Perhaps one of the best examples in NI of the being-with of individuality and collectivity, or of individuals and community empowering one another through improvisation, is John McGurgan and Kris Stronge's *Carousel*, a periodic event taking place at the Black Box in Belfast.[67] In McGurgan's words:

> The concept is simple, put high quality and proficient improvisers in a circle with musicians and songwriters who wouldn't normally engage with improvisation. They then have the chance to hear their music interpreted by a large ensemble of quality players and see what happens. From the first event we've always included an element of live visual art. The songwriter angle as well as the live art projections also helped to keep Belfast audiences onboard, as for the most part improv is still an alien

concept to the general public here. For the audience to have a melody or song structure, as well as something to look at, we felt we could hold their attention through some of the more aggressive and experimental improvisational moments that would naturally occur at such an event. Over the last 7 years we've programmed over a dozen carousels and booked well over 100 musicians to play from all levels of ability.[68]

The collisions of sometimes up to twenty musicians responding to an individual's initial offering frequently have surprising results. It is not always a friendly and supportive sonic environment. Subversion and care are handed out in equal measure. Factions can form and take the music in a new direction. In these ways it sometimes feels like a version of John Zorn's *Cobra*, a game-based performance piece in which a set of visual cues (e.g., symbols) provide instructions for musicians to respond to in their ongoing performance—but more anarchic without *Cobra*'s prompter role. At other times, however, the accompaniment sounds convincingly precomposed, with more consonant reverence than dissonant dissidence. Neither of these methods is always successful musically, but the drama of the exchange consistently seems to hold the attention of the equally diverse audience. Each piece is relatively short for an improvisation, or relatively long for a folk song, typically clocking in somewhere between five and ten minutes. Each new offering is as different as the individual musicians. And yet somehow this format provides a sense of cohesion; this is not a unified single voice but a community that enjoys a tense but productive coexistence.

Thinking about ethics as a hospitable (non)listening to others or otherness, musical improvisation can be seen as a means of generating an "ethics of cocreation," or finding "a way out of no way," a playing for keeps, in a society divided by difference and intolerance.[69] As Daniel Fischlin, Ajay Heble, and George Lipsitz argue, "improvisation accentuates matters of responsibility, interdependence, trust, and social obligation. Through the development of new, unexpected, and productive cocreative relations among people in real time, improvisation aligns with the broader rights project of promoting a culture of collective responsibility, dispersed authority, and self-active democracy."[70] Just as the being-*with* of collective individuality entails both connection and separation, the *co* of *cocreation* marks a simultaneous unity and division. This is extremely important in a society such as NI in which the relational aspects of creation are often ignored or trivialized.

The example of *Carousel* above suggests the importance and necessity of improvised musical practices in guiding NI toward an ethics of (non)listening and the cocreation of a shared future based not on *unproductive* conflict but on an attentive listening to those voices that typically go unheard or are silenced, particularly in divided societies. (Non)listening is always already a listening-*with* (others). Not entirely intuitive, it must be learned and honed. Improvised musical practices thus speak not only to music but to other realms as well, such as that of law and justice, as our recently concluded research project Into the Key of Law: Transposing Musical Improvisation; The Case of Child Protection in Northern Ireland, sponsored by the UK Arts and Humanities Research Council (AHRC), confirms.[71]

One key finding arising from the Into the Key of Law project is the importance of listening—*really* listening—to the voices of others, looking specifically at the context of NI child protection law.[72] Responding to Pauline Oliveros's keynote address, "Safe to Play," at our Just Improvisation Symposium, held at the SARC on May 29–30, 2015, Judge Patricia Smyth, a NI district court family law judge, says this about the importance of listening:

> If people genuinely feel they have been listened to, that the judge has understood their point, that the judge has given it proper consideration, even if they lose, they can deal with it . . . because they have been listened to. . . . And, it is a key task for any judge to not just listen, but to convey the fact to the person that they have been listened to, and, in my own experience in the family court, I think it is an absolute priority that the vulnerable parents are made to feel that they matter, that they are treated with dignity and respect, and I consciously speak directly to parents, for example. I do it deliberately and consciously so that they understand, and very often some of the vulnerable people who find their way into court, they've never been listened to by anyone, they've been treated like a piece of dirt by authorities everywhere all their lives, and, as a judge, I make it a priority that in my court they will not feel like that.[73]

Judge Smyth's sentiments, powerfully expressed, are equally applicable to both the local improvised musical practices and the wider NI society. If one aspires to play for keeps, or to listen attentively to what is actually being said about listening, its role in cocreating a more just and equitable future is indisputable.

In summary, while people living in NI are often skilled at listening *for* difference, continuing conflict in the region reveals that more work is needed on listening *to* difference and otherness, particularly if NI is ever going to move from a state of prepeace to one of postconflict. As it stands, NI remains ever on the brink of crisis. And political responses to these crises, as the examples that opened this chapter illustrate, seem almost invariably to involve a pulling away, stepping down, or basically not listening to the voices on the other side, or outside, of the political, religious, and cultural divide. As noted above, nonlistening is not necessarily or inherently unethical, but, as is the case in musical improvisation, politicians must share responsibility not just for their own actions (that is, for not listening) but also for the way these decisions may affect others and society as a whole. This is where NI politicians have much to learn from improvising musicians in NI. It is well documented that improvisation can play a vital role in crisis response.[74] Further, we have provided many examples that illustrate how musicians and audiences alike in NI have, notwithstanding, or perhaps because of, the divisions and hostilities existing outside the musical venues, embraced the sounds and voices of otherness, honing their attentive listening skills and practicing an ethics of (non)listening. Always a listening-*with*, this can teach us much about responsibility and hope, and ways to adapt to change, especially in times of crisis.[75] The ethics of (non)listening promotes multivocality and being-with-difference, rather than falling back on polarized dominant narratives. It teaches us when to listen and when not to, and it encourages cocreative, improvisatory solutions to unproductive conflict, which is undoubtedly desperately needed in prepeace NI.

NOTES

Both authors have lived in Belfast, Northern Ireland, for over ten years. Sara is extremely grateful to Dr. Kathryn McNeilly, senior lecturer at the Queen's University Belfast School of Law, for her excellent research assistance and to Maurice Macartney for his stimulating and enlightening conversations about Jacques Derrida, jazz, and Northern Irish politics. Paul would like to thank Steve Davis, Barry Cullen, Phil Smyth, Saul Rayson, John McGurgan, and Brian Carson for providing insider perspectives on improvisatory musical practices in Belfast through interviews. Both authors appreciate greatly the exchange of ideas that has taken place at the Translating Improvisation Research Group gatherings, particularly the contributions of the regular attendees, namely, Robert Bentall, Steve Davis, David Grant, Mark Hanna, Adnan Marquez-Borbon, Aoife McGrath, Ruth Morrow, Thomas Muinzer, Seamus Mulholland, Simon Rose, Franziska Schroeder, Phil Smyth, Maruška Svašek, and Simon Waters, as well as the discussion generated at the Translating Improvisation International Colloquium and Concert, held at SARC on May 29, 2014, by participants such as Ajay Heble, Marcel Cobussen, Eric Lewis, Daniel Lametti, and others. Last, but certainly not least, we would like to thank Matilde Meireles for her assistance with pretty much everything else. As always, any mistakes are our own.

1 The Belfast (or Good Friday) Agreement was the result of multiparty peace negotiations, which took place in the late 1990s. Among its provisions the agreement established

a new power-sharing executive framework for NI and provided for a number of formal North-South and East-West links to be established and a number of new safeguards in relation to rights and equality. For further discussion see Wilford, *Aspects of the Belfast Agreement*. On the marketing of NI as an "unqualified case of successful post-agreement peace," see Bush, "Politics of Post-conflict Space," 167.

2 Since its inception in the 1920s, NI has been characterized by (and more recently is emerging from) ethnoreligious social conflict between two factions or identity groups: Unionism/Loyalism (traditionally associated with Protestant identity) and Nationalism/Republicanism (traditionally associated with Catholic identity). See McGarry and O'Leary, *Northern Ireland Conflict*; McKittrick and McVea, *Making Sense of the Troubles*; Tonge, *Northern Ireland*; and Guelke, *New Perspectives*. Unionism/Loyalism seeks to maintain NI's constitutional position as part of the United Kingdom. Nationalism/Republicanism, in contrast, identifies with Irish identity and seeks to achieve inclusion of NI within a wider united Irish Republic. Mainstream, elite-level politics in NI largely remains drawn along these lines, the main Unionist parties being the Democratic Unionist Party (DUP) and the Ulster Unionist Party (UUP), the main Republican party being Sinn Féin, and the main Nationalist party being the Social Democratic and Labour Party (SDLP).

3 Parades have been a contentious and divisive issue throughout NI's history. See Jarman, *Material Conflicts*. Following the 1997 report of the Independent Review of Parades and Marches in Northern Ireland, the Parades Commission was established as a quasi-judicial nondepartmental public body under the Public Processions (Northern Ireland) Act 1998. The commission is made up of seven members appointed by the secretary of state for NI with the role of reviewing and placing conditions on any planned parades it considers to be contentious. The commission has come under fierce criticism since its establishment, especially from the Protestant fraternity the Orange Order. Kaufmann, *Orange Order*, 236–66. See also McDonald, "Northern Ireland Unionists Urged."

4 In 1997, for example, the DUP and UK Unionist Party (UKUP) walked out of peace talks following discontent over details of decommissioning and the admission of Sinn Féin into the talks process.

5 Brexit is the current process in which the United Kingdom is negotiating to withdraw from the European Union (EU). Confidence and supply is the process by which a minority UK government retains power through the support of other parties or independent members. This is a less formal arrangement than a coalition government.

6 Morrow, "Epilogue," 343. We are extremely appreciative to Morrow, a professor at the School of Planning, Architecture and Civil Engineering (SPACE) at Queen's University Belfast, for alerting us to this interesting distinction.

Religious, cultural, and political differences collected around Unionist/Loyalist/Protestant and Nationalist/Republican/Catholic community identities in NI have led to a long-standing sectarian conflict that has manifested itself in profound social division, discrimination, and violence. See Whyte, *Interpreting Northern Ireland*, 1–94; Tonge, *Northern Ireland*, 27–30; and Anderson and Shuttleworth, "Sectarian Demography." While progress is being made on bridging this divide, events such as the 2012 Belfast flag protests and current NI Assembly crisis demonstrate how polarized social, cultural, and political identities remain strong in many parts of NI society. This divisive and regressive mentality, while widely rejected by the vast majority of individuals we have encountered while living in NI, still acts to characterize politics and social life in the region and has translated not only into instances of sectarian violence and exclusion but also into forms of racist violence. See Hainsworth, *Divided Society*; and McVeigh and Rolston, "From Good Friday to Good Relations." Combined with conservative and heteronormative values present in local political party politics and other institutional settings, similar attitudinal problems are present in relation to gender and sexuality, leading to significant levels of homophobia and the marginalization of women. See Kitchin and Lysaght, "Heterosexism"; Duggan, *Queering Conflict*; Roulston and Davies, *Gender, Democracy and Inclusion*; and Sales, *Women Divided*.

7   The Troubles broadly refers to a period from the late 1960s into the 1990s–2000s transition to peace when NI was characterized by severe sectarian violence that claimed over 3,700 lives across the community divide. McKittrick et al., *Lost Lives*, 13. The NI civil rights campaign, which aimed to end social and political discrimination against those from a Catholic background, and the violent response it provoked from 1968 onward marked the trigger for sustained violence throughout the subsequent three decades. See Tonge, *Northern Ireland*, 35–49. Other notable events included Bloody Sunday (1972), when twenty-seven civilians were shot dead by British paratroopers in Derry/Londonderry during a civil rights march; unrest caused by the policy of arrest and internment without trial of those suspected of paramilitary involvement; Republican prisoner hunger strikes in the early 1980s; and the Omagh bomb (1993), which killed twenty-nine civilians and injured hundreds more.

8   On the current nonviolent conflict, see Knobel, "Paradoxical Peace," 91. She writes, "Like many outsiders to Northern Ireland, I considered the current status of the political environment to be 'post-conflict,' but once I arrived, I understood that the conflict is still very present on the ground, though primarily nonviolent. The most significant indicators of this I encountered were the sectarianism and conflicting political aspirations that continue to divide society." See also the work of Cynthia Cockburn, who writes that "peace is not post-violence." Cockburn, "What Became of 'Frontline Feminism'?," 111. For an interesting discussion of the use of sectarian/political murals as a (nonviolent) means of surveilling or monitoring and controlling the NI population, see Johnston, "Foucault, Crime Control and Paramilitaries."

Note that engagement with the "other," even if conflictual and combative, can be productive. As Rebecca Jane Weinstein asserts in another context, "productive conflict resolution does not deny control, it permits planning and strategy. It also embraces emotion, is tolerant of change, accepts mistakes but attempts to correct them, and is a collaborative effort." Weinstein, *Mediation in the Workplace*, 13–14.

9   For more on postagreement violence in NI, see, for example, MacGinty, Muldoon, and Ferguson, "No War, No Peace"; Howarth, "Connecting the Dots"; McAlistair, Haydon, and Scraton, "Violence in the Lives of Children"; and Cockburn, "What Became of 'Frontline Feminism'?"

10 Our use of the term *(non)listening* is based on Marcel Cobussen and Nanette Nielsen's book *Music and Ethics* (2012), which develops the idea that *nonlistening* can be just as appropriate a course of action as *listening*.

11 Daniel Fischlin, Ajay Heble, and George Lipsitz list "careful listening" as one of the "core elements of the *most achieved* improvisers." Fischlin, Heble, and Lipsitz, *Fierce Urgency of Now*, 71.

12 The "other" is that which "resists, escapes definition whenever definition is put in place." Cobussen, "Music," para. 3.

13 On the ethics of cocreation, see Fischlin, Heble, and Lipsitz, *Fierce Urgency of Now*, 198. See also Lipsitz, "Improvised Listening," 11.

14 This account has been constructed through our direct experience with improvised music in Belfast over the past decade—as audience members and, in Paul's case, as a performer. These experiences have been augmented by interviews with local musicians and promoters, as well as the limited existing literature.

15 Belfast's metropolitan area has a population of approximately 580,000. After Dublin, Belfast is the second-largest city on the island of Ireland, which has a total population of roughly 6.3 million with less than 2 million residing in NI.

16 Ó Súilleabháin, "All Our Central Fire," 340.

17 Ó Súilleabháin, "Crossroads or Twintrack?," 175.

18 Kerr, "Belfast," 19.

19 Kerr, "Belfast," 19. Moving on Music is the leading NI promoter of electronic, jazz, folk, trad, contemporary classical, and world music. For more information, see their website at www.movingonmusic.co.uk.

20 In March 2015 Queen's University Belfast withdrew funding for the annual Belfast Festival at Queen's, owing to financial challenges, and it is now named the Ulster Bank Belfast International Arts Festival.

21 Born, "Music and the Materialization of Identities," 378.

22 For more information on SARC, see their website at www.sarc.qub.ac.uk.

23 Quoted in Lewis, "Mobilitas Animi," 114.

24 Derrida, *On Cosmopolitanism and Forgiveness*, 17. For more on the relationship between the thought of Derrida and Levinas in relation to ethics, see Critchley, *Ethics of Deconstruction*. In this chapter, following Cobussen and Nielsen, we hold "ethics" to be an "indeterminate concept, capable of referring to a variety of practices"; generally speaking, then, ethics means "doing the good thing, doing the right thing." Cobussen and Nielsen, *Music and Ethics*, 3, 16. Problems arise, however, when trying to provide content for what it means to be "good" or "right," as there is no universal conceptualization of this (16).

25 De Ville, *Jacques Derrida*, 39.

26 The quoted phrases are from Derrida and Dufourmantelle, *Of Hospitality*, 77 (emphasis in original). In "Force of Law: The 'Mystical Foundation of Authority,'" Derrida refers to "the Law" as "justice" in opposition to more generalized "law." For more on this distinction as it relates to improvisation, see Ramshaw, "Deconstructin(g) Jazz Improvisation." For more on the relationship between absolute hospitality and justice, see Derrida, "Hospitality, Justice and Responsibility"; and de Ville, *Jacques Derrida*, 38–39.

27 Alterhaug, "Improvisation on a Triple Theme," 113 (citing Derrida).

28 Finn and Cobussen, "InterMezzo," s.12. See also Coleman and Derrida, "Other's Language." One local example of (an attempt at the impossible) absolute hospitality is the Household Art Festival in South Belfast, which "encourages audiences to re-negotiate

how they view and interact with art in urban and domestic spaces" and "offers an opportunity to experience new work in an unrestrictive and non-commercial context by inviting members of the public into artists' homes." For more information, see Household, "About."

29 Derrida and Dufourmantelle, *Of Hospitality*, 77.
30 Room does not exist in this short commentary to explore law as absolute hospitality further. See de Ville, *Jacques Derrida*, for an extended and compelling discussion.
31 Maurice Macartney concurs: "The collaborative, shared act of music-making provides a face-to-face encounter with the other." Macartney, "Different Drums," 96.
32 Quoted in Kernfeld, *What to Listen For in Jazz*, 119.
33 Barrett, "Creativity and Improvisation," 610. See also Fischlin, Heble, and Lipsitz, *Fierce Urgency of Now*, 204.
34 Cobussen and Nielsen, *Music and Ethics*, x (emphasis added). On unconditional hospitality as creating a space for ethics to happen, see Cobussen and Nielsen, *Music and Ethics*, 10. For more on the significance of listening in relation to improvisation, see Monson, "Hearing."
35 Cobussen and Nielsen, *Music and Ethics*, 30.
36 Cobussen and Nielsen, *Music and Ethics*, 33.
37 Fischlin and Heble, "Other Side of Nowhere," 11.
38 Oliveros, xxv. For more on the philosophy and work of Pauline Oliveros, see McMullen, "Subject, Object, Improv."
39 Cobussen and Nielsen, *Music and Ethics*, 31.
40 Fischlin, Heble, and Lipsitz, *Fierce Urgency of Now*, 203. See also, in relation to jazz, Balliett, *Collected Works*; and Cotterrell, *Jazz Now*, 6.
41 Fischlin, Heble, and Lipsitz, *Fierce Urgency of Now*, 217.
42 Crawford, "AMM Moving on Music Festival." The group AMM was founded in London, England, in 1965. In a 2001 interview with Dan Warburton, guitarist Keith Rowe explained the history behind the group:

> We were visual artists who also played musical instruments. We wanted to move on from what jazz was about. We were inspired by what black American musicians had done, but we found the jazz form terribly limiting. AMM was based on a philosophy whereas free jazz was based on performance of music. We knew what we wanted to do. Invent a music that would be ours—AMM music. Music that would fit into no category. We were outside the scene of improvised music. We still are. We've always been perceived as arrogant (maybe you have to be to say you're going to invent a new music), though personally I've never felt arrogant in my life. (Rowe, "Keith Rowe Interview")

43 Crawford, "AMM Moving on Music Festival." The Belfast-based magazine *Fortnight*, founded in 1970 by Queen's University Belfast academic lawyer Tom Hadden and ceasing publication in 2012, offered an alternative to the polarized newspaper press, which were either unionist or nationalist (O'Doherty, "Fortnight's Reading"), and provided "analysis and criticism of politics, culture, and the arts from those from both inside and outside the local mainstream" (Irish Left Archive, "*Fortnight Magazine*").
44 Crawford, "AMM Moving on Music Festival."
45 Steve Davis, interview with the author, July 2, 2014.

46 The quotation is from Cobussen and Nielsen, *Music and Ethics*, 59. The ethical act of listening in relation to improvised music is directed not only at the audience but also at the musicians themselves (59–60).

47 Born on April 13, 1939, in Castledawson, NI, Heaney studied and lectured at Queen's University Belfast before being awarded the Nobel Prize in Literature in 1995. He passed away in Dublin, Ireland, on August 30, 2013, at the age of seventy-four.

48 Davis, interview.

49 Kerr, *Collective 4tet*.

50 Quoted in Cobussen and Nielsen, *Music and Ethics*, 60.

51 Cobussen and Nielsen, *Music and Ethics*, 60.

52 Cobussen and Nielsen, *Music and Ethics*, 11 (emphasis added), 62. Cobussen and Nielsen point out that determining what is an "acceptable musical result" is extremely difficult, and there is no universal definition: "It differs between musicians mutually, as well as between musicians and audience and members of the audience mutually. Expectations, desires, knowledge, mood and so on—they all play a crucial role in this." Cobussen and Nielsen, *Music and Ethics*, 62n7.

53 Cobussen and Nielsen, *Music and Ethics*, 65.

54 The Listening Project episode in which "Fi Glover and guests explore lyricism and storytelling in Derry/Londonderry" aired on August 3, 2015. To listen to the episode, go to http://www.bbc.co.uk/programmes/b063zt9p.

55 According to his website: "Brian McGilloway is the New York Times bestselling author of the critically acclaimed Inspector Benedict Devlin and DS Lucy Black series. He was born in Derry, Northern Ireland in 1974. After studying English at Queen's University, Belfast, he took up a teaching position in St Columb's College in Derry, where he was Head of English until 2013. He currently teaches in Holy Cross College, Strabane." See McGilloway, "Bio," for more information.

56 Derry/Londonderry is located in the northeast of Ireland. Its name is disputed in the sense that generally speaking, although not always, nationalists favor the name Derry, while unionists prefer Londonderry.

57 For an online version of the poem containing this line, see http://www.blueridgejournal.com/poems/sh-what.htm.

58 Prévost, "Discourse of a Dysfunctional Drummer," 358.

59 Cobussen and Nielsen, *Music and Ethics*, 72, 74, 75, 77.

60 On improvisation as freedom, see Stewart, "Freedom Music," 96.

61 Cobussen and Nielsen, *Music and Ethics*, 80.

62 Nancy, *Being Singular Plural*, 3 (emphasis in original).

63 Nancy, *Being Singular Plural*, 5 (emphasis in original). See also Fischlin and Nandorfy, *Community of Rights*, on relational contingencies.

64 Stapleton, "Autobiography and Invention," 169–70.

65 For more on community in Nancy's philosophy, see Nancy, *Inoperative Community*.

66 Cobussen and Nielsen, *Music and Ethics*, 81.

67 A recent all-female version of *Carousel*, titled *carousELLE*, was cocurated and directed by composer and violinist Gascia Ouzounian. In addition to being a highly successful performance, such an event is remarkable on at least two other levels. All-female musical improvisation groups are rare in a field that continues to be largely dominated

by men. The late 1970s England-based Feminist Improvisation Group (FIG) is one of few examples.
68 John McGurgan, interview with the author, July 6, 2014.
69 Fischlin, Heble, and Lipsitz, *Fierce Urgency of Now*, 198; and Neal, "'A Way Out of No Way,'" 195.
70 Fischlin, Heble, and Lipsitz, *Fierce Urgency of Now*, 198.
71 For more information on this project, see www.translatingimprovisation.com/ahrc.
72 On really listening, see Caines and Heble, "Prologue," 2.
73 Video documentation of this keynote address can be found at http://translatingimprovisation.com/portfolio/symposium. The transcript of this discussion is with the authors. For video documentation of the panel discussion in which Judge Smyth participated, see Panel 3, "Imagining the Future," at http://translatingimprovisation.com/portfolio/symposium.
74 Adrot and Garreau, "Sense as a Bridge."
75 Caines and Heble, "Prologue," 2–3.

BIBLIOGRAPHY

Adrot, Anouck, and Lionel Garreau. "Sense as a Bridge between Crisis and Improvisation: How People Make Sense of a Crisis to Improvise?" Semantic Scholar, 2009. Accessed July 19, 2019. https://www.semanticscholar.org/paper/Sense-as-a-bridge-between-crisis-and-improvisation%3A-Garreau-Adrot/34ca0ab7d4e147762b72dd1d50b8ad7e5c41cc6f.

Alterhaug, B. "Improvisation on a Triple Theme: Creativity, Jazz Improvisation and Communication." *Studia Musicologica Norvegica* 30 (2004): 97–118.

Anderson, James, and Ian Shuttleworth. "Sectarian Demography, Territoriality and Political Development in Northern Ireland." *Political Geography* 17, no. 2 (1998): 187–208.

Balliett, Whitey. *Collected Works: A Journal of Jazz, 1954–2000*. New York: St. Martin's, 2001.

Barrett, Frank. "Creativity and Improvisation in Jazz and Organizations: Implications for Organizational Learning." *Organization Science* 9, no. 5 (1998): 605–22.

Born, Georgina. "Music and the Materialization of Identities." *Journal of Material Culture* 16, no. 4 (2011): 376–88.

Burgess, Marya, prod. *The Listening Project Live*. BBC Radio 4, August 3, 2015. https://www.bbc.co.uk/programmes/b063zt9p.

Bush, Kenneth. "The Politics of Post-conflict Space: The Mysterious Case of Missing Graffiti in 'Post-Troubles' Northern Ireland." *Contemporary Politics* 19, no. 2 (2013): 167–89.

Caines, Rebecca, and Ajay Heble. "Prologue: Spontaneous Acts." In *The Improvisation Studies Reader: Spontaneous Acts*, edited by Rebecca Caines and Ajay Heble, 1–5. New York: Routledge, 2015.

Cobussen, Marcel. "Music, Deconstruction, and Ethics." In "Deconstruction in Music," by Marcel Cobussen. PhD diss., Erasmus University Rotterdam, 2002. Interactive version available at http://www.deconstruction-in-music.com/navbar/index.html.

Cobussen, Marcel, and Nanette Nielsen. *Music and Ethics*. Farnham, UK: Ashgate, 2012.

Cockburn, Cynthia. "What Became of 'Frontline Feminism'? A Retro-Perspective on Post-conflict Belfast." *Feminist Review* 105 (2013): 103–21.

Coleman, Ornette, and Jacques Derrida. "The Other's Language: Jacques Derrida Interviews Ornette Coleman, 23 June 1997." *Genre* (Summer 2004): 319–28.

Cotterrell, Roger. *Jazz Now: The Jazz Centre Society Guide*. London: Quartet Books, 1976.

Crawford, Mairtín. "AMM Moving on Music Festival." *Fortnight* 354 (October 1996): 40.

Critchley, Simon. *The Ethics of Deconstruction: Derrida and Levinas*. Oxford: Blackwell, 1992.

Derrida, Jacques. "Force of Law: The 'Mystical Foundation of Authority.'" Translated by M. Quaintance. In *Acts of Religion*, by Jacques Derrida, edited by Gil Anidjar, 230–98. New York: Routledge, 2002.

Derrida, Jacques. "Hospitality, Justice and Responsibility." In *Questioning Ethics: Contemporary Debates in Philosophy*, edited by R. Kearney and M. Dooley, 65–83. New York: Routledge, 1999.

Derrida, Jacques. *On Cosmopolitanism and Forgiveness*. Translated by M. Dooley and M. Hughes. London: Routledge, 2001.

Derrida, Jacques, and Anne Dufourmantelle. *Of Hospitality*. Translated by R. Bowlby. Stanford, CA: Stanford University Press, 2000.

de Ville, Jacques. *Jacques Derrida: Law as Absolute Hospitality*. London: Routledge, 2011.

Duggan, Marian. *Queering Conflict: Examining Lesbian and Gay Experiences of Homophobia in Northern Ireland*. Farnham, UK: Ashgate, 2012.

Finn, Geraldine, and Marcel Cobussen. "InterMezzo: Creativity and Ethics, in Deconstruction, in Music." *ECHO: A Music-Centered Journal* 4, no. 2 (2002). http://www.echo.ucla.edu/volume4-issue2/intermezzo/index.html.

Fischlin, Daniel, and Ajay Heble. "The Other Side of Nowhere: Jazz, Improvisation, and Communities in Dialogue." In *The Other Side of Nowhere: Jazz, Improvisation, and Communities in Dialogue*, edited by Daniel Fischlin and Ajay Heble, 1–42. Middletown, CT: Wesleyan University Press, 2004.

Fischlin, Daniel, Ajay Heble, and George Lipsitz. *The Fierce Urgency of Now: Improvisation, Rights, and the Ethics of Cocreation*. Durham, NC: Duke University Press, 2013.

Fischlin, Daniel, and Martha Nandorfy. *The Community of Rights, the Rights of Community*. Montreal: Black Rose Books, 2012.

Guelke, Adrian, ed. *New Perspectives on the Northern Ireland Conflict*. Aldershot, UK: Avebury, 1994.

Hainsworth, Paul, ed. *Divided Society: Ethnic Minorities and Racism in Northern Ireland*. London: Pluto, 1998.

Heaney, Seamus. "Whatever You Say, Say Nothing" (1975). Accessed July 19, 2019. http://www.blueridgejournal.com/poems/sh-what.htm.

Household. "About." Accessed July 19, 2019. https://householdbelfast.co.uk/about.

Howarth, Kristen. "Connecting the Dots: Liberal Peace and Post-conflict Violence and Crime." *Progress in Development Studies* 14, no. 3 (2014): 261–73.

Irish Left Archive. "*Fortnight Magazine*." Accessed March 8, 2016. http://www.clririshleftarchive.org/publication/111/.

Jarman, Neil. *Material Conflicts: Parades and Visual Displays in Northern Ireland*. Oxford: Berg, 1997.

Johnston, Stephanie. "Foucault, Crime Control and Paramilitaries." Essay submitted in partial fulfillment of the requirements for LAW7045 (Philosophy of Law), Queen's University Belfast, 2014. Cited with permission and copy on file with authors.

Kaufmann, Eric. *The Orange Order: A Contemporary Northern Irish History*. Oxford: Oxford University Press, 2007.

Kernfeld, B. *What to Listen For in Jazz*. New Haven, CT: Yale University Press, 1995.

Kerr, George. "Belfast, Home of Amazing Jazz." *Fortnight* 410 (2003): 19.

Kerr, George. Liner notes to *Collective 4tet: Live at Crescent*. Leo Records, 1997, compact disc.

Kitchin, Rob, and Karen Lysaght. "Heterosexism and the Geographies of Everyday Life in Belfast, Northern Ireland." *Environment and Planning A* 35, no. 3 (2003): 489–510.

Knobel, Ariel Heifetz. "A Paradoxical Peace in Northern Ireland." *Praxis: The Fletcher Journal of Human Security* 26 (2011): 89–96.

Lewis, George E. "Mobilitas Animi: Improvising Technologies, Intending Chance." *Parallax* 13, no. 4 (2007): 108–22.

Lipsitz, George. "Improvised Listening: Opening Statements. Listening to the Lambs." In *The Improvisation Studies Reader: Spontaneous Acts*, edited by Rebecca Caines and Ajay Heble, 9–16. London: Routledge, 2015.

Macartney, Maurice. "Different Drums: Development Education through Interactive Music Experiences (A Response to Chaib and de la Torre)." *Policy and Practice: A Development Education Review* 11 (2010): 92–98.

MacGinty, Roger, Orla T. Muldoon, and Neil Ferguson. "No War, No Peace: Northern Ireland after the Agreement." *Political Psychology* 28, no. 1 (2007): 1–11.

McAlistair, Siobhán, Deena Haydon, and Phil Scraton. "Violence in the Lives of Children and Youth in 'Post-conflict' Northern Ireland." *Children, Youth and Environment* 23, no. 1 (2013): 1–22.

McDonald, Henry. "Northern Ireland Unionists Urged to Return to Talks after Parade Ban Walkout." *Guardian*, July 3, 2014. http://www.theguardian.com/uk-news/2014/jul/03/northern-ireland-unionists-pull-out-all-party-talks-after-parade-ban/print.

McGarry, John, and Brendan O'Leary. *The Northern Ireland Conflict: Consociational Engagements*. Oxford: Oxford University Press, 2003.

McGilloway, Brian. "Bio." Brian McGilloway. Accessed July 19, 2019. http://www.brianmcgilloway.com/bio.

McKittrick, David, Seamus Kelters, Brian Feeney, Chris Thornton, and David McVea. *Lost Lives: The Stories of the Men, Women and Children Who Died as a Result of the Northern Ireland Troubles*. 2nd ed. Edinburgh: Mainstream, 2007.

McKittrick, David, and David McVea. *Making Sense of the Troubles: A History of the Northern Ireland Conflict*. London: Viking, 2012.

McMullen, Tracey. "Subject, Object, Improv: John Cage, Pauline Oliveros, and Eastern (Western) Philosophy in Music." *Critical Studies in Improvisation* 6, no. 2 (2010). DOI: https://doi.org/10.21083/csieci.v6i2.851.

McVeigh, Robbie, and Bill Rolston. "From Good Friday to Good Relations: Sectarianism, Racism and the Northern Ireland State." *Race and Class* 48, no. 4 (2007): 1–23.

Monson, Ingrid. "Hearing, Seeing, and Perpetual Agency." *Critical Inquiry* 34 (2008): s36–s58.

Morrow, Ruth. "Epilogue: Lessons from the Peripheral." In *Peripheries: Edge Conditions in Architecture*, edited by Ruth Morrow and Mohamed Gamal Abdelmonem, 339–46. London: Routledge, 2012.

Nancy, Jean-Luc. *Being Singular Plural*. Translated by R. D. Richardson and A. E. O'Byrne. Stanford, CA: Stanford University Press, 2000.

Nancy, Jean-Luc. *The Inoperative Community*. Edited by P. Connor. Translated by Peter Connor, Lisa Garbus, Michael Holland, and Simona Sawhney. Minneapolis: University of Minnesota Press, 1991.

Neal, M. A. "'A Way Out of No Way': Jazz, Hip-Hop, and Black Social Improvisation." In *The Other Side of Nowhere: Jazz, Improvisation, and Communities in Dialogue*, edited by Daniel Fischlin and Ajay Heble, 195–223. Middletown, CT: Wesleyan University Press, 2004.

O'Doherty, Malachi. "The Fortnight's Reading That Lasted 40 Years." *Belfast Telegraph*, December 19, 2011. http://www.belfasttelegraph.co.uk/opinion/news-analysis/the-fortnights-reading-that-lasted-40-years-28693590.html.

Oliveros, Pauline. *Deep Listening: A Composer's Sound Practice*. Lincoln, NE: iUniverse, 2005.

Ó Súilleabháin, Mícheál. "All Our Central Fire: Music, Mediation, and the Irish Psyche." *Irish Journal of Psychology* 15, nos. 2–3 (1993): 331–53.

Ó Súilleabháin, Mícheál. "Crossroads or Twintrack? Innovation and Tradition in Irish Traditional Music." In *The Crossroads Conference 1996*, edited by Fintan Vallely, Colin Hamilton, Eithne Vallely, and Liz Doherty, 175–99. Dublin: Whinestone Music, 1996.

Prévost, Edwin. "The Discourse of a Dysfunctional Drummer: Collaborative Dissonances, Improvisation, and Cultural Theory." In *The Other Side of Nowhere: Jazz, Improvisation, and Communities in Dialogue*, edited by Daniel Fischlin and Ajay Heble, 353–66. Middletown, CT: Wesleyan University Press, 2004.

Prévost, Edwin. *No Sound Is Innocent: AMM and the Practice of Self-Invention*. Essex, UK: Copula/Matchless Recordings, 1995.

Ramshaw, Sara. "Deconstructin(g) Jazz Improvisation: Derrida and the Law of the Singular Event." *Critical Studies in Improvisation* 2, no. 1 (2006). DOI: https://doi.org/10.21083/csieci.v2i1.81.

Roulston, Carmel, and Celia Davies, eds. *Gender, Democracy and Inclusion in Northern Ireland*. Basingstoke, UK: Palgrave, 2000.

Rowe, Keith. "Keith Rowe Interview." By Dan Warburton. *Paris Transatlantic Magazine*, January 2001. http://www.paristransatlantic.com/magazine/interviews/rowe.html.

Sales, Rosemary. *Women Divided: Gender, Religion and Politics in Northern Ireland*. London: Routledge, 1997.

Stapleton, Paul. "Autobiography and Invention: Towards a Critical Understanding of Identity, Dialogue and Resistance in Improvised Musics." *Contemporary Music Review* 32, nos. 2–3 (2013): 165–74.

Stewart, Jesse. "Freedom Music: Jazz and Human Rights." In *Rebel Musics: Human Rights, Resistant Sounds, and the Politics of Music Making*, edited by Daniel Fischlin and Ajay Heble, 88–107. Montreal: Black Rose Books, 2003.

Tonge, Jonathan. *Northern Ireland: Conflict and Change*. 2nd ed. Harlow, UK: Longman, 2002.

Translating Improvisation: Beyond Disciplines, Beyond Borders. "Just Improvisation: Enriching Child Protection Law through Musical Techniques, Discourses and Pedagogies." Symposium, May 29–30, 2015, Queen's University, Belfast. http://translatingimprovisation.com/portfolio/symposium.

Weinstein, Rebecca Jane. *Mediation in the Workplace: A Guide for Training, Practice, and Administration*. Westport, CT: Quorum Books, 2001.

Whyte, John. *Interpreting Northern Ireland*. Oxford: Oxford University Press, 1990.

Wilford, Rick, ed. *Aspects of the Belfast Agreement*. Oxford: Oxford University Press, 2001.

Zorn, John. *Cobra: John Zorn's Game Pieces*. Vol. 2. Tzadik Records, 2002, compact disc.

Contributors

REEM ABDUL HADI is cofounder and executive director of the Al-Mada Association for Arts-Based Community Development. She has overseen the growth and development of the organization since its inception in 2009. Under her direction, Al-Mada established the first music therapy center in Palestine, which provides music therapy services benefiting children, youth, and women throughout Palestine and Jordan. In addition, Abdul Hadi has more than twenty-five years of experience in the fields of development, human rights, and gender equity. She served as a program analyst at UNDP for fifteen years and as a human and women's rights researcher at Al Haq. In this capacity, she developed the Gender Mainstreaming Training Manual. She is a specialist in communication strategy planning and serves as a member of the Global Technical Network for WHO-Geneva, representing the MENA Region. She is also an expert in monitoring and evaluation and serves as external evaluator for projects and programs. An experienced copywriter in Arabic, Abdul Hadi holds a BA in Arabic literature and linguistics from Birzeit University and an MA in international cooperation and development from Bethlehem University. She currently serves as manager of institutional development at the Palestinian Museum in Bir Zayt, West Bank (Palestinian Territory), an institution dedicated to supporting Palestinian culture nationally and internationally.

RANDY DUBURKE has been a professional illustrator for twenty years. His work includes comic book art, animation, editorial illustration, book covers, and children's books. His work has been published by DC Comics; Marvel Comics; Hill and Wang; Farrar, Straus, and Giroux; Macmillan; Chronicle Books; Scholastic Books; Lee and Low Books; the *New York Times*; and MTV Animation. DuBurke received the 2003 Coretta Scott King–John Steptoe Award for best new talent in illustration for his first children's book, *The Moon Ring*. He is also the author of the highly acclaimed *Malcolm X: A Graphic Biography* (2006), a collaboration with writer Andy Helfer. Randy has illustrated the 2018 Grammy-winning instrumental jazz/graphic album *EMANON* by the composer-saxophonist Wayne Shorter.

RANA EL KADI grew up in Lebanon and recently completed a PhD in music (ethnomusicology) at the University of Alberta in Canada. Her research focuses on the role of participatory music making in negotiating intercultural identities and social relations in the context of migration, war, and political conflict. Her projects have been funded by Canada's Social Sciences and Humanities Research Council, and her doctoral research was recognized by the Society for Ethnomusicology through the Bess Lomax Hawes Award in Applied Ethnomusicology. Her work has been published in *Popular Music and Society* and *Review of Middle East Studies*.

KEVIN FELLEZS is an associate professor of music at Columbia University, where he shares a joint appointment in the Institute for Research in African-American Studies. His book *Birds of Fire: Jazz, Rock, Funk, and the Creation of Fusion* (Duke University Press, 2011), a study of fusion (jazz-rock-funk) music of the 1970s, won the 2012 Woody Guthrie Book Award. He has published articles in *Jazz Perspectives*, the *Journal of Popular Music Studies*, the *Journal of Metal Music Studies*, and numerous anthologies. His book *Listen but Don't Ask Question: Hawaiian Slack Key Guitar across the TransPacific* (Duke University Press, 2019) is on the circulation of contemporary Hawaiian slack key guitar in Hawai'i, California, and Japan.

DANIEL FISCHLIN, university research chair, is a leading Canadian humanities researcher who has produced important cross-disciplinary work, including some twenty books with a wide variety of international presses. His most recent books include (with Ajay Heble and George Lipsitz) *The Fierce Urgency of Now: Improvisation, Rights, and the Ethics of Cocreation* (Duke University Press, 2013) and a coauthored book with Martha Nandorfy entitled *The Community of Rights • The Rights of Community* (2011), the third in a trilogy of books cowritten with Dr. Nandorfy on rights issues. Fischlin has received several major awards for teaching excellence and is to date the only winner from the humanities of the prestigious Premier's Research Excellence Award. As a musician and community organizer, he chairs the board of Silence, a community art space in Guelph, and is also the founding director of the newly launched MA/PhD program in critical studies in improvisation at the University of Guelph.

KATE GALLOWAY is a lecturer in music at Rensselaer Polytechnic Institute. She specializes in North American musical environmentalisms, sonic cartography, radio, musical expressions of Indigenous modernity and traditional ecological knowledge, sound studies, science and technology studies, new media studies and audiovisual culture, and the digital humanities. Her monograph *Remix, Reuse, Recycle: Music, Media Technologies, and Remediating the Environment* examines how and why contemporary artists remix and recycle sounds, musics, and texts encoded with environmental knowledge. Galloway's work has been published in *Ethnomusicology, Intersections, MUSICultures, Tourist Studies, Resilience: A Journal of the Environmental Humanities,* and *Sound Studies.* She has forthcoming essays in *The Oxford Handbook of Hip Hop Music, The Oxford Handbook of Music and Advertising, Nuclear Music: Sonic Responses to War, Disaster, and Power,* and *Music in the Role-Playing Game: Heroes and Harmonies.* She previously held a postdoctoral fellowship at Memorial University of Newfoundland's Research Center for Music, Media, and Place.

VIJAY IYER, a composer-pianist, is the Franklin D. and Florence Rosenblatt Professor of the Arts in the Department of Music at Harvard University, where he also serves as the graduate adviser in creative practice and critical inquiry. One of the leading musicians of his generation, he has released twenty-one acclaimed albums of his music, tours internationally as a pianist and bandleader, and has received composer commissions from ensembles, soloists, and festivals around the world. He has been voted *DownBeat*'s Jazz Artist of the Year four times, and he has received the Alpert Award in the Arts, a US Artists Fellowship, the Doris Duke Performing Artist Award, and a MacArthur Fellowship.

MARK LOMANNO is an ethnomusicologist, jazz pianist, and an assistant professor of music at Albright College. Currently the associate editor for the peer-reviewed journal *Jazz Perspectives,* he also served as chair of the Society of Ethnomusicology's Improvisation Section, cofounded the Jazz Studies Collaborative, and curates The Rhythm of Study, a website focused on improvisation in the arts, academia, and activism. In addition to ongoing ethnographic and performance work in the Canary Islands, Lomanno's current projects include a monograph on intercultural jazz collaborations and an edited volume titled *The Improviser's Classroom: Pedagogies of Adaptive Performance, Social Engagement, and Creative Practice.* Lomanno is a former Mellon Foundation/Consortium for Faculty Diversity postdoctoral fellow and was awarded the Livingston Fellowship for his work in the Canaries during his doctoral studies at the University of Texas at Austin.

MOSHE MORAD is a radio broadcaster in Israel, hosting a popular daily world music program. He lectures at Tel Aviv University and at Ono Academic College, where he teaches courses on African music and on gender and queerness in the music of Africa and the Middle East. Morad completed his PhD at SOAS University of London, in 2013. He is the author of *Fiesta de Diez Pesos: Music and Gay Identity in Special Period Cuba*, based on his PhD dissertation, winner of the 2015 Alan Merriam Prize honorable mention awarded by the Society for Ethnomusicology and the 2016 Herndon Book Prize awarded by the society's Gender and Sexualities Section. He is also the coeditor of *Mazal Tov Amigos! Jews and Popular Music in the Americas*, winner of the 2018 Jewish Music Special Interest Group Prize of the Society for Ethnomusicology. His career in the media and music industry includes presenting TV and radio shows in Israel, presenting "on location" *World Routes* programs on BBC radio 3 in the United Kingdom, serving as managing director of NMC Music, global marketing director at EMI Music in the United Kingdom, and head of EMI's world music label Hemisphere. He has produced and compiled numerous CDs in various genres.

ERIC PORTER is a professor of history and history of consciousness at the University of California, Santa Cruz. His research and teaching interests include black cultural and intellectual history, US cultural history, jazz and improvisation studies, urban studies, and critical race and ethnic studies. He is the author of *What Is This Thing Called Jazz? African American Musicians as Artists, Critics, and Activists* (2002), winner of an American Book Award; *The Problem of the Future World: W. E. B. Du Bois and the Race Concept at Midcentury* (Duke University Press, 2010); and, with the photographer Lewis Watts, *New Orleans Suite: Music and Culture in Transition* (2013).

SARA RAMSHAW is an associate professor at the University of Victoria Faculty of Law, Canada, following previous appointments at Queen's University Belfast and the University of Exeter (United Kingdom). She was called to the Bar of the Law Society of Upper Canada in 2000 and worked for the Ministry of the Attorney General at the Superior Court of Justice, Family Court, in Toronto before completing a PhD in law at the University of London (Birkbeck) in England. During the 2008–2009 academic year, Ramshaw was a postdoctoral fellow with the Improvisation, Community, and Social Practice (ICASP) project in Montreal. Her research explores arts-based approaches to justice, and she is particularly interested in the relationship between improvised music and law. Her first monograph, *Justice as Improvisation: The Law of the Extempore*, was nominated for the 2014 Socio-Legal Studies Association Hart Book Prize. In 2014–2015 she was the principal investigator on the project Into the Key of Law: Transposing Musical Improvisation; The Case of Child Protection in Northern Ireland, funded by the Arts and Humanities

Research Council (UK). Ramshaw has published widely in numerous international journals, given invited talks, and held visiting positions throughout the Commonwealth and beyond.

MATANA ROBERTS is a self-taught mixed-media composer who, as a musician, has performed with Vijay Iyer, Roscoe Mitchell, Greg Tate, Nicole Mitchell, Henry Grimes, Jayne Cortez, George Lewis, Pauline Oliveros, Savion Glover, Anthony Braxton, Amina Claudine Meyers, Quest Love, Bill T. Jones, and many others. She is a past member of the Black Rock Coalition and the Association for the Advancement of Creative Musicians, and a lifetime member of the Tri-M Music Honors Society. She has taught at the Banff Creative Music Workshop, the School for Improvised Music, and Bard College. Her numerous awards include the Alpert Award and the Doris Duke Artist Award, and she held a residency at the Whitney Museum of Art in the summer of 2015.

DARCI SPRENGEL is a junior research fellow in music at St John's College, University of Oxford. She has published in *Popular Music*, *The International Journal of Cultural Studies*, *Sound Studies*, *Égypt/Monde Arabe*, and *Ethnomusicology Review*. She received her PhD in ethnomusicology with a concentration in gender studies from the University of California, Los Angeles, and has taught at Beloit College, the American University in Cairo, and the University of California, Los Angeles.

PAUL STAPLETON (born in California, based in Belfast) is professor of music at the Sonic Arts Research Centre, Queen's University Belfast, working primarily in the areas of new musical instrument design, music performance, sound design, and critical improvisation studies. He designs and performs with a variety of modular metallic sound sculptures and custom-made electronics in locations ranging from *Echtzeitmusik* venues in Berlin to the International Conference on New Interfaces for Musical Expression and has received critical acclaim for his sound design and composition work as part of the immersive audio-theater piece *Reassembled, Slightly Askew*. Paul has (co)directed several interdisciplinary research projects funded by the Arts and Humanities Research Council (UK) and the European Commission, on topics ranging from the relationship between music improvisation and law to the development of new methods for studying social interaction and entrainment in music performance. www.paulstapleton.net

ODEH TURJMAN is a Palestinian musician, composer, and music educator. He is the cofounder and artistic director of the Al-Mada Association for

Arts-Based Community Development. Turjman has significant professional experience of more than thirty years, including being the first person to initiate, design, develop, and implement music education programs in Palestinian schools. He has trained hundreds of teachers and helped in developing music education resource materials for primary education. Turjman was the director of the Music Department at the Ministry of Culture for three years and the former director of the Palestinian National Music Committee affiliated with UNESCO. He is a key founder of the Palestinian music group Sabreen. Currently, he is a member of the International Music Council and the International Society for Music Education. Turjman has extensive experience in developing community music programs, performing, participating in international festivals, and composing music for film, theater, festivals, and dance, for both adults and children. He was awarded first prize for music composition in the documentary *Ordinary Day*, directed by the Palestinian filmmaker Rashid Mashharawi. In addition to his work as a musician and community organizer, Turjman is a researcher and has completed research titled "Consciousness: A By-Product of Two Mirroring Processes." He holds a BA in business administration from Birzeit University and an MA in music education from Reading University in the United Kingdom.

STEPHANIE VOS is a postdoctoral fellow at Africa Open Institute, based at Stellenbosch University, South Africa. She spearheads the Interdisciplinary Forum for Popular Music, a project that develops critical perspectives on popular music from a South African vantage point. Her research interests in South African jazz and the politics of place stem from her doctoral research at Royal Holloway, University of London, where she wrote about exile as a discourse in South African jazz, with a particular focus on the pianist Abdullah Ibrahim.

Index

Abdelnour, Christine, 133–34, 136–37
Abdul Hadi, Reem, 192, 196–97, 200–201, 212–24
Aburedwan, Ramzi Hussein, 201
acoustemology, 278, 294
Adam, Omer, 268
Afro/Canarian identity, 55–60, 64–65; erasure of, 60–62, 73; and improvisation, 58, 61–64, 66–68, 72–73. *See also* Canary Islands; "cut, the"
Aharon, Dudu, 264
aislamiento, 62–63, 68, 70–71, 77n10
Ait Nahaya, 56–59, 62, 72, 76n3
Akel, Sara, 6
Al-Mada Association for Arts-Based Community Development, 17–18, 192–95, 198, 204–5, 224, 231, 238–41, 245n4, 247n34; creation of, 215–16, 232, 234–35; methodology of, 200–201, 206–8; workshops run by, 202–3, 207–14, 220–22, 226–29, 241–42
Amari Camp, 203, 207, 210–11
AMM, 306–8, 317n42
Anderson, Laurie, 101
Animism (2014), 114–15
Apex Jazz Band, 302
Arab music, Eastern vs. Western, 250–52, 262–64
Argov, Zohar, 257–60, 268, 271n29, 272n39
Ashkenazi culture, vs. Sephardic culture, 18, 250–52, 255–56, 260–64, 266
Ashraf, Ramez, 160, 182n4
Association for the Advancement of Creative Musicians (AACM), 14
A Trio, 137–47, 149, 151, 153. *See also* Kerbaj, Mazen; Sehnaoui, Sharif; Yassin, Raed
autophysiopsychic music, 41
avant-garde, 75, 101, 129, 134–37

Bailey, Derek, 35, 42, 46, 303
Ballard, Jeff, 67
Bang, Billy, 90, 93n2
Baramawy, Yasmine El, 176–80, 186n92
Barber, Diego, 55–59, 67–72, 74, 76n1, 78n33
Barenboim, Daniel, 200, 212
Barot, Ranjit, 192, 208
Beamer, Keola, 285–87, 292
Behrend, Ina, 192, 203, 221, 223
Beirut, free improvisation scene, 129, 134–37
Belfast, history of improvisation in, 302–4
Belfast Agreement, 300, 301, 313–14n11
Belfast Festival, 303, 316n20
Ben, Zehava, 257–61, 268, 271n29
Ben Ari, Mosh, 266–67
Bennink, Han, 303
Best Hawaiian Music Album, 277, 287–93
Björk, 97, 99
Blake, Seamus, 69
Blood, Black and Blue, 91–92
Botaraste (1992), 64–65
Bourne, Matthew, 303,
Brian Irvine Ensemble, 303
Brothers Cazimero, 288, 292
Brotman, Charles, 287–88, 290, 292
Brötzmann, Peter, 134, 303
Buber, Martin, 310

Calima (2009), 67–69
Canary Islands: cultural composition of, 55–57; relationship to Africa, 55–57. *See also* Afro/Canarian identity
Carousel, 310–11, 318–19n67
Carrere, Tia, 291–92
Carson, Brian, 303, 306
Carvin, Michael, 90, 93n2

Charke, Derek, 94, 96, 99, 104–9, 111–12, 115, 117n28
Chillingworth, Sonny, 291
Choice, The (2011), 69
Cipres, Hugo, 69
civil rights movement, American, 121–28
Civil War Tapes, 150–51
Coleman, Ornette, 303
collective memory, improvisation and, 130, 141, 149–53, 157n84
Collective 4tet, 307–8
colonialism, 1, 3, 7–9, 18–21, 95, 110, 130, 276, 281, 288–89, 296n15; and the Canary Islands, 57–61, 64
Coltrane, John, 33, 41, 47, 51n38, 134
Compton, Jimmy, 302
Constitution, United States, 25–28
Corea, Chick, 67
Cotsiolis, Costas, 68
Crescent Arts Centre, 306–7
crisis, improvising in response to, 1–2, 4–6, 11–12, 14, 29–30, 34–35, 42, 47–49, 81, 130, 153, 192–93, 196, 201, 212, 229, 234, 236, 300, 313
Critical Studies in Improvisation/Études critiques en improvisation, 13
Cullen, Barry, 303
"cut, the," 59, 61, 71, 74–75

Dancing Cat Records, 291–92, 297n34
Davin, Nicholas Flood, 20
Davis, Miles, 68
Davis, Steve, 303, 307
Decaul, Maurice, 83, 90–91
decolonization, 6–8
deep listening, 162, 168–69, 178, 180, 306
division of the sensible, 44–46
Domínguez, Chano, 70
Dörner, Axel, 149
Du Bois, W. E. B., 7
Dutt, Hank, 104

Eastley, Max, 303
Edward Said National Conservatory of Music, 201, 206, 212, 242–43

Egypt, music scene, 164–65
Ellington, Duke, 75
Eminem, 5
Endresen, Sidsel, 303
Essam, Ramy, 174–75
ethics: of hospitality, 305–6, 308, 311, 316n26, 317n34; of (non)listening, 305–13, 318n46
Evers, Medgar, 16
Exhibition of Vandalizm, The, 30, 32–33, 49n1; and crisis, 47–49; filming of, 36–39, 52n59; and healing, 39–41, 44, 49n6; improvisation of, 33–34; and ritual, 39–48, 51n38, 51n46; South Africa as context for, 14–15, 30–32, 37–39, 43–45, 50n12

Fernández, Luis, 66
First Intifada, 204, 262; impact on music scene, 236–38
Fischlin, Daniel, 11, 17, 22n22, 32, 45, 50n20, 147, 276, 279, 311, 316n11
Flaherty, Robert J., 108–11, 113. See also *Nanook of the North* (1922)
"For My Identity, I Sing!," 222, 239–42
4th Dimension, 192, 194, 201, 203

Gallery MOMO, 30, 37, 39, 49n6
Geffen, Aviv, 266–67
Geisser, Heinz, 307
gender-based violence, 163–64, 173–76, 180–81, 185n66, 220
Ghirass Cultural Center, 205
Good Friday Agreement. *See* Belfast Agreement
Grammy Awards, 277, 287–93, 295, 297n35
Grenadier, Larry, 67, 69
Grendizer Trio, 144, 150–51, 153
Guindy, Sabrin el-, 166
Guindy, Safinaz el-, 166
Guy, Barry, 134, 304

Haber, Charbel, 144, 148
Haber, Khaled el, 133, 154n11

Hadad, Sarit, 266, 268, 273n59
Hānaialiʻi Gilliom, Amy, 288, 292
Hancock, Herbie, 2
Hared, Yigal, 257–58
Harlem Stage, 90, 93n1
Harrington, David, 96, 102
Hawaiian Renaissance, 276–77, 285–86, 290, 292, 295n3
Hawaiian slack key guitar. See *Ki hoʻalu*
Heaney, Seamus, 307, 309, 318n47
Heble, Ajay, 11, 22n22, 45, 50n20, 147, 276, 311, 316n11
Helm, Raiatea, 287, 292
Hennen, Mark, 307
Hennessey, Rebecca, 19
Herman, Ruskin, 64–65
Highway, Tomson, 95
Hill, Lynn, 83–86, 90–92
Ho, Daniel, 290–93
Hoenig, Ari, 69
Holding It Down: The Veterans' Dream Project, 15, 81–83, 86, 92–93, 93n1; audience for, 84–85; improvisation's role in, 81, 84, 87, 89
Hoʻokena, 288
Hopkins, Billy, 302
Hoyer, Jeff, 307
HPrizm, 92
Hui, Melissa, 95
Husband, Gary, 192, 208
Hussain, Zakir, 194, 245n4

Idrissen, Kino Ait, 62–63, 76n3
Ilzghayyer, Ibtisam, 205
improvisation: as accommodation, 277–78, 287–93; Arabic, 165–70, 183n20; and collective memory, 130, 141, 149–53, 157n84; and the commons, 4–6, 11; and composition, 36, 243, 255; defining, 88–90; ethics of, 301–2, 305–6; of film, 36–39; free, 15, 17, 19, 29–31, 35, 43–47, 98, 111, 114, 129–30, 133–34, 137, 139–41, 144–45, 147, 149, 152–53; and freedom, 15, 87–88; as healing, 29, 38–41, 48, 214, 227–28; and indigeneity, 1, 3, 16, 18–21, 275, 281; as interaction, 34–35; and intersectarianism, 137–39; liminality of, 42–44, 46, 48, 51n46; as marginalized practice, 9–10; and music education, 241–43; and performance of identity, 139–40, 147, 149, 152; as response to crisis, 5, 14, 29–30, 34–35 47–49, 81, 193; and risk, 305, 308; as ritual, 31, 39–48, 51n38, 51n46; and trauma, 1–2, 6, 9, 15, 18, 83–86, 145, 153, 192–93, 201, 207–8, 212–21, 226–29, 233–34; and war, 144–45, 147–51, 207
Improvisation, Community, and Social Practice (ICASP), 3, 13–14
indigeneity, 94–95, 99, 102, 105, 109–14, 118n51; as improvisation, 1, 3, 16, 18–21, 275, 281. See also *Kanaka Maoli*; Tagaq, Tanya
Indigenous modernity, 94–95, 98, 115, 116nn2–3, 326
International Institute for Critical Studies in Improvisation (IICSI), 224, 226, 238
In What Language?, 81–82, 93n1
Irtijal, 129–30, 136, 143, 149, 154n1
Israeli Black Panthers, 259, 261, 263

Jazzahead Festival, 194, 239
Jazz Borondón, 64–66, 68–69, 71, 77n22
Johnstone, Keith, 6
Jost, Ekkehard, 30

Kaganof, Aryan, 30, 32, 49n1, 49n7
Kahumoku, George, 290, 293
Kanaka Maoli, 18, 275–77, 282–83, 288–89, 295n1; as improvisers, 278–81, 284–87, 291–95
Kane, Raymond, 280, 285, 291, 294, 297n37
Kerbaj, Mazen, 133–34, 136–42, 144–53, 156n56
Kerr, George, 302–3, 307–8
Khalife, Marcel, 133, 154n11
Khalil, Kamal, 199
Khan, Deeyah, 192, 194, 201

Ki ho'alu, 18; appropriation of, 287–91; as commercial genre, 283–84, 291–93; commodification of, 288; as gentle, 279–81, 296n15; history of, 281–84; improvising in, 275, 277; origins of, 277; popularity of, 276; revival, 277, 284–86; as safeguarded tradition, 285; as tied to geography, 279, 294–95; and tourism, 285–86, 295n4; visibility of, 276, 281–85, 287
King, Thomas, 1, 19–21
Koh, Jennifer, 90
Kronos Quartet, 94, 96, 99–107, 115

LaBarbara, Joan, 101
Ladd, Mike, 81–84, 87, 91–92, 93n1
Langevin, Hector, 20–21, 22n35
Lateef, Yusef, 29, 41, 47, 51n37
Lau, Milton, 290
Lebanon: civil war, 17, 129–30, 132–35, 144, 150–51; cultural identity of, 131–34, 137–39
lenguas cortadas, 58–61, 63, 68–72, 74, 77n12
Lepore, Joseph, 55
Le Trio Joubran, 230–31
Levy, Etti, 268
Levy, Ofer, 268
Lewis, George E., 42–43, 45, 87, 290, 304
Lipsitz, George, 11, 22n22, 45, 147, 276, 311, 316n11, 316n13
Listening Project, 309, 318n54
Llanos, Alfredo, 64

Machado, José Carlos, 64
Mahadevan, Shankar, 195
Mahavishnu Orchestra, 64
Makdisi, Samir, 132
Makdisi, Saree, 18
Martin, Jean, 108–9, 111
mawwal, 252–58, 271n13
M'Bappé, Étienne, 192
McGregor, Patricia, 83
McGurgan, John, 303, 310–11
McLaughlin, John, 192, 194, 201–3, 212, 221, 223, 239

Medina, Avihu, 264, 268
Mehldau, Brad, 67
Mingus, Charles, 305
Mini Mobile Concerts (MMC), 160–61, 163–66, 168–70, 175–81, 182nn3–4, 183n14, 183n22, 184n31; affective potential of, 176–79; audience role in, 161, 167–72, 176–80, 184n31; as improvisational, 165; as site-specific, 17, 167, 170
"Mississippi Goddam," 121–28
Monk, Meredith, 93, 101
Morris, Butch, 90, 93n2
Moten, Fred, 59–61, 64, 71, 73–75, 78n30, 78–79n47
Moving on Music Festival, 303, 306–7, 316n19
Murad, Leila, 144
Murad, Said, 225
music therapy, 192–95, 203, 212–22, 226–29, 233–36, 239. *See also* improvisation: as healing; improvisation: and trauma
Musique Improvisée Libre au Liban (MILL), 136–37
Muslim Brotherhood, 172
muzika mizraḥit, 250–52, 270n3; exclusion from the mainstream, 258, 261–67, 271–72n39; features of, 253–54, 257; politics of, 259–62; popularity of, 268–69, 273n59

Nandorfy, Martha, 32, 42, 210
Nanook of the North (1922), 108–13
Nanook of the North (2012), 95, 108–9, 111–14
Ngqawana, Zim, 29–30, 32–36, 39–43, 45, 47–48, 49n1, 49n4, 51nn37–38
Nilsson-Love, Paul, 303
Noland, Brother, 294–95
nonlistening, ethics of, 305–13, 318n46
North, the, 94–96, 99, 103–4; contemporary, 115, 116n3; field recordings, 104–5, 107–9; representations of, 106–15, 116n1
Northern Ireland, conflict in, 300–301, 311–12, 313–14nn1–4, 314–15nn6–8
Nunavut (2006), 95, 99–104; as improvisatory, 100–101

obligate mutualism, 11
Oliveros, Pauline, 168, 312, 317n38, 319n73
Olsen, Keith, 288

Pahinui, Charles Philip "Gabby," 280–81, 283, 285, 291–92, 297n36
Palestine Liberation Organization (PLO), 132–33
Palestinian National Music Council, 214
Parades Commission, 300, 314n3
Parker, Evan, 134
Parker, William, 307
Perdomo, Enrique "Kike," 55–59, 62, 64, 70–73, 76n1, 77n22, 78n34
Pérez, José Pedro, 64
performance ecology, 96–98, 116n3
Porter, Eric, 22n22, 41, 279
Potts, Tommy, 302
Power, Teobaldo, 65–66
Prévost, Edwin, 300, 306
Pure Gabby (1978), 281, 284

Rahbani, Ziad, 133, 154n11
Rahbani Brothers, 133, 146, 154n10
Rancière, Jacques, 15, 31, 44–47, 51n55
Reichel, Keali'i, 288
Remember Shakti, 194–95, 239, 245n4
Return to Forever, 64
Rodney Foster band, 302
Rowe, Keith, 306, 308, 317n42

Saade, Bechir, 144
Sabinosa, Valentina la de, 65–66
Sabreen, 201, 215, 225, 229–33, 245–46n16
Salman, Abraham, 257
Sanders, Pharoah, 41
Savall, Jordi, 198
Schafer, R. Murray, 99, 111
Second Intifada, 193, 209, 212, 233, 268–69; music scene impacted by, 236–38
Sehnaoui, Sharif, 133–34, 136–42, 144–49, 153, 155n41
Selvaganesh, V., 195
Sephardic culture, vs. Ashkenazi culture, 255–56, 260–64, 266

Seroussi, Edwin, 251, 260, 262
Shabbat, Shlomi, 266, 272n54
Shepherd, Kyle, 30, 32–36, 38, 42, 49n7
Shepp, Archie, 29, 41, 51n37
Shimabukuro, Jake, 286, 296–97n24
Shorter, Wayne, 2
Silence (Guelph, ON), 19, 236–37
silsulim, 18, 250–53, 258, 268–69, 271n13, 272nn54–56; emotional impact of, 256–57; as improvisatory, 254–57, 271n20; in media, 264–67; as resistance, 259–62. See also *muzika mizraḥit*
Simone, Nina, 121–28
Smith, Wadada Leo, 3, 87
Sonic Arts Research Centre (SARC), 304, 312, 316n22
South Africa, 14–15, 30; poverty in, 31–32, 37–39, 43–45
Srinivas, U., 195
Still Life with Commentator, 82, 93n1
street, as site of performance, 170–81
String Quartet in Her Throat, A, 100. See also *Nunavut* (2006); Tagaq, Tanya
Stronge, Kris, 310
Sudden Rush, 286, 297n36
Sun Ra Arkestra, 303

Taborn, Craig, 69
Tagaq, Tanya, 94–104, 106–9, 111–15, 116n3, 118n49
Tales (2014), 69
taqsim, 154n1, 253, 255, 257, 262
ṭarab, 161–69, 184n31; as affective politics, 179–81; as social change, 174–79; and the street, 170–74
Teyssot-Gay, Serge, 91
Threadgill, Henry, 90
throat singing, 94–96, 111, 117n28; contemporary, 99–106; improvisational, 97–98, 100, 102–4, 108, 115. See also Tagaq, Tanya
Tilbury, John, 306
Toop, David, 21n5, 303

trauma, improvisation and, 1–2, 6, 9, 83–86, 145, 153, 192–93, 201, 207–8, 212–21, 226–29, 233–34
Tribe Called Red, A, 94
tricontinentalidad, 62–63, 68, 77n10
Trio, A. *See* A Trio
Troubles, the, 301, 309, 315n7
Truth and Reconciliation Commission of Canada, 20
Truyen, Joseph, 55. *See also* "Volcano Music"
Tundra Songs (2007), 95, 104–9; improvisation in, 106–7
Turjman, Odeh, 17, 192–93, 200–201, 203–6, 211–16, 224–25, 229–33
Turner, Mark, 69
Turner, Victor, 31, 42–46, 51n46
22 Inuit Throat Games (2002/2005), 105–6, 117n28

Umm Kulthum, 168, 256, 258, 263, 268, 271n25
UNICEF, 194, 245n4
United Nations Relief and Works Agency (UNRWA), 194–95, 197, 201, 203, 207, 214, 223, 245n4
Uzuri, Imani, 92

Virginians, the, 112
Voice, The, 265–67, 272n54, 273n59
"Volcano Music," 55–58, 62, 70–72, 74

war, 82–83, 90; improvising with, 144–45, 147–51, 207
Weather Report, 64
Weidenmueller, Johannes, 69
When You Were Gone, 19–21
White, Billy, 302
Winston, George, 291–92
Women's Program Center, 203, 207, 210–11

Yamauchi, Yuki "Alan," 294–95, 297n37
yam-tichonit. See *muzika mizraḥit*
Yassin, Raed, 133–34, 137–41, 143–47, 149–53, 155n49

Za'arur, David Regev, 257
Za'arur, Yosef, 257
Zeigler, Jeffrey, 103–4
Zerang, Michael, 141
Zimology, 29, 41
Zimology Institute, vandalism of, 29–30, 32–33, 38–39, 45, 47–48, 49n1
Zorn, John, 311
Zubot, Jesse, 107, 109, 111

www.ingramcontent.com/pod-product-compliance
Lightning Source LLC
Chambersburg PA
CBHW032013300426
44117CB00008B/1013